As its performance in the Gulf War amply proved, no organization, whether Japanese or American, has done a better job in Quality than the Tactical Air Command of the U.S. Air Force. Yet in no organization could it have been more difficult to install and to maintain Total Quality Management—because of the size of the organization, its diversity, its being widely scattered, and because of the resistance of a military organization to drastic changes in behavior, habits, relationships.

This achievement was the work of one man, Bill Creech. He did the job not by preaching, not by giving orders, not by grandstanding. He did it through the relentless pursuit of the basics, The Five Pillars of TQM. Success, indeed, survival of any organization—and especially of any business—in a competitive world economy will increasingly depend on installing quality throughout the entire organization and on maintaining it. This book by Bill Creech tells how to do this in simple, clear, and persuasive prose. It is must reading for every manager.

—PETER F. DRUCKER

This book, in and of itself, should be the shot in the arm the American quality movement needs to move forward.

TQM has made an enormous difference. But companies are finding that TQM is not a technique but a way of life as they struggle with the nitty-gritty of implementation. Thus TQM is under widespread attack for not universally delivering on its promises. But the real problem—as always—is management. Or rather the absence of visionary leaders willing to bite the whole TQM bullet.

Enter Bill Creech. He's been there. His revitalization of the giant Tactical Air Command is perhaps the single most impressive "corporate" revolution we've witnessed in this century.

Bill Creech may have retired from the fighting business, but he's still at war—he's a passionate, persistent foe of centralized, authoritarian, functional organizations. It was his mettle in that respect that first attracted my attention to him in 1984, and he has gone on to a second career as a premier advisor to corporations on quality, productivity, and performance.

"Centralism is a bankrupt approach," he writes—it has crippled American industry. The alternative, he says, is to trade "organizing big" for "organizing small." He begs us to tear down all the functional walls, and change from big functions to small teams. Why? To release the awesome power of "the human spirit."

Brimming with practical advice and proven examples, this is much, much more than a how-to book, it's a helpful guide with strong philosophical underpinning. Creech discusses traits such as character, integrity, and leadership—and matches them with overarching concepts of organization, empowerment, and teamwork.

Supervisor or CEO, *The Five Pillars of TQM* is meant to change your life. It's the most important book on corporate transformation to appear in a long while.

—TOM PETERS

BILL CREECH, a former four-star general, used his TQM principles to make over the Air Force in time for its stunning success in the Gulf War. Today, he advises companies in a wide mix of industries and speaks on business leadership to diverse audiences here and abroad. *Inc.* magazine named him as one of six members of its Management Dream Team for the '90s. He lives in Henderson, Nevada.

THE FIVE

*How to Make
Total Quality Management
Work for You*

PILLARS

OF

TQM

BILL CREECH

TRUMAN TALLEY BOOKS/PLUME
NEW YORK

TRUMAN TALLEY BOOKS/PLUME
Published by the Penguin Group
Penguin Books USA Inc., 375 Hudson Street,
New York, New York 10014, U.S.A.
Penguin Books Ltd, 27 Wrights Lane, London W8 5TZ, England
Penguin Books Australia Ltd, Ringwood, Victoria, Australia
Penguin Books Canada Ltd, 10 Alcorn Avenue,
Toronto, Ontario, Canada M4V 3B2
Penguin Books (N.Z.) Ltd, 182–190 Wairau Road,
Auckland 10, New Zealand

Penguin Books Ltd, Registered Offices:
Harmondsworth, Middlesex, England

First published by Truman Talley Books/Plume,
an imprint of Dutton Signet,
a division of Penguin Books USA Inc.
Previously published in a Truman Talley Books/Dutton edition.

First Truman Talley Books/Plume Printing, December, 1995
10 9 8 7 6 5 4

The quote on page 347 is from *The King and I* by Richard Rodgers and
Oscar Hammerstein II. Copyright © 1951. Published by
Williamson Music, Inc.

The Library of Congress has catalogued the Truman Talley
Books/Dutton edition as follows:

LIBRARY OF CONGRESS CATALOGING-IN-PUBLICATION DATA
Creech, Bill
    The five pillars of TQM : how to make total quality management
work for you / Bill Creech.
        p.   cm.
    ISBN 0-525-93725-0 (hc.)
    ISBN 0-452-27102-9 (pbk.)
    1. Total quality management—United States.   I. Title.
HD62.15.C74   1994
658.5'62—dc20   93-28570
                                                 CIP

Printed in the United States of America
Original hardcover design by Eve L. Kirch

Contents

Introduction to the Plume Edition

There's no shortage of talk about "change" these days. But it's not nearly as successful as is purported. John Kotter of Harvard wrote in April 1995: "Over the past decade, I have watched more than 100 companies try to remake themselves. . . . A few have been very successful. A few have been utter failures. Most fall in between, with a distinct tilt toward the lower end of the scale." There's lots of other proof of that. For example, the 1994 *Survey on Change Management* published by the AMA/Deloitte & Touche revealed a similar picture: Companies attempting to change are having far more failures than successes. Why? The survey findings say it this way: "It seems that many organizations have to change in order to change. Their present structures and cultures tend to disallow the successful implementation of change initiatives." Well said; I find the same.

Moreover, there's another aspect to the problem. The majority of the current literature espousing change is too narrowly focused for change to have a chance—even if you put forth your best efforts. There is certainly no shortage of hot new fads, but then they wear thin and America's managers move on to another. There's a huge difference between fads and fundamentals. Some of the evidence of that now comes from James Champy, the coauthor of *Reengineering the Corporation* (which set off a huge "reengineering" craze across the nation). His movement, also, has yielded puny results. Champy confirms that. His consulting firm (CSC Index) did a sweeping survey of companies that had "reengineered" themselves—and they found virtually none had changed for the better. Champy now admits the focus on the "operational processes" simply isn't enough. In his new book, *Reengineering Management*, he addresses that very issue. These quotes provide insight into his change of heart:

> Reengineering is in trouble. It's not easy for me to make that admission; I was one of the two people who introduced the concept. . . . Anything less than a fundamental revolution in actual management practice, we discovered, is like a communist regime introducing free enterprise into a controlled economy while trying to hold on to power. . . . Our earlier book was largely about reengineering *work*—the operational processes. Now, in this book, I must shift my focus. This book is not about operational processes. It is about managing, written for managers. It is about changing management itself.

He's on the right track this time around. And Champy also now says: *"The old ways of managing no longer work."* He's also dead right about that. In this regard, the Hammer/Champy book promulgated the explicit idea that changes of processes yield, in turn, a host of improvements in many other organizational and performance aspects. They could not and did not describe how all that follow-on magic was to occur, because it was a hollow premise from the outset. Alas, their book was just the latest in a long stream of "process-centered" literature promising change that has proved to be illusionary.

Are you one of the many who have grown skeptical of this huge parade of new "brand-names"? (MBO, BPR, TQM, Reengineering, etc.) If so, that's understandable. I'm skeptical, too. And with good reason, because some involve valid new concepts, but most don't. As Peter Drucker said in his opening endorsement, you need to address the "basics." That's why fads that ignore fundamentals won't work.

In that spirit, what I'm espousing here needn't be called "TQM." I named my new management approach that, but I tell businesses to put their own name on their own program. So substitute your own phrase. However, the evidence shows that for change efforts to succeed they must be based on the solid foundation I discuss here. Therefore, please look for the underlying (and highly consistent) themes in the host of examples I provide in these pages. They disclose a distinct pattern—a pattern to be followed if your own change efforts are to be anything other than a hollow exercise.

For all these reasons, I believe you will find ideas here that will help you succeed. So if you, too, are interested in achieving organizational greatness and personal success, read on.

—Bill Creech
Henderson, Nevada
October 1995

TQM: The Need, the Issues, the Shape It Must Take

A BRIEF OVERVIEW OF WHAT IS TO COME

Not every book needs to start with an overview to explain what it's about. However, it is useful for this one to do so. If the advice it provides is to prove valuable to you, it can best be absorbed in the light of the overall picture. Experience shows also that readers have heightened interest in the book's message if they are convinced of the author's credibility. So I will provide insight later into my credentials and extensive background as a successful practitioner of *Total Quality Management*. Obviously, my voice is but one of many on this popular, widely misunderstood, and often misrepresented subject. So, right from the start, you need to know where I'm coming from on TQM—on the need, the issues, and the shape it must take. There's a growing crescendo of voices speaking out now on quality management and TQM. A few know what they're talking about, but frankly, many don't. I'll explain why I say that in the chapters that follow. You can decide who is right, and who is wrong—a decision critical to your own success.

This book is about the management problems of our country—and proven solutions to them. The problems seem especially daunting and highly resistant to correction, but that need not be the case. So the book is aimed at every level within every organization, because that is where the change for the better must begin, whatever the organization's nature. Let's start with TQM, and begin untangling the issues.

TQM IS AN IDEA WHOSE TIME HAS COME. BUT THERE'S CONFUSION OVER WHAT IT IS, WHERE IT CAME FROM, AND WHAT IT CAN DO

There is confusion in the land over what deficiencies in the current American management style TQM should address, if any. One need not be an avid reader to be aware of the ongoing debate over what's still right with that traditional style and what's wrong with it. Almost everyone involved in the management business agrees some sort of change is required. It's difficult to come to any other conclusion. But when it comes to introspection in individual businesses, you find everything from denial that management change is needed *there*, to uncertainty as to what is broken, and on to serious doubts about how to fix it even if it is. This book addresses those issues.

There's not a lot of doubt about America's need to improve its competitive edge. There's also little doubt about the wisdom of questioning America's traditional management approach as a major culprit in the nation's growing problems. Those problems, at least those of economic origin, are steadily increasing as globalization unfolds. That need not be the case. The *Globalization Age* offers even greater—not less—opportunity for national success and well-being. That's not the way it's unfolding, but that's our own fault. One result of globalization is the exposure of management inadequacies that have long lain hidden. They were not easy to spot before because local comparisons, colored by identical cultural influences, have been insufficient to reveal them for what they are: They are the products of a management culture that developed in older, less complex times. Those times—of comparative economic isolation and insulation—featured advantages of special industrial know-how that have now evaporated, and an absence of strong outside competition to force introspection and change. Those days are over everywhere and over as dramatically and completely in America as anywhere. America is not faring well in the glare of those new circumstances and new comparisons.

It's a new game, and the nation has yet to awaken adequately to its new rules, and their portent for the future. I am convinced that getting back to a position of leadership in international competitiveness—including against the Japanese—is well within reach. But we can't go on as we are. Our management practices must change. Adequate though not ideal for earlier times, they are thoroughly unsatisfactory in an era of intense competition. The proof is in. This new era presents new realities such as borderless marketplaces and discriminating consumers who are unmoved by appeals to select home-built products for patriotic reasons. Consumers look for the best value (quality and durability considered) and buy that product. In doing so they are indifferent to the macroeconomic effects of their decision. However, the cumulative effects of their individual decisions are profound—that's all too clear. And the trend toward choosing foreign-made products in America is accelerating, not diminishing. The effect eventually reaches every business and every individual in the society, not just those involved in international commerce.

Therefore, the need for change is clear. But the responses at the moment range from making excuses to explaining the problems away. None of that helps. The need is for objective introspection, candor regarding shortcomings, and a readiness to change. And few companies are exempt from that need. Therefore, this book contributes to the dialogue on the interaction between our national competitiveness and our traditional management style. That dialogue increases in intensity by the day, as it should, because it's increasing in proportion to the growth in our problems.

The whole country can't get better overnight. But it can start getting better, piece by piece, right away. Each business makes its own decisions. That's the American way, and it's the right way. So I speak in this book to each of those businesses—and to every organizational element within every business. Each can be substantially, even dramatically improved. However, the extent of the success in each case depends on the willingness of the management to abandon the traditional American approach for a new and better way. By definition that also makes it a book about the management system, structure, and style most widely practiced in the United States. I explain what's wrong with that traditional approach. There are many things to undo as well as to do. However, the book is weighted far more toward *what to do*. If you're like me, you've heard a lot about what not to do. Therefore, the book primarily concerns old practices and new realities—and creating new practices to suit those new realities. Specifically, it's a book about a type of TQM that few are now practicing.

In that respect, change advocacy comes these days in many faces. In fact, there is a parade of new buzzphrases used to describe a new type of quality-oriented management. Thus, the quality movement literature now covers a very broad tent encompassing all sorts of management practices. In my advisory activities I run into scores of these different programs. Few are alike, and those varied programs have a wide variety of features—a mixture of the old and the new—with, in more cases than not, very little of the new. In short, not all the change concepts loose on the management scene work all that well, and some don't work at all. This being so, has TQM lost its usefulness as a term? No, it's a great rallying point for what is needed to provide a competitive edge in these new times. However, I forewarn you there are almost as many different change programs—under various names including ''TQM''—as there are companies that started them because that creates confusion about what to do in your own case. There is, however, a healthy aspect to that array of differences. It shows overdue convergence on the notion that change is required. Needed now is greater convergence on the best way to go about it.

I'm not suggesting there are truly bad forms of TQM. If there are, I haven't seen them. But I've seen many incomplete forms that fall well short of producing substantial improvements. Those results are particularly anemic when compared to the quality and productivity improvements which the most savvy practitioners prove are possible. However, those forms of incomplete change are so widespread, and are yielding such minimal results, that we're in danger this particular management crusade could become another of America's many short-lived crusades of the past.

I've found a viable change program must meet four criteria if it is to succeed. First, it must be based on a *quality mindset* and *orientation* in all activities at all times, including in every process and product. Second, it must be strongly *humanistic* to bring quality to the way employees are treated, included, and inspired. Third, it must be based on a decentralized approach that provides *empowerment* at all levels, especially at the frontline, so that enthusiastic involvement and common purpose are realities, not slogans. Fourth, however named, it must be applied *holistically* so its principles, policies, and practices reach every nook and cranny of the organization.

In short, the revised approach must shape all parts of the management system, structure, and style—not some pieces in some ways. That may sound daunting, but it's not complicated, mysterious, or hard to achieve. And it doesn't all have to be done at once. It is this holistic, humanistic kind of management approach that I have used in many successful management transformations. It's also the kind I now see in use by the Japanese. (In fact, they are virtually identical —the story later.) And I've found this same kind of approach in other highly successful companies in the United States and abroad, further confirming its worth.

The Japanese didn't invent this style of quality-focused, team-concept management, though they are very good at it. And it didn't spring full-blown from the American quality pioneers who took process quality techniques to Japan in the fifties. They got the ball rolling there, but there's ample proof the same ideas were being adopted in other places as well. But whatever the parentage, this new decentralized way admits to no national origin nor exclusive use by anyone. It works successfully in any organization, whatever its size, whatever its nationality, whatever its product or service, whatever its industry, and whatever its market niche. Still, what makes it all work, and the scope of the principles behind it, are widely mischaracterized. My goal is to add clarity to the dialogue, and insight to you regarding how a change program must be structured if it is to succeed.

THE FIVE PILLARS OF TOTAL QUALITY MANAGEMENT—THEY PROVIDE THE STRONG FOUNDATION UPON WHICH THE SYSTEM MUST REST

A holistic, humanistic management system is required that blends these new principles into every aspect of the organization. I have long used the "Five Pillars" as a way of describing the need for that broad foundation. In fact, the depiction opposite is of the slide I used in my first speech to a business seeking my advice when I joined the business world (from the Air Force) in early 1985.

There have been many such businesses asking for my advice since. So I've seen a wide array of management practices in action. But I've seen nothing that changes my opinion about the need for all Five Pillars; in fact, I'm more convinced of their worth than ever—and of their relevance to today's quality dialogue. All these pillars are necessary for organizational greatness. In fact, if there is one thing I've learned in the management business, and in working with organizations large and small, public and private, it's this:

> *Product is the focal point for organization purpose and achievement. Quality in the product is impossible without quality in the process. Quality in the process is impossible without the right organization. The right organization is meaningless without the proper leadership. Strong, bottom-up commitment is the support pillar for all the rest. Each pillar depends upon the other four, and if one is weak all are.*

The chapters that follow expand on those themes and provide advice on how to blend the principles involved with that foundation into your entire management system.

I concocted the TQM logo on the book's jacket early in the '80s, and for my speech slides such as this one, when I gave the first of many speeches to business audiences on the subject. "TQM" wasn't a term in use back then. The literature on the quality approach,

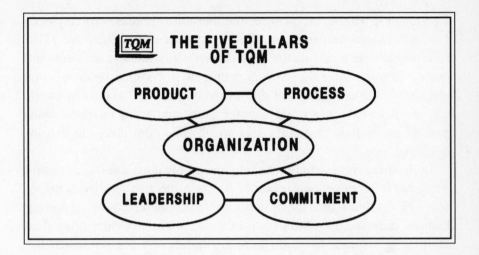

such as it was, centered on such overarching descriptors as *"Concurrent Engineering,"* *"Design-build Teams,"* and *"Lean Production."* The great success of the Japanese in grabbing U.S. market share with high-quality automobiles was the attention grabber for the new attention to the subject. And descriptors such as those were a natural consequence as people started looking for the reasons behind that Japanese success. (They didn't look quite far enough. I will explain that later.) I knew from my own success in many settings that the techniques described within the rubric of those terms, even in combination, would not suffice to create successful organizational change. So I dubbed the successful new management ways I had developed "TQM." I emphasize that Deming, Juran, et. al. were not my source. I hadn't heard of them then. Rather, I coined the phrase TQM because it best seemed to capture what was involved: A **total** approach to put **quality** in every aspect of **management**. (Thus, the Five Pillar foundation.) The TQM name spread, first through DOD, and then widely from there. (Story later.) Though now it's shrouded in ambiguity, I use it here to reflect what *any* serious change effort must encompass—if it's to work.

Everyone is welcome to do the same, in fact, they're doing that. "Quality Management" and "TQM" is much in the air these days, and the management literature is full of notions and nostrums on how to go about it. However, most of that literature addresses mere pieces of what's required to build a ''Total'' system that carries the TQM principles to every part of the organization. It is for that reason—and because of our country's growing problems in competitiveness—that I decided to write this book. I don't pretend to have the only answers. I do claim to have a special vantage point and solid business management credentials to qualify as a worthwhile contributor to the ongoing dialogue.

In dealing with business executives and business audiences, I find four general groups when it comes to the subject of quality management. First, there are those who are not interested in exploring change—they see no reason for it in their own case. (More often than not, they're wrong.) Second, there are those who are interested but confused about what it is and how they could put it to work. (So they haven't even started a process of change.) Third, there are those who have adopted some form of QM, as TQM or other names—at least they've put up the banners—but have applied only pieces of the involved principles to some pieces of their organization. (As this was being written, that was about 35 percent of companies, and the number taking the piecemeal approach was growing.) Fourth, there is a handful of American companies, some 2 percent or fewer, that fully understand the bold new principles and understand that applying them must involve the entire management system not just pieces of it. Successful though they are, they're always interested in capturing even greater success by learning from others. In fact, the lack of the *not invented here* reaction—so widespread elsewhere—is one of the key characteristics that makes them successful. While this book is aimed at all four groups, I'm especially concerned with the first three. I draw on the fourth group for examples.

I was emboldened to write the book not so much by my own success (or I would have written it several years ago), as by the extensive evidence I've continued to run across of that same new style successfully at work in the hands of others, including the Japanese. As that evidence has grown it has become increasingly obvious that those successes involve the use of a style that's a radical departure from the traditional management style widely practiced in the

United States. I've also learned the various aspects of that traditional American style are not well understood in most circles—much less the damage they cause, or why. This book looks at those issues in detail. Here's a brief preview.

THE TRADITIONAL AMERICAN MANAGEMENT STYLE FEATURES CENTRALISM PRECEPTS AND SMALL REGARD FOR THE HUMAN SYSTEM ASPECTS

Various surveys show that a mere 5 percent of American workers are organized into work teams. Indeed, I'm convinced the major reason for America's lack of competitiveness with the Japanese is that the team-based approach is widely practiced in Japan—and narrowly practiced in America. The long-standing American preference is for organization by *functions*, with a vertical, centralized structure to provide the oversight. The affinity for that type of organization stems from the American management fixation on *centralization* and *consolidation*. Always around, those precepts of an ideal organizational approach took on a new "matrix management" form and came into even more widespread practice in the sixties and seventies—and that's still the case. Those precepts are now so embedded in American management theory and practice I call that mindset *Centralism*. You'll hear a lot about Centralism in these pages—what it is, where it came from, and why it's fatally flawed as a basis for organizing in this fast-moving Globalization Age.

Webster's tells us that an "*ism*" is a "*doctrine, school, theory, or principle*." Centralism is all that, and far more. It has long been the dominant catechism shaping the American management style. As is the case with nearly all such isms, the seemingly inexhaustible longevity of Centralism is based on the true faith of its parsons and practitioners—not on empirical evidence of its worth. It's America's greatest handicap because its precepts inescapably lead to *organizing big*, all in the name of economy and efficiency. But it produces neither. In fact, Centralism has such a stranglehold on American management thinking that the country is full of *centocracies*, large and small. (Centralized, functionalized bureaucracies held together by managership.) Like the principles that build them, they glitter in the abstract but fail in practice. Accordingly, this book shines a spotlight on the Centralism precepts, and on the practices they yield. It also examines the comparative merit of centralized and decentralized management. That's critical to the story because the choice of the organizational system, structure, and style ends up deeply affecting the *psyche* and *spirit* of all employees. There's insufficient recognition that the most important system of all is the *human system*. Every company, every organization, has one. It supports, or fails to support, all the other systems. However, few make any attempt to define it or shape it in positive ways.

There is all sorts of untapped potential in the American work force. It's easily unlocked. The success stories I will provide contain the proof of that. So the solution to our growing national problems is up to America's managers. By adopting a holistic, humanistic foundation they can provide success in their own case—and make a positive contribution to resolving the current national dilemma. That's the central message of this book. It provides tips on how to build a new but well proven system that will work in any organization, whatever its size, market, or challenges—including yours.

That's the overview. To get to the details, let's turn first to a discussion of the management system, structure, and style that makes it all come alive and succeed. It's appropriate to start that discussion with the issue of organizational structure. That's pivotal to everything else because some structural arrangements lend themselves to organizational greatness—and others quite clearly do not.

ORGANIZATION IS THE CENTRAL PILLAR OF TQM'S FIVE PILLARS

The way you organize profoundly affects all other elements and activities. The organization is the framework on which the entire management system depends for efficient operation. For that reason it more than anything determines the overall health and vitality of the system. Experience shows that some organizational structures are suited only to a centralized system, while others are suited only to a decentralized system. Centralism's fixation on inputs and its reliance on excessive regulation depress the human spirit. Its cavalier treatment of human system factors produces alienation and stifles motivation. As a result, the products of a centralized structure and system fall woefully short. Sadly, what's needed is well within the potential of the same work force, but it remains mere potential. In contrast, a decentralized structure facilitates leadership and unleashes creativity. Indeed, the key question is whether the organization serves or squashes the human spirit. Therefore, how you choose to organize can either make you or break you.

In that regard, it's traditional to think of the structure of an organization in vertical terms—as a pyramid with a top, a bottom, and with "management" layers in between. But it also can be (and should be) thought of as a triangle, lying on its side—with a front and a rear. And the shorter the span from front to rear, the higher the "*teeth-to-tail*" ratio of the organization. Without question, the intensifying competition of globalization requires more teeth and less tail. It also requires employees at the front—at the cutting edge of the organization vis-à-vis customers and competition—to be as inspired and determined to succeed as those at the rear. That seems obvious, but I don't see many businesses that look on it that way, or take action to give that principle meaning and substance.

Sure, most American businesses call their employees at the bottom working level the *frontline*, but that's about as far as the front-to-rear thinking goes. (Most of them call it that because everyone else does.) I will be mixing metaphors in these pages like most do in talking about the "frontline level." (It's a contradiction in terms, but one that's well understood.) Wars are won, in the final analysis, by what goes on at the front. The outcome of economic competition between organizations, and between countries, is determined in exactly the same way. I'm not shrugging off the importance of planning and strategy or the importance of the leadership from the top down—I'll address those subjects in some depth. However, it all boils down to execution at the cutting edge. Accordingly, conceptual thinking about organizations should start at the bottom (at the front) and proceed from there, with intense focus on how the organization can best be structured and managed to provide the frontline competence, creativity, and commitment that are requisite to success.

Change is now in the air, and "*process quality*" is on many lips. But there's little real change. That's because most companies now examining their processes are not extending their inquiry to their entire organization. That's a serious omission because that is Centralism's most grievous flaw. The structure it yields—and depends on to support its precepts—is the antithesis of responsiveness and flexibility. And that makes it archaic and ill suited to the fast-paced competition of the Globalization Age. While some of the ardent practitioners of Centralism are professing to support change, in most cases those changes involve mere *patchwork* on a system so fundamentally flawed that the patches are of little utility. They simply don't come to grips with the core problem creating their organizational ills. And the issues are dimly understood, though that is changing.

THE GROWING RECOGNITION: ORGANIZATIONAL CHANGE IS IMPERATIVE, AND THE TEAM APPROACH IS THE MOST EFFECTIVE WAY TO REORGANIZE

There is increasing recognition that how one organizes profoundly affects everything else, and that the team approach produces by far the best results. Even the business schools are coming around to that point of view. In doing so, they are recognizing that much of what they taught in the past had little utility, or was even counterproductive. Rosabeth Moss Kanter, formerly of Yale—who provides excellent management insights in her books and her discourses in the *Harvard Business Review*—was quoted in the April 1989 *INC.* magazine: "Now, I'm at Harvard—which 10 years ago was the antithesis of the new approach to business." It was indeed. And it wasn't alone.

But now a new outlook is sweeping large segments of the academic community. Spurred by Japanese success and our growing problems in competitiveness, research and retrospective analyses have provided increasingly compelling evidence of the need for a change. An example of this fresh insight can be found in an excellent *Harvard Business Review* article, "Why Change Programs Don't Produce Change" (November–December 1990 issue). Written by Professors Michael Beer and Russell Eisenstat of Harvard and Bert Spector of Northeastern University, the article addressed many of the reasons that change programs go astray. The authors' conclusions were formed in a major four-year study of organizational change at six large corporations. Among their major observations were these:

> Most change programs don't work because they are guided by a theory of change that is fundamentally flawed. According to this model, change is like a conversion experience. Once people "get religion," changes in their behavior will surely follow. . . . In fact, individual behavior is powerfully shaped by the organizational roles people play. The most effective way to change behavior, therefore, is to put people into a new organizational context, which imposes new roles, responsibilities and relationships on them. . . . Task alignment is easiest in small units . . . where goals and tasks are clearly defined. Thus the chief problem for corporate change is how to promote task-aligned change across many diverse units. . . . Without strong leaders, units cannot make the necessary organizational changes, yet the scarcest resource available for revitalizing corporations is leadership.

You do need to put people into a new organizational context that creates new roles, responsibilities, and relationships if you are to affect their behavior. Also, your approach must feature goals and tasks which are clearly defined. Finally, success indeed depends on sensitive and focused leadership—which I agree is a resource in very short supply. That's because America's management practices turned to an ineffective form of *managership* over the past several decades that puts *leadership* in short supply. In subsequent chapters I will address the organizational reasoning that led to that focus on managership, and examine the distinct differences between the two forms of carrying out human endeavor.

Further evidence of this new thinking and insight in the academic community is reflected in the findings of the MIT Commission on Industrial Productivity. The commission did in-depth research on a large sample of American firms in eight separate industries to look behind America's growing problems—especially those in international competitiveness. A major conclusion of that exhaustive study was that the way America manages is a primary source of its problems. The commission's 1989 book *Made In America* said: "As things turned out, the weaknesses we discovered concern the way people cooperate, manage, and organize themselves, as well as the ways they use technology, learn a new job, and interact with the government." The commission expanded on that theme: "Organizational structure . . . varies considerably from industry to industry and from small firms to big ones. In virtually all successful firms, however, the trend is toward greater functional integration and fewer layers of hierarchy, both of which promote greater speed in product development and greater responsiveness to changing markets." The rewards, indeed, are *speed* and *responsiveness* not only to changing market conditions, but also to the day-to-day job of getting the product out the door or the service performed—to the customer's satisfaction. The focus, sense of purpose, agility, and responsiveness the team arrangement offers simply can't be matched by other structural approaches. Companies have discovered that fact after realizing that organizing by functions creates separation, not integration.

DESPITE THE GROWING EVIDENCE, THERE IS AS YET LITTLE CHANGE FROM ORGANIZING BIG TO ORGANIZING SMALL

According to survey results recently released by the Department of Commerce, a scant 5 percent of American employees are organized in a team. According to the same surveys, only 27 percent of American employers use any variant of team organization at all, and they use it for less than one-fifth of their workers. Clearly, the team approach is not spreading rapidly or widely within American management circles. That's despite the abundant and increasing evidence that it's the most powerful and motivational way to organize human endeavor. Peter Drucker, the brilliant and insightful management visionary, has said about teams, "Every business—and every other institution—has been using teams all along for ad hoc, nonrecurrent tasks. But we have only recently recognized what our nomadic ice-age ancestors knew: the team is also a principle for permanent structural design." Peter Drucker is right, there has been recent recognition of the utility of teams as a principle for permanent structural design. And those who have put those team principles to work in that permanent structural manner have succeeded handsomely. However, the statistics show that very few have even reached that recognition, much less done anything about it.

Of course there has been lots of talk about "quality management," and about the use of "teams" in that context. "Cross-functional Teams," and "Product Improvement Teams," along with quality "Councils" and "Committees" are springing up all over the business world. But that's not the same as a team-based, *permanent* structure. Therefore, most who have recently seized on the team concept are simply using teams in another ad hoc variation. While that's useful in treating Centralism's symptoms, it doesn't cure the disease. The reader is asked to be alert to that important distinction as this narrative unfolds.

Though Centralism comes in many guises and applications, the basic notions that fuel it are remarkably consistent—as are the results. For example, Centralism's tenets lead to organizing big wherever they are applied, regardless of the setting. And organizing big, with functional building blocks, is the American preference and has been for decades. That leads to what I have termed the *centralized, managership* approach, which is the one most widely used across America —in organizations large and small.

CENTRALISM PRECEPTS LEAD TO A MANAGEMENT
SYSTEM BASED ON FUNCTIONS, INPUTS, AND JOBS—
HELD TOGETHER BY MANAGERSHIP

While the centralist approach varies slightly from business to business, it has certain features that one finds in all of them—so consistently, in fact, that in the early eighties I developed the depicted organizational model to describe it:

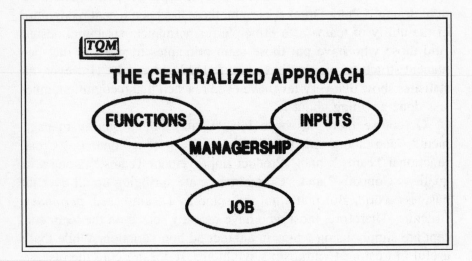

Since joining the business world I have discovered this model to be equally descriptive and applicable there. In this now traditional American approach the organization's structural modules are functions (usually oriented vertically—more on that later). The managers of those functions focus on the inputs, the input parameters, and the input rules. Each worker in each functional array focuses on his or her job. And it's all held together by conformance rules, strict procedures, and pervasive managership. It yields a *centocracy*, no matter the organization size.

In some cases an elephantine approach to organization is not inspired by slavish devotion to centralization concepts; it's just inattention, even indifference, to the human system factors. Groups are lumped together willy-nilly based on the size of the *job to be done*, not on thoughtful treatment of the interactive dynamics that come into play in that approach versus some alternative. But that's a minor part of the pattern and the problem. This centralized, managership "organize big" approach mostly flows from conscious decisions at work, not inadvertence or inattention. The great majority of managers structure their organizations thoughtfully and deliberately. And the evidence shows they do so for the most part in accordance with the highly touted Centralism principles. Thus is formed the parade of America's organizational elephants.

The advocates of Centralism use narrow, sacrosanct criteria in shaping how to organize. Their litany includes "*economy of scale*," "*economy of effort*," "*preventing duplication*," and others of that same nature. Those criteria lead inexorably to organizing big. They produce a continual search for, and satisfaction with, organizational centralization and its companion pieces of excessive consolidation and the use of functional building blocks. It sounds good to many, particularly in the abstract, because it's all couched in extravagant though unproven claims of greater economy and efficiency. In later chapters I will provide numerous illustrations (and rationale) of why it doesn't work as advertised—and show that, in fact, it produces significant diseconomies and inefficiencies.

In examining the differences between centralized and decentralized systems, as we shall, one should look at three key issues that help define each. The first is the size and orientation of the organization building blocks. The second is the way those blocks are internetted to produce the most efficient mutual support and harmonious interaction. The third is the matter of authority—how much authority is distributed and to whom. And that decision involves far more than abstract debate about the relative efficiency of decentralized teams versus centralized functions—it involves *power*! In fact, if there's one piece to the puzzle of why centralization fails so badly and decentralization works so well, it's the issue of *empowerment*. So it's not only a question of how to shape the building blocks, it's also one of distributing authority. The principal questions are: *How wide? How deep? How much? How is it being done? Where is the authority—and accountability—vested? Who is being empowered?*

Before turning to the decentralized approach and its features, let's examine the three issues mentioned above (size and orientation, internetting, and authority) as they are addressed by the centralized, managership model. Let's begin by looking at the urge to organize big, not small.

When one embraces the precepts of Centralism it can lead in no other direction than organizing big. If *"economy of scale"* is a major tenet of that brand of management thinking, and it is, then scale is not reasonably associated with diseconomy and inefficiency. If *"consolidation wherever possible"* is another sacred tenet, and it is, pressure is constantly exerted toward building bigger organizational blocks—and, of course, bigger blocks within them. Accordingly, consolidation as a sacred tenet deserves a close look. Is it the right thing to do? The short answer: *Some* may be good or may be bad, but too much is always terrible.

CONSOLIDATION OFTEN CAN BE USEFUL—BUT THE CONSOLIDATORS RARELY KNOW WHERE TO STOP

There is undeniable merit in avoiding unnecessary duplication. Unfortunately, most who adhere to the Centralism principles don't know where to stop their consolidation efforts, or, for that matter, how to weigh the trade-offs involved in assessing how far to go. Using consolidation to get rid of duplicative layers or segments is fine, with an important caveat. You usually can gain cost efficiency and process efficiency from consolidating, say, eight similar segments to four, or four to two. However, my experience is that consolidating down to one is exactly the wrong number. And only one is precisely what most consolidation efforts aim for. The problem with *one-of-a-kinds* is the damage they do to objectivity and motivation. Macro-consolidation within organizations provides an ideal breeding ground for insulation, isolation, and illusion. Those, in turn, produce poor quality and a lack of responsiveness to customers, internal and external. The irony is that although the stampede into the one-of-a-kinds has been set in motion in the name of economy and efficiency, there's little evidence that, over time, such macroconsolidation produces either one. Indeed, I have found them to be consolidation's principal casualties.

Comparison is the only true litmus test of *objectivity*. Without it, subjectivity reigns supreme, and the one-of-a-kinds, isolated from comparative reality, grow increasingly subjective and so, inefficient and unresponsive. Nevertheless, as Centralism exerts its influence, such one-of-a-kinds spring up everywhere. I found them all over the Tactical Air Command before we restructured. Each one thought it was great, but wasn't, and the internal customers had neither a basis for comparison nor a serious audience for their gripes regarding the poor service. I'm convinced the thrust to build one-of-a-kinds is Centralism at its worst. To illustrate the point, I call it the *Aeroflot Syndrome*. How would you like one airline in this country? Ask anyone who rides on Aeroflot.

It's useful to remember that a key to the underlying genius of the free enterprise system is the beneficial stimulus of comparison and the continuing competition of ideas and results. Most managers subscribe to that notion in its larger sense, but fail to translate its application to their own internal organizational dynamics. Having two "where one would do" offends the sensibilities of the centralizers. So, the reasoning goes, consolidate everything you can, and to the fullest possible extent. This does not necessarily mean businesses must avoid all such one-of-a-kinds whatever their nature. But it should not be a preferred mode of organization, as it is in the nation's centocracies. And if a bit of macroconsolidation does make sense, all issues and circumstances considered, companies must provide for ample, objective comparison of the resulting performance—quantitatively and qualitatively. Also, special scrutiny must be given to the growth of large, consolidated blocks within those one-of-a-kinds because they greatly compound the felony. Therefore, as managers consider how far to carry their consolidation efforts, it's important to recognize that they stem from the urge to *organize big*. And that's an urge that yields unfailingly bad results when carried too far. In fact, the best companies do the opposite. *They are succeeding by turning big piles into little piles, not the other way around.*

Damaging though it is, the consolidation precept is not the only culprit in creating barriers to organizing small or in stopping efforts to change well short of what's needed. For example, some believe that "flattening" an otherwise centralized organization is all that is needed, and that all the other centralization edicts can still apply. And many in the change frame of mind do exactly that. But that's not enough.

IT'S MORE THAN FLATNESS—THE HORIZONTAL IS EVERY BIT AS IMPORTANT AS THE VERTICAL, OR MORE SO

Most centralized organizations have too many managers, and too little management. There are too many managers because the system produces more, and fatter, layers of hierarchy as time passes. That growth is fueled by the rationale that more and more people are needed to chase inputs, ensure conformance, and keep up with the paperwork. And that creates a paperwork deluge, flowing from the constant addition and revision of complex rules of behavior, and from constant kibitzing. It also flows from all those layers interacting with the others, not much of which has anything useful to add to the accomplishment of work at the frontline levels. Once the process is under way, empire-building adds fuel to the fire, and more fat to the bureaucracy. So cutting out unnecessary layers and thinning out the staffs are normally useful things to do. The catch is that one must also cut out the "*busywork*" that produced all those people in the first place. That will help get rid of too many managers. However, that's just half the problem.

Centralization produces too little management—despite layers of managers—for two reasons. First, it simply does not create and foster the active, sensitive involvement by managers that is needed. Second, in a centralized system the "management," in the proactive sense, is not found at the frontline level where the things to be done need to be managed. Obviously there's more to management than telling people what to do and keeping track of the inputs from ever loftier vantage points above the core, frontline level. And in cases where the management stops at the demarcation line between labor and management, the level that needs to be doing the most managing is doing the least. For example, a frequent remark at the bottom of a centralized system is *"Somebody ought to do something about that!"* In fact, those at the bottom are the ideal ones to do something about that—if only they were empowered to do so.

Current management literature has a lot to say on the merits of flatness and streamlining. Virtually all of it is right—as far as it goes. It does help cull out unnecessary layers and reduce staffs. But that's just the start in getting into a more interactive management system. Therefore, a litmus test businesses should use in their flattening is this: Did the decisions previously made at the extinct layer gravitate downward or upward? In most cases organizations that have flattened still suffer blind spots on what else centralization is doing to them. With such blind spots there is no other fundamental change, and there is no empowerment to make management a frontline matter, too. Consequently, reducing the number of vertical layers often has little practical effect on overall management efficiency—except to reduce overhead costs. That, of course, is worthwhile on its own merits—but more is needed. A short, fat elephant is still an elephant. And it's only marginally more nimble!

Some managers say, *"Well, my company is not organized by teams, but we're still not centralized."* I've heard any number of such assertions. They prove hollow, however, when the inquiry is extended into whether or not the organizational approach features and facilitates decentralized empowerment and ownership. Moreover, to use functions as the organizational building blocks, as nearly all American businesses do, is by definition to centralize. And Centralism has served those businesses poorly. More and more are recognizing that, but still not nearly enough to create the massive change that is required to make America more competitive. It was obvious to me that patchwork changes would never fix what ailed the Tactical Air Command—that we needed a holistic approach that looked at TAC's entire management system in a different light. That different light was focused on the human spirit and the operation of the human system aspects in ways that would create the necessary spirit.

No one yet has found a way to put human spirit aside—nor can they. But people keep trying. In that respect, the centralized managership approach was alleged to offer significant efficiency and productivity improvements for all those who adopted it. (That's why the Air Force, GM, and countless others bought into it.) How has the nation fared with those promises from the purveyors of the centralized style? In a word, miserably.

THE EVIDENCE SHOWS THAT CENTRALISM AND ITS TRAPPINGS HAVE BEEN A GREAT DRAG ON AMERICA'S QUALITY AND PRODUCTIVITY

Is there any hard evidence that this tide of centralization and functionalization has carried any real improvement to the American business world? Not really. If there is, I haven't seen it. And I *have* seen lots of evidence to the contrary. In fact, there's a strong case to be made that the application of centralist thinking has been the principal culprit in America's flat productivity growth—and in our growing problems in international trade just as globalization gathers steam.

Ponder this: At the end of the eighties the Brookings Institution did a study on America's productivity trends since 1945. Among the findings: The annual productivity growth in the United States in the two decades following World War II averaged 3.2 percent. From 1965 through 1989 it averaged 1.4 percent. (Please note when it started falling off.) The difference between 3.2 percent and 1.4 percent does not appear to be much to the casual eye. In fact, it's profound. By way of example, Brookings calculated that if U.S. productivity growth had simply been sustained from 1965 on, the U.S. GNP of $5 trillion in 1989 would have been $7 trillion. The average American income of $31,000 a year would have been $45,000. That's a sad commentary on opportunities lost.

And the situation is barely improving, if at all. During the first three years of the nineties productivity growth averaged a still paltry 1.4 percent—continuing the pattern. As this was being written, productivity growth was up some, but it remained anemic compared to Japan's running average of 5 percent growth. It also was anemic compared to the means needed to cover profligate government spending and persistent deficits (more in chapter 12). The debate on causes and cures goes on, but there is simply no question that American productivity growth turned anemic at the very time it needed to grow substantially. The sobering fact is that jobs are leaving our shores in droves in the new global game of wage scales versus productivity in determining where to locate production plants. Unless U.S. productivity increases substantially, those job losses stand to get worse.

Some economists, commenting on the phenomenon of lackluster productivity growth in the last twenty-five years, have pointed to factors other than management style and efficiency. They include discourses on macroeconomic dynamics at work domestically and worldwide. However, I have yet to find those factors persuasively explained or packaged. Such factors may well have existed, even if they are difficult to identify and calibrate. If so, I am convinced they contributed to the destructive influence of Centralism, rather than moving it off the list of causes. Also, most of those economists—like the academicians—now are beginning to recognize the strong influence of the nation's management weaknesses on collective productivity.

There's further evidence that the centralist management style has had a detrimental effect on employee competence and commitment. (I will explain why both are substantially affected in chapters 9 and 10.) Why then, one might ask, hasn't overall national productivity declined under the influence of Centralism oriented policies and practices, rather than shown meager growth? For the answer, we must turn to the factors that have made each labor hour more productive since the sixties. The national figures, after all, represent the sum of all the varied influences on productivity, good and bad.

Not the least of the positive influences is the explosive growth in the use of computers and information-processing technology. That technical surge has touched literally every business in the country and resulted in all sorts of workplace applications. Examined in microcosm, that has had a very positive effect. Surveys in one company after another reveal that computer-based technology has made work easier, less time-consuming, and more accurate, and has thus made each labor hour more productive. Indeed, there seems little doubt those modern tools in human hands have contributed materially to greater knowledge, creativity, and productivity in the workplace.

This technology infusion logically has had a comparably beneficial effect on the nation's productivity. Though no one yet has developed a good way to measure that overall effect, I've heard no one mount the argument that the impact of those technological advances has been negative, not positive. These impressive advances in workplace technology have generally been as well understood and as available for affordable application in this country as anywhere in the world. And they are in widespread use. So why hasn't there been a surge in national productivity since the mid-sixties? Why haven't the past twenty-five years put the previous twenty-five to shame? We're getting better at everything else, why not in productivity?

Clearly there are causes at work dragging productivity down—stifling its growth in ways that largely offset the many positive contributions. That leads one to a search for those major negative factors. Blame our education system or other combinations of causes that strike your fancy. There's no shortage of culprits or people willing to point to them. However, I strongly believe the biggest culprit of all, greatly overshadowing all the others, is the way most American businesses are managed. The business success stories I present in these pages have been achieved in the face of the same American cultural limitations and influences that all others face. If they can overcome them, others can as well.

But most others haven't been overcoming them. The Brookings analysis provides a revealing glimpse at our national productivity scoreboard. It suggests that America has been hurt, not helped, by the shift in the sixties and seventies to another form of organizational Centralism—one in most respects more damaging than the types of centralized management used earlier (partly because it became more widely used than before). Also, the Brookings report spells even bigger trouble ahead if the country doesn't awaken to the problem. I will tell the General Motors story in chapter 2 as a metaphor for the widespread shift to the centralized, managership approach beginning in the sixties. However, GM has had lots of company. In chapter 7 I will provide the ''smoking gun'' evidence that there was such a shift back then—and provide insight into what propelled it. The GM story, the TAC story, and others in these pages set the scene and provide insight into the makeup of the now traditional centralized management style. To deal with Centralism you must recognize it for what it is.

Fortunately, this bleak national productivity picture can be brightened appreciably. There's a better way of approaching the matter of managing human endeavor, and thereby the matter of human productivity. That way involves combining principles of decentralization with quality improvement initiatives into a decentralized, leadership approach that replaces the centralist approach root and branch. It takes no less. Yet many try to get there in a quick and easy way—and many fail. Some talk big—but do too little. As an example, the Wang motto is ''*Quality Begins Where the Buck Stops.*'' I can't think of a better or more realistic one. However, Wang's corporate performance after globalization grabbed hold of its industry—dismal, leading to bankruptcy court—helps prove that success in building a TQM-like system involves serious organizational restructuring as well as greater quality focus throughout. One of the two, or both merely as slogans, won't get the job done. So the conditioning of American managers to the highly touted merits of Centralism must be overcome. That includes overcoming the perceived advantages in organizing big. So let's look at what's wrong with organizing big—and why organizing small is the better way.

THE DIFFERENCE BETWEEN ORGANIZING BIG AND ORGANIZING SMALL IS GREAT—AND INVOLVES THE HUMAN SPIRIT

I am convinced that the way to win big and grow big is to organize small. My advice to organizational leaders over the years has been: *Think big about what you can achieve; think small about how to achieve it.* That's because you get things done through individuals and small groups of individuals. The macroorganization gets most of the attention. But it is far less important than the microorganization, regardless of the organization's overall size. Therefore, again, in structuring the organization it's important to start from the point of view of the human spirit, and from the bottom up. First things first. That's where the real work gets done—or undone. Any organization will be only as successful as those at the bottom are willing to make it. Their focus, spirit, enthusiasm, objectivity, and motivation are matters that transcend all others in importance.

The centralized, "organize-big" approach stifles rather than fosters those very qualities. It overlooks the critical human spirit aspects. I've heard many of Centralism's pitchmen over the years, and they all have one failing in common: They work on the assumption that the spirit and motivation of the employees will be unaffected by the structural measures taken to comply with Centralism's precepts. Lots of empirical evidence says that's just not so. Study after study shows that employees are powerfully affected by the organizational principles and structure that shape their roles, responsibilities, and feelings of fulfillment. Studies also show that organizing small, in a small-group and team context, creates far greater bonding, involvement, and commitment. In that regard, the aircraft autopilot serves as a useful metaphor in examining the issues involved, the flaws in the Centralism precepts, and the appreciable benefits derived from organizing small.

THE CENTRALIZERS HARBOR AN AUTOPILOT MINDSET—THEIR MEANS OF TRYING TO RUN EVERYTHING FROM THE TOP

The more I lived with the centralized approach, the more convinced I became its proponents harbor an autopilot mindset. Their actions reflect the belief that if one can centralize the rules, regulations, and other input controls, and tweak them right, then the organization will run on autopilot with great efficiency and effectiveness. While autopilots are useful in aviation, you still need human intervention. The degree varies with the mission and circumstances, but intervention is still required. For example, in flying an airliner from New York to London one can envision the Captain putting it on autopilot for the entire trip. In a fighter aircraft—where the mission is more complex and the maneuvering far more dynamic—an autopilot is present, but it's rarely used. It can't be programmed to handle the repeated need for human judgment and human intervention in order to get the required results.

The fighter is small, quick, and agile. It's designed to react to rapidly shifting circumstances and conditions, and must be operated in the same way. Organizations have similar characteristics. Nothing goes perfectly for long. Needs change. Circumstances change. Machines break. People make mistakes. Human intervention is required again and again, and intervention is needed at the level where these problems are arising. If the reaction to changing circumstances must come from the top, the system is simply too cumbersome, too slow to react. That's especially true in a centralized system. It's not built for quick reaction; it's built to run on autopilot. Toiling for years in such a centralized system, I became a keen and disenchanted observer of that clumsy way of doing business. When problems arose, those on high would initiate a predictable flurry to reprogram the central autopilot: *Change the rules. Write tighter regulations. Idiot-proof the procedures. Reprogram all the mindsets.* That response nearly always lagged far behind the need and rarely reached the actual cause of the trouble. As a result, today's solutions became tomorrow's problems. Those closest to the problem, who understood it best, were not empowered to fix it before it grew—so it did.

My philosophy was far different. I not only expected human intervention at the lowest levels—using creativity to react to changing circumstances—I considered it imperative. Therefore, when I reached positions of authority, I followed the "think small" approach and created an organizational structure of small teams and collections of such teams. Each team was given unambiguous achievement responsibility, commensurate authority, and uncluttered accountability. I then did all I could to make the achievements of those teams highly visible, and fully assessable in a comparative way. Recognition and reward were the primary tools for "sending messages" to the entire system.

On autopilot? Never. The team approach provides the flexibility, and the focus, to cope with constant change, shifting needs, and ever-growing challenges from competitors. The best organizations use the team approach to stay agile and adaptable. They outthink, outplan, and outmaneuver their opposition because they change and adapt from the bottom up, as well as from the top down. They have everyone involved to the fullest possible extent. They're not behemoths lumbering along on autopilot. They swarm all over any opposition, with everyone playing a creative role, just as the fighter forces did to Saddam Hussein's vaunted war machine. They achieve the competitive edge because everyone is helping to achieve it.

Among the many problems that Centralism and the centralized, managership approach create, unfailingly, is a huge gap in trust, perspective, and purpose between the managers and the managed. As a preview, let's briefly look at some evidence.

SURVEYS SHOW THAT CENTRALISM HAS EXACTED A HEAVY TOLL IN EMPLOYEE APATHY—WHICH CREATES LACKLUSTER PERFORMANCE

Well over half of America's workers indicate they "only work hard enough to hold onto their jobs"; 44 percent say "management is getting worse"; and 27 percent say they would not buy the products they make. Moreover, management and labor are not communicating well on these issues. As but one example of a pervasive problem, an extensive sampling a few years ago by the Louis Harris organization of the *Steelcase Office Furniture Company* found a growing "perception gap" between what employees really want and what top management thinks they want. There's abundant other evidence of underlying attitudinal problems stemming from centralized management styles which undermine commitment—and provide too much distance between managers and workers for common perspectives and common purpose to emerge.

Survey after survey reveals the ravages of America's favorite management approach on the attitudes of the nation's workers. That disaffection increasingly is extending from the frontline level into higher echelons. For example, the Hay Group in a wide-ranging 1988 survey concluded that the attitudes of middle managers and professionals toward the workplace are becoming more like those of hourly workers, "historically the most disaffected group." As a result of still other surveys, the Hay Group has written, "Repeated findings show that missives from the boardroom are met increasingly with disbelief by everyone below VP level." The Hay Group terms this a "growing fraternity of skeptics," and attributes it to "mounting employee awareness of inconsistencies between what management says and what it does."

Little is being done to create better communication or other policies that close that gap in American companies—they are isolated from those issues by their traditional management style. Foster Higgins, a nationally known employee benefits consulting firm, found that only 45 percent of large companies make regular use of worker opinion surveys of any kind. And while Foster Higgins found that 97 percent of CEOs surveyed believe communicating with employees has a positive impact on job satisfaction and that 79 percent say it benefits the bottom line, only 22 percent actually do it on a frequent basis. Other surveys reflect that wide and growing gap in trust and perceptions—and that most of America's companies are taking no action to close it.

These are neither the kinds of attitudes nor the kinds of gaps that you encounter in the best companies. In becoming the best companies it is these attitudes that they seek out and take action to change. In every case where I find such good things happening, I find organizations that have changed the supervisory focus and means from managership to *leadership*. That brings us to the *decentralized* approach —and the interactive model that supports it, as depicted on page 30.

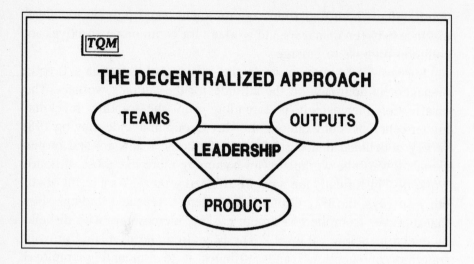

CHANGING TO A DECENTRALIZED APPROACH
BUILDS AND SUPPORTS TQM PRINCIPLES
THROUGHOUT THE ORGANIZATION

The decentralized approach is radically different from the centralized approach discussed earlier. In fact, it's the virtual antithesis, and the differences from the centralized, managership approach show up sharply. The structure is based on *Teams* not *Functions*. The supervisory focus is centered on *Outputs* not *Inputs*. The work-accomplishment mindset is on the team *Product*, not on each person's *Job*. That decentralized orientation affects every aspect of the management system operation and interaction—not only the structure, but also all facets of organizational character, culture, and climate. It takes the *human spirit* and the *human system* aspects into full account—in fact it's based on them. Its great and proven strength lies in the creation of new motivation and commitment among all employees and of proactive leadership from the bottom up.

A model is said to be useful as a means of depicting how its various elements work together interactively to form a coherent whole. Webster's tells us that a model also is "representative of others of the same kind.'' That definition fits my use of these models also. I've seen the centralized model at work in lots of settings—along with its lackluster, even dismal results. I subsequently saw the same interactive elements of the decentralized model at work, producing similar successes—in Japanese companies and in a range of American and foreign companies in various industries. I introduce these centralized and decentralized organizational models here so those contrasting features can be understood in the examples I present in the chapters to follow. In chapter 11, I will return to a portrayal of the primary differences between the two approaches and discuss the proven advantages of the *decentralized, leadership* approach—built on *The Five Pillars of TQM*—for all types of organizations, including yours. Leading to that, I will provide abundant empirical evidence of the success of that approach in action.

I've found the resistance to changing the centralist style is less a matter of hardheaded intransigence than of a lack of insight into the problems it produces. The resistance is buttressed by dim understanding of how a decentralized approach can improve matters. Most believe decentralization means loss of control. They believe they can't afford to lose that—not in the face of their other problems. They are wrong about equating decentralization with loss of control. I will explain why.

On that and kindred subjects in ensuing chapters you will find me challenging the wisdom being set forth by a host of this nation's self-proclaimed ''management experts''—including many laying claim to the true gospel when it comes to ''quality management.'' There is a bewildering array of such advice available now. Some of it is quite good. Much of it is off the point. And some of it is the worst advice you could take. Also, much of the advice found in one book directly contradicts that found in another. If you get confused by that you're not alone. So, now that you've had a brief taste of the advice to come, a few words are in order regarding my credentials to offer such advice. Credentials matter. You will find how much they matter when in ensuing chapters I take on a wide variety of the half-baked, quarter-baked, and unbaked ideas floating around these days about change and how to achieve it. The bottom line is this: *The most important step of all in a successful change journey is to first sort out who to believe*. I'm but one voice. Since it is directly relevant to your decisions as I present the differing opinions in pages to come, let me turn to some of the "battle testing" of my ideas on the subject of how to bring about productive change.

For those interested in the message and not the messenger, please skip or speed-read this section. I feel it necessary to include it because self-appointed "experts" and advisory firms on these same matters have popped up all over the place. And books featuring various names and concepts are flying off the nation's word processors by the hundreds. Since I directly contradict much of that advice (as well as the conventional management wisdom that has shaped the American style) it raises credentials to a matter of appreciable importance. In that spirit, it's appropriate to expose you to some of mine.

MY VIEWS ON TQM-STYLE MANAGEMENT WERE SHAPED BY EXTENSIVE EXPERIENCE AND SUCCESS IN CHALLENGING LEADERSHIP POSITIONS

The principles I set forth in this book have proved their worth in a number of challenging settings in both the public and the private sectors. The public sector challenges came in the thirty-seven years I served in the United States Air Force. I started out as a buck private and served in five different enlisted grades before becoming an officer. I then rose through ten officer grades to become a four-star general. Along the way I saw organizations from lots of vantage points, bottom to top. If I learned nothing else, it is that what goes on at the front is what determines organizational success—all the rest is background music. Recognizing that, as I rose in rank I kept in mind that I was not only moving from the bottom to the top but from the front to the rear. That meant the further I moved to the rear the harder I needed to work at staying in touch with those at the front, and keeping them the center of my attention—the stars of the overall show. That belief, more than anything, led to my management theories.

However, there's a legitimate question at this point: Is this Creech guy for real, or just another of the host of self-appointed experts with little in the way of hands-on success to commend his nostrums and theories? To answer it, let's turn to the views of some others you may have reason to believe. Chuck Yeager, who gained lasting fame for his achievements as an experimental test pilot, has written:

> I have known and admired Bill Creech for many years. He was an outstanding fighter pilot who proved his mettle in a variety of tough assignments, including two wars. What sets Bill apart most, however, is his great ability as a leader, and his insight into the right way to manage people. He believes very deeply in a decentralized style that gives maximum latitude to the folks down below—so that they can be aggressive and innovative in getting the job done right. His many successes with a variety of organizations, including his sweeping changes in the Tactical Air Command, help prove conclusively that is the best way to manage. No doubt about it, Bill has the "right stuff" both as a fighter pilot and as a leader. Those who follow his decentralized leadership ideas will be a lot better off.

I was privileged to use the leadership principles Chuck Yeager describes in leading radical transformations in four major Air Force organizations. Two were fighter wings. In each case they went from worst to first as the Five Pillar principles were applied. The third turnaround was of a large, highly troubled government procurement organization. The fourth was the radical transformation of the Air Force's Tactical Air Command (TAC). TAC wasn't troubled exactly, at least not in comparative terms. In fact, it was no better and no worse than other Air Force major commands. But it dramatically improved when the same Five Pillar foundation was applied in reshaping its management approach. The settings and challenges in these four cases were all different. The quality management principles used in each case were the same.

This, I emphasize, is not a book about military management. It is a book about management—the right kinds and the wrong kinds—in any kind of endeavor. So I'll touch only briefly on those military turnarounds, and only then for the lessons they hold for the business world at large.

Were those turnarounds real, or a figment of the author's imagination? General David C. Jones, former Chairman of the Joint Chiefs of Staff, has written:

> If Bill Creech had been born thirty years earlier, I believe his name would be widely recognized alongside the great combat commanders of World War II. The bigger the challenge, the greater the success achieved by this remarkable leader. When an Air Force organization, large or small, was in trouble, the first person we turned to was Bill Creech. He was a premier 'turnaround artist' long before that term came into popular use.
>
> Whether involved in planning or talking to the workers in a maintenance shop, his broad perspective, integrity, and personal attributes have made him the best at whatever he does. And he's a master at instilling motivation in people to enthusiastically pursue much higher standards than those he inherited. In fact, of the hundreds of top leaders I have known and observed under the most trying situations—heads of state, corporate CEO's, military commanders, and others—three truly stand out. Bill Creech is one of those unique three. He's a truly superb leader no matter what the challenge.
>
> The amazing results Bill obtained by restructuring the Tactical Air Command is but one more in a long trail of his impressive accomplishments as a planner and leader. As one who has now spent ten years in the corporate world I am convinced that his successful management concepts are every bit as applicable—and as necessary—in the private sector as they were in the Air Force.

That's high praise, especially since I did not create those transformations and turnarounds—the people in those organizations did, using the decentralized, leadership management principles I introduced and instilled. Instructively, they also worked every bit as effectively in other major Air Force commands, and other parts of the Department of Defense, when they saw the TAC results and adopted the same principles. In fact, the civilian official who exercises cognizance over all DOD installation matters worldwide said this in a January 23, 1989, speech: ''There are lots of defense people who are committed to this quality revolution. It started with General Bill Creech when he was Commander of Tactical Air Command.''

Let's fast forward to the recent Gulf War performance and quote another top military leader. What he says shows the principles involved in the TAC transformation are fully relevant (and topical) to our current national dialogue on quality management. General Merrill A. (Tony) McPeak, the U.S. Air Force Chief of Staff, wrote me a letter on January 16, 1991—the very night the Gulf War started. He closed with this: ''We are about to harvest the results of years of hard work and leadership by you and a handful of other great airmen. We will do well. But we need to recognize that we are beholden to you, because you really built this magnificent Air Force we have today.''

That's generous praise—delivered at an extremely busy time in his life. Those Air Force forces did do well, in fact, spectacularly well. They gave new meaning to the phrase ''competitive edge.'' Lots of others contributed to building that Desert Storm Air Force, of course, but the quality principles that started in TAC and spread across the Air Force unquestionably were major contributors (I'll explain in chapter 4). But what, you might ask, does that have to do with insights into the business world—into the challenges of meeting a payroll and beating tough competition? That too is a relevant question, so, following is a synopsis of my credentials in that respect.

MY TQM VIEWS ALSO HAVE BEEN SHAPED BY NINE YEARS OF EXTENSIVE INTERACTIONS IN THE BUSINESS WORLD, AND IN PROVIDING ADVICE TO ORGANIZATIONS LARGE AND SMALL, TROUBLED AND UNTROUBLED

When we went to a decentralized management style in TAC, we increased productivity by a whopping 80 percent. We also doubled the command's combat capability. That was all done with no more people, and no special funding, through the power of decentralized, team-based management. Startling statistics like that (and the many others that went with them) are bound to attract attention. And they did. Management sage Tom Peters came to visit, examined the before and after, and spoke and wrote extensively about the power of those TAC principles in action. One example was his coverage of those TAC principles in his 1985 best-seller: *A Passion for Excellence: The Leadership Difference*. Other national publications and other authors of management books have commented favorably on the principles that powered the TAC transformation. As a result, when I joined the business world at the mid-point of the eighties, I was in demand as an adviser to businesses.

I welcomed the opportunity to spread the word and to broaden my knowledge about management approaches in the private sector. Over the past nine years I've had extensive opportunity to do exactly that. I've provided advice at the corporate level, or to one or more of the major subsidiaries, to such diverse companies as Ameritech, ArgoSystems, Avondale Industries, Ben Franklin Stores, Boeing, Centel, Comarco, DGA International, Dynatech, EG&G, General Electric, General Motors, Industrial Indemnity Insurance, ITT, Johnson & Johnson, Kaman, LAACO, Litton, Lockheed, National Semiconductor, Rockwell International, Southwestern Bell, Tech-Sym, and Weyerhaeuser. The list is merely representative. Those companies have revenues that range from millions to many billions. Yet, for reasons I'll explain later, one does not find all that much difference in the organizational problems. The issue isn't how big you are overall; it's how you organize inside that counts.

I have also provided advice to such foreign companies as BTR, plc (British), Hitachi (Japanese), and Panavia—a German, Italian, and British production consortium headquartered in Munich. Those foreign travels have provided insight into the effects of globalization, and the dynamics of the international competition it produces. I've also been privileged to deliver any number of speeches and seminars to companies and groups, and have given keynote and principal speeches for a wide variety of associations, clubs, and councils ranging from the American Society of Quality Control, to the Association of Banyan Users (Computer Networking), to the International Association of Fire Chiefs, to the Young Presidents Organization.

Those travels have taken me into companies involved in virtually all of America's major industries and a majority of the minor industries as well—ranging from autos to chemicals, construction to computers, forestry to health care, retailing to shipbuilding, telecommunications to wholesale distribution. In all cases I did my homework on the challenges and circumstances of the client company—and the industry within which it seeks its fortunes. I learned a lot in the process. And one important lesson I learned is that the management principles that succeed and fail in the private sector are no different from those that do and don't work in the public sector. You still have to get things done through people, and that's where all kinds of organizations make or break. I've found the same to hold true in the several foreign countries where I've also been privileged to offer advice.

To further round out that business world exposure, I have for nine years served as a director on several corporate boards, and on the audit committees of three such boards. Thus I'm no stranger to balance sheets, market fluctuations, stockholder issues, cash flow dynamics, tax and audit matters, labor legislation, and the wide range of other issues that business leaders must face. I've also had considerable success in helping turn troubled businesses from failure to success.

Those national and international advisory activities have given me exposure to executives, managers, and employees from a large variety of business endeavors. And the feedback on my understanding of their challenges, and the relevance of the remedies I propose, has been positive. The following feedback is representative, and sets the tone of those interactions:

Kerrie Stewart of *National Advanced Systems* wrote after one of my business advisory trips to England: ''Thank you for coming to London to address our Executive Seminar for CEO's from throughout the world. Most people tend to have a high expectation of a guest speaker of your reputation. But you did a lot more than fulfill those expectations—you exceeded them at every level.''

After a tour in Australia Stuart Mellings of *Hitachi* wrote:

Thank you most sincerely for coming to Australia and conducting seminars in our main cities for Chief Executive Officers and managers from an array of businesses. The issue of Quality Management is global, and the solutions you developed are just as applicable here. We wanted an event that was topical, of high quality, and one where they could immediately apply what they would learn. Those objectives were fully met, and exceeded. . . . From every event we received enthusiastic, positive reaction, and requests you come back for a repeat engagement.

After a series of speeches across the U.S. to Chief Executive Officer gatherings in Boston, Chicago, Dallas, Los Angeles, New York, San Francisco, and Washington, Joseph R. Mancuso, national president of the *Chief Executive Officers Clubs*, wrote:

We have been addressed by the top business speakers and most successful entrepreneurs in this country from Ted Turner to Boone Pickens to Clement Stone to Zig Ziglar—and many others of that stature. Without question, no one delivered a more concise and well-delivered message than you. What was especially relevant was the "take-home-put-it-to-work" value of your ideas on quality and productivity. The feedback from our members was extensive and resoundingly positive in all seven major cities where you spoke. Without any doubt, Bill Creech is a true Superstar.

I lay no claim to being a superstar. I do lay claim to having successfully applied decentralization and quality-oriented management principles that made *Superstars* out of every organization where they were applied.

As those activities have granted me access to the inner workings of businesses large and small, in many industries, cultures, and countries, I've greatly broadened my understanding of management styles and their effect on employee attitudes and business outcomes. I've also made it a point to study the Japanese management style in depth, including visits to their transplant auto plants that have mushroomed across the United States. I will discuss that style in depth, because it also is widely misunderstood—and it holds valuable lessons for managers everywhere. Finally, since joining the business world I have read hundreds of business management books, old and new. That has added significantly to the experience base from which this book is drawn, and I will cite many of those authors to amplify various themes within these pages.

In this overall regard, in April 1989, *INC.* magazine presented its *"Dream Team of the Decade." INC.* said it had been carefully made up from a long list of those who had excelled in American business leadership. The final *Dream Team* choices were said to include: ''The ideal people to lead a company facing the challenges of the Nineties.'' Six business leaders from across America were named to the team. I was one of the six.

So much for my credentials to offer you advice. I could have given more, or given less. I gave this much because those contemplating starting a change program (or improving one already started) must sort among the widely different views to be found in the current literature. Thus my sensitivity to establishing my own credentials at the outset, and also to providing you abundant evidence as we go along that the approach I espouse has been proven successful in many business settings and in many different hands. You must decide whose advice to follow. Given the conflicting opinions, that's not the easiest decision to make. So I'll provide lots of evidence, and I'll also examine the most substantive differences in opinion.

The first critical step is to decide a change is needed from your current style—and surveys make clear that some 90 percent of America's managers have not even taken that first step. (Or at least done enough to amount to anything.) They appear to need more convincing, even though it's hard to understand why. A good way to start adding to the persuasion is with examples of ''Japanese Management'' in action, examples that provide still more evidence of the merit of changing to an approach that differs dramatically from the traditional American style. However, the exact nature (and full extent) of the Japanese management style is not well understood. Some of that is due to indifference to the subject. Part of it is attributable to omissions in the current literature, most of which addresses the macroeconomic issues in Japan's success or provides hopscotch glimpses of a few features of the Japanese style. Little of it examines the Japanese approach as a *holistic* management system at work—and understanding that is essential to appreciating how Japan's change from shoddy to superb products was based on TQM-style management principles that are available to all.

Chapter 2 examines Honda and Toyota as illustrative examples of the Japanese style. The traditional American way is then addressed, using GM as the metaphor to bring to light its principal features and failings. That juxtaposition reveals the marked contrasts between the two. Later, I will provide lots of American success stories. The Japanese have no corner on good ideas or the use of decentralization, team-based organization, and strong quality focus to build a *competitive edge*. But they're very good at it, as the record shows. Chapter 2 is titled *"Lessons from Japan's Success and American Failings."* If we're to cope with the new realities of globalization, those lessons must be taken to heart. So far, they haven't been.

2

Lessons from Japan's Success and American Failings

WHY ARE THE JAPANESE SO SUCCESSFUL?
I WENT TO LOOK FOR MYSELF

I wanted to look at the principles by which the Japanese manage because of their dramatic success. There are scores of apologists for that success in the United States, and most gloss over the Japanese management approach. Their focus is on other factors, with their own favorite getting star billing. Those most cited:

1. "Cultural advantages" such as the work ethic, savings ethic, and company loyalty.
2. The role of the Ministry of Industry and Trade in avidly promoting domestic cooperation—and foreign trade.
3. The extensive and cozy working relationships between the other government agencies and the various business sectors.
4. The useful, interlocking *keiretsu* relationships between and within industries—which extend the overall network.
5. Japan's use of unfair trade practices, which produce an "uneven playing field" in bilateral trade with the United States.

I fully agree those factors play a role, singularly and in combination, in Japan's economic success. However, Japanese firms must manage well or they would not put out such high-quality goods. Whatever else they do, the Japanese government and the Ministry of Industry and Trade can't build the products!

I lived in Japan and its environs for two years, and I'm sensitive to the cultural differences between America and Japan. I also understand the many strengths of the Japanese culture, including the work ethic. But for all its strengths, I don't agree that the Japanese culture has sweeping, perhaps insurmountable advantages over the American culture, as many portray it to have. Each culture has its own strengths and weaknesses. America is no different, and Japan is no different. However, many of America's unique cultural strengths—which can greatly improve workplace performance—simply are not being put to good use.

I have now had the opportunity to study the Japanese management style in appreciable depth. In that pursuit I have extensively examined their management approach in action with American workers; thus, the cultural differences in the workers themselves are set aside, reducing the matter to how effective their management principles are or are not. A corollary reason was to look for patterns in the Japanese approach which differ from those most widely used by American companies. Honda, for example, is a worldwide success. It has as many employees in countries around the world as it has in Japan. Therefore, the Honda management style and principles must work in many different cultures, including our own, not just in Japan. They do work successfully in that wide array of national cultures. There's a moral there.

Much of the research on management structures and styles over recent years reveals the Japanese approach is markedly different from that widely used in America. Nevertheless, I wanted to look with my own eyes. So I visited the U.S. *"transplant"* auto plants of Honda and Toyota to see their management style—and the concepts underlying it—in action. I found their decentralized, quality-oriented approach, carried out through a team-based structure, is conceptually sound, human nature based, and highly effective. Its effectiveness is reflected in the spirit and commitment of the employees—and that, in turn, shows up in the superb quality and high productivity for which the Japanese have become famous.

There's no mystery about their approach. In fact, it turned out to be virtually identical to the one I used in carrying out several major transformations over the years. I didn't get those concepts from the Japanese. Neither did the many other companies I will cite that have had great success using the same management approach. I freely admit I didn't go to their plants expecting to find such remarkable similarity. But that's what I found. So others can ascribe the Japanese success to any of the reasons they find persuasive, but no one should overlook how they manage. Based on all the available evidence, it is that, more than anything else, that is the underlying engine of their startling success. Honda America provides some of the proof. It also provides useful insight into that now renowned Japanese management style.

THE HONDA SUCCESS STORY: HIGHLY EFFECTIVE APPLICATION OF QUALITY MANAGEMENT PRINCIPLES ACROSS THE ENTIRE ORGANIZATION

I was aware of Honda's credentials before I visited their factories in America because of the success of Honda's products, and what knowledgeable observers have said about them. Lee Iacocca said in his book *Talking Straight* that "*Honda is probably the best company in Japan today*," and he has praised Honda's management strengths in other forums. Also, review of the highly respected annual ratings by J. D. Power & Associates reveals that in product quality Honda is "world-class" and has been for decades. The medium-priced Honda Accord ranked number one in the J. D. Power surveys among all worldwide model contenders for several years in the early to mid-1980s. Then the Accord jousted for number one with a Mercedes model that costs more than twice as much. Soon thereafter the two fought for the top position with a completely new entry in the auto quality derby—another Honda product—the Acura. Perhaps the most telling endorsement of all is that the Honda Accord has been America's favorite automobile for several years and now jousts with the Ford Taurus for number one. Let's look at some of the management magic that lies behind that performance. It's an interesting and impressive story, with lots of lessons for managers mired in the traditional American style.

HONDA CREATED, ON ITS OWN, THE FIRST JAPANESE TRANSPLANT AUTOMOBILE FACTORY IN AMERICA

Honda was the first of the Japanese automotive companies to establish transplant plants in the United States. They came in cold, without a U.S. partner to steer them through the thicket of U.S. work legislation and the intricacies of the American culture. That's a major handicap to overcome in order to compete in a foreign setting, much less to excel in it. Honda began production of motorcycles in a new facility in Marysville, Ohio, in September 1979. (That plant produces 60,000 motorcycles a year and exports them to fifteen countries worldwide, including Japan.) In November 1982, another new facility opened in Marysville, this one producing Honda automobiles. That was followed in mid-1985 by production of engines and other components at a new factory in Anna, Ohio. Finally, at the end of the decade, a second automobile production plant began operation in East Liberty, Ohio. As they and the other Japanese transplants thrive, the Big Three U.S. automakers are closing plants all over America. There's also a management moral there. Let's see if we can find it.

My review of the Honda management style started with the Accord plant in Marysville. The president of Honda America, Yuki Yoshino, warmly welcomed my visit to all their plants and gave generously of his own time for touring and detailed explanation of the way Honda does business. He accommodated my every request, as did everyone else at Honda. The candor of the Japanese in explaining how they go about achieving their success is refreshing in this competitive world. However, there's little evidence it sticks to the ribs of America's business leaders. Perhaps my explanations can provide additional insight into what is involved—and greater interest among America's managers in adopting a similar system. It's not complicated. But it is fundamentally different from the traditional American approach.

HONDA AMERICA: AN AMERICAN SHOW, BUT IT'S MANAGED ACCORDING TO THE HONDA PRINCIPLES

There are 5,500 "associates" building Hondas at Marysville, and all are American except for a handful of Japanese. The factory manager is American, as are the other key leaders at all levels. (The same is true in all the Honda America plants.) Scott Whitlock, Marysville's factory manager, proudly explained the entire operation. He also covered in appreciable depth Honda's underlying management principles and how they are put to work with an American work force. Marysville turns out a new Honda Accord every minute. I've been in well over a hundred manufacturing facilities throughout U.S. industry, and Honda's operation takes the *blue ribbon*. You can see and feel the energy and commitment those Honda America "associates" put into their endeavors.

(I found a similar picture in the Toyota-managed facility at Fremont, California—a joint venture with General Motors. The Honda operations in America were all "greenfield" start-ups, with new, nonunion, employees. Indeed, there are those who ascribe Honda's success in America to that factor. Toyota's success at Fremont belies that view—it has been achieved in a preexisting American plant with a unionized work force of long standing. I found the Honda and Toyota management principles essentially identical. So as I describe Honda's system, structure, and style, think in larger terms of "Japanese Management"—and zero in on its features. You'll find them repeated when I describe how Toyota does it.)

Here's what I found: Honda organizes by teams, not by functions. The team approach is used in every activity, not just on the production line. Each of the team members is multiskilled. Every team has a leader. There is no gap between labor and management, as there is in virtually all of America's plants. Empowerment and ownership are real, not slogans. In fact, Honda pays close and continuing attention to all the human system factors. Also, every team has goals that give meaning and substance to *"Kaizen"* (the Japanese term that essentially means "continuous improvement"). One finds measurement at all key product-process interface points. The results of those measurements and assessments are analyzed comparatively with history, goals, like shifts, and like teams. Scoreboards reflecting those results and standings are everywhere. The *objective feedback* to the employees is relevant, rigorous, and rapid.

As a result, leaders at every level display impressive, in-depth understanding of the subcomponents at each of the various assembly stages of their final product: a quality-built automobile. That understanding and insight extend to all the attendant process issues, refinements, and subtleties. To ensure such detailed understanding at all levels—including the frontline—Honda trains, trains, and trains some more, and special training emphasis is placed on *team leaders* at every level. You also see the famed Japanese quality mindset (*Jidoka*) in every facet of every operation.

Honda's *"just-in-time"* production arrangements extend well beyond component supply to virtually all aspects of its operations. They are highly efficient and especially adroit at cutting out excessive steps and cumbersome procedures. They "waste not, want not," a key feature of the Japanese approach. For example, all scrap metal from machining processes is carefully gathered in below-floor collectors and recycled through Honda's own collocated foundry. All these features provide a pervasive air of excellence, reflected in everything from plant upkeep to the purposeful bustle of the employees. The organization's character, culture, and climate are keyed to the American culture, not the Japanese; and our American culture acts in harmonious concert with the Honda management principles and style—not in conflict, as some would try to make you believe.

Each of the Honda principles and the methods used to carry them out are fully oriented to the customers, internal and external. And, Honda is absolutely unyielding on the quality of the product. The employees *build* the quality in—not *inspect* it in—at the various subcomponent stages. They do it right the first time and every time to every possible extent. Even so, they won't let any Honda out the door until it has passed the most scrupulous final inspection I have seen. The final inspectors reject and send back for rework cars with even the most minor defects and blemishes—including those a customer would be highly unlikely ever to notice. They enter each of those defects immediately into their plantwide computer data system. They then analyze performance trends by teams, and strive continuously for even higher first-pass yield efficiency.

Many reporters and other observers go to the Japanese transplant auto plants and see each production line worker's "ability to pull a cord and halt the production line at any time for quality reasons" as a principal metaphor for the Japanese management approach. Often they see little else (except for the lack of special robotics or exotic technologies at work). In contrast, I don't see that "stop the line" business as particularly descriptive of their management system and its principal features. That's because I see a rich array of other signs of decentralized management and quality commitment that are far more illustrative of their underlying principles. One such example is Honda's extensive employee involvement program.

HONDA'S INVOLVEMENT PROGRAM IS PERVASIVE AND EFFECTIVE—AND GOES BROADLY BEYOND A SUGGESTION PROGRAM

Upon entering the foyer of the Marysville plant, one sees a large display of pictures of rank-and-file associates. (No, not of the founder, the top managers, or the board of directors.) Pictured are those who have excelled in providing improvement ideas in Honda's *Voluntary Involvement Program.* The top prize each year is a new Honda, only one of numerous awards and participant recognition features associated with the program. This *"speak up and speak out"* part of their approach to detailed employee involvement supplements the team-based quality circles—which also are a rich source of improvement ideas. And, those two fit nicely with the ownership features of Honda's regular team-based structure. It's that combination that makes Honda's employee involvement approach so successful.

That combination also markedly differentiates Honda's approach from that found in most businesses. For example, many American managers quickly soured on the use of quality circles. In virtually all cases it was because they had implemented the concept with no other substantive management changes. Not surprisingly, they saw few tangible results. Consequently, company after company has tried it and cast it aside. Yet the Japanese make it succeed. Is it a cultural difference? Not at all: It works well with Honda employees in nations around the globe. What is most instructive is that Honda's success with quality circles is due to their being but one of four key parts in Honda's overall approach to detailed employee involvement.

In fact, the Honda approach is more closely aligned with the broader *"participatory management"* movement, which became a vogue in many American companies in the seventies and early eighties. However, unbuttressed by sufficient supporting changes, that also marched off into the mists with other management theories perceived to be of little worth. There it resides with other slogans of bygone crusades. Some richly deserved to be abandoned. Participatory management did not. It made great sense. It just didn't go far enough. The employees are the real test of whether an involvement program is substantive and effective or mere hyperbole and atmospherics. All the many associates I questioned on the subject supported the Honda approach with enthusiasm. You won't find that enthusiasm in most American companies. Indeed, most companies' principal contribution to employee involvement is a *"suggestion program"* and little beyond that.

To make the matter of the employees' perception of their involvement even worse, traditionally managed American companies share any bounty from improvement with their "managers" but not their "workers." That's a shortsighted form of exclusion that businesses can ill afford as America goes forward in an increasingly competitive world. It's not only shortsighted, it reduces the bounty for everyone —including the top managers and all the other shareholders and stakeholders. (I will provide the proof that supports that conclusion later.) Nevertheless, that exclusionary compensation approach is deeply embedded in the American management style. As a precursor to a detailed discussion of that subject in chapter 10, let's look at how Honda approaches the matter. The fourth element of Honda's overall involvement program is to link all associates at all levels, through monetary rewards, to the company's success.

HONDA'S INVOLVEMENT PROGRAM EXTENDS TO ITS COMPENSATION SYSTEM—ALL OF THE ASSOCIATES HAVE A STAKE IN THE OUTCOME

The associates share in the monetary rewards of success because Honda clearly understands the motivational aspects of a *pay-performance link*. For example, the basic wages paid Honda's front-line employees are the lowest in the U.S. auto industry. *The total compensation is the highest.* Two bonus programs fill in that gap: First, Honda pays an attendance bonus. Go thirty days without being late or absent and you start drawing the bonus, day by day. Be either late or absent and the thirty-day clock begins all over again. It's very effective. Absenteeism runs 2 percent or less—extraordinary for an American automobile plant. Also, more than half of the associates can boast of perfect attendance records. Second, every associate from the president to the newest hire gets an annual bonus from Honda's profit-sharing program. As one would expect, the bonus is scaled to the level of responsibility as salaries are, but the bonus distributed to each production worker is substantial. Clearly, there is motivational power in Honda's profit-sharing and total compensation approach. In contrast, well under 10 percent of American companies have any form of incentive compensation for their workers. That's not because they are indifferent to the motivation such incentive schemes can provide as virtually all have bonus systems for their managers. (There will be more on the problems that traditional approach causes—and the opportunities it creates—in chapter 10.)

In summary, Honda's wide-ranging involvement approach provides significant psychic and monetary rewards for employee industriousness, initiative, and innovation. Honda uses those positive tools and a decentralized, team-based system as the key engines of stellar performance. (Centralism's negative tools make a marked contrast.) Honda America employees come across as cheerful and committed —especially when compared with the atmosphere I've found in touring scores of American manufacturing plants. I've seen that same marked contrast in lots of other settings, including in the Tactical Air Command when comparing employee attitudes before and after we reorganized. All kinds of statistics back that up (more in chapter 4). So Honda's ''greenfield'' operations in Ohio should not be written off as atypical. It's the management system and the way employees are organized and treated within that system that count. And that applies everywhere.

HONDA BUILDS QUALITY IN, NOT INSPECTS IT IN, AND ALL EMPLOYEES KNOW HOW WELL EVERYONE IS DOING

I was also interested in the way Honda went about ''building quality in'' at every stage and in every component. At Anna, Ohio, the Honda engine factory manager, Al Kinzer, explained their approach in detail. As one example, when operations began at Anna in 1985 every engine was test-fired before sending it on to ''final assembly.'' Over time, quality improved, and when I visited, Anna was test-firing only one in ten for sampling purposes. That had been their goal, and it was achieved on schedule. Were they satisfied? Not at all. Their eventual goal is to test-fire one in every hundred. They know that goal is achievable because it's the practice in Honda's main engine plant in Japan. But Honda America has gone about those performance improvements in achievable increments, not in a frantic rush.

That's just one example, among many, I saw that illustrates their approach to *continuous, measurable*, and *incremental* improvement. I am of a similar persuasion, and used the same approach to continuous improvement. As Phil Crosby advises on this same subject, *"You have to eat the elephant a bite at a time."* Also, even though the Honda engines built at Anna are for low- and medium-priced markets (Civics and Accords), Honda measures component tolerances in *microns* and weight tolerances in *grams*. And they expect those reaching final assembly to be of such high quality that the defects can be measured in a *few parts per million*. Obviously, the engines are run after they are mated to the automobile, and rejected out of hand if the least thing is wrong. But catching the defects at that final product stage is aptly called "inspecting it in." That's not the Honda way.

I found this same pattern throughout the Honda operation: the same commitment to quality and the same use of goals. Everyone I talked with talks goals in numbers as well as in words, from the bottom to the top. And every time they showed a team goal they had reached, they described a still higher goal related to the same subproduct. (Most American employees don't talk numbers as well as words, nor most managers either. I will elaborate later on why that's a fundamental weakness.) The Honda associates are justly proud of their accomplishments, but I detected no tendency to rest on their laurels. Honda uses great care to make the goals reasonable and attainable, and the top leaders are especially sensitive in that regard. I also was struck by the objectivity of the appraisals, and the widespread incorporation of useful facts, not mere opinion. The honesty, openness, and lack of pressure with which it is all handled also are most impressive.

CREATING THE QUALITY MINDSET, AND A VALUE, NOT COST, ORIENTATION

The Japanese say *"Quality is not a cost issue."* They say the real costs, the unseen and usually ignored costs, come from poor quality, which drives up costs by producing excessive scrap, rework, and warranty repair caseload. Beyond those, they cite the high costs of customer disaffection, which drives down both profit margins and market share. Therefore, the Japanese practitioners of quality management believe it's not only possible, it is imperative to use quality to drive costs down while simultaneously driving up product worth and market share. In most American management circles those have long been considered inherently incompatible goals. I agree with the Japanese view. But to make that formula successful, leaders must create an abiding belief in the value of quality in every aspect of every operation.

The Japanese call that *"Jidoka,"* the "quality principle." Two examples of many I saw illustrate Honda's application of *Jidoka.* First, Honda's factories are spotless—you can eat off the floor. All the equipment is the same, and the associates look just as sharp—reflecting the same quality consciousness. Honda provides comfortable two-piece white work suits for every associate from top to bottom. The associate's first name is embroidered on the jacket. (And that's for everyone, including the factory manager and the president of Honda America. In Honda plants, unlike other American plants, the associates don't talk about the "suits"—meaning the managers who stroll through from time to time.) Each employee gets seven work suits, for an ample supply. Honda does the laundering daily and returns each personalized suit to the associate's locker. Obviously it costs extra money to do that. Few American firms would do it, or if they did, I doubt it would long survive some *beancounter* in corporate heaven who would ax it without a second thought as an "unnecessary expense." Honda understands those cost-versus-value trade-offs, and the critical importance of the quality mindset. They believe the quality principle starts in the minds of the employees. So do I.

(We had a similar program in TAC's automotive repair activities, instituted along with our other changes. As you would imagine, TAC had a huge automotive fleet. We called that program *Proud Look*. It featured newly spotless facilities and special work uniforms for all the mechanics. Once it was in place, quality and productivity soared. That same approach was followed in all the TAC workplaces. Those programs, designed to create pride, played a key role in our huge improvements in quality and productivity. Weighed in terms of the beneficial returns and the savings they generate, the costs to create the quality mindset are minuscule. We proved that in TAC. So does Honda. More on the subject, and the importance of *pride*, to come.)

The second story illustrating Honda's approach to *Jidoka* in all things involves automobile body sealant. While touring the Accord plant, we stopped to examine the body shells as they enter the production line. The factory manager said Honda recently had developed a new sealant in order to have the best in the entire industry in its quality and longevity. I asked, "How is it better than the old one?"

He responded, "Previously, it would prevent any rusting at all for at least nine years, in any climate. The new one is good for more than fifteen years, and probably will resist rust and corrosion beyond that."

I pursued the matter. "This costs you more to use?"

His quick reply was "Yes, but we won't pass it on. We won't because our overall approach to quality helps keep costs down, so we can absorb higher costs in some items."

I went on, "I assume this is something the owner can't see, is not used in your sales pitches, and would not show up in most cases until the second or third owner?"

He lit up at that question and replied, "That's right, but over time people will notice how many old Hondas there are on the road. That will affect customer perception not only of our quality but also of our durability."

Contrast that way of thinking with the "planned obsolescence" so long a reputed (and visible) part of Detroit's approach. The story also illustrates what it means to make Quality a way of life, not just a claim for factory banners and sales brochures. And that intense commitment to quality is why American consumers find the quality in Japanese products real—and to their liking. In fact, it's the primary reason they have flocked to those products. So the track record reinforces the Japanese belief that quality can be used to drive costs down and market share up at the same time. It can be, that is, when the quality mindset is instilled and applied conscientiously throughout the organization.

HONDA'S OVERARCHING MANAGEMENT PRINCIPLES PROVIDE THE BASIS FOR ALL THEIR POLICIES AND PRACTICES

Principles operate top to bottom. Decisions operate bottom to top. I've applied that philosophy since my earliest years in management positions. I see its efficacy at work in the best organizations, and I saw it in abundance in Honda's plants. Therefore, I had no doubt the right kinds of overarching principles were flowing from the top of the Honda hierarchy. That was confirmed when I read a September 1988 speech by Tadashi Kume, president and CEO of Honda Motor Company, given in Dearborn, Michigan, to an international audience of automotive executives. The following excerpts pertain:

> There is a relationship—almost a human relationship—between the automobile and the people who use it. . . . It reflects individual tastes, desires, emotions, feelings and lifestyles. The automobile has become *humanistic*. [Therefore] we must have a *humanistic* system to produce it. [To succeed in that] each component must possess the same three characteristics. They must know and understand the common objectives, work as a team, and have the independence and freedom to be flexible. It is the last characteristic which is so important to the future well-being of the organization, and the success of its products in the marketplace. Now it is usually true that the larger an organization becomes, the more conservative it becomes, the more bureaucratic it becomes, and the more rigid it becomes. So it is my responsibility as President of Honda to continually spark the human spirit within our organization.

After I had seen the vitality of the Honda operation in America, it came as no surprise to hear Honda's CEO using terms, and philosophies, related to his own responsibility for attention to the human spirit.

Honda's management principles start in the right place: with the human spirit and with intense attention to all the human system factors. Moreover, the quality of Honda's products built in America proves that good management principles such as these transcend national, cultural, and corporate boundaries. In that respect, in mid-1990 I went to Australia to deliver a series of speeches on quality and productivity—and the management principles that produce them. On arrival in Sydney, I was handed the Sunday morning paper. My attention was captured by a full-page ad proudly proclaiming that the Honda Accord had just won Germany's top prize for automobile quality, the *Golden Steering Wheel Award*. The ad explained that ''twenty-five distinguished Judges from all over Europe'' weigh every facet of an automobile's performance, quality, and durability. From that intense scrutiny emerges the winner, among all comers, of Germany's top automotive award. I can think of no better way of underscoring what's happening in globalization. It's also an appropriate way to end this segment on Honda. Honda's management principles and their demonstrated success provide lots of lessons for America's managers. They are working for Honda all over the globe.

But do they work with union employees and with a work force of a different demographic mix than that found in midwestern Ohio? And do they work in other than a ''greenfield'' operation? The answer to these questions is a resounding yes. A look at Toyota in operation in California will reveal why. Later, I'll cover the success of the same principles in action at *The Boeing Company*. The world's leader in the production of commercial airliners, Boeing is a homegrown American firm if ever there was one. Therefore, as you read how Toyota applies its principles, please zero in again on the overall pattern of quality management ''Japanese-style,'' and keep in mind its essential features. You will read much more in later chapters about that decentralized, team-based style at work by other than the Japanese, in companies large and small. Neither its use nor its successes have ever been confined to the Japanese. They just use it more than most.

THE NUMMI STORY: TOYOTA'S DECENTRALIZED
PRINCIPLES SUCCEEDING WHERE GM'S CENTRALIZED
PRINCIPLES HAD FAILED

Fremont, California, thirty-five miles southeast of San Francisco, is the site of the joint GM-Toyota venture, *New United Motor Manufacturing, Inc.* (*NUMMI*). Production began on December 10, 1984. When I visited it the plant was producing just under 200,000 automobiles a year, about 40 percent Toyota Corollas and 60 percent Chevrolet GEO Prizms (they are interleaved on the production line). NUMMI has been a rousing success, and that success is occurring in a plant that previously was an abject failure. It was so bad, in fact, that in 1982 GM shut it down completely. According to GMers, it had the poorest record in the entire GM system in every category. Not the least of its problems was extreme alienation between labor and management. That manifested itself in a lack of motivation and commitment in the work force. There were problems everywhere. So much so, there is ample indication Maryann Keller was not exaggerating in the least in her 1989 book *Rude Awakening*, on GM's "*Rise, Fall, and Struggle for Recovery*," when she characterized those problems in this way: "[The Fremont plant] was notorious as being one of GM's most unmanageable. Before the plant was closed, daily absenteeism was regularly over 20 percent; beer bottles littered the parking lot; and even the slightest dispute had to go to the bargaining table."

General Motors and Toyota had extensive discussions leading to their February 17, 1983, agreement to create a joint operation at Fremont. Each had a good reason. The agreement gave GM a chance to learn about Toyota's "production and management techniques" and why they were so effective. It provided Toyota the opportunity to learn how to do business in the United States—as a precursor to opening its own transplant plants there and in Canada. For understandable reasons, Toyota wanted no part of the Fremont location and its history of intractable problems. However, General Motors insisted. So the new joint venture—to be managed by Toyota—started with a formidable challenge. It had to succeed in the very location, with the same work force, that had failed so spectacularly under GM. Therefore, as at TAC, there was a stark contrast in management styles at work in Fremont: the *centralized, managership, functions* approach on the one hand, and the *decentralized, leadership, teams* approach on the other. Despite the considerable obstacles and challenges involved, Toyota pulled it off. Automobiles produced at Fremont soon moved to the head of the pack in GM's quality derby, suggesting Fremont wasn't so bad after all—if managed right.

TOYOTA'S DECENTRALIZED MANAGEMENT APPROACH IS SIMILAR TO THAT OF OTHER JAPANESE COMPANIES, INCLUDING HONDA

In the Japanese manner, Toyota, like Honda, uses teams as the organization building blocks. From NUMMI's literature on the subject:

> By design, the team concept is the key factor in the manufacturing process and not only applies to small teams in the plant, but throughout the company. Each team is responsible for performing company and section objectives in areas such as quality, cost, production and safety. . . . The team concept supports the basic attitude that the company belongs to each and every team member, not just management.

Some 2,700 "team members" are employed at NUMMI, including 340 "team leaders" and some 100 "group leaders." The average size of a team is six members. More than forty team rooms have been built in the plant—for team meetings, briefings and debriefings, and work breaks. As at Honda America, the Japanese president of the NUMMI operation, Kan Higashi, was extremely gracious and hospitable. He also contributed generously of his time in explaining the Toyota management philosophy. The other NUMMI team members at every level, from Toyota and GM alike, were similarly helpful.

Toyota's principles and their results were much in evidence. They include high standards, excellent management-labor relations, a well-motivated work force, outstanding planning, smooth integration of the various elements, and the pervasive use of goals, measurement, and feedback to employees at all levels. The actions taken to ingrain the quality mindset also are impressive and form a backdrop for everything else. They call their approach the "Four S's." *Seri* means "clearing." *Seiton* means "arrangement." *Seiketsu* means "cleanliness." *Seiso* means "sweeping and washing." Toyota pays lots of attention to the Four S's. Also, as I had seen in Honda's plants (and in TAC and other settings after we created a new spirit), there is an atmosphere at NUMMI that comes from people who know they're winning, and who reflect justifiable pride in their accomplishments.

TOYOTA HAS FORGED A NEW PARTNERSHIP BETWEEN MANAGEMENT AND LABOR—UNDER GM IT WAS STRAINED TO THE BREAKING POINT

Like Honda, Toyota uses *multiskilling* as a key feature of its team approach. All team members learn one or more additional skills related to their team's responsibilities. That provides greater flexibility, and allows team members to trade off to avoid boredom. Such multiskilling was out of the question in the old GM Fremont days, since it was specifically prohibited in the union contract. As part of the negotiations for the NUMMI start-up, Toyota had agreed to hire back the bulk of the previous GM work force, and to have it represented by the UAW. But Toyota extracted certain agreements from the UAW in return. In particular, the union agreed *"to the adoption of the Toyota production system which is based on using a team concept and broad job classifications."* How was that generalized statement translated into action? The more than 120 job classifications the UAW had at the Fremont plant were reduced to only 4.

Also, Toyota made it clear in the application letter sent to former GM employees that NUMMI would not be bound by any of the former agreements between GM and the UAW. This was to be a new deal, and a new partnership. The letter also said, *It will be essential for everyone to contribute to an environment based on mutual trust, respect and cooperation if the company is to be successful.* It went on, *Past mistakes such as high absenteeism and poor quality will not be tolerated by the new company.* Those don't seem like terribly quaint ideas—just good common sense. However, in the context of the climate that had previously existed at Fremont, this was radical stuff indeed. Nevertheless, Toyota was swamped with job applications.

Naturally I was curious as to how all of this was working. So I asked for a one-on-one session, behind closed doors, with the chief representative of UAW Local 2244. NUMMI's Japanese president was all for it, as was George Nano, UAW chair of the bargaining committee. My discussions with George Nano were wide-ranging, and I gave him every opportunity to express dissatisfaction. He did not. In fact, he praised the *"new partnership"* and the results it was achieving. Having been in the UAW leadership in the pre-NUMMI days at Fremont, he recited some horror stories regarding absenteeism and lackluster performance which outdid Maryann Keller's. He also said the situation had changed completely and characterized that change as like *"night and day."* I was especially interested in the issue of multiskilling. Nano said, "Though we fought it tooth and nail, it's the best thing that ever happened to a union member." I asked why. He replied, "Because it makes the job more interesting, and it makes our union members much more employable if they have to change jobs or relocate for some reason—and many do."

George Nano was not suggesting that all is perfect at NUMMI. Neither am I. What Nano did say is that the Toyota management principles have created a climate for employee involvement and performance that is light-years better than what existed before under the GM management principles. (The union now gets along with the many GMers in NUMMI, and there is a moral there also.) That new partnership goes a long way in explaining the greatly improved quality and productivity at Fremont. Also, with job classifications and multiskilling being but cases in point, the management principles used by the Japanese are providing valuable lessons for American labor as well as for management. America needs to heed those lessons.

One of our country's greatest needs is for more harmonious labor-management relationships—based on a new partnership. That will involve significant change from the separation, suspicion, and even outright confrontation that have existed for decades. This may be the most important of all the many lessons the NUMMI experience at Fremont provides. Good labor-management relations are simply not America's strong suit—and that's true whether the business is union or nonunion (see the statistics in chapter 10 that support this conclusion). A thorny aspect of the problem is that most American companies believe relations in their company are as good, and productivity is as high, as they can get; but 95 percent of them are wrong. That won't be solved by discourses on America's aggregate competitiveness; however, it can be solved if each of those companies worries about its own fortunes and recognizes the potential for improvement under its own nose. The nation won't awaken all at once. But it's difficult to explain why so many businesses are sleeping through the Japanese wakeup call. A big part of that is a failure to recognize how far our society has gone toward building a *two-class* system in the workplace.

CEMENTING THE NEW PARTNERSHIP BY ELIMINATING THE GAP BETWEEN "MANAGERS" AND "WORKERS"—WHY THE JAPANESE EXCEL IN THAT

One important aspect of the Japanese approach, seen in all their transplant plants and also in Japan, is important for America's managers to consider. That aspect gets to the matter of the two-class system. Specifically, it addresses how the managers treat themselves on the one hand and the workers on the other. Many observers have written in detail about such Japanese practices as open offices, wearing no neckties, all eating in the same cafeteria, and having no special parking places.

I saw many such practices at both Honda and Toyota. At NUMMI, Kan Higashi, the president, has his office out in the open. It's the same for all the others in the managerial hierarchy, from Toyota and GM alike, no walls at all. The previous GM walled manager's offices are now used extensively for training sessions and other employee meetings.

In contrasting the American and Japanese management approaches, some call this the *egalitarian* issue. However, that's a misnomer. More importantly, it misses the point. Because it's not an egalitarian issue at all. For example, I presumed before my visits that those Japanese practices were aimed at creating trust, open communication, and a seamless network of leadership. After I saw them in operation and discussed the underlying thinking with the NUMMI and Honda presidents, my presumption was confirmed. They believe you use them to ensure a free flow of ideas, build involvement and trust, and avoid a huge gap in communication and perspective between labor and management. The numerous Japanese executives with whom I have discussed this subject believe that that gap is a natural consequence of allowing fault lines to develop between the two groups and then doing little or nothing to remove them. (That's my own experience as well.) So, they believe, top management has to work hard continuously at bridging that gap in every aspect of the operation.

By way of example, Kan Higashi at NUMMI explained that the open offices and companywide dining are merely the start. It's an important way of making the leaders, the most senior ones included, accessible and approachable. It replaces the usually empty phrase *"open door"* with lots of opportunities for personal interactions. Those practices demonstrate with actions—not just with words—a readiness to listen with interest not aloofness. Higashi further explained that all of the NUMMI supervisors have the obligation to follow through in that same spirit in every activity. When the top leader places that kind of premium on seamless communication and openness, it sets the tone for everyone. It's not that hard to instill in the organizational culture, but it has to come from the top.

For the tastes of most American managers the Japanese go too far with these practices. However, they work. And the objectives involved are of critical importance. Indeed, all businesses would benefit greatly if their managers got more involved and took similar steps to open up the stilted lines of communication. Numerous surveys reveal that the "trust gap" is one of the biggest problems that confronts American management. Thus, considerable movement in the direction of the Japanese style is direly needed, even for companies not prepared to adopt their approach wholesale. The techniques may vary, but the results need to be the same. And, those critics who scoff at the Japanese approach as more atmospherics than substance are just plain wrong. The Japanese do walk the walk even more vigorously than they talk the talk.

Finally, no one should confuse these Japanese methods with an excessively permissive approach, which creates ambiguity about authority. Every American employee in these Japanese companies knows who's boss, as well as the important role he or she plays in the exercise of overall authority. I'm convinced the employees in those companies acknowledge the chain of authority and its legitimacy even more than in an American counterpart company. It is apathy and alienation that erode organizational discipline, not improved communication and cooperation.

Although I have used Honda and Toyota as examples, I have by no means reached my conclusions regarding "Japanese management" from those two companies alone. They merely provide an instructive window into the successful Japanese approach. Every American manager should also keep in mind the dramatic change the Japanese have wrought from the days when a *"Made in Japan"* label inspired derision not respect. We're talking the effectiveness of management systems here, nothing else! Toyota's success at Fremont, on the heels of GM's failure, makes that point as powerfully as anything can.

TOYOTA'S MANAGEMENT APPROACH
WAS THE DIFFERENCE IN THE CHANGE
OF FORTUNES AT FREMONT

Toyota's approach was radically different from that of GM, and it has resulted in far better quality and much higher productivity. NUMMI officials provide ample comparative data to show how much better the Fremont plant is performing than before. That data ranges from far fewer employee hours to turn out a car, to impressive improvements in first-run efficiency, to quality and customer satisfaction ratings that far surpass Fremont's earlier ratings. And yet, as at Honda, one finds at NUMMI no differences in the robotics or any other technological secrets. It's the same plant GM used, with the same employees. The difference? *The management approach.* Nothing more, nothing less.

Maryann Keller summed it up well in *Rude Awakening*: "For those who believed that the Japanese industrial edge rested solely in technological prowess, the NUMMI experiment was a real revelation. The Toyota secret was, finally, no secret at all, and it was as old as history." She also quoted Al Warren, vice president of labor relations for GM: "I'm glad they did it, because it demonstrated that a work force we thought was unmanageable could be managed." That pretty well sums it up. But this also raises an important question. Why couldn't GM have brought about the same turnaround without any Japanese involvement? They could have, of course, if only they had chosen the same management approach that Toyota uses. Why haven't they? Centralism in their bone marrow? Relationships with the union beyond the point of no return? Lack of conviction there was a better way? Only GM knows. In that regard, it's especially instructive to take a look at the origins and makeup of the General Motors management style. It's the antithesis of that used by the Japanese.

GENERAL MOTORS: A PAINFUL EXAMPLE OF ORGANIZATIONAL CENTRALISM AT WORK—AND A METAPHOR FOR ALL SUCH ORGANIZATIONS

Almost everyone knows of the trials and tribulations of General Motors. However, most cannot divine the underlying causes for GM's failures vis-à-vis its competition. There's a great deal to the story—and it provides lessons for other businesses all over America. The bottom line is that General Motors heeded the siren song of management Centralism in the mid-sixties. Like the others who adopted Centralism, GM has paid a stiff price for the experience. It's an interesting story. And it's not over yet.

It begins with Alfred Sloan, who became president of GM in 1923 and chairman in 1937. Sloan deservedly is credited with the vision, strategy, and management acumen that built GM into the giant of the automobile industry—and the world's largest corporation. GMers confirm that perhaps Sloan's greatest talent was his understanding of people. He was sensitive and dedicated to staying in touch with their thinking (impressively so, given the autocratic management style of the era). And Sloan demonstrated impressive leadership skill in building a system that took their feelings, aspirations, and need for involvement into account. His own writings reflect his view that a mammoth corporation such as GM had to be managed in a way that was highly people-conscious and in ways that brought forth their creativity and commitment. As an example, he extolled the concept of *employee ownership* long before that became a buzzphrase in management literature (a comparatively recent development).

In keeping with that thinking, Sloan believed in decentralization and ran GM that way. He and a small corporate staff set overall strategy and goals, but the company subsidiaries had full authority to make their own decisions in pursuit of those goals. Those subsidiaries—Cadillac, Buick, Oldsmobile, Pontiac, and Chevrolet—essentially were self-sufficient. They had the internal decision power and the resources to control their own engineering, assembly, and sales.

In due time the helm of GM was turned over to others. By the mid-sixties GM's chairmanship had passed to Fred Donner. Donner was the first of what would be a long string of GM CEOs to come up through GM's financial hierarchy. That string did not end until Roger Smith, another CFO promoted to CEO, stepped down at the end of the 1980s. Over more than twenty years they perpetuated a Centralism-based system that has been a prime cause of GM's trials and tribulations. When Fred Donner took over GM the nation's business schools were abuzz with the alleged advantages of Centralism and its family of beguiling precepts. So while GM wasn't broke, Donner decided to fix it. He did so by launching a massive reorganization.

The themes? As you would expect: centralization, consolidation, vertical alignment, and the use of *functions* as the building blocks at all levels. Following the Centralism catechism, Donner fractured engineering, assembly, and sales—formerly integrated in the car companies—into separate functions, each consolidated internally to every possible extent. For example, since assembly was a *function* in centralist thinking, the gospel said there was great waste in having five such functions in the separate car companies. So assembly was taken away from each company and housed in a single large functional silo: the *General Motors Assembly Division* (*GMAD*). Just think of the economies of scale! I'm sure they broke out the champagne in GM's accounting departments, as visions of sugarplums danced in their heads.

The engineering and design function was likewise consolidated into a single vertically aligned group. That left "sales," which was also consolidated into a single group—a functional silo comprising five "nameplate" sales divisions (Cadillac, Buick, etc.). A very small engineering staff was left in each nameplate division, for example, a "Chevrolet Chief Engineer" with a few helpers. But that voice was purely advisory, not controlling. As events would prove, it was a frail umbilical cord from the customer to design and manufacturing. In both the pre- and post-1965 reorganization GM had lots of other divisions, in keeping with its leaders' steadfast belief in vertical integration—building as many components as possible in-house. Delco, Hydra-matic, and other such component divisions continued to serve as the privileged in-house vendors. However, now their internal customers were GM's vertical functional silos, Engineering and Assembly.

Commonality quickly took priority over distinctiveness. And the competing drive for ever better features by the individual car companies soon became a relic of the past. That drive for commonality took the *zing* out of the creative process and seriously dampened the competition of ideas. It also stifled originality in the now consolidated design studios. Also, it's fair to say—and GMers say it—that the drive for continuous improvement gave way to the *pressures for continuous cost savings from the finance side of the house*. So cost-cutting drove quality down, the reverse of the Japanese approach. And GM's customers increasingly became aware of the resulting decline in the quality and distinctiveness of GM's products.

The stage had also been set for stout functional walls to appear, and, as always, they did. The necessary bridging both within and between those new vertically aligned, functional silos was left to "matrix management" principles. (More on the problems with the matrix management approach in chapters 3 and 7. It doesn't get the job done.) GMers familiar with the way the matrix arrangement worked candidly admit that disputes between the functional arrays— and there were plenty—had to go all the way to the presidents of the functional silos for resolution. And then the resolution didn't always stick. This all made accountability a noticeable casualty of the Donner organization, by admission of the same GMers. One such GM executive says, "Somebody always had somebody else to blame!" The ambiguity in the flow of authority made that a difficult defense to challenge. You couldn't pin responsibility down because it was too diffused to track.

As a result of this sweeping centralization and functionalization, harmony and effective integration suffered greatly, as did quality. Others of GM's traditional strengths were significantly diminished as well. All that reached a nadir at the very time GM needed to be sharper and quicker, not duller and more sluggish, to retain its dominance in an increasingly competitive market. Donner had fixed GM all right. He had set it up for a kill by the Japanese. And the Japanese obliged.

GM HAS DISCOVERED HOW TENACIOUSLY
CENTRALISM HOLDS ON AND RESISTS CHANGE—
OLD HABITS DIE HARD

There's no need to dwell further on GM's shortcomings, since all GMers agree that the new organization served the corporation poorly. In fact, by the mid-eighties, after being in that organizational structure for nearly twenty years, the GM brass were at long last beginning to see, as then chairman and CEO Roger Smith put it, *"the handwriting on the wall."* Smith, previously GM's chief financial officer, was another in the long line of Donner protégés. Nonetheless, Smith was outspoken in denouncing the centralized organization of his mentors. While announcing a sweeping 1984 GM reorganization, he openly and pointedly questioned, "How could the company of Alfred Sloan have become so centralized?"

Though Roger Smith's question was rhetorical, there's an answer to it: Many hundreds of businesses were centralizing in that same way in the sixties and seventies. They were egged on by the promises of greater efficiency as the pipe organs swelled to a crescendo and the centralizers mounted their pulpits and recited the gospel of Centralism. They were very persuasive, and the congregation of believers grew and grew (more in chapter 7). In fact, the techniques of centralization became so widespread that they came to enjoy, and still have, the trappings and status of *traditional management*. It took GM a very long time to awaken, even partly, to the problems Centralism was causing. Most others are still sound asleep.

Roger Smith perceived, accurately, that solutions could be found in decentralizing what Fred Donner had centralized. Maryann Keller, commenting in *Rude Awakening* on that 1984 GM reorganization, quoted Roger Smith on how the reorganization decision was reached: "We got together and said, 'Hey, we've got to push this decision making back down to where it was. We've got to get the market responses faster. We've got to decentralize.' " Keller also commented that "Alfred Sloan was undoubtedly turning over in his grave" from watching all that had happened to GM after the Donner reorganization. However, if Alfred Sloan or anyone else concluded from Roger

Smith's statement that GM was really going back to pushing the "*decision making back down to where it was,*" they were to be disappointed. The 1984 reorganization, massive though it was, stopped well short of the Sloan model. While no one could reasonably expect that it would mirror the Sloan approach exactly, it was logical to think that it would squarely address the issue of the vertical, functional alignment. It didn't live up to its billing. The culture of Centralism had become deeply embedded at GM, and it exerted itself forcefully in the 1984 reorganization. Indeed, Roger Smith's version of decentralization took some strange twists and turns.

Smith had become convinced, and said in strong terms, that the functional silos of the engineering and assembly groups had become *powerful, bureaucratic fiefdoms* that needed to be broken up. Notwithstanding that recognition, he decided it was impractical to break them into more than two pieces. Two new overarching groups were formed, each having full authority and wherewithal for engineering, assembly, and sales. The first group, called BOC, was composed of the Buick, Oldsmobile and Cadillac products. The second, CPC, included the products associated with Chevrolet, Pontiac, and GM of Canada.

So far, so good. But the engineering and assembly functions within those groups remained centralized. And the sales function remained in the "nameplate" divisions. In fact, the latter remained essentially as Donner had created them, but they now reported to one of the two separate groups, BOC or CPC. At the same time, they lost their own engineering department. While it had not been terribly effective, it was the sales group's only input mechanism, in a qualified engineering way, from its dealers and customers to the designers and assemblers in the other functional silos.

To complicate matters further, both BOC and CPC continued to build both small and large cars. Therefore, they found themselves needing to cross the group boundaries in getting products engineered and assembled. All of that was still to be done in a context of economy of scale but, it was hoped, in a way that would avoid the look-alike syndrome that had been so detrimental to consumer acceptance of GM's products.

In all these senses, the new organization retained most of the features of the organization that had just been abandoned. Indeed, it retained more vestiges of Donner's organization than of Sloan's. Some claimed that GM had not decentralized at all—it had simply been broken into two parts instead of one, and the other *Centralism* precepts essentially were left intact. Subsequent events were to reinforce that view.

Once it snuggled into its 1984 structure, GM kept chipping away at the organizational issues. The BOC group re-formed the *Cadillac Car Company* and took steps toward giving it somewhat more wall-to-wall product authority. These and related steps led to Cadillac's winning the *Malcolm Baldrige Quality Award* in 1990. Also, GM's actions to improve process quality and its partial success in getting more flexible work rules from the UAW have slowly improved quality and productivity. That has happened in sporadic and patchwork fashion, but there have been improvements in most plants. GM also has adopted various pieces of quality management principles. For example, the corporation has formed numerous cross-cutting, cross-functional teams to improve coordination between the functional silos. One case in point is the formation of "segment teams" to look searchingly at diverse customer likes and dislikes, by product segment, and to feed those data and assessments into the overall system. I have provided advice to some of the major GM divisions in that regard.

I've also recently visited all GM's design studios. GM has separated them one from the other, reinvigorated each, and reintroduced a spirit of originality. That's working, and I saw many exciting and innovative future products there.

However, quality is needed throughout the organization as well as in the products to drive costs down as product quality goes up. Indeed, it is overall organizational quality—and the drive, determination, and efficiency it produces—that stands the old adages about quality on their heads. And in that larger context it's quite clear that GM has not mastered all aspects of the quality management equation. Therefore, serious questions remain as to when GM will apply all the lessons from its NUMMI venture. After all, GM's prime objective in that venture was to find out what was behind the Toyota management approach. Now they know. And they know it relates to how you manage people, not exotic technologies or techniques. Yet one can find the full range of the principles that powered the NUMMI transformation only at GM's new Saturn facility in Spring Hill, Tennessee. That being the case, it's appropriate that GM has chosen to call Saturn *"A different kind of car company."* It certainly is a different management approach than the one GM traditionally has followed. And it's also different from the rest of GM—which continues to be managed more in the old way than the Saturn way.

Hoping as I do that American managers will see the light, I have been perplexed by the raft of articles that talk of GM's "management experiment" at its new Saturn plant. But the press is not making that up. When the Saturn project was launched in the mid-1980s, Roger Smith called it *"the key to GM's long-term competitiveness, survival, and success."* GM has done nothing since to change that spin on what Saturn represents. The trouble with that is if Saturn succeeds it just piles more evidence on the abundant evidence that's all around us. The same "Japanese-style" management principles being used at Saturn have proved themselves in too many other settings for GM to look on Saturn as a laboratory on their worth. Or, for that matter, for anyone else in corporate America to do so. There's no reason these principles can't work every bit as well for Saturn as they do for Honda and Toyota (and as they do in the other companies I will discuss in later chapters). The Japanese do not have a corner on good management principles. They are there for anyone to use.

Therefore, the right question is not, *Will Saturn succeed?* (And we all wait with bated breath for the answer.) The right question is, *When is General Motors going to Saturnize its entire operation, and how quickly?* A second important question is, If General Motors is still not convinced after all its travails, then how about the host of other companies that manage as GM does but are still to be hit by the battering ram of globalization? It's not a comforting thought.

GM'S CHANGES HAVE NOT MATCHED THEIR COMPETITIVE CHALLENGES—A LESSON FOR EVERYONE USING A CENTRALIZED, MANAGERSHIP SYSTEM

The 1984 reorganization, and the revisions since, cured a few but not all of the old ills. And GM's financial fortunes have not noticeably improved since Roger Smith said he saw the *"handwriting on the wall,"* and presumed to have taken appropriate action to respond. In fact, since then GM's downsizing has continued— and even accelerated—in hope of stanching the financial bleeding. It has gone on and on and on. For example, in GM's 1990 round of downsizing (which by then had become an old-hat exercise), four more assembly plants were closed, 6,000 more people were laid off, and GM announced elimination of 15,000 more white-collar workers by 1993. That announcement was still producing shock waves when GM announced in December 1991 that it would close twenty-one plants and slash 74,000 jobs. That level of cuts equals the Chrysler Corporation's entire payroll and directly affects one out of five of GM's automotive workers. As a consequence of all these closings, GM's North American automotive operations will be half the size they were in 1985. So much for GM's love affair with organizational Centralism and its halfhearted reorganization in 1984.

Then, in April 1992, GM made still another announcement, this time of a shakeup in the top management structure—and another reorganization. The long-slumbering GM board awakened and played the key role in the additional moves. Robert Stempel was out as chairman of the board's Executive Committee, replaced by GM board member John G. Smale (former chairman and CEO of Procter & Gamble), but Stempel remained GM's chairman and CEO. (Only six months later, in October 1992, Robert Stempel was out completely, resigning under pressure.) John F. Smith, Jr., from GM's European operation, was named president.

GM also said it is abandoning the 1984 organization (BOC and

CPC, etc.) in favor of consolidating all automotive operations into a single organization. The new arrangement has four group executives responsible for *"Parts Making," "Truck Making," "Car Making,"* and *"Sales and Marketing."* Saturn will remain as an "independent subsidiary"—another telling indication that in GM thinking Saturn is *different.* Therefore, except for Saturn, the new organization sounds more like the failed Fred Donner model of 1965 than Roger Smith's 1984 model, which, though halfhearted, was an improvement over Donner's excessive centralization.

The issues involved are not new. It had become abundantly obvious to GM's top managers in 1984 that the corporation should not have centralized as it did in 1965. They said so. It has become even more painfully obvious now. It can be fixed, but not by the same formula GM has applied to date. So GM is right in calling, as it has, for *fundamental changes.* And the changes must extend to GM's entire management system—from top to bottom.

It is significant that GM's problems have not been and are not now caused by a lack of talent. I would stack the GMers I know up against the best and brightest of any corporation in America. Instead, GM's problems have stemmed from poor integration and orchestration of that talent. And a serious question remains as to which way GM is moving, toward the old-time Centralism religion—*more rigorously applied*—or to a new management system better adapted to our times and circumstances? That's hard to tell. If GM does what it did in 1984, it will be a largely ineffective mixture of the two. Let's hope that this time GM can turn its fortunes around under a new chairman and president and with its new organization. I'm strongly rooting for them. Everyone should be.

GM has tried to carry out its repeated downsizing actions, especially recently, with a human face. The techniques employed include early-retirement options and "job banks" for employees no longer needed but who still draw their pay and do "community service work" rather than build cars. GM's agreements with the UAW also provide for a period of GM augmentation of unemployment checks for those who have been released outright. With regard to GM's 1992 announcements, *Business Week* reported that the company will further slash its white-collar ranks by ''offering attractive early-retirement terms to workers as young as 51.'' Those clearly are humanistic and equitable actions. However, they further increase GM's production costs—still the highest in the industry—with no offsetting productivity contribution in return. Indeed, GM's worker-retiree ratio is rapidly approaching one to one. So those economic dynamics contribute to a continuing downward spiral. It's very difficult to overcome tough competition by paying more and more people *not* to produce cars. If there is a success formula in that it has yet to be demonstrated. That's a harsh fact of life that GM—and many others in the *Fortune* 500— will be confronting so long as they continue to manage in their old centralist ways.

Many people, including within GM itself, avoid the gut issues involved in GM's dismal modern track record by contending that the decentralized, team-based approach will not succeed with America's workers on a large scale. They also argue that it won't work in long-standing plants that are unionized, as opposed to new start-ups out in the boondocks. That's the ''greenfield'' argument. (And presumably that's why GM went to a greenfield in Tennessee to establish its ''different'' Saturn plant.) Those holding that view are not persuaded by the NUMMI success story in the old GM plant at Fremont, with the same work force that had failed under GM. In fact, many trash the Japanese management style as incompatible with American workers. They portray it as a mass-calisthenics, one-two-three kick-or-get-kicked approach. (I fervently wish it were: Then the Japanese would be easy to beat.)

The soothsayers hold that it's immensely difficult to change the management culture, even if it were necessary—and, according to them, it probably is not. They marshal all sorts of strained arguments. These include the observation that American worker productivity is the *highest in the world*, and proceed from there to blame our burgeoning difficulties on everything other than our productivity and quality. None of those arguments are valid; indeed, most are specious. But they extend the nation's slumber.

Quality and productivity problems, leading to loss of market share and accompanying downsizing, are becoming increasingly obvious (and onerous) across the American business landscape. The lesson that needs to emerge is that the Centralism-driven centocracy approach clearly hasn't been the answer—and that it definitely does not fit with any viable version of quality management. They won't fit together because they are complete contradictions in styles. But judging from the dogged persistence of the traditional American style there are few signs this lesson has emerged. If it has, it hasn't been heeded—except by a very few.

SUCCESSFUL CHANGE DEPENDS ON ABANDONING THE TRADITIONAL STYLE

This is not a book about the Japanese management style—except for using it, and its demonstrated success to illuminate the book's central premise. There is little question that America has been slow to catch on to the Japanese style and what makes it so successful. For a while, in the seventies, there was an abundance of facile answers for the Japanese seizing more and more U.S. market share, particularly in the automobile market. As a relevant piece of history, the Arab-Israeli War of 1973 spawned the 1973 oil crunch, and the birth of controlled oil prices by the OPEC cartel. After the brief 1973 "oil embargo" by the Arab states was lifted—and the shock waves it produced in the West subsided—the Arab oil-producing countries had leveled their supply to world markets at 14 million barrels per day. That was a dramatic decrease from the 21 million barrels per day before the embargo began in 1973. Consequently, with supply controlled by OPEC manipulation of individual producer country "quotas," the price of oil skyrocketed from less than three dollars a barrel pre-1973 to more than thirty dollars a barrel when the dust settled. Gasoline prices rose accordingly. Everyone in the West, America included, suddenly became conscious of fuel efficiency. For most it was now a personal pocketbook issue, not some abstract exercise of failed diplomacy in a far corner of the world creating worldwide economic dislocations (though it was certainly that, too).

Therefore, the first Japanese cars to be met with widespread consumer enthusiasm were small, and fuel-efficient models like the Honda Civic and equivalents from other Japanese producers. Thus, the conventional wisdom was born that this created the opening for the Japanese. The fact that "Detroit" got stuck with its fleets of "*gas-guzzlers*" was somehow its own fault. (Never mind that such models long had been in favor with the American consumer, and were now abruptly out of favor.) Critic after critic piled on Detroit as being slow to react. So, the conventional wisdom said, this was an issue largely reduced to the myopia and inertia of the Big Three automakers.

Most pundits saw few if any ramifications for other American industries. But as the years unfolded, that superficial explanation fell away. The Japanese started penetrating, year by year, other parts of the domestic automobile market until they covered the spectrum from compact, to midsize, to luxury models, to minivans, to pickup trucks—and Japanese dealerships mushroomed across America. (As oil prices stabilized near eighteen dollars a barrel, consumers' taste for larger models returned.) And then, in the mid-eighties, Japanese *transplant* production plants began popping up across the United States and Canada. (As this was written there were ten, and more were on the way.)

Meanwhile, we were witnessing a similar and steadily growing Japanese incursion into the American consumer electronics market—demonstrating that a process of globalization was under way that had nothing to do with fuel-efficient cars. That market incursion also demonstrated that the Japanese were not dependent on such extraordinary events as the OPEC phenomenon to penetrate and even dominate worldwide markets. That penetration and dominance extended to autos, electronics, shipbuilding, heavy machine tools—and a long list of other industries in which Japanese products replaced domestic products because they offered higher quality and value. The seventies-style facile answers no longer sufficed to explain our problems and Japan's success. But new answers sprang up to take their place. And most have little to do with how the Japanese manage. The sad fact is that we are amazingly persistent at missing the point. The point is this: There are good and bad ways to manage, and the Japanese are using the good ways.

By 1995 all the Big Three had staged a comeback in sales and profits. Even GM, after its long siege, had edged into the black. Although this is heartening, we must not overlook the dominant factor at work here. U.S. quality and productivity certainly improved (varying by company)—but the comeback primarily has been due to the plunging dollar/soaring yen. In only 10 years (1985–1995) the yen/dollar ratio went from 240Y/$1 to 80Y/$1. This essential tripling of yen value has given the Japanese a formidable array of cost/price challenges. The Japanese call this phenomenon *endaka*. And it has provided American competitors with a breathing spell from the Japanese market onslaught. But don't take solace from that as being permanent. Most believe the falling dollar has bottomed out.

Also, the respected consulting firm *Harbour & Associates* reported in 1995 the results of a broad study on comparative productivity, and it provided little solace. *Harbour* reported that the Japanese have improved further, and use less than 18 hours to build a car. In contrast, the best U.S. firm (Ford) in 1995 is at 25 hours, and GM, the worst, needs 30.1 hours. The report said that if GM were as efficient as Toyota, it could reduce its annual costs by $4.2 billion. I shudder to think of GM's fortunes had its costs more than doubled in 10 years versus Toyota, not the other way around. As more food for thought, despite the great boon to our competitiveness from *endaka*—our trade deficit in 1995 stood at an *all time high*. Thus, the key message in this book remains highly relevant: The old ways of managing, widely practiced, are simply unsuited to our times.

Clearly, the Japanese success alone has been insufficient to direct America's attention to its own management shortcomings. So in chapter 3 I want to change gears and bring the contrasts in management system approaches back solely to American case histories—and cover successes not failures. The chapter contains several examples of winning big by organizing small including three well-known American businesses that once were centralized, their elephantine management systems adopted when it was all the rage. However, during the eighties each abandoned the centralized, managership approach completely. Each replaced centralization with decentralization as their dominant organizational principle. Each switched from functions to teams as the building blocks. Each created strong, unwavering commitment to quality throughout. Each adopted distributed leadership to replace the managership of old. And all have achieved great success by doing so.

One studied the Japanese and adopted their methods. The other two determined that change was needed and carried out their successful transformations without any Japanese influence whatsoever— either as catalyst or model. These stories hold many lessons for America's managers.

Why are only 5 percent of America's employees organized in work teams? Tradition. Inertia. Most managers don't see a problem. Others remain uncertain about what to do. They await more proof there's a better way, and a clear picture of how to go about it. It might be said they are zealously applying the *First Law of Wing-Walking: Hold tightly on to what you have until you get a firm grip on something else.* (And that's not a bad idea.) Many also have a visceral feeling that ''Japanese practices'' simply do not fit *their* employees. That's largely because they don't understand it, and their scorn is heightened by the many who trash those Japanese practices.

To address such concerns, chapter 3 starts with two case histories from my own leadership experiences. They are included to provide insight into the conceptual underpinnings of the team-based, decentralized approach. They also provide the first elements of proof the management approach I commend for your consideration is grounded in successful application, in numerous highly challenging settings. All five of the stories in chapter 3 set the stage for later discussion of team-based quality management and the best ways to implement it. It's not new, the Japanese didn't invent it, and they're not the only ones to practice it. It works well for everyone.

Winning Big by Organizing Small: More Key Examples

It really doesn't matter who invented them, they work. But it's important to understand that they're not new, even though many now perceive them to be. That view is encouraged by some who, for their own reasons, portray these ideas as innovative new contributions to management knowledge. I learned early in my military career the value, and necessity, of strong leadership and commitment from the very bottom up—at all levels and in all activities. I also learned the value of using a team-based organization to facilitate that leadership and commitment. Those lessons—learned in vividly challenging settings—later proved invaluable in achieving the same synergy and results in organizations of ever-increasing size and complexity. The first such lessons came at the age of twenty-two when I was leading flights and sections of fighters in combat missions over North Korea. Then as now, those flights were organized as teams.

Successful fighter tactics against enemy threats depend upon intricate and cooperative *teamwork*—the basic reason for the team approach in the first place. They also depend on each member operating within that team concept at all times. To illustrate, in Korea our fighter pilot credo was "Every Man a Tiger." That meant we wanted every flight member to exercise the utmost in creativity and aggressiveness. However, it was also understood there would be no "Lone Wolves." A hard-won lesson of combat is that the team concept is absolutely dependent upon mutual trust, mutual respect, and mutual support.

You also learn in combat that your flight is only as strong as its weakest link. Therefore, the leadership challenge is to have no weak links. When your life is on the line that takes on special emphasis. Although only a second lieutenant, because of heavy combat losses, by my fifteenth mission I found myself in the flight lead position, and I led the rest of my 103 combat missions over North Korea. I learned a lot about teamwork, responsibility, and leadership. And I saw the tragic consequences to other flights and individuals when one element or another of that important synergy broke down.

After returning from Korea and a stint as a flight commander in a fighter gunnery school in Arizona, I was selected as a wingman on the USAF jet aerobatic team, *The Thunderbirds*. The competition was stiff, and I was delighted to be selected. After an exciting and demanding two-year tour flying the first year on the right wing and the second on the left, I was reassigned to Europe. There I was to have the chance to put my own organization and leadership theories to the test.

PUTTING TEAMWORK, LEADERSHIP, AND QUALITY PRINCIPLES TO WORK SUCCESSFULLY IN A HIGHLY DEMANDING SETTING—JET AEROBATICS

Soon after my arrival at a fighter wing in Germany, I was advised that I had been chosen as Leader of *The Skyblazers*, the European edition of *The Thunderbirds*. It was the same mission, but for European not U.S. audiences. I was twenty-eight years old and eager to accept the challenge to be the boss both in the air and on the ground. The prospect of more exposure to the aerobatic mission was welcomed, even though I knew a more dangerous peacetime pursuit could not be found.

Simply flying jet fighters in those early days involved high risk. Performing high-speed aerobatics in close formation, low to the ground, increased those risks many fold. In fact, we once computed the risk, based on casualties versus events, of jet aerobatic flying in that era versus the risk in Grand Prix racing. As dangerous as Formula One auto racing was in those days, the risk to the pilots performing on the jet aerobatic teams was more than twenty times greater. I recount those statistics simply to underscore the risks and challenges involved for every member of the team. Having just faced them for two years—and having seen numerous close calls, incidents, and accidents in my tour with the *Thunderbirds*—I did not discount the risks or the challenges. However, I was confident they could be overcome by concentrating on all the various "teams" within the team. I knew that leadership, professionalism, and commitment would need to emanate from every segment of the organization. For such high-risk activity one can't afford even one weak link.

We met those challenges. We did it by "organizing small" within the team. We emphasized that each team element was just as important as any other, and instilled the pride and professionalism of ownership in all of them. And it worked. As but one example, over four years, despite the dangers involved, we had *zero* major accidents resulting from our risky airshow mission. To place that record in perspective, the other premier aerobatic teams of that era, including the *Thunderbirds* and the Navy's *Blue Angels* in the United States, were averaging over two aerobatic-related major accidents *each year*. This alone suggests our approach was different, and how well it worked.

The *Skyblazer* performance record was even more impressive when contrasted with the European aerobatic teams of that era. Every NATO country had one, and we competed against at least one—and usually several—of those teams at every airshow. (Their accident records were comparable to those of the Thunderbirds and Blue Angels—or in most cases worse.) Because of the quality and precision of our performance, we were always the featured final event at every multi-team international airshow. That helps demonstrate we did not sacrifice the quality of the team's performance. In fact, we constantly improved it. However, we stressed risk control not risk aversion.

Traveling throughout Europe, from Scandinavia to the Mediterranean, we were almost always isolated from U.S. support. Despite that, we had no performances canceled or curtailed for maintenance reasons, thanks to the extraordinary dedication and determination of the Skyblazer maintenance people. So the team had lots of reasons to be proud of its record. We flew a very complex maneuver sequence, and during the four years I was privileged to lead the team we flew 399 official airshows—an average of 100 per year. We had about twice that many practice missions. Therefore, we had more than 1,000 opportunities to get it wrong. And make no mistake about it, formation aerobatics are not for the faint of heart.

Over the years, I have often been asked to explain what is involved in layman's terms. This is one way of explaining it: Imagine four race cars driving in a precise formation at over 200 miles an hour. The lead car has a car on either side, three feet or less away, and nestled between them is a car riding on the rear bumper of the lead car. Imagine the cars making turns, circles, and figure eights, all still at 200 miles an hour. Now, to make it even more interesting, have the cars maintain the same close spacing but constantly change their formation. One minute they are in the precise *diamond* formation just described, and the next they are in *trail* with one another after abrupt changes of position. The minute after that they are all *line abreast*, and still doing complex maneuvers. Now triple the speed, include the vertical, and add strong centrifugal force at all times— and you have a general idea of what's involved.

Maneuvering in the vertical from a mere 15 feet above the ground to an altitude of 7,000 feet and right back down again, the wing men must totally trust the leader not to fly them into the ground. Their eyes are fixed on him, and on one another, and the ground and sky are just a swirling kaleidoscope in their peripheral vision. For that matter, each pilot in the formation must totally trust the others. A mistake by one can mean catastrophe for all. The equipment must operate flawlessly as well. It's one thing to drop out of an auto race.

That's not an uncommon occurrence, even today. It is quite another to drop out of the sky. Those challenges and our success in meeting them greatly reinforced my convictions regarding the importance of trust, and of the dignity and worth of every team role and every team member.

As another significant measure of the professionalism of all the team members in the four years during which we traveled through Europe and Africa we did not have a single incident of untoward behavior by any member of the Skyblazer team. That includes both the job settings and social settings involved in performing in foreign countries. Since these were high-spirited young people, subject to the various temptations of constant traveling and extensive interaction with the public, that was a remarkable record—particularly for the era.

(A prevailing management theory of that era, at least in the post–WWII military forces, was that if one placed too much insistence on professionalism it would squash spirit and individuality—and thereby performance. And that excuse was used by many for lax supervision and standards, which resulted in all sorts of immature behavior—sometimes reaching bizarre proportions in ignoring flying rules and in other behavioral violations on the job, as well as in social settings. I considered that unprofessional, inappropriate, and totally unnecessary. We were able to instill that same attitude in every team member, leading to pride and professionalism in that respect also. That part of the team's record was enviable, and different, also.)

I am convinced that our success in the Skyblazers—which, comparatively speaking, blew the opposition away—can be attributed to the level of leadership and commitment emanating from every member of the organization. My contribution was the principles, the policies, and the organizational arrangement which fostered that collective commitment and performance. Those challenging years also convinced me of the great power of the quality mindset, and that leadership at *every* level is essential. I also learned in my four years in that pressure cooker how the competition from the European national teams helped keep us on our toes. They provided an objective standard by which we could judge ourselves. We were highly motivated toward constant improvement because they were improving all the time. The competition made us our own toughest critics—there was simply no room for complacency.

That, no doubt, helped shape my views on the value of comparison and the ills that arise when an organization is shielded from comparison. Though I didn't use the term at the time, I was using the TQM principles I later applied successfully in other settings. In the Skyblazer case I was the boss of ninety people. Later I was to command thousands, and then nearly 200,000. In all those cases I found that the matter of overall size was far less important than the *organization* and *orientation* at the lowest, frontline level. I saw in case after case that if you can create teams of people who care about and trust one another, and get leadership and commitment operating from the bottom up, you can create feats of quality and productivity that appear miraculous when compared to the levels that others are achieving.

Later I put to work those same convictions and principles to meet leadership challenges in four different settings that called for radical transformation. But the last three were well in my future, and not even remotely anticipated, when I stepped through the door to take on the first of the four. That story also helps explain what the decentralized, leadership approach is all about—and how effective it can be in creating a top-notch organization.

FORMING A FIGHTER WING FROM THE GROUND UP AND TAKING IT TO THE TOP IN RECORD TIME, USING THE SAME PRINCIPLES

After my six years in jet aerobatics I had a series of other interesting assignments. They included three years as the Dean of the Air Force's "*Top Gun School*," three years as executive aide to the then TAC Commander, graduation from the *National War College*, and two years as a staff assistant in the Office of the Secretary of Defense. During that time I went from captain to full colonel. I then volunteered to go to Southeast Asia. After five months and flying 177 fighter combat missions (yes, some full colonels fly combat, too), followed by seven months at the headquarters of 7th Air Force in Saigon, I went to Europe to be a fighter wing commander. I looked forward to the challenge. Little did I realize how much of a challenge it was to be.

The place was Zweibrücken, Germany, near Saarbrücken on the French border. There was nothing there—at least no people were there, and no fighter wing was to be found. My job was to build one from the ground up. The air base selected had been used by the *Royal Canadian Air Force* for many years but had been abandoned by them two years earlier. Understandably, the RCAF had spent little in up-keep money the last few years there, knowing it was leaving. To make matters worse, once the base was abandoned it had been extensively vandalized, picked clean by scavengers looking for anything of value, including electrical fixtures, wiring, heating ducting and the like. That wasn't the fault of the Canadians. They had offered the base to the United States before they left but the United States had declined. The decision to build up our forces in Europe came later, occasioned by increasingly bellicose Soviet behavior.

When I first walked onto the base my heart sank. It was over-grown with weeds and littered with refuse. Paint was peeling off inside and out, and there were signs of disrepair and neglect every-where. To add to the merriment, the decision to form the wing had been made after completion of the Washington budget cycle for the year. Therefore, I was informed we would have to get by on a budget considerably more austere than that of an existing fighter wing. Not-withstanding, I was told we had to build the wing from the ground up, work out by ourselves all the facilities and other buildup aspects, and have the new wing fully combat-ready—all in nine months.

I looked on that daunting prospect in a bad-news, good-news con-text. The bad news was that every detail and every problem would need to be satisfactorily resolved on a meager budget and on a very compressed time scale. Perhaps you're wondering what the good news was. It was that I could do it all in accordance with the decen-tralization and leadership principles I thought were important. It was to be a strenuous test of those principles. And they passed with flying colors.

High on my list was the *quality mindset*. I knew I could not build quality performance in such ramshackle surroundings. So I tried again at the headquarters to get at least a little money to hire some local laborers to help us in the badly needed repair and refurbishment. No luck. So we did it all ourselves, by putting in extra time and effort beyond the long and tiring hours already being devoted to putting the wing together from a mission standpoint. Everybody pitched in. I helped paint the exterior of the building I had selected as wing head-quarters, as did everyone for their own building. (I also painted and refurbished my own office and that of my secretary on several successive Sundays.) Everyone did the same. And it wasn't only paint; it was hammers and nails and installing building materials and electrical fixtures and countless things that you normally take for granted when you start a new job.

The base soon sparkled from end to end, and the facilities slowly took shape inside. The various pieces of equipment dribbled in from all over the Air Force. The vehicles and major items of equipment of all sorts arrived in extremely poor condition. Just one more hill to climb. It's not a surprising glimpse of human nature in action that we got the worst of the hand-me-downs. When people are asked to give something up, not many will send their best and keep their worst. Knowing that, later I always insisted we send our very best, not our worst, when we were called on. It builds character.

As we overcame obstacle after obstacle, our pride grew. Visitors started remarking favorably on what that enthusiastic crowd at Zwei-brücken was doing to catch up with the existing wings. However, almost no one thought we had any chance of passing the rigorous war-fighting inspection soon to come. Established wings struggled to do so, and failures were not uncommon. Two senior general officers at the European headquarters privately confided to me that no one would be terribly dismayed if we did not make it through the inspection—since all knew what we were up against. But as our pride grew along with our accomplishments, I became increasingly confident that we could make it, and with some room to spare. Like any organization, we had our setbacks. But we used them as incentive to charge even harder. We were determined not to fail.

The first indication that our hard work was paying off, and re- markably so in a comparative context, was when the inspection team came around to look at our maintenance activities, stem to stern. That same *Daedalian Award* team annually visited every U.S. base in Europe. They were professionals, and they knew what to look for. Imagine the surprise of the other wings in Europe when new-kid-on- the-block Zweibrücken was judged to have the best maintenance in all of Europe! That fueled our determination even more.

At this point I won't elaborate on the steps we took to build teams, internet them, and create leaders and leadership at every level. But that's what we did—from the bottom of the organization to the top. That was what I had earlier learned to do in order to appeal to the human spirit and create strong commitment. It worked here, too. But the proof of that—our big test—was yet to come. We asked for no delay and no quarter in that test of our mettle. As soon as the nine months were up, a NATO inspection team of well over 100 inspectors arrived to put the wing through every conceivable war-fighting test. It would take nearly a book in itself to explain the scope, rigor, and stress of those tests. They range from surging the aircraft over many days at very high sortie rates, to simulated bombings of the command post, preventing its use, to simulated destruction of many other facil- ities, to quick turnarounds of aircraft, all timed, to frequent checks of the condition of the aircraft to ensure that no corners had been cut, to detailed scoring and assessment, against strict standards, of the accomplishments of every sortie.

After nine full days at this frantic pace, the inspectors professed overwhelming surprise that this new wing had "maxed the course." In our inspection debriefing, the two-star general team chief bestowed praise on everyone involved. He ended his remarks by informing us that our aggregate inspection scores and final rating were the highest achieved by any NATO wing, U.S. or foreign, *in more than six years*. One high-ranking inspector from one of the other NATO countries even called it the "Zweibrucken miracle." But it was no miracle. It was just the right organization, leadership, motivation, and commitment in action—from every level and every person. We were all very proud of our accomplishment.

I didn't get to rest on our laurels. I was off, on a single day's notice, to an assignment as the new commander of a highly troubled Air Force fighter wing located outside Madrid, Spain. That wing had failed its last two war-fighting inspections, as well as an end-to-end management look-see by a special team from Washington. Two wing commanders in a row had been fired, and things were getting progressively worse. I was supposed to fix all that. I packed up my toothbrush and my leadership principles, jumped in a fighter, and took off for Madrid. The principles worked there, too. (I'll explain how later.)

What these stories about the Skyblazers and building a fighter wing from the ground up have in common is the organization and leadership approach that was used and the commitment, zeal, and outstanding personal performance that approach elicited from everyone in the organization. Since joining the business world I have seen similar techniques evoke similarly successful results. Let's turn to three such examples.

INCREASING NUMBERS OF AMERICAN COMPANIES ARE CHANGING TO A DECENTRALIZED, LEADERSHIP, AND QUALITY-ORIENTED MANAGEMENT SYSTEM—AND SEEING QUALITY AND PRODUCTIVITY CLIMB STEEPLY

Most American businesses are sailing along as before: no more inefficient than others in their industry. Oblivious to the rising tide of competition and its portent for their own future, they see no particular shortcomings in their traditional approach. Some other companies— still the tiny minority—have acted decisively, often without any spur from outside events. Their leaders have recognized the problems stemming from Centralism, and they haven't been fainthearted about addressing it. That has led them to the adoption of a decentralized, team-based, quality-oriented system. The increases in quality, productivity, and profitability have followed quickly, as case after case proves they do.

As noteworthy examples from this latter group of businesses, I have selected a regulated services company, *Florida Power & Light*; an industrial firm, *Boeing*; and a megacorporation dealing in a broad array of consumer products and services, *General Electric*. They are in different businesses. They have different challenges. But they have made similar changes in their management systems to become significantly better. Their success stories can help the undecided acquire the conviction to change, and provide a clearer vision of how to do it.

FLORIDA POWER & LIGHT: IMPROVING GREATLY— AND WINNING JAPAN'S PRESTIGIOUS DEMING PRIZE —BY IMPLEMENTING QUALITY MANAGEMENT PRINCIPLES THROUGHOUT THE ORGANIZATION

Most of the current quality management literature dwells on the processes dealing with durable goods. And most examples of successful decentralization unearthed by researchers involve manufacturing firms. That can lead to the mistaken impression that the principles do not fit businesses involved in services. Since nearly eight out of ten employees in America are engaged in services, that's a most unfortunate conclusion. Companies like FPL help prove how wrong it is. FPL's reputation is well established as a services firm that transformed its structure and style along the Japanese pattern, with impressive improvement resulting. Its experiences in doing so provide insight into what those quality management principles must entail to work effectively—in any business.

FPL is the nation's fourth-largest and fastest-growing electric utility. Its service area encompasses the Atlantic coast and southern half of Florida. Its *Odyssey of Quality* began in 1981. By all accounts FPL had lots of problems: There was widespread customer dissatisfaction.

Many FPL employees would not tell outsiders where they worked. Mistakes were rampant. And those are but the top three on a long list. Marshall McDonald, then president of FPL Group, the utility's parent holding company, encouraged the adoption of quality management principles. Consultants were hired, and *Quality Improvement Teams* were formed to look at the ways to improve various processes, such as reducing power outages. That helped but not that much. As one observer said, "By 1984, three years of tinkering with the culture had produced only lackluster results."

In 1985 FPL's improvement quest took a dramatic turn for the better. That was when John Hudiburg, chairman and CEO until his recent retirement, took key FPL executives to Japan to learn about Japanese methods and the reasons behind their success. In his 1991 book *Winning with Quality: The FPL Story*, Hudiburg put the genesis of his search for the secret of Japanese management principles in these terms: "In the early 1980's we didn't have this system, and we were in trouble. We were not coping very well with our problems [and] our customers were angry at us." As Hudiburg explained it further to me, he had started his search by reading all he could and listening intently to what the various American *"quality gurus"* were saying. But he and his colleagues just did not find enough there to latch on to.

He recounted to me his intuition that FPL needed a change in its entire management system. But in his search he could find only *pieces* of various techniques to improve quality and productivity. He went on to explain that those pieces—no matter how assembled—still fell significantly short of a *system* that would address all FPL's problems in productivity, quality, and customer dissatisfaction. So he went to Japan in search of a system. By that time he had the goal of making FPL the *"best electric utility in the world"* well ensconced in the corporate thinking. Obviously, that was going to be an extremely ambitious undertaking. So from the very start Hudiburg concentrated on visiting and studying the best of Japan's best—those companies that had won the Deming Prize. Established in 1951 and named after Dr. W. Edwards Deming, the renowned American statistician and a founding figure in quality-control and process-improvement techniques, the prize is administered and awarded by the Union of Japanese Scientists and Engineers (JUSE), an organization dedicated to improving product quality throughout Japanese industry.

Among that group of Deming Prize winners was Japan's largest electric utility, Kansai Electric Power Company in Osaka. Since it was in the same business as FPL, its management approach had special relevance and provided special insight. As Hudiburg's visits continued, and the patterns in those Deming Prize companies emerged, he came to understand that the Japanese had taken the seeds which Deming (and other Americans) had planted early in the postwar period to a higher level of development. Those companies called their broader application of the principles *"Policy Deployment,"* or sometimes *"Policy Management."* "Policy" meant that quality management principles were being applied everywhere in the organization—to every aspect of every segment and every operation. The principles shaped everything from system, to structure, to style—and everything in between, including human system factors—not just the tools of process improvement.

The process tools are of course one of the principal underlying themes in the Japanese overall management approach (as they had raptly learned them, at first from Deming and Joseph M. Juran after World War II, and later from their own "gurus" of process analysis and control, such as Kaoru Ishikawa and Genichi Taguchi). However, it was the broader understanding and application—an encompassing policy that extended to every organization element—that so impressed John Hudiburg. *He had found a system, not just pieces of one.*

To reinforce those lessons and conclusions, FPL hired some Japanese professors as advisers, led by Dr. Tetsuichi Asaka. All were well versed in Japanese-style quality management principles, and each had proven credentials in advising Deming Prize–winning companies. Their job was to keep FPL on the right track toward the holistic system Hudiburg had found so impressive—a system he was determined to apply to Florida Power & Light.

The FPL transformation effort started, as it always must, with training. Hudiburg explains that the training of FPL's people, extensively and at every level, played a vital role in their transformation from the old system to the new. FPL set up a systematic program of formal training that went far beyond anything it had done before. It reached everyone and concentrated especially on the various "management echelons" from top to bottom. In FPL parlance that meant training "executives, managers, supervisors, and team leaders." (Yes, the team approach was featured, just as it is by the Japanese.) Did that training cost more? Of course. But it still represented a minuscule proportion of the total costs—and the payback from improved quality and productivity dwarfed those costs many times over.

FPL also developed an entirely new system of measurement, assessment, and feedback to all employees. It proved especially effective in facilitating focused, in-depth management reviews. An even bigger benefit was the creation of a level of interest in improvement on the part of all employees that was instrumental—even central— to the entire change process. By 1989, the new structure, tools, and culture were all in place and producing impressive results. Administrative errors became the rare exception, not the rule. Errors in customer bills were reduced to only eight per million. Power outages were cut by more than half, to a point well below the national average, despite Florida's abundance of thunderstorms. As a result of such improvements, customer complaints went down by more than 70 percent. As an even more telling indicator of the cumulative effects, FPL was able to reduce the price of electricity to its customers—bucking an inflationary trend throughout the electric power industry.

More evidence of how well the new quality management system was working came that same year when FPL applied for and won Japan's Deming Prize. FPL did so only after the most intense examination by the same Japanese experts who pass judgment on the Japanese applicants—using identical criteria. By surviving that extraordinary scrutiny, FPL had demonstrated that it now excelled even in the comparative light of the best of the best in Japan. The student had joined the ranks of the teachers.

FPL CHANGED ITS ENTIRE MANAGEMENT SYSTEM
AND SUCCEEDED—PIECEMEAL CHANGES EARLIER
HAD FAILED TO MAKE A DIFFERENCE

To sharpen the lessons from all of this, I narrow to three the keys that made FPL's implementation of its Japanese-style, holistic quality management system so successful. The first, it seems to me, is John Hudiburg's openness to learning from others, wherever the best ideas and examples might be found. That ranks first because of the high "not invented here" quotient in most companies. Second is the understanding Hudiburg reached regarding the broad scope of management actions and techniques underlying the Japanese success (an especially important key given FPL's earlier lack of success in the application of the patchwork quality management ideas found in American management literature). Third, since the proof is in the pudding, is the way Hudiburg and his FPL colleagues exhaustively studied and diligently applied the principles they gleaned from their observations and tutoring. It wasn't haphazard, piecemeal, or halfhearted.

John Hudiburg summarized for me the events in his search and its successful conclusion:

> We had studied all of the American quality gurus, but it became clear that what they offered was not a system. What I found in Japan, on the other hand, particularly in their largest utility, was a complete management system. When I saw the synergy that it produced, and the remarkable effect that it had on their people, I knew that was the system we needed—and that's what we adopted. We learned from them and from some of the Japanese college professors who advised them. It all worked extremely well. Significantly, we did not go for the financial results. They were a byproduct that followed along. Our focus was on the quality, and on the system, and making sure it was producing the same synergy and effect on people that I had seen in Japan.

Hudiburg instinctively understood that it had to involve far more than piecemeal application of a few quality improvement techniques.

That understanding shaped the FPL approach properly from the very outset. There's a big lesson there for all companies contemplating change through the adoption of a new quality management system— by "TQM" or any other name.

Hudiburg issues this warning in his book: "The road we in the United States have been following will lead many a well-known American corporation to ruin." He also warns that virtually all "management experts" these days feel obligated to spout the latest slogans on quality management, but that very few understand what they're talking about when it comes to the holistic approach required. I have found ample evidence of the truth and timeliness of those warnings from Hudiburg. By way of ending the FPL story, it's useful to quote from Hudiburg's response to this question from the Deming exam team: What three pieces of advice would you give to any American CEO who was considering doing the same thing?

> First, I would strongly advise other CEOs to follow our experience because the results stood to be nothing short of spectacular. I would tell them that they could attain levels of quality and customer satisfaction greater than they had ever imagined. Moreover, they would enjoy work more than ever before in their life. . . . Second, they should be prepared to make a commitment to their employees in education and training beyond anything they had ever done before. . . . Finally, I said that anyone interested in quality management must consider it as a *complete management system.* . . . Quality improvement teams, and, indeed, all of the other parts of the TQM system are each well worth doing in their own rights . . . but it is all of them working together in a systematic way that produces the dramatic results companies really want.

Hudiburg's perceptiveness and Florida Power & Light's dogged persistence in pursuit of the ambitious goals he had set rocketed it to superstar status among utilities—and, for that matter, among businesses of any kind. Hudiburg and his colleagues throughout FPL proved that the principles work in service industries as well as they do in the manufacturing sector. Don't believe those who draw artificial distinctions between the two. Also, both *process improvement techniques and structural decentralization steps* must be involved. A seminal lesson of the FPL experience is that successful quality management simply cannot be narrowed down to either of the two alone. As Hudiburg puts it, it's a matter of putting lots of pieces together, in a systematic way, into a *complete management system*. That has been my own experience as well—reinforced by my interactions with scores of businesses.

Let's now move on to this chapter's other two examples. Their cases yield the same conclusions. I said in chapter 2, regarding NUMMI's great success at Fremont, that these same principles have worked in lots of other places, with unionized workers, and in the face of quality considerations not unlike those faced by America's Big Three automakers. For one such example, let's turn to The Boeing Company. Boeing needed neither Japanese competition nor a Japanese example such as NUMMI to see the light. *Hard times did not provide the motivation.* It came instead from astute observation of what does and does not work, and the recognition that the company faced new times and new challenges.

I find in my business travels that even a small amount of black ink on the annual balance sheet can be a large obstacle to change— so much so that I have come to call it the "black-ink barrier." The rationale in far too many companies is "We're doing all right—we're holding our own." As long as the profits are reasonable, the stockholders passive, and the management bonuses still flowing, there's little impetus for change. Boeing shows that's no excuse to stay mired in the practices of the past. It thrust aside one of the largest black-ink barriers to change in all of America, to completely revise its management philosophy and approach.

DECENTRALIZING THE BOEING COMPANY: ITS START WAS THE DECISION A NEW APPROACH WAS NEEDED

Frank Shrontz, Boeing's visionary chairman, saw the need to change from the "traditional" management style—centered on functional stovepipes—in the early eighties. By 1985, he had instituted a companywide program to change to a decentralized, team-based approach. He speaks convincingly and knowingly on the problems created by the "organize big," functional approach—even in the best of companies. His succinct discourse on the *"walls"* that are built, and how the functions then *"throw things over the walls to one another,"* should be heard in every corporate boardroom in America—at least, in every one where the board and the company still cling to the old ways. (And that's most of them.) During the course of a management retreat with top Boeing officials in Vancouver, Frank Shrontz invited me to take a close look at Boeing's new management program and to visit some plants where the company's new team concept organization is in operation. I did so, and I was impressed. But I wasn't surprised. I saw still another example of how well the underlying principles work, in any setting.

You'd think that if any organization has little reason to restructure, it's Boeing. It is, after all, the world's largest and most successful builder of commercial aircraft. Boeing built its first aircraft in 1916 and has been the industry leader since. Its impressive lineage has included the transoceanic *"Clipper"* flying boats, the 1954 introduction of the world's first jet airliner (the 707), and on to the popular 747 jumbo jet series. Boeing has delivered over 5,700 airplanes to more than 400 owners and operators and has a well-deserved reputation for the high quality and durability of its products. At the time Frank Shrontz decided Boeing must change, the company had an impressive balance sheet, some $4 billion in cash, and a firm backlog of more than $50 billion. Also, Boeing, which has long enjoyed a world market share of more than 55 percent, confidently expected an explosion in airliner demand accompanying globalization that would yield a $500-billion market by the year 2005. As this was written Boeing's order backlog is near $100 billion despite a worldwide recession. As Frank Shrontz put it at the outset of his changes, "We have plenty of business. Our big job is to execute."

To execute better, in the mid-eighties Shrontz launched Boeing's *Total Quality Improvement* program. That program features not only various process improvement techniques but also a fundamental change in the way Boeing is organized. Boeing's TQI program is spelled out in an excellent sixty-page guidebook, first published in 1985, with the subtitle "*A Resource Guide to Management Involvement*." ("TQI" gave way to "Continuous Quality Improvement" in 1990. Shrontz changed the name to emphasize that the quest goes on and on.) The guide outlines the company's goals comprehensively, and provides an abundance of wisdom on how Boeing achieves them.

The guide explains the essence of the plan as follows:

> To provide leadership in the continuous improvement process, managers must foster a climate of mutual trust and respect. . . . True quality improvement involves all employees working together in teams to search out the causes of [various inefficiencies]. This should be done on a daily basis so that quality improvement becomes an integral part of the way employees do their work. And it begins with the active involvement of every manager.

The guide warns explicitly that the traditional management system must be changed: "Pressure to work harder or better generally does not achieve much in the long term. Most people believe they are already doing the best job they can, often feeling that system faults frustrate their efforts to do better." Accordingly, Boeing set out to correct those "system faults" by changing its system. I chose two of Boeing's outlying plants for an in-depth look, so as to see how the changes fared in the far corners of the organization.

SUCCESS AT THE BOEING PLANT AT IRVING, TEXAS: CHANGING AN ESTABLISHED, UNIONIZED WORK FORCE TO THE NEW SYSTEM

The first of the two plants I visited is in Irving, Texas, the home of the *Dallas Cowboys*. Though wholly owned by Boeing, the plant is operated as an independent subsidiary as part of Boeing's decentralization philosophy. It is known as the *Boeing Aerospace & Electronics Irving Company* and has its own board of directors. Irving follows the broad Boeing management principles, but makes its own decisions and charts its own course. At Irving, Boeing manufactures avionics and flight-deck electronics (black boxes) for the entire Boeing commercial airliner fleet—737s, 747s, 757s, and 767s.

As an illustration of the complexity involved, there are 169 different electronic parts on the 767 alone for which Irving is responsible. Irving also builds, as needed, parts for the older Boeing aircraft still operating around the world, including the 727 and the 707, which are still active in many countries. As a result, the products at Irving cover a three-decade span of technology, and more than 7,000 individual electronics parts must be built right, the first time and every time. In one year alone Irving ships more than 70,000 end products, with timeliness of the essence, since all must meet new-aircraft delivery schedules or pressing customer needs in the field.

Irving was managed for many years in the traditional centralized manner. John Johnson, general manager, observed that the transition to the team-based structure involved some convincing. He said many Boeing Irving employees voiced the attitude: "Since Boeing has been so successful, why do we have to do this?" As he also put it, "Not everyone took kindly to the idea that Boeing needed to be in the forefront of change." So, Johnson said, previous conditioning was the most difficult of the many challenges to overcome. That was especially true for the managers. However, Johnson added, as events unfolded the new approach soon started to make more and more converts, until virtually all became strong supporters.

Irving started the entire change process by establishing *"common understanding,"* and by getting all employees involved. He stressed training, and covered the gamut from *Statistical Process Control* techniques to Boeing's concepts and goals for the new management system. He also emphasized training of the *"Team Leaders,"* who were to play key roles. Like Hudiburg at FPL, Johnson saw training as a key to their success. He also placed great emphasis on effective and unfettered communication. Irving set up lots of avenues for employee commentary and recommendations on how the change was going. Those same communication avenues remain active and include "town meetings" in settings ranging from a few teams to scores of them all at once.

To describe further what Irving did is but to repeat what I said about Honda and Toyota, so I will merely summarize. Irving did away completely with the functional alignments and matrixing techniques that had been used before. Teams were formed as the organizational building blocks. Most range in size from five to ten; a few are as large as fifteen. Each team has a leader. Where feasible, the teams are made up of many disciplines. All feature multiskilling. Each team member is trained in up to three different jobs within the team's overall product responsibilities. Team members stay in one job for several months, but can then change to provide fresh challenges and opportunities. Johnson said that from this they get a constant infusion of new ideas on how to improve the processes, along with greater flexibility.

Johnson, and many others at Irving, also extolled its virtue in building "team outlook and team productivity orientation." It's common for the team members themselves to recommend changes in assignments when it becomes obvious that one team member is far more productive in one task than another. In that respect, in keeping with Boeing's overall *Continuous Quality Improvement* program principles, the Irving executives take great care to make the *ownership* and *empowerment* of the teams real. The authority they exercise is far greater than anyone could have dreamed of in the pre-1985 organization. Mindful of the lingering effects of the old conditioning, Boeing also goes to considerable lengths to instill a new orientation regarding authority, responsibility, and accountability. Johnson calls that "sizing the box." It's done with team charters that spell out what the team can do, not what it cannot.

Team member after team member whom I interviewed said how much more they liked the new system. Their empowerment is real, not a set of slogans. It provides a feeling of ownership and obligation that was missing before. As an illustration, one team bragged to me about raising its first-pass yield efficiency from 30 percent to 95 percent in a very complicated process. The team's new incremental goal was even higher than that. (Think of the rework considerations, and cost considerations, when the first-pass yield is only 30 percent!) Because of the new, positive team interaction at Irving, the teams repeatedly come up with suggested improvements in their processes and their team's product that were not forthcoming under the old system. That's the extra ingredient the team approach provides.

One of the Irving teams had a special challenge. It builds the handset for intercom announcements on the Boeing 767. Although sturdily built, the handsets were being returned because of cracking and splitting at the seams. The handset is installed near the galley. Investigation revealed that the 767 flight attendants were using it as an ice crusher to break up the ice that had slightly melted and fused together in the climb to altitude. Boeing left the wisdom of that to the airline officials and challenged the team to come up with an even sturdier model. The team did. The handset is now almost indestructible. The innovative approach cost only a small amount more, with no increase in price to the customer.

As the team members told the story and showed the before and after handset models, they exhibited pride in their *ownership* of the problem and their *empowerment* to find the solution. In the old function-oriented system it would have been left to engineers somewhere, who might or might not have had the insight to come up with the same simple but effective fix. And the employees building it wouldn't have viewed it as their problem. As one of those team members put it, "In the old days our job was to just 'put 'em together'— and that doesn't build the same sense of product ownership or interest in improvement."

Irving also pays great attention to the interaction and synergism among the teams. Each "upstream" team is a supplier at Irving, and each "downstream" team is a customer. For example, an upstream team might be building circuit assemblies that a downstream team installs in a finished subcomponent. The quality is not left to inspectors. Each team has a direct and vested interest in the quality and delivery performance. Frequent face-to-face meetings iron out any problems and come up with interface and process improvements. In that same vein, Irving has *"Manufacturing Improvement Teams"* comprised of representatives from all teams involved in the production of a specific component. They meet on call to present and analyze recommended improvements of the interaction of the teams or of specific production processes. The representatives brief their own teams and thereafter keep them informed. A formal tracking and feedback mechanism follows up on recommendations.

This is similar to the *"Cross-functional Process Improvement Teams"* that receive so much emphasis in the current spate of quality management books and articles centered on process issues. The difference at Irving is that such cross-cutting teams work against a backdrop of actual team organization, rather than being *cross-functional* as they are in traditionally managed companies. The Boeing experience shows that the team-based structure adds far more in the way of positive dynamics to that cross-cutting process (just as it does at Honda and Toyota). Also, when decisions based on that analysis process are made, they get implemented rather than lost in the functional silos. Beyond those positive aspects, the best way to prevent process breakdown is to organize in a way that gets everyone involved in making processes better all the time.

You still have occasional problems, to be sure. But you don't have the same pressing need for ad hoc, cross-functional teams of *"Code Blue"* specialists dashing about giving emergency surgery to the stream of flawed processes that come from insensitive centralized management and the employee apathy and alienation resulting from it. Making the "great process improvement hunt" far more effective is interesting and useful, but it just scratches the surface of the underlying problem. Companies must address those larger issues—including the nature of their entire management system. If they don't, then by all means they should get better at their reactive *"Code Blue"* response techniques—they will continue to need them. And as competition continues to intensify, that will prove the biggest "continuous improvement" treadmill of them all. Boeing Irving is one more bit of proof there's a better way.

The upkeep standards throughout the Irving plant are most impressive, rivaling those of the Japanese. As one of the Irving executives put it, "It's important that we look professional as a necessary condition of being professional." I also found widespread use of goals, measurement, and feedback through scoreboards. The omnipresent scoreboards at the team level are augmented by frequent overall scoreboards in common areas, such as the company cafeteria.

Everyone at Irving talks numbers as well as words, and the objectivity regarding how well they are doing shines through in every conversation.

In my discussions with team after team at Boeing Irving, and with employee after employee, I found the support for the new system enthusiastic and convincing. The new system also has led to a far more harmonious relationship and a better partnership with the *International Association of Machinists Union* local there. It was done right: The IAM local was involved every step of the way. The Irving experience shows, as does that at NUMMI, that an established, unionized work force need not present a permanent obstacle to this kind of change. Indeed, that it works so well in such settings—historically the most difficult in creating harmonious labor and management bonding—provides all the more proof of its merit.

But is it working by other important measures? Yes. For example, in 1985, coincident with the reorganization, Irving "signed up with its sole customer"—the Boeing Commercial Airplane Company—to a 21 percent reduction, in constant dollars, in its entire family of parts over five years. Irving met that ambitious goal in only four. And the plant continues to bring the cost curves down. Clearly, the reorganization has been a success.

THE BOEING PLANT AT CORINTH, TEXAS: STARTING FROM SCRATCH, SAME SUCCESS

The Corinth plant: same story, different setting. Ron Riedasch, since moved to a higher Boeing executive position, was the Corinth general manager from its start-up in 1987 through its early years. He is proud of Corinth's accomplishments and flew there to show me around. As we first approached the plant he said, "Let's begin by looking around back to see how they're maintaining the rear of the building and the garbage can area." (It was spick-and-span.) Satisfied with what he saw, he explained, "You don't reflect the quality mindset in some places and not in others. High standards in all things not only send a message to our customers, they send a message to ourselves.'' It's obvious from my travels that not everyone understands that, but I have yet to see a hugely successful organization that doesn't stress that quality mindset. Believe me, Ron Riedasch doesn't look on it as ''atmospherics'' (as some would have it), but as a key stepping-stone to across-the-board quality.

Corinth has the same independence as Irving. This plant also builds complex *black boxes*. But Corinth has a different customer, the Boeing Space and Defense Group. Corinth products find homes in a wide variety of government space and aircraft systems instead of on commercial airliners. In some cases—space systems especially—the quality standards are particularly demanding. (There aren't many 25,000-mile screwdrivers around, so they must be both reliable and durable.) Like Irving, Corinth has a numbing variety of electronics parts in its product inventory.

Corinth was a greenfield start-up, in a brand-new facility. Despite that, its challenges in overcoming prior managerial conditioning were like those experienced at Irving. Ron Riedasch addressed that aspect in explaining how he started as Corinth's first employee, and how it was built from there:

> We first hired managers. Some were from Boeing, some from other major U.S. corporations. Then we isolated ourselves and worked day and night on our mission statement, on our principles and the like—so we could get started right. In that process, we found our largest single obstacle was overcoming our traditional management thinking. Again and again, whether the managers came from Boeing or other U.S. corporations, we found ourselves reverting to the old ways of thinking. Fortunately, we were able to overcome that conditioning, but it was not a simple or speedy process. . . . What made it especially hard was that it was as if you had lost your anchor. We had to rethink the issues and create new touchstones. . . . Not only that, we constantly had to tell ourselves that the entire process must pivot off of respect and trust—if you violate that it breaks down completely.

Riedasch repeatedly emphasized to me, ''This was not the easiest thing to do for managers brought up to think differently.'' But they were able to do it, as their very real empowerment and ownership programs attest. The Corinth executives thoughtfully "*size the box*" in distributing the authority and in providing ample latitude for its exercise. Along with that empowerment, they have achieved a healthy state of organizational cohesion and discipline. As Riedasch said, with emphasis, "*We were looking to achieve all the benefits of decentralization. We were not looking for anarchy.*" That they succeeded under his leadership and that of his successor is obvious in every facet of the Corinth operation.

Corinth's organizational building blocks are teams, not functions —and not only the multidisciplinary teams that build the black boxes. The support functions are divided into teams as well. All are given clear-cut linkage to their internal customer. As an example, they have broken the *purchasing* activity into teams. In the old system, that would have been a single, homogenized function located in a single large functional pile somewhere. In contrast, Corinth's purchasing teams are separated and collocated in the plant with the specific black-box production teams they support. That way, when you call purchasing you don't get a disembodied and disinterested voice. It's now person to person and face to face. The linkage between the teams is clear and distinct, as is the obligation for responsive service. The interactions have been considerably improved and unnecessary coordination removed from the interface. Moreover, by this means Corinth has tied the support people directly to the integrated group product, and to the customer. I was told they quickly built far more identity with the production teams they support than with the others in the purchasing specialty. And that's the main idea!

Everyone at Corinth expressed enthusiasm about the improved harmony and responsiveness in that arrangement. I could understand why. We had done the same in TAC with equally beneficial results (story later). It's the most powerful way to internet and integrate the organization. Also, this type of networking greatly improves the *mission identification* and *common purpose* of the support people—as well as their incentive to do a good job. Unfortunately, one rarely sees that same decentralized networking approach in use elsewhere in corporate America. It just doesn't fit with the precepts of Centralism. Indeed, if centralizers found purchasing distributed in that way they would smash those separate purchasing activities together into one consolidated functional pile, recite their mantra on economies of scale, and go off to do damage elsewhere—never looking back. It's time to clean up their damage. Boeing has.

Corinth, like Irving and other Boeing plants, places great emphasis on communication. "Town meetings" happen every other week. They include a segment called "message box," in which every complaint or suggestion placed in the box is answered. There's also an open discussion period. Tom O'Fallon, Riedasch's successor as general manager at Corinth, gave a telling testimonial of the way the system, particularly its measurement and feedback aspects, provides objectivity and motivation to the employees at all levels, specifically including the frontline. As he put it, "The old system did not have the ways to try out new ideas that the new system has—ways that can help convince everyone whether they work or not." O'Fallon explained that no matter how appealing the concept on the surface, the new measurement system provides for an objective litmus test. Does it drive quality and productivity up or down? That objective appraisal considerably dampens the usual subjective debate regarding the worth of such proposals.

As an example of O'Fallon's point, at the time of my visit Corinth was experimenting with a ten-hour-a-day, four-day work week. The employees had requested it, and the deal was that if it improved "P&Q" it stayed, if it didn't it went. The employees understood that. (It's a tribute to the sincerity of Boeing's decentralized approach that corporate headquarters allows such autonomy and experimentation.) As this is written, Corinth is still using the four-day work week. But the scoreboards are a continuing reminder they have to make it work, and deliver the goods.

Parenthetically, the evidence shows that to be effective, the *common purpose* must be directed toward a high-quality product and a satisfied customer. If that can be accomplished with work rules the employees prefer, so much the better. So those whose knee-jerk reaction is to reject ideas like *flextime* and *four-day weeks* would be well advised to consider the value of measurement systems in that context. Who knows, they may be resisting some idea that could greatly improve matters, even though their instincts say it would not. Rare is the manager who has not had at least one retrospective change of heart, after seeing the success of a new idea in the hands of others. *Better a leader than a follower be—and better a system that provides for objective appraisal than endless subjective debate across bargaining tables.*

And who says scoreboarding is resented by the employees? Many do, of course. Actually, measuring and scoreboarding make life better for everyone. I fear that some critics have developed their fixations based on observations of the combination of measurement and the old-time centralized management religion. In fact, their lexicon would suggest that's the case. I agree that measurement doesn't work well there. Why should it? The employees have no special stake in the outcome, so they just view measurement tools in a context of piecework. When continuous improvement is reduced to "Do more, do more, do more" for the same recognition and the same rewards, anything you do to measure is about as popular as it would be in an industrial plant outside Minsk. Boeing hasn't made that mistake. And neither have the Japanese. So whom are you to believe? It's either wrong to have goals, measure, and compare, as a few management gurus allege—or it's a principal, even indispensable key to an effective quality management system. *Each company's own choice is important because it will determine the success or failure of organizational change.* This issue is so important I will address it in greater detail later.

The enthusiasm of the Corinth employees for the decentralized, team-based system was as widespread as it was at Irving. I talked at length with Carol Murphy, president of the IAM local at Corinth. She said the union members like the new system very much. While she saw a continuing need for the union "to protect the worker's interests," she also praised the harmonious relationship with Corinth's crop of top managers—one more example of how the decentralized, team-based approach helps labor relations in addition to all its other benefits. Beyond the anecdotal evidence, are Corinth's overall performance results from this system noteworthy and demonstrable? They certainly are—even better than had been hoped. Boeing set very optimistic performance goals for the Corinth facility when it was established. At the time of my visit, the plant's *"efficiency rate"* was running 23 percent higher than those projections—and it keeps improving.

BOEING CLEARLY IS BENEFITING FROM
THE NEW APPROACH

A look at Boeing's overall performance indicators shows that it is far better positioned for the rapidly intensifying competition as a result of its CQI restructuring initiatives. Its competitive challenges are many. The defense side of its business has been heavily affected, as all defense firms have been, by steep reductions in defense spending. Indeed, Boeing's new improvements in quality and productivity can spell survival in that tough marketplace. On the commercial airplane side, the competition also steadily increases, coming from Boeing's main U.S. competitor, *McDonnell-Douglas*, and increasingly from Europe's *Airbus Industries*.

Airbus is the creation of a consortium of European countries that have heavily subsidized its operations from its very start. In fact, Airbus Industries has yet to make a dime, and it is not even projecting a profit before 1999, if then. Airbus keeps predicting that it will go into the black in five years—but that goal line keeps moving, and the heavy subsidies from the sponsor governments go on and on. Also, Airbus profits from the active arm-twisting of prospective airliner customers by the government leaders of those European sponsor countries. In contrast, Boeing cannot count on U.S. government subsidies so that it can slash its prices, offer concessionary financing terms, or benefit from such governmental sales pressures. It just has to be better enough to make up for those significant Airbus advantages.

(The subsidized Airbus is the tip of a large iceberg of unequal and unjust trade practices. They present a dilemma that won't soon be resolved, since every nation practices subsidies and import restraints to one degree or another—all the more reason America must be more productive. More on this issue in chapter 12.)

Boeing read the warning signs, determined what was wrong with traditional centralized management, and made the necessary changes. Despite its great past success, Boeing managed to avoid the "everything's just fine" and "not invented here" way of thinking that characterizes so many businesses. In fact, Boeing borrowed from everyone it could in putting together its new approach. Its executives acknowledge such help from studying such diverse companies as *Armco, Hewlett-Packard, Honeywell*, and *Motorola*. Now people should study Boeing. And they should start by asking Frank Shrontz why he didn't need to have a house fall on him to get the inspiration to change.

Boeing is only one of a growing number of American businesses that have been greatly improved through the adoption of decentralized, leadership management principles. General Electric is another. As one of America's largest corporations, GE provides still more proof of the benefits of organizing small, showing that it works no matter what the company size. (In fact, to generalize, the bigger you are the better you get by organizing small.) As in the Boeing case, GE overcame its own imposing black-ink barrier to bring about the needed changes.

THE GENERAL ELECTRIC STORY: DECENTRALIZING, DELAYERING, AND ADOPTING A NEW QUALITY MANAGEMENT SYSTEM TO GREATLY IMPROVE PRODUCTIVITY AND PROFITABILITY

Jack Welch, the dynamic chairman of GE, also read the signs and took visionary and vigorous action. He has radically altered GE's entire management system over the past decade. His goal has been to make giant GE into "a $50 billion enterprise as lean, as agile and as light on its feet as a small company—a big company with the heart and hunger of a small one." Since GE long has ranked among America's ten largest corporations and was managed along traditional centralized lines until the Welch-inspired changes began, such a revision was not a simple undertaking. But Welch demystified it by basing it on a clear, well-articulated vision and the right principles. His changes weren't just a bit of tinkering, but went directly to the gut issues of GE's *character, culture,* and *climate.* How he went about it is an instructive story, and might get a few more fence sitters to commit themselves to similar change.

Jack Welch launched the GE restructuring program in the early eighties, and by the middle of the decade it had built up considerable momentum. The changes were *sweeping.* Management layers were reduced from nine in number to four—including removal of the entire second and third echelons of GE management. What GE called ''sectors'' and ''groups'' simply disappeared. Welch describes the resulting structural arrangement as ''breathtakingly clean, simple and effective,'' one in which ''ideas, initiatives and decisions move, often at the speed of sound.'' GE aptly called those initiatives ''delayering.'' According to informed reports, no one misses the subtracted layers, and GE is far better off without them.

Early in the restructuring process Welch called for a stem-to-stern review of GE's conglomerate makeup. He and his colleagues zeroed in on the product mix and examined why GE should be in each of its many businesses. It was decided that a major restructuring of the business base was in order. Accordingly, during the eighties GE carried out a massive $18-billion-worth of acquisitions and $9 billion in divestitures. When the smoke had settled, GE had shaped a diverse mix of 350 businesses or product lines into a more tightly knit 13 core businesses. According to Welch, those 13 emerged as the favored businesses because they are among the leaders in their field and are ''closely knit by common values and shared technology.''

Welch also worked hard on changing the GE style from *managership* to *leadership.* A major part of that approach was to create change in the attitude and orientation of the division and corporate staffs. He puts it this way:

> We found ourselves in the early 1980s with corporate and business staffs that were viewed—and viewed themselves—as monitors, checkers, kibitzers and approvers. We changed that view and that mission to the point where staff now sees itself as facilitator, adviser

and partner of operations—with a growing sense of satisfaction and cooperation on both sides. Territoriality has given way to a sense of unity and common purpose.

GE is teaching its approach to leadership at Crotonville, its large corporate training facility in Ossining, New York. The attendees come from all levels of GE. Special emphasis is placed on the leaders at all levels who must bring to life the necessary changes—philosophically and substantively. Welch personally participates and ''almost never misses a class.'' He explains the new GE leadership approach, and he also carefully listens in a freewheeling exchange with those in each class. That interactive, open-minded style sets the tone for all of GE's leaders, at whatever level.

Welch also clearly understands there's more to *organizing small* than focusing on core competencies, delayering, reorienting the staff mindsets, and introducing proactive leadership—as important as those are. He also has aggressively addressed the frontline level, where the products get built and the services performed. To create the responsiveness, agility, and speed he wanted throughout the huge GE organization, he adopted teams as the organizational building blocks. They replaced the functional, structural approach that GE, along with almost everybody else, had been using.

As those sweeping changes took effect, the many beneficial results created more and more believers within GE's ranks. They also attracted considerable outside attention. *Business Week* commented on GE's new team-based organization in an article in the July 10, 1989, issue titled ''The Payoff from Teamwork.'' It quoted Robert Erskine, GE's manager of production resources, on one of the driving ideas behind GE's approach: ''We're trying to radically reduce the work cycle needed to produce a product. . . . When you combine automation with new systems and work teams, you get a 40 percent to 50 percent improvement in productivity.'' *Business Week* also gave an example: ''A General Electric plant in Salisbury, N.C., typically changes product models a dozen times a day by using a team system to produce lighting panel boards. This plant has increased productivity by a remarkable 250 percent compared with GE plants that produced the same products in 1985.'' There are any number of other indications of GE's success in eliminating wasted steps, complex procedures, and needless bureaucracy.

Jack Welch also appreciates the need to keep a flow of new ideas coming (from everyone in the organization) as the catalyst for constant renewal and rejuvenation. One of GE's key programs in that regard is called *Work-out*. It was first launched in the autumn of 1988. Simply described, it's a mechanism for getting ''issue teams'' together to brainstorm ideas for improvement and for intense interaction with the senior leaders who have the authority to make changes. Those Work-out teams cut across all kinds of boundaries and departments, as appropriate to the issues being addressed. GE even includes customers and suppliers in some of these soul-searching sessions (an inspired addition). Often the participants go off-site for several days, roll up their sleeves, and go at it no-holds-barred. Then the senior leader who has decision-making authority comes in to hear the Work-out team's recommendations—and is expected by Welch to make the decisions then and there. This Work-out approach is an important means of waging war against outmoded notions and dumb practices across GE. As such, it has important symbolic as well as great practical value.

Another such program is what GE calls *Best Practices*. It is aimed squarely at the heart of the ''not invented here'' resistance that abounds in most companies. Like many good ideas, it's simplicity itself. Jack Welch started the program by calling for a search for companies worth emulating. He wanted the names of companies that were doing better than GE in various areas, especially in productivity and productivity growth. The searchers found about a dozen that fit the ''worth emulating'' criteria. You can guess the next step. Welch contacted the leaders of those companies and proposed an exchange of ''best practices.'' GE learns from them, and they learn from GE. Everybody benefits. It's still another mechanism for constantly challenging long-held beliefs and practices and for propelling the continuous improvement process.

As part of the Welch restructuring plan, a series of initiatives have been taken to reorient GE's historic *reward system*. Examples of the new thinking are on-the-spot bonus awards to teams and individuals that make a significant contribution beyond normal expectations. Since the program's adoption, GE has made such awards to "tens of thousands" of employees. And stock options, for decades reserved to the top 400 executives, now have been opened up far wider. For example, by 1992 more than 13,000 GE employees held stock options. The program continues to unfold. A greatly improved pay-performance link is part of GE's new management approach, and Welch is unequivocal in both saying so and doing something about it.

A fundamental strength of the Jack Welch approach to the massive cultural change at GE is that he moved out aggressively but thoughtfully, and with due attention to persuasion, not dicta. His vision of change has been made clear from the very start, but he didn't try to get it all done overnight. And in its implementation he remained attuned to all the *human* aspects, specifically including the way the rate of change was affecting acceptance. Though he has tuned the timing to fit the human dynamics, he has presented throughout a clear vision of where GE is headed. The following quotes provide insight:

> [Writing in 1989:] As we succeed . . . in ridding our Company of the tentacles of ritual and bureaucracy, we are now better able to attack the final, and perhaps the most difficult challenge of all. And that is the empowering of our 300,000 people, the releasing of their creativity and ambition, the direct coupling of their jobs with some positive effect on the quality of a product or service. . . . Their roles, responsibilities and rewards must become clear to them and to everyone.

> [In a 1990 speech to shareholders:] The simplest definition of what we are trying to create—what our objective is—is a boundary-less Company, a Company where the artificial barriers and walls people are forever building around themselves or each other for status, security, or to keep change away, are demolished—and everyone has access to the same information, everyone pulls in the same direction, and everyone shares in the rewards of winning—in the soul as well as in the wallet.

Note the emphasis on *everyone*. I can't think of a better vision for GE, or for corporate America.

THE NEW ORGANIZATIONAL APPROACH HAS MADE A BIG DIFFERENCE AT GENERAL ELECTRIC—AND THE RECORD PROVES IT

This has not been empty rhetoric at work or a bunch of new slogans with no accompanying systemic changes. Welch's changes at GE have been real, sweeping, and highly successful. And they have been lasting. Among the abundant proof of that has been the change in GE's bottom line. Few if any American companies can point, as GE can, to *forty consecutive quarterly earnings increases* during the eighties. Moreover, as the GE program for change unfolded, those increases grew. By the early nineties GE's annual growth rate had reached 16 percent—remarkable for a corporation of its size. The cumulative effect provides an even more impressive testimonial. GE began the decade of the eighties ranked *eleventh* among U.S. corporations (at $12 billion in market value). By 1995 GE was valued at $89 billion—and first place in the U.S. pecking order. Once mighty GM was worth less than half that. Do you think that's just luck? Or are you prepared to believe that Jack Welch, and those who think like him, may really have something going?

General Electric, like Boeing, is heavily involved in international markets. Its new "heart and hunger of a small company" and its restructuring have paid off handsomely there as well. In 1985, GE earned some 20 percent of its profits beyond America's shores. By the end of the decade that had increased to 40 percent. In fact, Jack Welch says, "Globalization is no longer a lofty ideal. It is the key to the future for nearly every business in this company." In keeping with that part of the vision, GE is moving aggressively to take advantage of the dramatic opening of Eastern Europe.

For example, GE's lighting business bought Tungstram, the Hungarian lighting manufacturer. GE expects big things in the Eastern

European marketplace once Tungstram is humming according to the GE management principles. (While *Communism* is dead there as it is everywhere else, GE still will need to overcome the ravages of *Centralism* in that work force, just as it overcame another strain of the Centralism virus in its U.S. enterprises—more to come in chapter 7 on the lessons about Centralism embedded in the collapse of Communism.) As still another sign of its aggressiveness in exploiting that market, GE has booked a $150-million jet engine order from Aeroflot. In that same vein, GE is actively seeking opportunities for involvement in the huge markets its executives see opening over the next decade in Mexico and India. It's not just the Japanese who can export good management practices to other countries in the world and bring the fruits home in greater capital formation and a positive balance of payments. GE proves that every day.

To summarize, GE, like Boeing, saw that the old way of managing was hurting, not helping, so its leaders changed to a new way. Both companies overcame large black-ink barriers in making the decisions to change. Both used principles of decentralization to restructure their organizations. Both adopted various quality tools and greatly improved communication to further improve matters. Both realized that the latter steps could not succeed on their own without organizational decentralization. Both took the *holistic, humanistic* approach. Both are thriving as a result. And both are making impressive contributions to America's balance of payments. Alas, not many in the *Fortune* 500 resemble them in that respect.

That must change if America is to withstand the effects of globalization. A good catalyst for change is for the business community to take careful note of how Boeing, General Electric, and a few others like them have reorganized to stay in the forefront, not the backwash, of the wave of globalization. All who look will learn what's wrong with the way most American businesses are being managed. It's not hard to spot. That's the same way GE and Boeing were being managed before each determined there was a compelling need for a better way.

This chapter has provided a variety of examples of how to win big by organizing small. Speaking of big—and the manifold benefits of organizing small—I turn next to the story of the dramatically successful transformation of the Tactical Air Command. When I took charge of TAC on May 1, 1978, it was devoutly practicing centralized management—just like GM and most other American businesses. It got that way thanks to top-down edicts from the secretary of defense in the mid-sixties (note the date). It's a story of change from centralization to decentralization in our nation's largest bureaucracy. If it can happen there, it can happen anywhere.

This TAC transformation story involves *Five Pillar TQM* principles in action. Thus, it further sets the stage for later discussion of the other four pillars. Note the principles that were used: later chapters will elaborate on the way those principles are knitted together.

A TQM Turnaround
in Our Biggest
Bureaucracy

THE TAC STORY—A BRIEF INTRODUCTION

When I assumed command of the Tactical Air Command it epito-
mized the *centralized, managership* approach. We radically changed
its fortunes for the better by installing the *decentralized, leadership*
approach instead. The ripples from the dramatic improvements this
change brought about spread the same principles elsewhere in the
Department of Defense, and created many similar successes. I won't
dwell on those aspects because this isn't a book about management
in the government, and I'm not holding it up as the example for all
to follow. However, it is instructive that some big slices of the DOD
got much better through application of these principles, long before
"Japanese management" became a hot subject in American management circles. So this isn't a story about TAC's transformation alone
—but it starts there.

And, in this case—as with Boeing and GE—note the striking
before-and-after contrasts in the same huge organization. That puts a
different slant on it than the contrasts between the traditional American style as practiced by GM and the by now traditional Japanese
style as practiced by Honda and Toyota. The TAC case, therefore,
provides additional insight into why you should choose to combine
decentralization with far greater emphasis on quality in a *Five Pillar*

TQM approach, and illuminates the ways to go about it. Though TAC is a military organization in a huge bureaucracy, the lessons to be drawn from the TAC experience have practical application to all sorts of organizations, whatever their size, whatever their business.

THE TRANSFORMATION OF TAC: CHANGING FROM A CENTRALIZED SYSTEM TO THE DECENTRALIZED, LEADERSHIP APPROACH—AND INCREASING QUALITY AND PRODUCTIVITY DRAMATICALLY

During my tenure at TAC it had 180,000 people at more than 100 operating locations in forty-six of the fifty states and five foreign countries. About one-third of that total was in the *active reserve* forces, with the other two-thirds in active Air Force units. (The reserve units wore the TAC patch, trained to TAC standards, policies, and procedures, and were inspected by TAC inspectors to ensure they met the same high standards as the active force.) TAC also had the leadership role for all USAF tactical forces worldwide on equipage, training, and doctrinal matters. Besides providing some eighty-nine squadrons of fighters to be deployed rapidly, if needed, to trouble spots worldwide, TAC also had responsibility for the fighter forces and forward-deployed radar systems that provide for the air defense of the United States. The point is that TAC was and is big, with all kinds of challenges and internal dynamics. If judged as a corporation it would be among the world's twenty largest.

The highly centralized management system, structure, and style TAC was using when I arrived in 1978 were just like those of the other Air Force major commands, and like major elements throughout the Department of Defense. That was in keeping with the centralization doctrine that had been brought to the DOD from the American business world in the mid-sixties. Having watched the centralized approach in action throughout the Air Force for more than a decade, I was convinced it was strangling motivation, leadership, and creativity—and thereby wreaking havoc on quality and productivity. So, even before I went to TAC to take over, I asked for the authority to do a wide scale *test* of a far more decentralized, team-based system. In part because of credentials I had established in three earlier turn-arounds and in part because of the strong support of the Air Force Chief of Staff (who was as disenchanted with the centralized approach as I was), I was given the authority to conduct the test.

What did we do? Simply stated, we implemented the decentral-ized, leadership approach in all TAC elements and activities. As it had for me in challenging settings before, that made a huge difference. Overall productivity climbed by 80 percent (with no more people and no special funding). One of TAC's major shortcomings—mainte-nance of its huge fleet of aircraft of all types—improved dramatically. For example, we cut the number of aircraft *out for maintenance* at any given time by three fourths. That, and a number of other im-provements I will discuss later, produced equipment availability and combat capability that would have cost well over $12 billion if we had gone out and bought it. Indeed, we were able to double the com-bat capability in less than four years (based on the same size force; there were only minor changes in that regard). Moreover, the vast bulk of those improvements occurred well before the Reagan admin-istration defense-buildup dollars started kicking in. (That wasn't until 1983—from 1981 budget year appropriations—it takes a while to get things on contract and see tangible results from appropriations by the Congress.)

No mistake about it, that defense buildup helped fill the parts bins, bought improved systems, increased pay and morale, and thereby pro-vided even greater capability. But the great majority of the improve-ments I cite here were not the result of those buildup actions. I make the point because the centralizers are always looking for reasons to refute decentralization, even when they aren't there.

These impressive results attracted lots of attention within the DOD, and in the national media (partly because TAC wings earlier had served in the media as egregious examples of poor readiness and the contrasts were not to be ignored). As one example, in January 1987, *INC.* magazine carried a feature article on my role in trans-forming TAC titled "*Four-Star Management.*" That article quoted a high-level Department of Defense official as follows: *His may be the most important U.S. military victory since MacArthur's Inchon Landing.* That is generous overstatement, but the results indeed were sweeping as TAC's new management system model spread elsewhere.

For example, as it spread to the other Air Force major commands their improvements in quality and productivity were much like those of TAC. Tellingly, however, those improvements occurred only as that transformation in their management system approach actually took place. There is abundant data to show any skeptics the correlation between the marked improvement and the change in their management system, not other factors. In all those cases it produced impressive improvement in the peacetime performance statistics. However, peacetime is one case, and wartime is quite another. Did any of this have any effect on the extraordinary performance of the Air Force in the Gulf War? Let's look at that briefly, because actual combat provides a demanding test of whether those management system changes made a difference.

THE TRANSFORMATION RESULTS AT WORK IN THE GULF WAR—PUTTING THE NEW MANAGEMENT SYSTEM TO THE ACID TEST

As all will recall, the date was January 16, 1991. It was early evening on the East Coast of the United States, late afternoon on the West Coast, and 3:00 A.M. in the darkened skies over Baghdad, Iraq. In Kuwait, the illegal and immoral Iraqi pillage continued unabated. Baghdad was serene. Saddam Hussein and his ruling clique had defied the United Nations deadline to pull out of Kuwait or face the consequences. Amidst ringing pronouncements about *endless streams of body bags* if war was to come, Saddam was saying that Americans would not have the courage to act—or to stay the course if they did. He and his Revolutionary Council expressed supreme confidence in their ability to stand up to the United States and its coalition partners. Both the serenity and the bravado were about to change.

High over Baghdad in his F-117 Stealth fighter, a U.S. Air Force fighter pilot peered intently into the infrared scope that outlined the main buildings of Baghdad below, including his specified target, the main Iraqi communications building (dubbed the *"AT&T building"* by the targeting staff). That was the communications hub that linked Saddam Hussein to all of his forces in the field. Minutes before, a joint Army–Air Force helicopter raid in southern Iraq had taken out two early-warning radar sites. So the Iraqis were alerted; however, their Baghdad area radars could not pick up the stealthy F-117, which had penetrated Iraq well before the helicopter attack. Confident of his equipment and his training, the pilot locked his gunsight cross hairs onto the building's roof antennas and, one after the other, released two 2,000 pound laser-guided bombs. Both were direct hits, as he knew they would be. The bombs thundered through the roof and into the complex communications equipment on the floors below. Communications routed from that building to the Iraqi forces in the field would not be a factor for the rest of the war. The Desert Storm air campaign had begun. The other fighters, striking targets throughout Iraq, achieved comparably precise and devastating results.

It was not obvious to Americans in those dramatic opening hours, but the overall tone of the air campaign had been set. Purposeful professionalism, operating in the framework—and with the accumulated benefits—of a *QUALITY* approach to all aspects of the demanding business of air combat was to prove its worth again and again in the stressful days that followed. That quality approach encompassed all the elements required for success; there were no weak links. It embraced the *people*, the *equipment*, the *training*, the *planning*, the *strategy*, the *tactics*—and especially the approach to *organization* and *leadership* that had to pull all of those elements together into a collective and focused team effort.

Those multiple factors, operating interactively, were not fully appreciated by most outside observers, then or now. But the increasingly impressive war-fighting results strongly implied their presence somewhere in the background. And the quality of that performance confounded those throughout the nation conditioned to the notion, spread by the critics, that the Air Force had long been asleep and was outright remiss because it was preparing to *"fight the last war,"* not *"the next one."* They were wrong.

That air campaign went on to play the major, definitive role in determining the ultimate war outcome and the speed with which it was achieved. Make no mistake, it was a joint and coalition air-land-sea effort that eventually liberated all of Kuwait. That effort was superbly orchestrated and executed by General Norman Schwarzkopf and all concerned in *Operation Desert Storm.* All of the U.S. services performed with distinction. However, virtually all knowledgeable observers, uniformed and civilian, agree that the pounding from the air, along with cutting off the battlefield from resupply, increasingly turned Saddam Hussein's ground forces into the underfed, disheveled, and demoralized crowd they had become at the start of the ground campaign, with little effectiveness or resolve remaining. Reinforcement for that view came from the wholesale Iraqi battlefield desertions and from the eagerness with which those forces surrendered once the four-day ground campaign began. In fact, a senior Iraqi commander, when asked during the surrender talks why his army had collapsed, responded simply, *"The airplanes."*

Saddam Hussein had over 15,000 Surface-to-Air Missiles of all types, and more than 6,000 Anti-Aircraft Guns, in addition to his large air force. Despite those formidable defenses, the U.S. Air Force, over forty-three days of intense day and night combat, lost a grand total of only thirteen fighters. That's an average of only one every three days, or *only one shot down for each 3,200 combat sorties.* That was by far the lowest loss rate of any of the U.S. services or the air forces of the international coalition partners participating in air operations in Iraq and Kuwait. Even more impressively, U.S. Air Force fighter forces suffered *only three deaths.* Considering the widespread havoc they caused, never in the history of warfare has there been such a tremendous disparity between opposing military forces in terms of the damage inflicted on the one hand and the damage incurred on the other. It can justifiably be said, therefore, that the Gulf War air campaign gave new meaning and dimension to the phrase *"the competitive edge."* And the lessons of how the Air Force fighters were structured for success—through a new management system that greatly improved quality and productivity—have direct applicability to America's problems in competitiveness.

I wish to reiterate that the U.S. Air Force by no means did the air campaign job all by itself. However, it had a lead role, particularly in the highest-threat areas, and it delivered three-fourths of all the munitions delivered from the air. Of special importance, the Air Force also delivered more than nine out of ten of all the *precision-guided munitions*. It was no accident that Air Force fighters were the *heavy hitters* in the precision business. That had been a key part of the TAC stress on *quality*, and of doing it right the first time, every time. *When you don't have to do it over, it yields great mission efficiency, effort efficiency, and cost efficiency*. Indeed, that's the troika that gives the quality approach its enormous leverage. And that's as true in business as it is in combat.

As that first bomb was dropped on Baghdad, I had no doubt about how those Air Force forces would perform. I was confident the results would be spectacular. I also was confident they would amaze an American public conditioned to viewing its military (and the Air Force emphasis on quality, not quantity) with jaundiced eyes. Sharing my confidence were scores of other Air Force leaders. Indeed, they had played instrumental roles in the design and implementation of our new management system and combat tactics. Among them was the commander of all Desert Storm Air Forces, Lieutenant General Chuck Horner. Horner was the principal architect of the air campaign and orchestrated its execution. As such, he has impeccable credentials as a commentator on the reasons underlying its success. In the course of a long and detailed letter he sent to me soon after the war was over, he provided his reflections on that subject. He has synopsized those reflections as follows:

I want everyone to know of the monumental contribution made by General Bill Creech to the success of our air campaign in the Gulf War. I was in the Tactical Air Command both before and after he brought us fresh ideas on how to organize and lead in the late seventies, and I can tell you the difference that it made—to our spirit and our capabilities—was like night and day. He untiringly taught all of us, over and over, what to me were three essential points: *The first*: The critical importance of decentralization in the way you organize, to ensure a maximum in flexibility, responsiveness, and feelings of ownership. *The second*: The absolute necessity of getting leadership and commitment from everyone—and I do mean everyone. *The third*: the power of quality in everything that you do.

The great success of our air campaign flowed from a strong quality foundation, shaped on those three basic points. It produced: Quality in the weapons we conceived, and had built. Quality in our insistence and insurance they would work as advertised—and they did. Quality, and maximum realism, in our training. Quality in the way we treated and supported our people. Quality in our team structured and team oriented organization. And quality in our leadership at every level which had been unleashed by that new organization. It was all of those, and the other important improvements that came with them, that blended together to build peak performance and strong, unwavering commitment from everyone involved.

Though the equipment got most of the headlines, it was far more than the smart bombs and the Stealth fighters, as important as they were. It was a quality approach across-the-board. It ranged from the clear-cut goals and objectives set by the President, to the empowerment all the way down through the system to get them done, to the way our people maintained aircraft, and loaded bombs, and carried out the myriad support activities, and on to the execution of the combat missions themselves. They exercised all sorts of initiative and creativity, they thought for themselves, and they had great confidence in their cause and their capabilities. That wasn't by accident—it was just what the training and the organizational approach had been designed to produce.

Their performance, courage, and perseverance under often stressful, and always austere conditions were magnificent, and they deserve the bulk of the accolades and our lasting gratitude. Having said that, I am convinced our Air Force forces would not have performed even remotely as well under the old system, and the old way of centralized thinking. It yielded inefficiency, apathy, and disunity—the very things we did not see in action in the Gulf. And it was General Bill Creech who set us on, and kept us on, that new track to organization and leadership that proved so successful in everything that we did.

It's hard to sum up the importance of that aspect of our success in a single sentence, but one of our commanders came as close as anyone can. A few days after the war was over I was visiting one of our bases. The wing commander and I were visiting with the people who had performed so brilliantly, basking in the glow of our success, and reminiscing about the events that had contributed to it. As we talked more and more about how it had all been put together the wing commander turned to me and put it in these words: *"You know, General Horner, after all that General Creech did for us, we couldn't miss."* I strongly echo his sentiments.

The American people gave us unashamed and unwavering support, and General Bill Creech gave us the organization and training that made the success of our crusade possible. I can't thank him enough for that.

Before turning to the steps that were taken to transform the Air Force forces—which led to the impressive capabilities on display in the Gulf—it's appropriate to sort out why that is relevant to our discussion of the effects of *Five Pillar TQM*.

THE INDIVIDUAL U.S. SERVICES ORGANIZE, TRAIN, AND EQUIP THEIR FORCES—THE JOINT COMMANDERS EMPLOY THEM AS REQUIRED

Our country was fortunate to have General Norman Schwarzkopf as the Commander-in-Chief of the U.S. Central Command when Saddam Hussein invaded Kuwait on August 2, 1990. (Schwarzkopf was promoted to four-star general and assigned as CINC, USCENTCOM on November 23, 1988. He retired on August 1, 1992. His last two years were to prove highly eventful, for him and the country.) I watched his performance throughout the Desert Shield and Desert Storm sequence of events with the critical eye of a senior military leader well schooled on that part of the world. I was impressed. His performance was particularly outstanding in the light of the multinational complexities involved. (Many fault the overall war-fighting strategy that came down from Washington. But you can't blame

Schwarzkopf or the fighting forces for those decisions—heavily weighted as they were to international political realities. Those forces did what they were empowered to do in the time given to them, and they did it well.) General Schwarzkopf deserves the widespread acclaim he has received.

What does TAC have to do with all of that? It's an appropriate question to answer because few Americans understand how our overall joint system operates. Here, in a nutshell, is the story: In the U.S. system, and under U.S. public law, the individual services are responsible for organizing, training, and equipping their forces. Those forces are then employed, as required, by the various U.S. joint commanders. As an example of this arrangement of "Joint Commands" in action, TAC provided forces to Atlantic Command (LANTCOM) for the operations in Grenada, to Southern Command (SOUTHCOM) for the operations in Panama, and then to Central Command (CENTCOM) for Desert Storm. Under that arrangement, there's no practical approach other than to make the individual services responsible for the *organization, training*, and *equipping*.

Said simply, it's the job of the services to get themselves ready for use in crisis or combat, and it's the job of the joint commanders to do the area-related planning and provide the overall direction of the actual fighting if the need arises. In that sense, it's fair to observe that success in actual combat operations is not only a matter of the quality of the coach (the joint commander), it's also an issue of the quality of the team elements being coached. That's where the TAC story and the Gulf War example come together.

THERE ARE MANY LESSONS EMERGING FROM THE NATIONAL RESOLVE, COHESION, AND SUCCESS SHOWN IN DESERT STORM—AT LEAST THERE OUGHT TO BE

It has been proclaimed that the Gulf War has helped lay to rest the "ghosts of Vietnam." True or not, the Gulf War most certainly has proved the worth of laying to rest the ghosts of *centralized man-*

agement systems—in all their forms. That critical need is obvious from abundant other evidence, but the Gulf War provides emphatic verification.

In that regard, many who worry, as I do, about our growing problems in economic competitiveness are calling for a second Desert Storm—at least in the spirit and resolve we exhibited there nationwide. Obviously we can't simply call out our fighters again. The means of establishing national hegemony—and protecting the nation's well-being —increasingly are shifting from the military to the economic sphere. And that is where the new global economic competition must be waged and be won or lost. You can't look at the growing evidence—including the specter of Japanese transplant auto plants mushrooming across the United States while the Big Three U.S. automakers close plant after plant—or compare the *logos* on the goods that fill shelves all over America, or look at our persistent trade imbalance, and fail to recognize that we're in a tough new economic battle.

Some apologists say not to worry; "It creates new jobs for American workers" (and other such soothing pronouncements). But that leaves aside the issue of where the profits go. The same apologists blithely explain away our huge trade imbalance and express unconcern over the Japanese buying up everything from CBS Records, to Pebble Beach, to the 7-Eleven stores, to Rockefeller Center, to large chunks of real estate in downtown Los Angeles, Honolulu, and elsewhere. I'm not sure what it takes to arouse concern in such *Pollyannas*. It seems obvious to anyone who will look that America is getting the worst of the transfer trends in national wealth. That's one of our biggest exports! So it's neither xenophobic nor alarmist to say positive action is needed now.

Again, this isn't a book about military management, at TAC or anywhere else. However, as a lesson for all kinds of organizations in all kinds of businesses, it's useful to take a look at the centralized, managership approach as it operated in TAC, and thereby shed light on the principles to be used to dismantle it and replace it—wherever it's found. The place to begin is with the difference between functions and teams as an organizing principle.

CHANGING FROM BIG FUNCTIONS TO SMALL TEAMS —UNDERSTANDING AND CONFRONTING THE ISSUES INVOLVED

The efficiency of the interactive dynamics between individuals and departments determines organizational success or failure. The building blocks must mesh smoothly with all the other building blocks, both vertically and horizontally. That sounds self-evident. Yet inattention to the size of the building blocks and to their integration with other organization elements is the rule not the exception in traditionally managed organizations. TAC was by no means the only place I have found such inattention. (It's all over the place.) But TAC's experience can help illustrate the point. Upon becoming the TAC commander, I examined and found widely varied sizes of the building blocks. As I sought the rationale for those differences, I encountered an analytical roadblock. Neither consistency nor a coherent underlying rationale could be found. Instead, I encountered bromides such as *"economies of scale," "consolidation rules out duplication,"* and *"centralization yields efficiency and cost savings"* (the familiar litany of Centralism). As I examined TAC's historical trends, the data showed that those bromides were yielding continuously lower productivity and less cost efficiency—not exactly the results promised by Centralism's champions.

Yet TAC was no worse in that regard than the other major agencies within the Department of Defense. It certainly was no worse than other Air Force major commands. As mentioned previously, the strong, *from-the-top* impetus for sweeping centralization had come from the then secretary of defense and his staff in the mid-1960s. However, the Air Force leaders of that era embraced it in a big way. In fact, they embraced it so enthusiastically they set out to be better at it than anyone in the DOD. They may have been. And the better at it they became, the worse they got (a story now also familiar to me in American businesses of all kinds). So all Air Force major commands were in the grip of the same centralist-produced malaise—and they felt powerless to change it even if they were inclined to do so.

And they were not so inclined: They had fallen into a rut of acceptance, some even of outright advocacy, just as it was (and still is) in the bulk of corporate America.

I did not share that enthusiasm, and had long since been convinced that the philosophical underpinnings of Centralism were seriously askew. Therefore, a key part of my approach in taking over a new organization during the Air Force's "Centralism era" was to challenge each of its treasured precepts and their applications in that setting. Accordingly, I immediately set out to do that in TAC, and to hold those precepts up to the light of fresh, objective perspective. *I knew I would need to persuade, not order, if change was to be effective.* I also knew that one of the big obstacles to overcome would be the old conditioning.

The employees at all levels had been steeped for so long in centralization's reputed brilliance that few questioned its efficiency. It was just the way things were. In some circles, particularly among the various *technicians* in their functional silos, it went well beyond acceptance. It had been fully embraced as the *true faith.* Fortunately, that level of devotion was rare. Even the technical specialists later were to become some of the strongest proponents of the new approach. But there was much to do before reaching that point.

I knew from experience that objective performance data would be needed in overcoming that prior conditioning. The precepts of Centralism rest heavily on a base of *ad hominem* argumentation, not on empirical evidence of their effectiveness. It follows that facts and comparisons are the best assault forces on the rampant subjectivity that supports it. I also was convinced that empirical, before-and-after evidence would be required to fend off the zealous champions of Centralism in Washington, who I was sure would swoop down on us with a vengeance when they got wind of what we were doing. (And they did. And it was.) In that quest, our first step was to begin gathering comparative performance data across the breadth of TAC. We then analyzed that data in the light of history and like activities, and published the results for all to see. It wasn't easy, especially at first. There simply was no data available for comparison of similar activities. I did not find that surprising. Centralism does not prize comparison. Since it does not, its alleged efficiency is effectively shielded from comparative evaluation. The little data available was all at the macro level and *worthless* in analyzing performance within the organizational depths.

So we set to work to develop tools of *output* measurement and comparison where they really count: down where the work is done. As that data began flowing in, it did not surprise me to find results —outputs—that varied widely between like units, and with little rhyme or reason to them. Some activities in one part of the country were doing extremely well, while those at other locations, similarly structured and equipped, were doing terribly. Those variances simply could not be explained on any rational basis. That attracted lots of attention throughout that nationwide organization. Everyone was scratching their heads trying to explain it. Some even tried, but their explanations were hollow, and even they soon came to realize it. The old conditioning began crumbling.

To augment that investigation, we soon had decentralized models in operation at several locations to provide an even more illuminating *benchmark* for comparison. We kept pushing for data—hard, irrefutable, comparative data—for use in exposing the difficulties in the existing organization. As that data base grew, here's what we found: Large, functionally oriented building blocks are unwieldy and unproductive. They are focused on the *functional specialty* and on the *job* for each member within that functional array. However, they are not focused on the integrated final product or the subelement products within it. Also, because of their vertical orientation, they mesh imperfectly with the other building blocks similarly structured.

In theory, if everyone carries out his or her own job and function properly, it will all fit together like a Swiss watch. *In practice, it does not.* In that same vein, the more we studied TAC organizations near and far, the more we became painfully aware of an absence of ''focal points''—that is, focal points at which we could get an accurate sense and an accurate measurement of the integration of effort at the various levels in a product-process context. Our reorganization fixed that.

A STORY OF HOW GREAT QUALITY AND PRODUCTIVITY GAINS CAN BE ACHIEVED BY CHANGING FROM BIG FUNCTIONS TO SMALL TEAMS

As an example, let's look at the before-and-after of maintaining TAC's complex fighter aircraft. In keeping with the precepts of Centralism, TAC maintenance was organized big and by function. For example, all electricians who worked the entire flightline—on seventy-two fighters—were in one functional silo, and all reported to a chief electrician. They were dispatched in trucks, when called on, from a central shop to wherever their services might be required. The hydraulic specialists were organized in the same manner, as were the aircraft mechanics, and so on. As you would expect, that approach required lots of telephone coordination, paperwork, and going to and fro. Nevertheless, Centralism's advocates prized its *flexibility* in moving people around. They also applied their beloved *"economy of scale"* argument. But it was neither economical nor flexible.

Our new architecture broke up those functional fiefdoms and broke down those functional walls. All flightline maintenance was organized by teams. The specialists were moved from their functional silos into those teams and integrated fully with all other maintenance technicians. Most were given elementary training in another technical skill to facilitate harmony and cross-utilization. And all helped, when necessary, with uncomplicated maintenance tasks. In other words, they helped the crew chiefs where required, as well as one another. Thus, technicians of all kinds worked together in a close-knit, focused group. Integrated, product-oriented teams replaced nonintegrated, job-oriented functions. *Teamwork became a reality and not a slogan.*

We also introduced *ownership* and the *empowerment* to go with it. There had been neither in the centralized system. To that end, the one large flightline-wide maintenance organization was broken into three identical "squadron" teams. Each was responsible for its own twenty-four aircraft, and each squadron was broken into four flights of six aircraft. Within each squadron and flight all the various disciplines worked together in small teams to get the job done. Each squadron had its own set of goals. Each did its own scheduling, which had been done centrally before. Each made its own decisions and charted its own course. And we carried those themes of ownership and empowerment down all the way to the frontline level.

For example, each fighter aircraft was assigned a *"Dedicated Crew Chief"* who, with an assistant, was totally responsible for that specific aircraft. We painted his or her name on the side of *their* fighter, and they went with it everywhere. To help them, within the small, integrated squadron teams were the various technical specialists required to keep the fighter and all of its systems in top-notch shape. When it needed maintenance it was fixed quickly and without extensive coordination and paperwork. We had gone from a vertical to a horizontal arrangement, and the authority flowed in that new manner. That gave focus to authority and accountability in an integrated product sense; and it removed the ambiguity about who was accountable for what. Before, the aircraft mechanics and various specialists might work on as many as six different aircraft during a day, and on a different six the following day. That approach of unfocused responsibility was replaced by the integrated teams, providing ample *focal points* at all levels for product focus and performance assessment.

Accountability for poor performance now was easy to track. It was equally easy to single out those who deserved recognition for stellar performance—both individuals and groups. Our measurements at those focal points soon began to reflect the power of motivation, pride, and commitment. It was flowing from decentralization and from the newfound ownership and empowerment that came with it. The cumulative results impressively followed suit, and that improvement could be found across the board.

THE ORGANIZE SMALL APPROACH CREATES
MOTIVATION AND PRIDE—AND CRISP LINKAGE
BETWEEN AUTHORITY AND ACCOUNTABILITY

The motivational aspects of the new approach can perhaps best be described by citing the insights of a young three-striper crew chief. Not long after we began, I was visiting one of TAC's many bases. As usual, I was mingling with the workers at the frontline level to find out *what was really going on.* The first crew chief I approached smiled as he shook my hand and said, "I really like the new arrangement and the dedicated crew chief program, General Creech." I said that I did too, and asked him why he liked it so much. He responded, *"When's the last time you washed a rental car?"* That said it all. He and his colleagues now exercised real *ownership.*

He went on: "I also like it because now my work shows up in one place, and when I take pride in it, it shows. Also, the people who were goofing off before without anyone being aware of it now have to put out or be found out. That's been a big morale booster." In those few words, that young sergeant brilliantly captured the power of ownership, of empowerment, and of clear-cut accountability. New meaning had been given not only to his own accomplishments, but also to the accomplishments of his aircraft flight. The peer pressure began working in positive not negative directions, and the multi-discipline teams produced far more effective interaction and integration. Problems started getting worked on and solved by those closest to them. They had understood those problems all along—even those that had long gone unrecognized at higher levels. Their insights and empowerment helped us get rid of lots of dumb practices, and to cut off problems at their source.

Another sergeant underscored the appeal of another aspect of our new system—that of empowerment to his level and below. He was a maintenance flight chief, a first-line supervisor. He cited their new-found authority to do their own work scheduling to make his point. He started by volunteering how much he liked doing their own scheduling, which had been done centrally before. When I asked why, he responded: "It lets us live with our own mistakes." Then, after a knowing smile, he added: "And we make fewer all the time." In those two sentences he summarized the whole point of decentralizing. We had integrated ownership, authority, and accountability at the lowest levels and the system became largely self-correcting. That's just one example of how we carried out the empowerment principle. The centralized approach works to separate the *thinkers* and the *doers*. That's one of the reasons it works so poorly. We let the doers do the thinking.

And it surprised many of centralization's devotees to see how smart those doers were. It didn't surprise me. They had the incentive to do it smart, and do it right the first time. And that incentive was increased when they got personal recognition and satisfaction from doing it better than ever before. Also, with our new focal points, where problems did emerge it was far easier to find them, and to get them fixed efficiently and rapidly. There was then no need for the *all points bulletins* (broad-based harangues) that were a staple of the centralized approach. And the scattergun approach to reacting to problems went into the trash can. A *humanized* system had replaced a *dehumanized* system. The problems of unwieldy structure, poor focus, and diffused responsibility became relics of the past. But none of that happened without running gun battles with the centralizers in Washington. Its advocates are found all over the place, all hoodwinked by Centralism's alluring sales pitch.

At the time I went to TAC the Air Force Chief of Staff was General Dave Jones, later to become Chairman, JCS. He strongly endorsed my radical restructuring of TAC's entire management approach. Indeed, he was equally dismayed with the centralized approach. We had worked together before. He took over as the CINC of USAF-Europe just as I was completing a turnaround of the wing at Madrid (story later), and I then spent three action-packed years on his staff as deputy for operations. I especially admired the way he challenged, and overcame, convention. For example, he led a host of *sweeping* changes that vastly improved NATO's war-fighting capabilities—particularly in command and control. Thus, he further enhanced my beliefs and perceptions regarding structural issues and the value of decentralization and empowerment (and how to overcome entrenched defenders of the status quo). Those who succeeded him as Air Force Chief of Staff followed his lead and were very supportive of what we were doing in TAC. Without that it wouldn't have worked. None of them intruded, but they helped us fight off the Washington bureaucrats so we could carry out our game plan. There's a big moral there: corral the staff kibitzers or your efforts to decentralize the operating units won't go anywhere. This need holds true everywhere. Witness Jack Welch's sensitivity to this issue in the transformation of General Electric.

THE INTERNETTING OF TEAMS: GETTING EVERYONE INVOLVED IN AN INTEGRATED EFFORT REGARDLESS OF THEIR SPECIALTY

As we broke up the large, unwieldy functional silos, we placed every specialty possible directly into the integrated squadron teams on the flightline. However, that wouldn't work in all cases. Sometimes, because of the nature of the function, it was not appropriate or feasible to fold it into the integrated team. Nonetheless, we formed teams in those functions also. And we then paid lots of attention to their connectivity—their *umbilical cords*, if you will—to the integrated teams they supported. For example, in breaking up the single, vertical functional silo in which all munitions specialists had been centralized, we took the *munitions loaders* and placed them directly into each of the three squadron teams. They integrated nicely because they load the bombs, missiles, and bullets onto the fighter aircraft in a beautifully orchestrated ballet of speed and safety to get the fighter ready as quickly as possible for another combat sortie. Therefore, they were key players in those new integrated teams.

However, the loaders comprise only one of two munitions specialties. The other specialty involves the buildup of the munitions that are stored in a remote area in disassembled form (for security and safety reasons). Those specialists were left functionally aligned, and remained in the remote storage area. But they too were broken out of a single function and formed into three separate teams. Each team was then tied to one of the three flightline squadrons—in a supplier-customer sense. That tied them directly to the principal mission and thereby provided a perspective and an immediacy that had been missing in the functional alignment. Also, since we now had three teams in munitions buildup rather than one function, we could measure and make comparisons as to how each was performing. Their spirit, focus, and productivity all rose significantly.

We used the same approach in the *Ground Equipment* function. (This is equipment not unlike that you see out the window of your airliner before it taxies, only more complex.) Again, three teams were formed out of one function. Each was tied to a specific flightline squadron as its internal customer. The results were the same as for *Munitions*. Quality and productivity greatly improved, as did the enthusiasm with which the newly formed teams carried out their work.

We did the same with *Supply*, which like everything else was centralized. All supplies and parts, from fighter radars to office supplies to paints and varnishes, were all held in a single supply complex and administered centrally. That system also was decentralized. For example, we moved the portions related to aircraft supply directly to the flightline. All the parts and pieces, along with "dedicated" supply specialists, were devoted only to that flightline customer. The direct linkage and face-to-face internetting with the people they supported allowed other steps to cut out unnecessary steps and streamline the entire process. Paperwork was reduced by 65 percent, and coordination greatly simplified. As a result, responsiveness to customer requirements and the speed of response improved markedly.

For example, at the time we began it took an average of three and one-half hours from the time a part was ordered until it was delivered. (Lots of time for the repair technician to lose interest, or go to another job and be replaced by someone who hadn't done the troubleshooting.) After our changes, delivery time averaged only eight minutes throughout TAC. No waiting, no handover to other maintenance technicians, and just one supply technician involved, not many. We netted it together with small computers that rapidly revealed whether we had the part and where it was. The only two people involved were the person who needed the part and the person who had it. The theme was *Fix it now, fix it fast, and fix it right*.

Sounds so simple, one wonders why TAC didn't do it all along. I'll tell you why. With our new approach we shattered about every Centralism precept there is. I could tell by the yelps of anguish from the centralizers in Washington if by no other way. And yet it took even fewer people and was far more cost-effective—besides all its other advantages. We exploited the economies of small scale and laid to rest the diseconomies of large scale. So much for that precept.

With the internetting with the frontline mission teams came lots more *hustle* and a strong sense of personal obligation by the supply specialists in assuring that the parts were on hand when the maintenance person needed them. So they *bugged* the black-box repair folks when required, and took personal initiative to backtrack to the wholesale depots (and raise a ruckus) when we were short of some items. That was no longer left to "central computers" as before. We had *personalized* an impersonal system. Not surprisingly, our overall supply posture as well as its speed of response improved markedly.

A COMPARISON OF TAC BEFORE AND AFTER SPEAKS ELOQUENTLY TO THE POWER OF ORGANIZING SMALL

Our significant improvement in productivity allowed us to double the number of peacetime fighter pilot training sorties, an increase that was sorely needed. Before our restructuring, TAC had ample authorization and budget to fly more training sorties, but it simply could not maintain airplanes well enough to produce them. That negatively affected the combat readiness of the pilots and of everyone else involved. As their brilliant performance in the Gulf War later demonstrated so vividly, our new management system corrected that vexing problem. And not only productivity shot up. Quality in all areas soared to the top also. There was abundant evidence of that.

For example, we reduced by 73 percent the number of aircraft grounded for maintenance in that fleet of more than 4,000 aircraft. (That is a fleet twice as big as all the U.S. airlines combined.) And aircraft *"Hangar queens"*—those grounded for more than three weeks for maintenance or supply problems—were rapidly reduced from an average of 234 a day to only 8 per day once our new system was in place. The combination of those two improvements alone made ten full wings of fighters available to us that were grounded and unavailable before. The fighters still landed with problems from time to time, of course, as airliners do. But they were fixed and returned to service far more rapidly. For example, we improved by an astounding 270 percent the rate of fixing aircraft on the same day they landed "broke." We were now able to fix more than four out of five aircraft immediately, as opposed to only one out of five under the old system. That meant they were again available within minutes or a few hours, as contrasted to a day or days before. *We also more than doubled our ability to generate sorties in combat.*

All of that was on ample display, and proved its worth, when Saddam Hussein invaded Kuwait and refused to leave. The fighter squadrons deployed quickly to austere bases throughout Saudi Arabia and the Gulf Emirates. They bedded down quickly, and could have begun combat operations within hours if called on. When the fighting did start, they operated *"just like we do at home"*—a refrain heard over and over at the various locations. (And that was one of the ideas!) The deployment to the Gulf and the combat that followed showed the new management system's effectiveness in a stressful setting and its inherent agility and flexibility. Other evidence of its effectiveness included average fighter *"Mission Capable"* rates of over 95 percent throughout the conflict—in high-tempo operations. And that was remarkably different from the 50 percent and lower MC rates I found in TAC on my arrival to take over as commander.

That stark contrast was primarily due to the new management system and the way it made everything function better from the bottom to the top. A somewhat higher percentage of new-generation aircraft played a part. But that effect was measurable and simply did not provide a primary reason. The high mission capable rates in the

Gulf were achieved with old as well as new generation fighters. They also were achieved in peacetime in the same systems, old and new, years before the Gulf War loomed. Moreover, in the old centralized system, both the new and old generation fighters had the same abysmally low rates.

As proof of all that, six years after we reorganized and restructured TAC, we did a detailed analysis of the reasons for our impressive improvement. It turned out that our changed mix of aircraft during that period could be attributed to only 11 percent of our cumulative improvement in productivity. In other words, an overwhelming 89 percent of the improvement was due to our new TQM-style management system, not to a change in the equipment or greater equipment reliability. Those facts notwithstanding, many of the longtime external critics quickly seized on equipment reasons to explain why their previous gloomy analyses had been so wrong. For years they had harshly and loudly criticized the Air Force, particularly the fighter forces, for taking a "wrongheaded approach." Their rationale centered on quality issues.

As most readers will recall, those critics alleged that TAC was doggedly pursuing *"needless sophistication that won't work when called upon in combat."* In ascribing high fighter availability rates during *Desert Storm* to greater equipment reliability, they vitiated their previous argument. Not only that, they managed to be wrong a second time!

Far more than somewhat improved reliability of the equipment was involved—the vast improvement was due to the people and the way they were organized, and treated, and led, and how fast they repaired aircraft that still landed with problems needing attention. And that all traced back to the strong *Quality* improvement, over more than a decade, in all aspects of those forces. So the critics' arguments against quality proved to be off-base in every respect. This is worth dwelling on, because those who brush quality off as *unaffordable* abound in the business world as well. The same lessons apply.

Simply using the day-to-day statistics and deployment results under the old system for retrospective comparison, the centralized maintenance organization would have been an unmitigated disaster in the

Gulf War setting. And that's not just my view. It's also General Chuck Horner's view and that of many others who were on the scene in the Gulf and who are conversant with the capabilities of the fighter forces before that quality transformation took place. The centralized system didn't work in peace; it wouldn't have worked in war; and it doesn't work well anyplace it's tried—regardless of the business involved.

All businesses have different products, markets, and challenges. Therefore, not for a moment do I believe these examples from the Air Force fighter world serve as exact models for most businesses. However, they illustrate what can be achieved through the powerful effects of organizing small. Also, the problems we confronted in addressing Centralism, and our gains in doing so, are in no way unique to the military. I have seen the same organizational dynamics in action throughout the business world. The many examples of that provided in these pages help to prove the point. Therefore, the primary benefit of the TAC before-and-after story is to frame and sharpen the issues. The centralized, managership approach does its damage everywhere. And it's easily fixed everywhere. It just takes the gumption and guts to do it. An old fighter pilot expression applies: "*No guts, no glory.*"

SITUATION AWARENESS—KNOWING BOTH YOUR COMPETITION AND YOURSELF—AND THE IMPORTANCE OF PROPER PLANNING

Sun Tzu, the storied Chinese leader and philosopher of the fourth century B.C., handed down an abundance of wisdom about military strategy and tactics that have considerable application to all businesses. With regard to knowing the competition, he said:

> *If you know the enemy and know yourself,*
> *You need not fear the results of a hundred battles.*
> *If you know yourself but not the enemy,*
> *For every victory gained, you will also suffer a defeat.*

If you know neither the enemy nor yourself,
You will succumb in every battle.

In the fighter business astute knowledge of that kind is called *"Situation Awareness."* The phrase—and the notion behind it—grew from the fighter pilot adage in World Wars I and II to *"Check Six."* That meant that while on a mission you should constantly check behind you, at your six o'clock position, because the fighter weapons then were guns, and the kills were made from behind—more often than not on the unaware. Then along came hypersonic missiles that could kill at long range and from any direction. So *check six* wouldn't do anymore. The phrase became *situation awareness* because the enemy could be anywhere and you were threatened from everywhere. At the same time, on-board radars and other sophisticated sensors—such as devices to detect radars and missile launches—were added to the fighter pilot's ability to maintain situation awareness.

Of course, the gaining of appropriate situation awareness must start long before the pilot climbs into the cockpit. It must cover all aspects of the enemy's equipment, training, tactics, basing, vulnerabilities, and an accompanying host of information that can prove vital in sorting out the winners and the losers. That makes an indispensable contribution not only to the pilots but also to those who are doing the strategizing and targeting. Intelligence on the enemy is never perfect. But the harder one works at it, the better it gets. And we work hard at it in the fighter forces. Therefore, we're better than you might suspect at appraising what the enemy can and cannot do and what we must and must not do.

Two examples of before-the-fact *situation awareness* in the Gulf War help illuminate the point. First, the Air Force fighters used tactics—and had the weapons to allow such tactics—to stay above the Iraqis' main defensive strength, which was their Anti-Aircraft Artillery (AAA). Saddam Hussein had invested heavily in acquiring more than 6,000 AAA batteries. He also had bought some of the most sophisticated versions now available. (And, as the TV images of tracers criss-crossing and lighting up the Baghdad sky revealed, AAA is no respecter of pilot ability. Fly through it when it's as dense as that and you'll get hit.) The tactics to avoid that dense AAA—at targets throughout Kuwait and Iraq—account in large measure for the very low loss rates of the Air Force fighters.

As further proof of that, some of the coalition allies, in keeping with their own long-standing tactical doctrine, tried to "go low" against targets in Iraq. And they paid heavily in aircraft losses for the lesson that that was the wrong thing to do. So they changed their tactics to those of the USAF—so as to get up out of the AAA. But they then found their weapons poorly suited to that higher altitude. (That also accounts for why the Air Force had the "smart weapons," and not the others—at least not in appreciable numbers. They can't be used at low altitude.) So the Air Force's vigorous actions to obtain good situation awareness on enemy capabilities had paid off in developing the training and the weapons to make flexible tactics work. What the Iraqis could throw at them came as no surprise. And those fighters were ready for the "next war," despite what the critics said. The low loss rate and the damage inflicted on Saddam Hussein's forces in a short time showed it.

The second example of good situation awareness of enemy capabilities and vulnerabilities was on vivid display on network TV: a Stealth fighter placing a precision guided bomb exactly down the air shaft at Iraqi Air Force headquarters. The target planning staff knew about it and knew it was the best way to get the bomb to the bottom floor to wreak maximum damage to the building. Among other advantages, it eliminated the need for restrikes and any further exposure of friendly forces at the same target. So situation awareness is a fundamental part of organizational capability. It plays a major role in focusing energy in the right areas and on the right subjects.

There's a lesson in that for the business world. While I knew quite a bit about American business before I left the government, when I started seeing deeply inside various companies, to my considerable surprise I found a marked lack of competitive situation awareness. Most companies do not understand their competition as well as they could or should—as weighed against their own strengths and weaknesses. I've found traditionally managed, centralized organizations to be especially poor at that.

The Japanese are among the most astute and aggressive in the global community in obtaining situation awareness. Stories abound attesting to that. The latest such story concerns what Toyota's executives did to understand the luxury car market before entering it. They acquired and *reverse engineered* the top models from around the world to determine the strengths and weaknesses of each among that broad array of products. And they looked at what was good and bad about the sales and service outlets of those same manufacturers. They then crafted their new *Lexus* series in the light of that array of knowledge. They aimed for the best automobile in the luxury field, and built their dealer network in a way that would beat the competition in that respect as well. Mind you, this was an entry into an entirely new niche in the automotive market, and a highly competitive one at that. The *Lexus* series was an instant hit. And it shot to the top of the *J. D. Power & Associates* quality and customer satisfaction ratings right from the start—and has stayed there. That captured the attention of both German and American luxury car builders. I heard a senior GM executive muse over Toyota's success with the *Lexus* in this way:

> We should know more about the automobile business than any company in the world. We're the biggest, have been at it the longest, and have the largest data base on which to draw for improvement and refinement. We also have the talented people. But we don't know how to build a Lexus. And if we did, we couldn't price it competitively. Our big problem is our management system and old practices. They're giving us a competitive handicap that is very difficult to overcome. We're trying to fix it, but we're obviously not doing enough, fast enough.

GM is not alone in this dilemma.

To summarize, most companies don't use the entire cycle—*situation awareness, strategy, planning, tactics, training*—and use that action sequence for every product and product line. Sure, the operating divisions are tasked to develop the *Annual Operating Plan* (*AOP*) and even *"Five-Year Plans,"* which are reviewed thoroughly at the topmost level. I've helped in such corporate reviews, and many companies do it well. However, they are long on business outlooks (mostly predictions) but short on the background details that went into their calculations. Moreover, most are not good at taking periodic wall-to-wall looks at all aspects of the "business of their business" and how it is being affected by changing marketplace dynamics. I made that almost a religion in the organizations I headed, and it paid off on numerous occasions in many ways. My sensitivity in that respect started back when I was a young captain leading the Skyblazer aerobatic team. I got it from someone else— someone who had acquired it the hard way. There's an important moral to the story; at least there was for me and the organizations I later headed.

CONSTANTLY REAPPRAISING THE BUSINESS OF YOUR BUSINESS—ONE OF THE KEYS TO SUCCESSFUL TQM

During the four years I led the Skyblazer team I also put on numerous *maximum performance* solo shows. Their purpose was to show off the capabilities of our supersonic fighter, which was new to the Air Force and to the Europeans. Accordingly, the solo show was designed to take the aircraft to its maximum limits (whereas the team show displayed precision teamwork). One day, after just such a solo show at an air base outside Casablanca, Morocco, I was approached by the famous British fighter pilot Douglas Bader, who had watched the show. Bader had become a legend in aviation circles for becoming one of the RAF's leading Aces in the *Battle of Britain* even though he had two artificial legs. The legend grew based on his courage and tenacity after being shot down and imprisoned by the Germans. He made escape attempt after escape attempt until the Germans finally confiscated his legs. And then the RAF dropped him a new set, and he tried again. His amazing story was set forth in his book *Fight for the Sky*. Needless to say, his opinion carried a lot of weight with me.

He started with extravagant praise regarding the solo show that I had just flown, and capped it with: "I have never seen a more skillful display of pilot ability." He then asked whether he could offer me some advice. Naturally, I said I welcomed it. He then recommended that I consider cutting out the *"Derry turn,"* one of several maximum-performance maneuvers I was doing. He recounted how he had lost his legs: by getting too low and crashing upside down during a pre–World War II airshow—in a quest to impress fellow pilots. He said he had learned from that to design the maneuvers for the public, and then to fly them to satisfy the other professionals—not the other way around. As he put it, *"I became confused over what business I was in."*

His point on the Derry turn was well taken. It was designed by John Derry, the chief test pilot of DeHavilland Aircraft (who later was killed performing an aerobatic display at the Farnborough Air Show in England). The Derry turn called for the utmost in pilot ability. It looked deceptively simple. To do it you set up a horizontal figure-eight turning maneuver in front of the crowd. The idea was to use maximum aircraft turning capability in the turn (I used six Gs) and then to reverse direction to start the other half of the "eight" by rolling the aircraft *underneath* (toward the ground). Performed at very low altitude (about fifteen feet), it took great skill and timing to blend the controls from very heavy back-stick pressure (for the high-G turn), to heavy forward-stick pressure as you rolled underneath (to keep the nose up and not descend), and then again to heavy back-stick pressure to turn abruptly in the opposite direction. Extensive, rapid manipulation of the rudders also was required to keep the aircraft rolling on a "point" and not lose altitude. That, of course, would have been disastrous with the ground so close. To do it right was even more complicated than it sounds.

I grasped Doug Bader's point immediately. The public, not knowledgeable about the laws of aerodynamics, did not know it was immensely more difficult to reverse underneath than to reverse over the top. (Which is the normal turn reversal technique, and thus is a *"piece of cake."*) Bader was telling me I had lost sight of the true business I was in, just as he had on the day he lost his legs. He was right. The maneuver was designed to please the professionals—and few of them could fully appreciate the maneuver's difficulty factor. The public understood not at all.

I emphasize that Doug Bader was not addressing the issue of the risk to me. I was doing at least two other maximum-performance maneuvers in the solo routine that were, on balance, every bit as dangerous. One of those was to pull straight up at comparatively low speed, lose all flying speed and fall backward, cartwheel the aircraft from nose up to nose down, then regain flying speed—just in time to pull out to miss the ground. If you didn't do the cartwheel maneuver exactly right, or pulled back on the stick the least bit prematurely on the way straight down before you had adequate speed, you would buffet the aircraft and not make it out the bottom without crashing. (Patience, though a virtue, is sorely tried when the windshield is full of nothing but onrushing ground at very low altitude.)

When performed in a high-performance, swept-wing, heavy-weight fighter, it was a most demanding maneuver. And it was totally unforgiving of any loss of concentration or nerve. However, it made a graphic point about the "controllability" of that fighter at slow speeds. That point was useful to make, because it had quickly developed a miserable reputation in that respect with the pilots (and with accident investigators!). It was indeed cranky, but not impossibly so when handled right. Doug Bader didn't comment on that maneuver because he wasn't talking about risks that were within the business of my business, just those that weren't.

I never did another Derry turn. And ever since, I have tried to keep uppermost in my mind Doug Bader's point about the business that I'm in. Leaders of organizations, regardless of their business, have the same problem. They must not only *stick to their knitting*, but also frequently reappraise what their knitting is all about. The approach of BTR, plc, a highly successful British conglomerate, comes to mind. BTR does periodic, detailed *business reviews* in which its leaders take a *zero-based* look at each individual subsidiary, its products, and its market segment. They proceed from "*Why are we in this business?*" to a thorough review of "*Are we doing it right?*" In so doing, they put rigor into constantly refreshing their situation awareness and the analysis of their strengths and weaknesses in the competitive context.

As an example of that principle at work in TAC, our switch in combat tactics—to provide the flexibility to go in high as well as low—was a change we made (circa 1979) after I had initiated just such a zero-based review of the business of our business. We confirmed in that detailed look that we had what I termed ''go low disease''— brought on by a perceived need to fly under the enemy Surface-to-Air missile (SAM) coverage (a perception that pervaded the entire Air Force). As a consequence, we concluded that our focus on training in TAC to go in low was hampering our future flexibility and our survivability if we challenged dense AAA to escape the SAMs, and also was restricting our view of the equipment we needed to carry out our job. So we changed the philosophy. We then followed through in all our equipage and training programs, to ensure that we had the capability to take out the SAMs as a first order of business—and had the flexibility to operate at either low or high altitude in enemy territory, depending on the defensive array. That change in the way we viewed our business paid rich dividends in the Gulf War.

This is but one example. We constantly challenged and reviewed our own most devoutly held beliefs. Paying that kind of attention to the business of the business is fundamental to aware, proactive leadership. However, it simply doesn't get enough attention by enough leaders in enough organizations. Group Captain Douglas Bader, a consummate leader if there ever was one, brought that forcefully to my attention many years ago. It stuck with me.

If you are to make the business of your business successful, you must remain constantly and closely attuned to the cycle of *situation awareness, strategy, planning, tactics*, and *training*. When that's done right it produces the right calibration and an objective perspective on the actual business, and on the follow-up actions necessary to make that business successful. If it starts wrong, or proceeds in an unfocused way, it ends wrong. I've seen lots of examples of that as well.

Earlier I explained how the decentralized, leadership approach (embodying the principles of *Five Pillar TQM*) spread from TAC to other Air Force major commands with equally beneficial results. To conclude this chapter, I turn to another example of the ripples that spread from that TAC success. It helps explain the quote in chapter

1 about TAC having started a *quality revolution* within the Department of Defense.

Many researchers credit the defense industry with helping to invent what I call a centocracy—or at least giving that organizational structure its major push beginning in the sixties. In fact, I have the experience in government procurement to verify that a great many of the troubled defense industry programs over the years can be attributed to that management structure and style. In that respect, however, it's only fair to point out that the DOD and other government agencies over the past several decades have been vigorously promoting that very centralized management style. So the government has not been an active agent for a change away from Centralism either. At least it wasn't until the DOD launched a major initiative to spread "TQM" to its many vendors in March of 1988. Based on its own internal experiences, the DOD saw that as a means of improving the quality and value of the millions of products it buys each year. The story of how the massive Department of Defense came from its own long-standing Centralism ways to being a proponent of TQM-style management is relevant to this narrative for the many lessons it holds.

It's a story with special interest for the thousands of American companies that sell to the DOD, since they now are obliged to have a TQM program as a condition of selling the DOD their products. And virtually all of the *Fortune* 500 do so in one way or another—not to mention thousands of businesses of lesser size all over the country. (Some 33,000 vendors sell products to the Department of Defense, and the majority of them have subvendors to which the DOD TQM-edict, by extension, also applied.)

This story also holds interest for businesses not involved in defense products or services because it's an example of the constant struggle for decentralization concepts to survive in a society long hooked on Centralism. Thus, how the DOD came to its TQM beliefs, in several stages, holds important lessons for organizations of all kinds. That change didn't come about easily—and it almost didn't come about at all.

THE DOD TOTAL QUALITY MANAGEMENT PROGRAM: ADDRESSING ITS CONCEPTIONS—AND THE MANY MISCONCEPTIONS IN INDUSTRY ABOUT WHAT IS INVOLVED

It has been said that *success has a thousand fathers*. Similarly, all major change programs have tens if not hundreds of people claiming parentage (and legitimately so). Without staking any special claim to parentage, I will trace the lineage of a principal thread in the DOD's Total Quality Management initiatives, for the lessons it provides. That thread depended on a major revision of the Centralism orthodoxy in the DOD's upper sanctums. The story is instructive because it is at the top of the ladder that TQM management principles must be supported—even championed—if they are to be allowed to spread. The story begins in late 1982. The TAC transformation was well along, the results were impressive, and the TQM principles involved were rapidly spreading elsewhere in the Air Force and on to some segments of other military departments.

Meanwhile, in the DOD's upper hierarchy the centralizers were busy. They convinced then Deputy Secretary of Defense Frank C. Carlucci to sign a December 1, 1982, DOD Memorandum calling for the study of a single defense agency that would *"own and operate all DOD installations."* To the centralizers being able to carry that out was a foregone conclusion; they just needed the charter and a quick study to get started on it. That approach would have taken all the bases, posts, camps, and stations away from the military departments, to be centralized and functionalized under a single DOD czar. It was to be the *Mother of all consolidations*. Secretary Carlucci was understandably—and rightfully—seeking greater effectiveness and cost efficiency. The centralizers told him they had the answer. He later found a far better way—a decentralized, not centralized way— to achieve both. But it nearly went the way the centralizers had in mind.

I was aghast when I read the memorandum. So I invited the DOD officials who were behind it to visit TAC and see what we had accomplished. I wanted to show them firsthand what we had done to cure the ills created by past centralization and consolidation edicts within the DOD. That, I felt, was the best means of demonstrating the last thing DOD needed was more of it. To their credit, they came. And, to their credit, they examined the issues in detail. One of the many who came to look—and the highest ranking—was Robert A. Stone, the deputy assistant secretary who oversees all DOD installation matters worldwide.

Bob Stone is a DOD career civilian executive who knows all the ropes, old and new. Stone also candidly confesses that he was a centralizer, of the avid variety, and that he and his people in the Office of the Secretary of Defense (OSD) were behind both the memorandum and its objectives. But what Bob Stone and his principal assistants saw at TAC changed that point of view and changed it radically. In fact, they became fervent converts to the idea that centralization was exactly the wrong way to go. They then had the courage to act on that new belief.

Secretary Stone's principal deputy, Doug Farbrother, described what happened on that visit to TAC in a speech to an industry group on May 10, 1985:

About three years ago I experienced what I call my "management rebirth" in the TAC commander's office. Before I walked in there . . . I was a typically trained OSD-type who knew a lot about how things run in Washington but little else. So we came up with the idea of a Defense Agency that would own and operate all the bases. . . . Well, as soon as General Creech heard about it he summoned us to Langley Air Force Base. As you can imagine, it didn't take him long to shake the very foundations of my OSD management articles of faith. After hearing him talk, and seeing the evidence for myself, I lost interest in the "economies of scale" and all zeal for centralized functional management.

Secretary Stone also attributed his conversion to his trip to TAC and what he saw there. He said, for example, in a July 17, 1985, speech: "General Bill Creech, who commanded Tactical Air Command for six years puts it this way: 'There is a constant war between people who want to do things and people who want to keep them from doing it wrong.' '' He added that he was convinced by what he saw at TAC that the solution to effective management is to empower those who want to get things done and to get the useless rules and kibitzers off their backs. He also explained he now realized that he, and his fellow centralizers, had for years been following the wrong idea about how to create greater effectiveness and cost efficiency. I wish I could say it was my eloquence that effected these remarkable transformations—but I can't. Those changes in their thinking came from the proof they saw all around them, from talking to lots of people down in the trenches, and from seeing all the well-documented before-and-after statistics.

So all those who visited became convinced of the power of decentralization. That was of prime importance, because they would have to lead the charge in that opposite direction from the DOD's historical preference. And they did exactly that. To get it laid out in the most effective way, Bob Stone asked my advice. How could OSD best go about spreading those same TAC-style quality management principles throughout the DOD? In response, I reminded him of our use in TAC of "Models" of the new system, structure, and style. I explained how we used them as rallying points for persuading, not strong-arming, the employees regarding a need for change, as well as providing exemplary evidence of how to do it and how well it worked. Stone liked the idea of going at it a chunk at a time in the various military departments. (When you're dealing with an entrenched bureaucracy the size of the DOD, that idea has a certain appeal.) So in early 1984, Bob Stone created the DOD-wide *Model Installations Program*, or *MIP*.

Each of the services nominated five of their installations for participation. And Stone and his staff got busy empowering the commanders of those installations by relieving them of onerous DOD regulations that were stifling creativity and preventing innovative new solutions to old problems. Those regulations represented more than logical oversight—they long since had pulled all important decision-making up into OSD. (Centralism is a powerful siren song there, as it always is at the top.) Stone also started putting out an MIP news-letter for effective crosstalk between those model installations. He invited suggestions from each of the MIP installation commanders on other centralized practices and edicts that should be changed. And he solicited examples on what they were achieving in the way of greater effectiveness and cost efficiency with their newfound authority. He got a flood of responses. The program was as successful as it was popular. And there's plentiful proof of that for any skeptics.

Now we fast forward to March 26, 1986. Another deputy secretary of defense memorandum was signed out, titled *"Defense-wide Application of the Model Installation Management Approach."* The lead paragraph said:

Two years ago we gave a few so-called model installations an ex-traordinary degree of freedom from regulations and the added in-centive that they could use a share of any money they saved. The model installations have clearly demonstrated that this management approach yields more defense capability for the dollar. . . . It is time to apply these management principles to all installations.

The memorandum went on to instruct the departments and agencies on the details of Defense-wide application. Two sentences are rep-resentative of its flavor: *"First, give more authority to the doers, linking responsibility with authority and push both down to lower organizational levels. Redirect headquarters efforts away from re-stricting and toward facilitating the work that installation command-ers must perform."* (Emphasis added.) Believe me, that was a massive cultural change for the DOD, and particularly so for a DOD that had become fixated on the concepts of Centralism in the sixties and had proudly counted itself one of the nation's most devoted practitioners.

At about this same time, in 1986, the *President's Blue Ribbon Commission on Defense Management* was formed. Headed by David Packard of Hewlett-Packard fame, it was tasked by the President to look at every facet of defense management and report back to him with its recommendations. When Dave Packard and his commission members were briefed on what had happened in TAC and in the ensuing Model Installations Program, Packard expressed surprise and pleasure. In fact, he characterized that initiative as a "welcome breath of fresh air" compared to everything else they had seen. And in the commission's final report to the President, issued in June 1986, Chairman Packard said in his foreword:

> Despite formidable bureaucratic obstacles, I believe that a centers-of-excellence approach can tangibly improve productivity and quality. If widely adopted, and steadfastly supported, it could achieve revolutionary progress throughout defense management. The potential applications are almost without number. In 1984, for example, DOD began to apply this concept to managing its installations as potential centers of excellence, by according installation commanders much greater latitude to run things their own way, cut through red tape, and experiment with new ways of accomplishing their missions. As a result, commanders and their personnel have found more effective means to do their jobs, identified wasteful regulations, and reduced costs while improving quality. The program has shown the increased defense capability that comes by freeing talented people from over-regulation and unlocking their native creativity and enthusiasm. . . . Excellence in defense management will not and cannot emerge by legislation or directive. Excellence requires the opposite—responsibility and authority placed firmly in the hands of those at the working level, who have knowledge and enthusiasm for the tasks at hand.

David Packard, one of America's self-made billionaires, was uniquely qualified to render a judgment on defense management styles. He had refused to buy into sixties-style Centralism as Fred Donner of GM and so many others had—instead, he pursued the opposite course. And he made Hewlett-Packard both an industry giant and renowned for its team-oriented principles.

So the decentralization, quality-oriented initiatives that started in TAC and then became boldly reflected in the MIP approach were cited by the Presidential Blue Ribbon Commission on Defense Management as the model for the way all of the DOD should be managed. At the same time, the DOD revealed that from the MIP program's creation in 1984 and its expansion to involve all the DOD in 1986 more than 50,000 suggestions had been received on saving money, resulting in abundant and documented cost savings. Thus, the entire initiative was about greater cost efficiency as well as greater effectiveness.

If you think the centralizers in their lairs and warrens within the government were most unlikely to let such decentralization initiatives go by unnoticed and unchallenged, you're right. There was considerable sniping from the Congress, particularly from the staffers who cut their eye teeth on Centralism principles. But they were missing the entire point. Tom Peters, finding such myopia hard to believe, attacked the attackers in an *Open Letter to Congress*. Among other pithy points he made was this:

> I spent months reviewing hundreds of examples of excellence in the public sector for a recent PBS television special. I chose five on the air, and I selected the Model Installation Program to lead off. Why? Because I've long been aware that the chief impediment to getting lots of people excited—and thence elicit superior organizational performance—is the jumble of self-imposed Mickey Mouse rules and regulations that would demotivate a saint, let alone a sailor or a road painter. . . . Superb quality and ideas for increased efficiency cannot be "ordered" in the Army or at Ford; they can only come from committed people given the wherewithal to do whatever it takes to get the job done.

Peters went on to remind the Congress of the program's great success, and provided several examples. He ended his "open letter": "Any Congressman who wants to up the odds that we don't buy more $600 ashtrays, but do get more million dollar successes, should vote to keep the freshest breath of air in DOD alive." Congress went on to other things.

During all of this, TAC had continued to get even better—using the same array of principles that had started it all—under the highly capable leadership of General Bob Russ. I will cite two telling indications of that. First, in 1988, TAC won a new U.S. Air Force management award as the best of its best, called *The Productivity Enhancement Award for Professional Excellence*. And in 1990, the

President's *Award for Management Excellence* was bestowed on a Department of Defense agency for the very first time. (That presidential award is the in-government equivalent of the *Baldrige National Quality Award* for businesses.) TAC was the DOD agency so honored. Meanwhile, the DOD at large was making progress along the same path initiated by TAC: far greater quality focus, decentralize the decision-making, and the use of team-concept management. Encouraged by its successes from doing so, DOD in 1988 renamed its DOD-wide initiative *"Total Quality Management."* (I had been using that very name for 7 years by then.) And DOD also took action to extend it to all its vendors, nation-wide. A March 30, 1988 Secretary of Defense memorandum said this:

> TQM has already achieved reduced costs and increased efficiency and effectiveness in several DOD components. We now need to expand the TQM effort. . . . Quality is synonymous with excellence. It cannot be achieved by slogans and exhortation alone, but by planning for the right things and setting in place a continuous quality improvement process. . . . Quality in weapons systems is central to the DOD mission. Therefore, I have asked the Under Secretary of Defense for Acquisition to lead the TQM thrust by implementing it as an integral element of the entire acquisition process.

Thus was born the DOD's TQM outreach program to all its vendors, large and small. And the TQM banners went up all over America.

Before moving on to the results that ensued, let me express my great admiration for Bob Stone and the tireless way he and his colleagues in OSD have battled for a full decade to bring TQM principles into all facets of DOD management. Credit must also go to the secretaries of defense during that period, because without their strong support MIP and the TQM follow-on would have died on the vine. (That hasn't been easy for them, or cut-and-dried, given that any decentralization initiative is viewed with suspicion in most Washington quarters, including in Congress and the press.) Their persistence in supporting those initiatives had a big payoff in Operation Desert

Storm. Indeed, Desert Storm proved the validity of those TQM-style programs and of the DOD's support of them.

With that, let's turn to the industry aspects of the overall DOD TQM initiative. Certainly the TQM name got its big boost as well as its popularity in American industry from that March 1988 DOD memorandum. Interestingly, perhaps predictably, that DOD edict, applying TQM to all its procurement activities, was strongly opposed by virtually all the major industry associations. Nevertheless, companies large and small dutifully complied and initiated their own "TQM programs." (When it's either that or not sell to the DOD, there's an incentive at least to put up the banners.) Those companies also asked for like action from their subcontractors.

Through these means "TQM" spread to thousands of American companies. That has focused even more attention on the subject of quality management nationwide. But as I've said, the results have been mixed, and more often than not they have been anemic. That's because of the wide variety of programs that have been adopted— most of which involve new slogans, not system changes. (I will explain in chapter 6 the varied reasons for that confusion and the spotty patchwork in TQM application.)

In this overall regard, when DOD launched its program with industry it did not put out any definitive guidelines. That's completely proper because the government badly overreaches itself when it gets into telling companies exactly how to manage. However, the DOD did give broad hints of what was expected in the industry TQM initiatives, and it expanded on those hints in a DOD manual, dated February 15, 1990, titled "Total Quality Management Guide." Some 10,000 copies were sent out to the various DOD vendors. The TQM manual addressed the need for much greater focus on process quality, as well as the management system changes needed to ensure a viable TQM approach. That specifically included the *people* aspects as well as the *process* aspects of TQM. Regarding the people aspects, it spelled out the ideal means of *empowerment* as being the formation of *customer-focused, autonomous work teams* as the basic and permanent structure of the organization. It also called for broad-based *recognition* programs including *gainsharing* to create motivation. And on the subject of *management focus*, it called for *creating an envi-*

ronment for teamwork. Thus, there was little room for doubt that the DOD, based on its own internal experiences and successes, was strongly advocating the team concept—and the permanent structural and system changes that must go with it.

With regard to the many TQM achievements in the DOD, I would not want the reader to get the idea these TQM-style decentralization initiatives and quality-oriented principles reached every element of the DOD—or even most elements for that matter. The Department of Defense is far too big and the principles of Centralism far too entrenched for that to have happened. Also, in the massive DOD downsizing that started in 1987, there have been greatly increased pressures by the centralizers who still populate large parts of the department to return to macroconsolidation and the host of other centralist principles. The turmoil of reorganization always presents such opportunities. In a few cases they have won the day, and some new super agencies within the DOD have resulted (none of which are performing with particular distinction). Those philosophical retrenchments notwithstanding, in most DOD elements this radical conversion from the centralized to the decentralized style continues to exert a highly beneficial effect, especially in the military services. In other words, the new approach did get a large and a strong foothold in the DOD—and the successes it yielded were sweeping and substantial. Let's hope that new approach will expand, not shrink, in the never-ending battle with the legion of Centralists that abound in our public and private sectors.

Although I provided advice to DOD officials as this overall MIP and TQM initiative unfolded, I make no representation whatsoever as speaking for the DOD. It can speak for itself. I do feel obliged to point out, however, that most of the change programs one now sees in industry fall well short of what the best companies are doing. So more is needed. The following chapters will explain what and why. How difficult it will be has nothing to do with organization size. It's how well the top management understands the gut issues and gets involved. It's best if it starts at the top. But it didn't start there in DOD. Get it started, wherever you are—and then work hard to sustain it.

As a result of adopting this new decentralized, team-based approach the Department of Defense has demonstrated that it *can be* a positive force and a positive example for change—not the negative force and example it has been for all too many years. The Desert Storm performance and the reasons underlying it helped prove that.

Let's hope DOD will continue an outreach program to the businesses that sell to it and promote these principles there. Unless the emphasis and the heat stays on, however, I can assure the current Secretary of Defense that even the incomplete change found in most industries today will disappear in a flash as the centralizers reassert control. Indeed, the outcome of this struggle in the entire government—and throughout the business world—will be the key to America's success in the years to come.

Chapters 1 through 4 have focused on the *Organization Pillar*— the central pillar—of *The Five Pillars of TQM*. I've explained why, if the organization is wrongly structured, nothing else goes well either. The evidence that this is the case is simply overwhelming. The evidence is also abundant that the right organization—decentralized, team-based—provides the required framework for organizational greatness to flourish in all organization aspects, and every nook and cranny.

So, if your business, public or private, has launched a major process improvement effort—without serious revisions to its management system, its structure, and its style—don't expect much in the way of useful results. I'm not saying here that process revisions aren't important—they certainly are. (I'll address the subject, and give it its due, in chapter six.) However, we know from case after case that process revisions must fit hand-in-glove with precursor organizational revisions and restructuring if any change program is to be productive.

The moral here is clear: Contrary to the vast bulk of the current process-centered literature that espouses change (under a variety of brand-names), those process revisions simply cannot and will not lead you to other needed changes that will produce the efficiency, hustle, and competitive edge you need for our new times. You must address the people issues as well as the process issues. There's all kinds of proof of that—as James Champy of ''reengineering'' fame now attests.

In the Introduction I talked of a pattern that is distinctive in the best companies, and suggested you should look for that pattern. You've now seen it in these first four chapters. The pattern is quite clear in the most successful companies (including the Japanese). Each of them employs the *Teams-Outputs-Product-Leadership* model discussed in chapter 1. Each has their own small variations, to be sure. Nevertheless, the use of that team-based model is quite distinct. There are more examples of the success of that model to come.

I used GM as a metaphor for the *Functions-Inputs-Job-Managership* model that I also set forth in chapter 1. It no longer works, as GM helps to prove (and scores of others do, too). Yet, that very centralist approach remains hale and hearty across the U.S. landscape.

Even for those embracing change, a large compounding factor is the widespread preference these days to entrust change initiatives to a new hierarchy of committees and ''teams.'' Far more companies than not who have latched on to some variant of quality management have installed a new hierarchy of ''steering committees'' at various levels, plus ''cross-functional'' teams (for coordination between functions), and a new plethora of ''process improvement'' teams. That approach doesn't work out well on two counts: First, it fails to address the fundamental changes needed in the traditional system and style. (Indeed, it confuses those issues.) Second, this dual organization structure—this overlay—promotes the idea that change to improve quality (and productivity) is a separate set of activities rather than being a normal, natural part of the regular organizational structure. So that approach has become but one more *overlay* to the traditional centralist approach. And we know from sad experience such overlays just won't bring the right kind of changes.

Let's now turn to another of the Five Pillars. As important as the Organization Pillar is, it still needs strong support from the other four. Greater efficiency requires a Product focus, not a Job focus, and one simply doesn't find that in traditionally managed organizations. Chapter 5 explains why that's so, and sets forth what can be done about it.

Product: Focal Point for Purpose and Achievement

THE PRODUCT PILLAR PROVIDES ESSENTIAL CONCEPTUAL
AND PRACTICAL UNDERPINNING FOR THE
DECENTRALIZED, LEADERSHIP APPROACH

Product is the focal point for organization purpose and achievement.
And from *Product* flows important linkages, in every organization, to
the other organizational elements—and to the touchstones for their
improvement. That being so, over the years I have used (and now
find the Japanese using) a much broader conceptual application of
"product" than that found in traditionally managed organizations. To
describe that broader application in brief: When one makes product
the focal point for purpose and achievement, as should be done, it
also becomes the logical rallying point for quality and productivity.
That, in turn, makes it the obvious focal point for measurement of
organization effectiveness, in every element (an ingredient conspicuously missing in traditionally structured organizations). It is in that
broader conceptual construct that *Product* serves as one of the five
essential pillars of successful TQM. This chapter explains how that
broader application facilitates decentralization and greater employee
interest in improving quality and productivity. For that matter, that
broader view of product is essential to *any* organization regardless of

its structure or orientation, centralized or decentralized. But it rarely gets the status or the attention it deserves.

One's *job* is *self-centered*; the product is *group-centered*. It is the "we and our" not "I and my" mindset that leaders must build for effective interaction and integration within the organization—and that is dependent on the creation, through proactive leadership, of a product mindset. That's an important key because, when asked about their endeavors, nearly all employees will unfailingly respond in the narrow terms of their job, without relating it to any broader product context. And leaving that narrow focus in place is a sign of the failure to produce the bonding and teamwork on which a vibrant organization depends. How do I know that most employees think in narrow "job," not broader "product" terms? Because for years and years I have asked them. That's how they answered in TAC before we set out to create the group-oriented product mindset. I find the business world no different. In fact, the narrow job mindset is the rule. And that's not the fault of the employees.

That concept of product as the focus for employee motivation is not new. I once read a story that explained the difference in attitude (and motivation) in a memorable way. It did so by contrasting the answers from two workers who were busily wielding sledgehammers in a rock quarry. When the first was asked, "What are you doing?" he answered, "I'm breaking rocks." When the second was asked, "What are you doing?" he responded with enthusiasm, "I'm building a cathedral." Not everyone is building a cathedral, of course. But everyone is building something in the way of a product or providing a service. And it almost always involves an effort integrated with the efforts of others to form a combined final product. It is in this sense that *all* organizations, their subelements, and the individual employees within them have a *product*. That's true whether those organizations are public or private, whether they deal in goods or services. And it's true whether the product is durable or nondurable, a part or a whole.

That product can be identified and defined in terms of its customer, internal or external. I have yet to find a case where it can't be done. Accordingly, I asked the leaders in organizations I led to help create a product, not job mindset in our collective efforts to improve

the organization. Once done, with the involvement of all the employees, we placed great emphasis on each of those products as the focal
points for the integrated efforts of the groups that *owned* them. We
also identified the product of the team of teams as we ascended from
the micro to the macro level. However, that product context becomes
more and more abstract for the workers the further one goes up the
chain—not uninteresting, just less relevant. In all these respects, a
product mindset provides a pivot point for other vital ingredients of
success. To depict the synergism of those ingredients I use the Venn
diagram below. These ingredients reinforce one another, and you
can't improve quality and productivity without getting all of them
working for you.

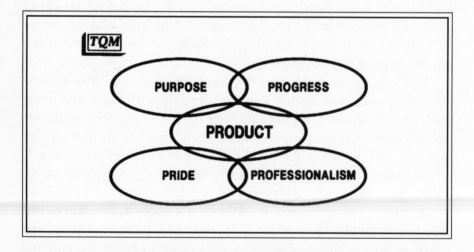

In that same vein, we emphasized the *product-process* linkage.
It's virtually impossible to evaluate the quality and sufficiency of the
process in any context other than the product, as I will further explain
in chapter 6. We also placed heavy emphasis on the most important
linkage of them all—the *product-customer* linkage. That linkage also
is ill-defined in most organizations, public and private. There's really
no acceptable excuse for that. Even in the military we could define
the specific customer and the product for that customer, and it's far
easier in a business. Yet most managers in most companies make no
serious attempt to do that. *Nothing in Centralism's precepts calls for*

that sort of definition and focus. So it's rarely found in traditionally managed businesses.

If the product is not well defined—along with the group that owns it, the organization has no clear-cut rallying point for purpose and achievement. That's why so much of the cheerleading and ringing exhortation used by managers in most organizations—*"We need more teamwork,"* for example—falls on unresponsive ears. Thus, these elements that pivot off a product focus require close attention by everyone—they will not spring to life on their own. Therefore, it's appropriate to discuss the importance of each of the "Ps" in the Venn diagram to success, starting with the important matter of *Purpose.*

COMMON PURPOSE MUST BE CREATED AND SUSTAINED—BUT TRADITIONAL, CENTRALIZED SYSTEMS FOIL IT, NOT FOSTER IT

A *common purpose* is essential for success, but few businesses are good at molding it. Indeed, common purpose gets very little attention, when it should be the principal focus of all managerial actions. And to successfully build strong common purpose leaders must recognize the realities surrounding the array of purposes at work in all organizations. There is, of course, the purpose of the organization—its mission and goals. But also at work are the varied purposes of the individual employees. These start with the need to care for themselves and their families. They go on to the desire and felt need for fair treatment, adequate compensation, appropriate recognition, professional surroundings, a harmonious workplace, and an opportunity to advance. Most also harbor, consciously or unconsciously, the need to feel pride in their activities, their colleagues, their management system, and their leaders. Others might construct a somewhat different list, but everyone could build one.

Good leaders understand those purposes can often work in discord rather than harmony—and most assuredly will, unless the leadership pays lots of attention to the matter. No organization can succeed—

against any kind of robust competition—where the purposes at the rear and the front are divergent or in outright conflict. Therefore, plumbing the extent of the common values, perspectives, and purpose is the surest way to judge whether an organization is being managed well or poorly. An objective assessment also can reveal whether the corrective action to forge a common bond lies in the hands of the workers or the managers. You won't often find it in the hands of the workers.

It's an observable phenomenon that when the relationship has deteriorated to the point the organization itself is struggling, the management will claim that the workers are responsible—and were all along—and for the workers to contend the opposite. Such a thorough rupture in relations might accurately be called the *Eastern Airlines Syndrome*. Sure, Eastern had many fundamental problems to overcome. It had a north-south route structure when most business travel is east-west; and it operated in what became with deregulation the most competitive of all U.S. industries. But Eastern had been losing money and failing in its goals for years and years under several different sets of top managers. A principal reason was that Eastern consistently had some of the poorest management-labor relations in all of America. Finally, the management and labor factions, having become increasingly polarized, fought to the death in failing to settle a nationwide strike. Each side was unyielding in protecting its position. So Eastern died—and everyone lost. Eastern is not the only place where one can see such a bitter division in action and such bitter consequences.

Indeed, such a division is visible in lots of companies, even where it has not reached the stage of being a terminal disease. General Motors provides but one of many examples of that malady in the corporate body. Even for casual observers the clues to its presence are abundant. For example, when GM made its December 1991 bombshell announcements of massive layoffs, the perception gap and the alienation between the labor and management "factions" once again went on vivid public display. UAW president Owen Bieber rushed forward with a statement condemning GM for "capitulating to Wall Street's short-sighted and greedy marching orders." And GM management insiders leaked to the press that the UAW's vice president, Stephen Yokich, was threatening a crippling strike at another GM facility unless GM reversed itself on its planned closing of a plant in California. In other words, there was lots of finger-pointing back and forth—and that was hardly anything new.

The depth of those poor relations took center stage during the network TV interviews of GM workers around the country after the announcement of massive closures. One GM worker from the Michigan Willow Run plant facing possible shutdown appeared to voice sentiments common to most UAW members when he was interviewed. Asked what he would do to help ensure the Michigan plant (and not a Texas plant) stayed open, he said, "I'll fight them. My Mom and Dad worked for GM, and they had to fight for everything we've got."

Lots of GM employees are second, even third or fourth generation workers from the same family. The long-standing distrust and alienation has been handed down. None of GM's management changes to date have overcome that to any substantial degree. That doesn't make GM's task any easier, or that of the UAW's top management for that matter. But if they can't form a new labor-management partnership and forge common purpose out of divergent purposes, we can expect lots more bad news from GM that will profoundly affect all the GM stakeholders—especially UAW employees. This challenge is not unique to GM and the UAW.

Earlier I provided examples of unionized plants at which the relationship between labor and management has been significantly altered by going to a decentralized system that treats the workers in a different way. Contrast the bottom-line performance of GM and GE. Also look at the NUMMI plant in Fremont, California, and the attitude of the UAW local members under GM management on the one hand and Toyota management on the other. *There's a lesson there that directly applies to America's future in the intense competition of globalization.*

I don't suggest that labor relations become perfect overnight in companies that change their traditional ways of managing. But it does start almost immediately to close the gap between the two factions, instead of perpetuating it. Those old animosities within the union leadership, as well as the rank and file, give ground grudgingly. But it's enlightening how quickly employees change their outlook and acquire a new sense of partnership when the frontline labor force is made a fully functioning member of the management. I've seen many such examples.

In *Beyond IBM*, an excellent 1989 book on modern management issues, authors Lou Mobley and Kate McKeown commented extensively on common purpose and why today's management systems must have that as their central objective. Kate McKeown, president of McKeown & Company, bright and insightful, helped Dr. W. Edwards Deming compile his notes and recollections into his massive 1986 book, *Out of the Crisis*. Lou Mobley was a member of the fifteen-man task force that developed IBM's first computer. He later helped to astutely formulate IBM's "Executive School," which trained the corporation's executives, and then supervised it for well over a decade. After that, he formed his own consulting company, where he saw firsthand the problems in companies across the business spectrum.

This background of the two authors of *Beyond IBM* lends authenticity to the book's observations on good and bad management styles. In that regard, Deming wrote a testimonial calling their book *"Beautifully done."* These excerpts from the book capture Mobley and McKeown's treatment of the pivotal matter of common purpose:

If Leadership in the Information Age is anything, it is the creation, articulation, and implementation of common purpose. . . .

Teleocratic leadership, leadership order by common purpose, is leadership that is future oriented, ever relevant, non-ritualized, non-habitual, always thinking, and always human. . . . There is no more effective way to insure commitment than to give people the opportunity to achieve their own purposes while simultaneously achieving the purposes of a larger community of which they choose to become a part. . . .

[To bring that about,] a purpose oriented management system must replace the autocratic and bureaucratic systems of the past. General Bill Creech built such a management system. This is the system that is right for our times. It is far and away the best we know.

Teleos is the Greek word for purpose. Mobley and McKeown use the term *"teleocratic"* throughout their book as one of many means of emphasizing the overriding importance of common purpose. Lou Mobley, the longtime IBM hand, also presented a persuasive case regarding the evolvement of management systems with which he had become intimately familiar—from the "autocratic system of Tom Watson, Sr." to the "bureaucratic system of Tom Watson, Jr." After describing those systems (and their shortcomings) in depth, the book chronicles the need for IBM (and other firms large and small) to now go well *beyond* such outworn management systems. Thus the book's title, *Beyond IBM*.

Lou Mobley's astute observations and visionary advice took on additional relevance in late 1991. That's when IBM stepped forth to announce its own need for a huge layoff of workers and to massively restructure the corporation and its long-standing practices. John Akers, then IBM's chairman, said the need was to unshackle IBM from its stifling bureaucracy and enable its separate divisions to become more agile and competitive against constantly improving rivals. That was the proper move to make, and better late than never. (John Akers was out as chairman and CEO soon thereafter because of continued financial hemorrhaging.) IBM—another of America's pantheon of centocracies—is but one more example of an admired U.S. corporation, hugely successful in the past, that has recently fallen on hard times. "Experts" rush in from all directions, invited and uninvited, to offer reasons and remedies. Most don't go to the heart of the matter as Lou Mobley did.

The fact is that IBM made the centralized, managership model work for a very long time, so there is a reluctance to give it up and an equal reluctance to see the problems for what they are. The rules have changed in the global business game and the centocracies like IBM and GM have simply been too slow to respond. They try, but too little is done because they won't confront the gut issues that are causing the decline in their fortunes. I'll give my own analysis of the disease IBM (and many, many others) is suffering from and provide my prescription for the cure: IBM will either organize small and become more agile and creative so as to handle the global competition or it will slowly perish. And to organize small means that its leaders must renounce their beloved Centralism precepts of the past. I wish them luck.

To get back to McKeown and Mobley's theme of common purpose (which has been the organizational centerpiece for me as well), leaders must work unceasingly to instill it, from the very bottom to the top. It takes actions, not slogans. And it takes making the frontline a part of the ''management,'' just as the Japanese have done. Leaders must also forge a common outlook regarding the achievement benchmarks by which everyone will judge the organization's *progress*. As purpose is instilled and progress achieved, that will build *pride* and *professionalism*, which also are key ingredients of success. That brings us to a discussion of their importance.

QUALITY IN THE PRODUCT FLOWS FROM QUALITY IN THE COLLECTIVE PERFORMANCE—AND THAT FLOWS FROM PRIDE AND PROFESSIONALISM

The *quality mindset*, which I commented on extensively in describing ''Japanese Management,'' manifests itself in the *pride* and *professionalism* the employees feel and reflect—or do not reflect. Absence of both or weakness in either indicates a weak quality mindset within the organization, and that yields meager motivation. *Pride is the fuel of human accomplishment.* I have believed that since my earliest days, and I have used it as a touchstone in all my leadership endeavors. I also have preached to all who would listen: *Unquality is unaffordable.* Never mind the grammar, it's catchy so people won't forget it. Also, never mind those who believe that quality costs, not saves, money—and is therefore nice to have but can't be afforded. They haven't tried it the other way.

I also have long since learned that *pride* and *quality* (in all things, not just some things) go together. You can't have one without the other. And you won't achieve adequate *professionalism* without both. I practiced that belief back when "*Made in Japan*" meant cheap and shoddy goods and Japan's signature product was paper parasols for variety stores, not high-quality automobiles. I freely admit that not everyone quickly understood, even in the late seventies when I took over TAC, why I placed such great emphasis on *quality in all things at all times*. And many were surprised that I meant it literally and applied it across-the-board. The emphasis and its effects were soon to be seen in everything—ranging from facilities, to tools, to equipment, to all forms of upkeep, to renewal and rejuvenation, and on to performance itself. In short, most had to learn that a pervasive quality mindset and the programs which instill it save, not cost, money. They also quickly learned how fundamental it is to building pride and professionalism. Making it much easier for them to make that connection was a huge surge of improvements in quality and productivity all around them. And once they made the connection, they embraced the philosophy as their own. I saw that same progression in every organization I led.

The Japanese now make that connection far more credible and understandable to America's managers, but only a small minority of America's managers work the quality mindset issue smart enough and hard enough. Often that's because policies from on high prevent them from doing so. This lack of sensitivity to the wellsprings of quality largely stems from shopworn but doggedly persistent ideas on where to economize. And it usually traces back to the *beancounters* found in nearly all companies, especially traditionally managed ones. *They know the cost of everything and the value of nothing.* And they exercise a hammerlock on all the cost and value trade-off decisions. Those beancounters don't fully understand the first effects of their decisions, much less the secondary effects, but those secondary effects most assuredly influence attitude, motivation, and pride. I've seen it work both ways again and again: inspiring when done right; demotivating when done wrong. The beancounters won't support what they can't quantify, so they line up in opposition. In fact, they're disinclined by nature to consider "squishy" things like the human spirit.

Therefore, the leaders must be the champions of the quality mindset and the ones to ensure the expenditures that create it.

YOU REAP WHAT YOU SOW IN QUALITY. SO YOU HAVE TO MAKE IT HAPPEN—IT WON'T HAPPEN ON ITS OWN

Dr. Genichi Taguchi is the director of the Japan Industrial Technology Institute. He's also an internationally renowned expert on process improvement methodologies and serves as a consultant to major firms worldwide, including several in the United States. He, as much as anyone, understands the fundamental change in thinking that created Japan's extraordinary success in shifting from shoddy to superior products. He says, "The most elusive edge in the new global competition is the galvanizing pride of excellence." I couldn't agree more. That's *rule number one* for managers to observe in the fast-moving Globalization Age. And achieving that competitive edge is elusive only because so few managers truly understand and employ to their benefit the *galvanizing pride of excellence*. Taguchi expands on that Japanese thinking with these words:

> In Japan, it is said that a manager who trades away quality to save a little manufacturing expense is "worse than a thief"—a little harsh perhaps, but plausible. When a thief steals $200 from your company there is no net loss of wealth between the two of you, just an exchange of assets. Decisions that create huge quality losses throw away social productivity, the wealth of society.

Taichi Ohno, former executive vice president of Toyota, who is also highly regarded in quality management circles, puts it in these forceful terms: "Whatever you believe the costs of poor quality to be, they'll be six times more."

It's not only the Japanese who understand that, of course. Norm Augustine, the thoughtful chairman of Martin Marietta Corporation, sums it up succinctly: "It costs a lot to build bad products." Some

American executives have learned that lesson the hard way, but learned it well. Donald Petersen, chairman emeritus of Ford and the man who led the Ford quality turnaround in the eighties, said it this way: ''There's no market anywhere in the world for poorly built motorcars. We know—we've tested the market.'' He has also often said, ''If we aren't customer-driven, our cars won't be either.'' Those are words to live by, and Ford profited by doing so.

Ford, though a fraction of GM's size, made far more profit during the eighties than GM did and, in measures such as return on equity, outclassed GM completely. It took a change of heart and a massive change in attitude to bring that about—because near the end of the seventies Ford was suffering huge monetary losses every month. That change and the reasons it worked were summarized in a 1988 speech by John Betti, then Ford's executive vice president, titled ''The Quest for Quality—A Key to the Corporate Turnaround at Ford Motor Company.'' These excerpts capture the spirit of his observations:

> At Ford, our quality commitment started in 1978. . . . But quality commitments and quality programs were not new to the company. In fact, we had a pattern of renewing our commitment every three to five years—bring out the bells and whistles with an occasional new slogan. It changed because we were in a crisis. When you're losing more than $4 million every day, you've got to believe it's serious. We had no choice—we had to improve quality, and we had to improve costs. When we cut through all the excuses we made for ourselves, we concluded that by eliminating poor quality and waste, we would indeed reduce overall costs. The tough part of that position was that quality decisions weren't all that apparent. . . .

So Ford took concrete steps to get the idea across to one and all. John Betti continued his speech in that vein:

> In 1980 our volume was down and we had to close an assembly plant. According to our financial analysis, the most effective action would be to close the 50-year old Norfolk, Virginia, assembly plant. [But] it had the best quality record among the plants under consideration. Recognizing our quality credibility was at stake, we decided

to close the Mahwah, New Jersey plant instead. Mahwah was a much newer and larger facility, but had the poorest quality record. . . . We made certain that as many people as possible in our organization knew that quality, and not cost, had been the factor that determined that decision. . . . Those actions were truly counter-cultural. There was no question in anyone's mind that something was different. They could no longer dismiss our statements about commitment to quality as mere talk. Our actions were in harmony with our words.

Betti then quoted two headlines to prove how well it had worked: "*Monthly Detroit*, April 1980—Can Ford Put It Back Together? Portrait of a Company in Trouble." The second headline: "*Newsday*, February 1988—Ford Still Most Profitable Carmaker." Because of its decisive actions, the eighties saw Ford hold on to its historic market share against the Japanese onslaught. Even more dramatic was the change in its profitability and prospects.

(With regard to the reference in chapter 4 to poor situation awareness in most American companies; a portion of this Ford turnaround story helps illustrate the point. Many will recall that Ford—spurred into action by losing money hand over fist—bought hundreds of different automobile models from U.S. and foreign competitors. Ford then took them apart piece by piece for the lessons they held in charting its turnaround actions. That Ford action became featured news in the business magazines, largely because vigorous efforts to obtain competitive situation awareness are not normal corporate behavior. The moral: Why wait until you're in trouble?)

Before leaving the Ford story, it's useful to contemplate John Betti's remarks contrasting the performance of the Ford assembly plants at Norfolk and Mahwah. Why would performance in a fifty-year-old plant in Virginia significantly surpass that in a newer, more modern facility in New Jersey? Look to the *human system* factors at work in the two plants. Perhaps, if Ford had been more astute about comparing and assessing those factors, and had taken more vigorous action to improve Mahwah's performance, it might not have been necessary to close either. We'll never know. But I raise the question because such comparisons, and sensitivity to such human system issues, have not been strong suits in the American corporate management style. However, none of that takes away from Ford's major accomplishment in the eighties of turning from losing to winning through a greater commitment to quality. Ford adopted the corporate motto *"Quality Is Job One"* and made sure it was not just another empty slogan like their quality slogans in the past. And John Betti's concluding observation on a principal reason that it all worked, *"Our actions were in harmony with our words,"* are words to live by as well.

Quality begets quality. And one cannot justifiably expect employees to appreciate quality, think quality, and produce quality if top management shows by its actions that it is indifferent to it. That was why I placed such great emphasis on creating the *quality mindset*. A case in point: When I took over TAC, the appearance and upkeep of the aircraft in that huge fleet could most charitably be described as *shabby*. The even larger ground vehicle fleet was as bad. Therefore, it did not surprise me to see maintenance statistics showing a poor *interior* condition of that same equipment. The same substandard appearance held true for virtually all of the TAC facilities as well. In fact, in my first swing around TAC's many bases nationwide, I found lots of *eyesores* which had no place in an outfit that ever hoped to be proud and professional.

That neglect in equipment and facility upkeep was all done in the name of economies, of course. And TAC was no different from other Air Force commands or other DOD elements in that regard. It was just part of the conventional centralist wisdom—only to spend money on "important things," not "atmospherics." (So I'm pointing a finger at the policies, not at the people who were carrying them out.) We in the restructured TAC were to prove that they weren't atmospherics at all—that these matters go to the very heart of the quality mindset, and thereby to quality performance.

I won't dwell on the actions we took. It suffices to say we launched a host of programs to rectify the situation. Not surprisingly, given quality's low priority, I found no formal upkeep plans or programs in place—or adequate facilities for that purpose. For example, less than 15 percent of TAC's bases had any facilities for painting and periodic touch-up of either vehicles or aircraft. Yet, deterioration spares no business, large or small, so it shouldn't be a surprise that if you don't tend to the upkeep, everything slowly grinds down to third-world standards. And then management's indifference to quality issues is on vivid public display, with all the attendant consequences. Prizing the quality mindset, we provided the necessary facilities and developed detailed five-year plans and budgeting on each base regarding upkeep schedules. Those schedules were sufficiently flexible that we didn't refurbish things that didn't need it. But we didn't have our heads in the sand regarding inevitable deterioration either.

To draw attention to our approach, I found in one of my forays to the field a beat-up old office chair in use by a maintenance supervisor. One of its four casters was missing, stuffing was coming out, and its general appearance was atrocious. He was responsible for more than 100 people and several hundred million dollars worth of matériel resources. In using that chair he was making a graphic statement regarding the quality standards he expected. I talked him out of the chair, and took it back with me to TAC headquarters. It became my symbol of the way we had been neglecting our people, their attitude, and the quality mindset. I placed the chair in the TAC conference room at the chief logistician's place at the table. It hadn't been his doing, just old, flawed policies, but he was the one who would need everyone's support if we were going to change matters. Everyone got the message. (Such symbols can be very useful in making sure everyone understands that there is a new approach to carrying out the business.)

We then searched for ways to carry out that upkeep in the most economical manner possible, and we found lots of ways. Largely they revolved around doing local refurbishment and renovation instead of replacement. (Replacement had been the principal practice in the past when either buildings or equipment were beyond salvation.) Equipment of all kinds will last a long time if you take care of it properly; it won't if maintenance and upkeep are ignored. That change in focus alone saved money. Also, since people took far more pride in their surroundings, they took initiative to fix a lot of things on their own.

(And we opened "Self-Help" stores all over TAC so they could do that without a lot of fuss and paperwork.) So, besides quality we're also talking basic economics here.

I knew all these changes would make a big difference, and they did. Improvements showed up in all areas. Those changes were reflected in the attitude and motivation of people throughout the organization. A year or so after we started this new approach a new phrase cropped up: When outsiders complimented TAC people on their base's new image or some outstanding unit achievement, it became the vogue to reply self-deprecatingly, "*It's just TAC standard.*" (The idea being you would find that pride and professionalism everywhere in TAC—it was both the expectation and the practice.) I don't know who came up with the phrase *TAC standard.* I do know that I was to hear it often as our changes improved matters still more. In fact, "Do it TAC standard" became a sometime admonition on how to carry out an activity. And that was music to my ears, because that was exactly the attitude we were trying to instill: that quality in all things was simply how we did our business.

MOST DON'T UNDERSTAND: THEY LET MISAPPLIED COST REDUCTIONS DRIVE QUALITY DOWN—NOT USE QUALITY TO DRIVE COSTS DOWN

I have no problem whatsoever with diligent efforts to save money. I do have problems—big problems—with insensitive bureaucrats who try to save money on the wrong things. The *Law of Unintended Consequences* comes into play and soon everything is going downhill, performance, quality, and productivity included. The costs involved in installing the quality mindset at TAC were trivial—especially when the cost savings they generated are considered. Moreover, TAC received not one extra dollar for that purpose. We funded those actions out of our many savings elsewhere, as our family of quality programs took hold. We just had a different view of priorities. In that respect, many if not most managers, when faced with a budget reduction, say they will start by "deferring maintenance." Their priorities are all wrong. What most cut first should be cut last. When times get tough and the need to cut operating costs looms, there's all the more reason to optimize the amalgamation and operation of your resources. But nearly everyone follows the course of making everything a little sick, so that the various parts add up to far less than an optimum whole. Why do you think everything throughout the old Communist bloc looked so bad? Because they were heavily into conformance, not spirit and enthusiasm. I'll have more to say on the right ways to improve cost consciousness and control later. It's an important issue, but the old-time religion doesn't get the job done. The key moral here is: *Be wary of cuts that affect the quality mindset—don't disable it.* If you do, the *Law of Secondary Effects* will drag you further down.

The story of Roger Penske's success in racing at Indianapolis and elsewhere underscores the point. Though I've heard the story many times, Mike Harris, an Associated Press writer, captured its essence in the fewest words in a 1990 story:

> When the now silver-haired "Captain" of Penske racing first came to the speedway in 1969 as a crewcut "college boy," his team polished the wheels of its race car and kept the floors of its garage clean and waxed. That was ridiculous. Polishing your wheels wouldn't make the car run any faster. Nor would cleaning the garage floor. "I remember we came here and they laughed at us for the way we did things," Penske said. "But we knew it was the right way for us." . . . Now everybody in Indy-car racing polishes their wheels and cleans their floors—at Indy and everywhere else. And nobody laughs at Penske anymore.

They shouldn't. He showed the Indy folks what the quality mindset and pride and professionalism can do. His team has won more Indy races than any other by far. And he now sits at the helm of a $2 billion business empire that includes truck leasing and auto dealerships. I hadn't read about the Penske style when we upgraded TAC's many aircraft hangars and put white polyurethane paint on the hangar floors to improve cleanliness and reflectivity—and to inspire the maintenance to be equally fastidious. Only later did I find that

Roger Penske and I think alike, and that we're in company with an awful lot of Japanese. I've never seen a sharp organization that didn't look sharp. That's just the start, of course. It must go on to professionalism in all things, but the quality mindset is the cornerstone of all professionalism.

As the executive said at Boeing's Irving plant, "A necessary condition of being professional is to look professional." Many scoff at that and belittle it further by calling it the *look good syndrome*. I know. At one time, they scoffed at my insistence in this respect, too. But somewhere along the line they stopped laughing when they compared their own results with what we were achieving. Obviously one does not want to paint unnecessarily, to "gold-plate" facilities, or to be wasteful in overly obsessive upkeep. But consider this: I knew of no way to tell a young technician working on a multimillion-dollar aircraft that although it looked lousy, was dirty, and had sadly deteriorated paint, he or she must ignore that and do fastidious, error-free work on the inside. Tom Peters says that when you see lots of coffee stains on the airliner's upholstery, start worrying about the engines. He's right.

These same principles apply to whatever one is working on, whatever the product or service. People are affected by their surroundings, the way they're treated, and the way they're led, either positively or negatively. It's up to the senior leaders to decide which it is to be.

That brings us to the important matter of *progress* and whether it is up or down. As proven by Lee Iacocca at Chrysler and many others who have forged extraordinary transformations, the organizational and leadership tone set from the very top makes a dramatic difference. Indeed, it makes all the difference between failure and success. To amplify the point, let's examine another dramatic corporate turnaround, every bit as sweeping and successful as the one at Chrysler. (However, the aftermath of the story received very little press attention. So, it's not a well-known or well-understood story.) This turnaround involved the *Lockheed Corporation*, and it took place at about the same time as the one at Chrysler. As in other turnarounds, the before-and-after aspects of the Lockheed story amplify how important the top leadership is to the organization's success or failure. It also illustrates again that transformations only begin at the top—they won't work unless everyone, at every level, gets on board.

THE LOCKHEED TURNAROUND: ASTUTE NEW LEADERSHIP AT THE TOP AND GREATER FOCUS AND COMMITMENT THROUGHOUT THE CORPORATION

Much can be learned from turnarounds because they shine a spotlight on the importance of the leadership dynamics. It's common that when companies are struggling or failing, internal apologists come up with an array of reasons other than the organization's leadership. Far more often than not, the reasons they cite are off the point—indeed, they miss the point entirely. (They're not likely to indict themselves.) I've seen that again and again in organizations large and small. And I've seen such organizations change quickly and dramatically for the better when the leadership dynamics are changed. So have we all. But not all draw from such stories the full implications they might, especially with regard to how instrumental the leadership patterns were in the change. The Lockheed turnaround fits the same mold.

Space doesn't permit chronicling all of Lockheed's problems in the 1970s, when the story begins, but they were thorny and pervasive. For a variety of reasons, Lockheed got into deep cost and schedule trouble on two major government programs—the huge C5A *Galaxy* transport aircraft for the Air Force and the *Cheyenne* helicopter for the Army. Lockheed's commercial airliner, the wide-body L-1011, got into similar serious problems. Those L-1011 troubles were exacerbated by the bankruptcy of England's Rolls-Royce company, which produced the engines, and no alternate engines were then available. These and many other lesser wounds had Lockheed bleeding so much financially there was serious question whether it could survive. Its stock was selling for $3 a share, and its credit rating had sunk so low it was impossible to raise capital.

The Lockheed board of directors finally set aside all the apologists' explanations for those problems and concluded that new leadership was required at the top. They found it within Lockheed's own ranks, in Roy Anderson. The corporation's chief financial officer before they made him CEO, Anderson was soon to prove that he was a superb leader and as astute regarding people and their motivation as he was about financial and accounting matters.

Roy Anderson faced a daunting array of challenges, and he tackled them with vigor. One of his first problems was to convince all the stakeholders that Lockheed could not only remain viable, but could actually turn matters around. The customer stakeholders included the U.S. government and the commercial airlines with standing orders, as well as a host of others then using Lockheed's products and services. The supplier stakeholders included the British government, which had stepped in to prop up the failed Rolls-Royce, and all the suppliers were skittish about staying the course, for understandable reasons.

Lockheed also desperately needed new capital to stay afloat, so Anderson sought a government loan guarantee for $650 million worth of commercial loans from a consortium of banks. Somehow Lockheed fought its way, under Anderson's leadership, through a thicket of skepticism by bankers, hordes of government auditors, not a few backbiting politicians, and a less than sympathetic press to get not only the government loan guarantee but also the breathing room from the other stakeholders that they needed.

(Like the government loan guarantee for Chrysler, this one attracted widespread national media attention to Lockheed's problems and a raging political debate about a *"government bailout."* The successful aftermath in the Chrysler case has been told and retold. The successful aftermath in the Lockheed case has barely been mentioned. In both cases it ended up not costing the U.S. government a dime, and in both cases this was because astute new corporate leaders changed the corporation from failure to success. *There are no poor outfits, just poor leaders.*)

Lockheed now had more capital, albeit with an accompanying heavier load of interest payments, but there still were problems everywhere. That was the biggest leadership challenge of all, just as it had been at Chrysler. Roy Anderson, and those who rallied under his leadership, proved equal to that challenge. He started, as positive change in the internal dynamics must, with the frontline employees. He preached their pride was at stake as well as their jobs. He got them much more heavily involved at all levels. And he kept them fully informed. They made sacrifices. They pulled together. And they started operating in focused team efforts rather than just reporting each morning to "do their job." As one Lockheed employee at the time put it, "It was a big change. Our management approach now featured good interaction and across-the-board involvement, not the distance and detachment of the management that got us into trouble in the first place." And in all of this, Roy Anderson took great pains to ensure there were no more surprises for any of the players in the unfolding drama.

Meanwhile, he and the top leadership bit some tough bullets in hard decisions that looked to the future health of Lockheed, not just to survival. For example, Anderson continued a high level of company-funded research and development, even though that was surpassingly difficult in the "cash poor" environment in which Lockheed had to operate. Slowly but inexorably, the more astute management and the new employee focus and commitment took hold, and the corporation climbed out of the hole it had dug for itself. And that provided the financial wherewithal to keep Lockheed's famous "Skunk Works" on the cutting edge of aerospace technology through innovative research (the very research that led to the Skunk Works building for the Air Force the F-117A Stealth fighter which performed so brilliantly in the Gulf War). Management continued to improve across the board, and success yielded more success.

This was a turnaround that profited everyone involved. Roy Anderson, who combines an unassuming nature with great intestinal fortitude, would be the last one to take any personal credit for it, but it clearly was the changed leadership that made the difference in the way the employees were being managed and motivated. They, in turn, unleashed the energy that brought about the dramatic difference in Lockheed's fortunes and prospects. And Lockheed's *shareholders* profited along with all the employees and every other stakeholder. From $3 a share at its low point the Lockheed stock by 1977 had climbed to $25. And by 1985 it had reached $150 a share, stock splits considered. By anyone's definition, that's a turnaround.

Roy Anderson also used great care in grooming leaders to follow him who would carry on the new Lockheed management tradition and success. By the end of the eighties Lockheed was making over $600 million a year on annual sales of more than $10 billion, and was keeping 100,000 Americans productively and gainfully employed. The corporate balance sheet also showed a steady and impressive growth in shareholders' equity over the years since Lockheed almost died. The moral here is the same as that from other turnarounds: The potential is always present; it just takes the right approach to bring it out. And when that is done you can snatch victory from the jaws of defeat, just as Roy Anderson did at Lockheed and Lee Iacocca did at Chrysler.

That's the difference the caliber of the leadership can make. Given such real-world examples, I'm continually surprised that the public, the press, and the corporate boards don't pay more attention to that aspect of what separates the winners from the losers. They keep looking for other reasons, and the real point keeps eluding them. That's why the *Organization* and *Leadership* Pillars are so vital to successful management.

LOCKHEED'S SKUNK WORKS PROVES THE IMPORTANCE OF THE LEADERSHIP—AND THE ORGANIZATIONAL PRINCIPLES THAT PRODUCE IT

Another Lockheed story is instructive on these same themes. It starts with the various conceptions and misconceptions about Lockheed's famed Advanced Development Projects organization, otherwise known as the *Skunk Works*. Lockheed's ADP has long been a model of a streamlined organization, with short cycle times, clear-cut authority and teamwork, and high-quality products. Kelly Johnson, the design and management genius who formed and ran the Skunk Works for decades, was years ahead of his time in both categories.

His ADP programs not only pushed the design state-of-the-art (such as the SR-71 reconnaissance aircraft which routinely flew at three times the speed of sound), but also were justifiably renowned for coming in on cost and schedule and performing as advertised—due to ADP's excellent management.

Kelly Johnson had fourteen published rules by which he ran the Skunk Works, and rule number one was: *The Skunk Works program manager will have complete control of his program in all aspects.* No ambiguity about who was in charge, and who was accountable for what, for Kelly Johnson. He had no patience for busywork or needless paperwork, and he was brilliant at what today is called *delayering* and *streamlining*, but he also was a stickler for pride, professionalism, and attention to quality—and all the critical details that produce quality in performance and product. The consistently high customer acceptance and value of ADP's products reflect the synthesis of those organizational and leadership aspects at work.

The organization got its name from Al Capp's *Li'l Abner* comic strip and its smelly *"Skonk Works."* (Near the end of World War II Kelly Johnson put together a team to design and build the P-80 *Shooting Star* as America's first production jet fighter. He had it in the air on its first flight 181 days from the go-ahead by the government. Because of a shortage of facilities at Lockheed, he put a lot of his design engineers into a large tent. It smelled bad. So one of the engineers started answering the telephone, "The Skonk Works here." The name caught on and later was changed to "Skunk Works.") Because of that name, some have wrongly interpreted the "Skunk Works approach" as providing an *ad hoc, cavalier, unstructured* environment—which they then proclaim as the organizational model necessary to give free rein to innovation and creativity.

The Lockheed Skunk Works certainly has fostered innovation and creativity over the years, but it was then, and still is, the antithesis of a loosely run organization full of cavalier individualists. To the contrary, the Skunk Works is to this day the epitome of close teamwork and distributed leadership that produces well-planned, coherent, and superbly integrated activity throughout the organization. And that proves, once again, that the right organization and leadership principles are timeless and adapt well to changing technological and competitive circumstances. However, most can't get behind ADP's doors for a look at these Skunk Works principles and practices because of the highly classified nature of ADP's work, so the myths continue to spread.

I've known a good bit about the Skunk Works and the way it operates over the years because of visits and interactions on various government programs. And I was the TAC commander during the period the F-117A Stealth fighter was developed and produced by Lockheed ADP for TAC and fielded by TAC. That provided for lots of intense interaction, and the opportunity to observe Kelly Johnson's ADP management principles in action. The F-117A came in on cost and schedule, and I assure you that was because the Skunk Works was well organized and well managed, not because it was the laid-back antithesis of that. In fact, I'm convinced that ADP's programs have been consistently successful because it has managed the way the bulk of the aerospace industry *has not*.

Let's now return to the matter of *turnarounds* of failing organizations. Here's a story about one of the many turnarounds in the business world in which I have played a hand. Turnarounds, in my experience, share one common element: a change in the way the organization's *human system* rallies itself—*under changed policies*—to bring forth unrealized work-force potential. That slumbering potential is always there.

THE CREATION OF NEW INVOLVEMENT, OBJECTIVITY, AND COMMITMENT IN THE BUSINESS WORLD—ANOTHER STORY OF WORST TO FIRST

A few years ago I was asked to provide strategic advice on how to save a dying company. Part of a larger corporation, it was in the metalworking business and had a formidable array of problems. It had been losing money every quarter for more than four years. Corporate officials had run out of patience and the will to support the cash drain.

Moving the company was not a viable option. Corporate leaders were planning to close it unless they could get significant wage concessions from the workers. The litany of problems they revealed to me can best be summarized as follows:

- *High costs*—so high they were not competitive. The company was competing with offshore suppliers, and with suppliers in the southwest United States whose labor costs were 25 percent lower.
- *Low productivity and poor quality.* Quality marks from the customers were very low, and in some contracts the company had received "cure notices," a precursor to cancellation.
- *Declining orders and backlog.* Much of the backlog was being delivered at a loss.
- *Acrimonious relationship with the union.* Bitterness stretched back several years. Each side had lost all patience with the other.
- *A demand by management for a $2.30-per-hour wage reduction.* Essentially the message was "Grant it or we'll close down."

Some at the corporate level thought the situation was unsalvageable. Bad as it was, I didn't think so—if the company would change its traditional, centralized ways. After appraising the situation, I gave the following advice:

- *Restore a relationship of trust with the union.* Open up your books to them. Show them how bad things are.
- *Fly the union leaders to face-to-face talks with the purchasing agents of your primary customers.* Have them hear from the horse's mouth why you're failing.
- *Develop some key measures of merit, and provide measurement and scoreboards on how you're doing.* Get the workers involved. Put the scoreboards on the factory wall, and keep them simple.
- *Provide goals, and incentives to reach those goals.* Give the workers a stake in the outcome. Provide a bonus system.

That's simplified, of course, but it wasn't a lot more complicated than that. The company officials were not thrilled with my advice. A lot of it ran counter to their intuition, and their frustration and alienation were just as strong as those of the workers. However, in desperation because they had tried everything else—and with a bit of corporate encouragement—they took my advice. And they implemented it vigorously.

It wasn't easy for them. They had some real conceptual hangups on opening up the books. But they did it. My last recommendation gave them the biggest conceptual problems of all. Here they were asking for wage concessions, and I was telling them to offer bonuses tied to new quality and productivity goals. But they did that, too. My point was that they could power their way out of their problems with the latent potential among the workers. And then they wouldn't need the wage concessions, which the workers were not going to grant them in any case. (I based that prediction on the alienation that had built up over the years.) Doggedly, they pursued the wage concessions anyway. In an election to decide the issue, the workers refused the concessions—even though the union leaders, now enlightened about the scope of the problems, had recommended approval. Earlier, such a negative outcome was believed to spell certain shutdown of the company. But weeks had passed, and the results from the new approach were starting to kick in. Let's now skip one year ahead. A feature article in the company newspaper said:

Let's review some of the results you have achieved during the past twelve months:
- Over 40% productivity improvement.
- More than 75% reduction in scrap.
- More than 90% reduction in past due backlog.
- Quarterly productivity bonuses increased from $0 to more than $800 average per employee.
- Continuing improvement in our quality ratings from our major customers.

A few explanations are in order: Reducing scrap was one of our four key measures of merit. In metalworking, your margins end up on the shop floor with even the slightest employee inattention. The bonus was pegged to a simple productivity scale everyone could understand. And it was calculated so that it would kick in after the company had received a fair return on equity to pay for things like renewal, new product development, and the search for new business. In that sense, what was being shared was a percentage of the *additional profit* being generated—by those who were generating it. That's how I recommended it be set up, because I was convinced the gains could take care of all of the above.

So, here's a case where the company didn't get its wage concessions and still survived. Not only that, but at the end of one year under the new system, each employee was getting an extra $3,200 a year. As for the company, it went from worst to first in the corporation—the best performer of all. It now stood out among its competitors as well—and that same year went from cure notices to a status of *Elite Supplier* with its biggest customer, a rare and coveted honor. The credit goes to the company executives who applied the new ideas, and to the workers, not to me.

Given my record of such turnaround involvement in the business world as well as in the government, in September 1988 I was privileged to give the keynote address at the first annual convention of a new association, the *Turnaround Management Association*. The association's stated purpose is to share the insights and expertise of turnaround specialists on why some companies are able to reverse stagnating performances while others are not (as well as analyzing the factors that started their decline in the first place). Its membership consists of leading turnaround specialists, corporate managers, lenders, investors, consultants, attorneys, accountants, bankers, and academicians. It's a great idea. America needs such sharing of ideas, particularly now, because if we don't hang together we most assuredly will hang separately. So I was most pleased to participate, and to help get it off on the right foot. The TMA's executive director, P. Scott Scherer, later wrote to me:

> I want to be President of the Bill Creech fan club. We had in the audience for your keynote address over 300 of the nation's leading

turnaround experts from the leading investment firms, the top commercial banks, and nationally recognized consultants. Their exuberant acceptance of your ideas indicated that you have become an expert in all aspects of their demanding business.

The association continues to thrive. And the more I hear of failing companies, and why they fail, the more convinced I am of the advice I'm offering in these pages.

These two examples from my extensive business world involvements are provided to help assure readers that these ideas don't just work in the military—or in Japanese automobile companies. Even so, all those cases remain relevant, because human nature doesn't change from business to business. The challenges may vary. But the techniques which overcome them are amazingly consistent, in businesses large or small, public or private.

Let me amplify that observation by providing the story of another of the turnaround situations I found myself in during my military career, in which a very troubled, very large, and very complex organization was transformed using these same principles.

CURING A TROUBLED FIGHTER WING BY CHANGING TO DECENTRALIZED LEADERSHIP—AND APPLYING A TEAMS-OUTPUTS-PRODUCT FORMULA TO BRING FORTH THE BEST FROM THE HUMAN SYSTEM

This challenge to fix a failing organization involved the Air Force fighter wing outside Madrid, Spain. As mentioned earlier, I was assigned on overnight notice to replace a fired commander—the second wing commander in a row to be fired. The wing had failed three recent major inspections, including two war-fighting inspections, called Operational Readiness Inspections, or ORIs. It also had failed a wall-to-wall management inspection by a special Inspector General team from Washington, D.C. The four-star boss of the U.S. air forces in Europe said this on the telephone when he told me to go to Madrid and take over:

> That wing can't manage and it can't fight. It has been sick for some time. Based on your impressive success at Zweibrücken, I believe if anyone can turn it around you can. I want you to go down there immediately and make it a healthy wing again. By the way, the wing will have a full-scale rerun of its failed ORI within four months. So you have your work cut out for you. Good luck.

We did have our work cut out for us. The wing, I found, had inadequate focus and a fuzzy sense of purpose. A product focus, team construct, and team-oriented motivation simply were not to be found at any level. That was largely due to the centralized organization mandated for all Air Force wings—and its damaging results. The wing's "managers" were using functional thinking, not team thinking. Also, they were thinking in terms of managership, not leadership.

Clearly, that was the place to start. I got the process rolling by talking directly to every person in the wing. It was a big outfit, so it took eight separate sessions in the base's 700-seat theater. I wanted to be sure each of them knew who I was, what I stood for, and what we needed to do to become winners instead of losers. My remarks focused on the "*will to win*," and I said that once we had that we easily would find the "*way to win*." I emphasized that it would be *their* leadership that would make the difference and that they would have ample empowerment to exercise it. I made a special appeal to the first- and second-level supervisors to take personal responsibility for improvement; they're the ones who make or break any organization. All the follow-through was in accord with these themes. And I made very sure that my actions supported those themes and my promises.

Rather than merely give my own version of what transpired, I have asked someone who was in the wing at that time to provide his account. Retired Major General Russ Violett—later to have many notable leadership successes himself—was then a major who ran the Wing Command Post. That is the nerve center, where score is kept on all wing activities. Therefore, Violett had an ideal vantage point, an eagle's-eye view, from which to judge the wing, its health, and its accomplishments, both before and after the transformation. Here is his account:

I was in the 401st fighter wing, as a major, when Colonel Bill Creech took over because of our failing record. The wing was disheartened and disoriented. We had failed three major inspections in a row. We were told that Colonel Bill Creech was being sent in to turn things around. When he arrived, he placed no blame on us, but rather on the way we were going about our business. He said that wasn't our fault, and that it was easy to fix. He exuded confidence, and somehow passed that on to the wing. He pledged to us that we would all start pulling together, and that we would pass the imminent readiness reinspection with top marks. He said that we would aim even higher and become the best wing in all of Europe.

His footprints were everywhere, yet his style was to bring out leadership, creativity, and initiative from everyone. We set goals for specific teams throughout the wing, and kept score on their progress. Clean, clear lines of authority and accountability were established. A new mood quickly came over the wing as people realized how extensively they were changing for the better. He praised, he counseled, and he taught. He lifted both our spirits and our expectations.

Our Operational Readiness Inspection was the toughest to pass of any Air Force wing. As part of the war-fighting test our wing elements were required to deploy to and then be tested at wartime operational tempo at bases in Italy and Turkey, as well as at the home base in Spain. Despite the challenges inherent in being split three ways, after an extremely tough nine-day inspection we were told that we had passed with flying colors. In their inspection debriefing, the inspectors recounted how "dazzled" they had been with the marked contrast from our previous failing efforts—and with the new competence, spirit, and enthusiasm which permeated all parts of the organization. They then revealed our scores in the various measured areas, and our overall rating. They were the highest to have been awarded any wing in Europe in over a decade! We had gone from repeated failures to highest marks in only four months. If I hadn't seen it I wouldn't have believed it. And the magic didn't stop there. The wing also started winning everything else in sight. In every measured area—operations, maintenance, and support—the statistics rapidly rose to top all wings in Europe.

The bottom line was that in a very short period of time, Colonel Bill Creech was able to turn the wing from the command's biggest loser to its biggest winner. As I reflect on it, those amazing results were centered on his ability to create a new feeling of commitment and confidence, and of eliciting enthusiastic, "can do" leadership from throughout the wing. He gave us a new set of principles, goals, and expectations which brought forth the best from each of us. What before had been thought to be difficult, or even undoable, suddenly became easy to do.

From where I sat that transformation was astounding. You could actually feel it as it unfolded, as well as seeing it in our results even before the inspectors arrived to confirm our vast improvement. Colonel Bill Creech fired no one, and the wing received no extra resources. Therefore, it was easy to figure out, he had made the difference. But in a greater sense it was as he chose to explain it in the aftermath analysis of our remarkable turnaround: "It wasn't me, it was all of you. I just showed the way." That he most certainly did.

As Russ Violett correctly perceived, the wing was far too large, the mission far too complex, and the details far too numerous for me to handle the needed improvements in an individual, hands-on way. I helped change the vision. I also worked very hard to foster the distributed leadership mindset. It sprang to life as people at all levels recognized that their empowerment and ownership were real and lasting, not just figures of speech. We made the frontline level a fundamental part of the "management." Those workers also learned the importance of fully embracing their obligations to other members of their team and to the team of teams. That propelled the new organizational focus, team spirit, and each employee's sense of personal responsibility.

It's appropriate to highlight one aspect of this story. We created and sustained that improvement enthusiasm by identifying the product of each team (after forming teams throughout), and then by dissecting and refining the processes each would use in creating maximum efficiency and responsiveness with its product. So please don't conclude that this was a successful cheerleading exercise. It involved lots of hard, detailed work down in the trenches to transform fundamentally the wing's basic way of doing business—its management system. And that's what produced the dramatically improved mission results, and the transformation from the command's worst wing to its best. I later was to learn the techniques employed in the case of this failing wing will work in any organization, even one of massive size, and move it from worst to first as well. And not a small part of those techniques involves using the product of each group as a definition point, focal point, and rallying point. It's a key to organizational success.

A SUCCESSFUL QUALITY MANAGEMENT SYSTEM INCLUDES A PRODUCT PILLAR—AND MEANS TO EVALUATE AND IMPROVE PRODUCT WORTH

Why a Product Pillar? Because a narrow focus on one's job does not create the broader perspective and common purpose that are essential to building commitment to the goals of the group. I've seen lots of evidence of that, and many polls and surveys show it's the case. Thus success lies in making each group's *product* the focal point for *purpose* and *achievement*. It also then serves as the logical rallying point for *quality* and *productivity*. Beyond those important considerations, giving the product such definition and preeminence provides the necessary linkage to other key elements of a system that breeds success, as I will explain in later chapters.

In this vein, the *product-process* link and its relationship to other organizational elements receives little attention in traditional American management. But now almost all the ''management experts'' agree—even when they can't agree on anything else—that it's high time to pay far more attention to each and every *process*, how it's shaped, how it's working, and how it can be improved. I agree with that. I always have. That's why years ago I made the *Process Pillar* one of the five key pillars to successful TQM. So let's turn now to the matter of process, and provide some much-needed perspective on its role. Is *process* the star of the show, as most of the current quality literature makes it, or but one important member of a larger cast? Chapter 6 addresses those issues—and explains its importance to your improvement efforts.

6

Process: Its Effectiveness Determines Product Worth

DETERMINING THE RIGHT PROCESS STARTS WITH APPROPRIATE PLANNING AND DEFINITION IN A CUSTOMER-PRODUCT-PROCESS CYCLE

The cycle that shapes the process can appropriately start nowhere else than with the customer's needs and wants. And it isn't an American management strength to seek those needs and wants out. That's what GM was addressing with the formation of its "segment teams" to determine the demographic composition, needs, biases, and buying proclivities of the customer base in each prospective product segment (such as that for family vans, sports coupes, and the like). At this point some might yawn and say the need to start that way is altogether obvious.

It should be, but it's not. Joshua Hammond, president of the *American Quality Foundation*, cites from the first findings of his organization's "*International Quality Study*," culled from the data bases of 583 global companies, that translating customer expectations into the design of new products or services is a habit in less than 25 percent of U.S. companies. The same study reveals that only 22 percent of U.S. companies regularly use process improvement. Other studies show that insensitivity to customer wants in product design, and inattention to improvement in processes, are more customary than rare in the traditional American management style.

Said simply, if you don't know what you're trying to achieve with the product, it follows that the process will be equally unfocused. That applies to both goods and services. An analogy, using our American educational system, can be useful in underscoring the *customer-product-process* definition cycle and its importance in meeting customer needs.

There are at least two "customers" of the American primary and secondary educational system: (1) the student, and (2) those who will use the services of that student. The first isn't complaining about the way the system is working, but the second is. Numerous surveys show how poorly equipped students are to enter a work force that faces increasing technical complexity and intensifying competition. Much has been written about our deficiencies in defining the product of that educational system, other than as graduation; the criticism includes concern over the lack of comparative national standards and the lack of countrywide testing against such standards. Indeed, there's a strong case to be made that it's the very absence of a satisfactory product definition that leads to policies like "*social promotion*" (moving a student on to the next grade because of age, not accomplishment). Many teachers decry the practice, but most school boards either champion it or tolerate it. To them it's an answer to alarming dropout rates and the perceived *right* for all students to graduate—with or without an education. Given that lack of focus on the customer and the product, when you move on to the actual educational processes, it's not surprising that they vary widely, have fuzzy definition and purpose, and often are geared simply to pumping students out the door.

Using this analogy, it's not difficult to understand what happens in any business when it's inattentive to the *customer-product* steps in defining its processes. Yogi Berra's oft-quoted admonition applies here: *If you don't know where you're going, you might end up somewhere else.*

Thus, all businesses need to pay intense and continuing attention to the entire *customer-product-process* cycle. And the cycle's key "product" step must lead not only to product conceptualization but also to specificity. Once those processes are specifically defined, disciplined execution is the next vital ingredient. And that, too, depends on a clear definition of what is expected and the means of determining whether it is being achieved. Rosabeth Moss Kanter of Harvard, writing in the "From the Editor" section of the *Harvard Business Review* (January–February 1992), made these cogent observations regarding workplace discipline:

> Shared disciplines facilitate teamwork and allow organizational flexibility. People can get to work faster—and more easily work together in new groupings—when they share a methodology, or planning and problem-solving framework. While different approaches might work equally well, the important thing in a disciplined organization is that everyone uses the *same* approach. People can stop wondering about how to get started, or arguing about whose way is better, and just get on with it. . . . Teamwork goes up and costs go down in disciplined organizations. . . . When people share a methodology, they can check each other's work and count on each other's results. To do this effectively, however, they need performance data. Professional discipline is aided by measures that enable professionals to monitor and correct their own work.

It's in this context that adequate insight into customer needs, adequate product definition, and full description of process parameters are so important. Parenthetically, I don't believe Kanter suggests here, and I certainly don't suggest, that this means the process is thereafter inflexible. It does mean that you determine the "best way" for that activity for that particular process until a conscious decision is made to change it. As Lee Iacocca says, you can't have a system where the workers decide one morning to come in and paint all the convertibles baby blue.

Once the processes are defined and set in motion, the question becomes the efficacy of the execution. That involves the *process-product-customer* result, as seen at each of those stages. (This is the reverse of the definition cycle.) Thus, the entire product circle, including both the definition and execution cycles, begins and ends with the customer, with "process" at the fulcrum. If process is not viewed in that larger context, and constantly monitored in that light, there's small hope that the products will be sufficiently responsive to changing market dynamics.

IT'S MORE THAN DEFINITION: IT'S ALSO EXECUTION —AND THUS THE COMPLETE CYCLE RUNS CUSTOMER–PRODUCT–PROCESS–PRODUCT–CUSTOMER

Is the process adequately defined? Is it working? You should have means of assessment both before and after product delivery. If it doesn't meet the company's expectations, the process needs to be fixed. If it meets the company's expectations but not the customer's, it's time to recalibrate the product definition. The workers can help in both cases. Indeed, the reason you need talented and well-trained people is so they can be *producers*, not just *processors*. When properly trained, focused, and motivated, they provide the spirit and intent to a process that helps ensure a satisfactory product. Webster's tells us that product is "the thing that is produced by labor or effort" and process is "a series of progressive and interdependent steps by which an end is attained." So there's no good reason to confuse the two. But many do. In my experience, those long conditioned by Centralism are the worst offenders. They primarily focus on how you get there, not on where you're going. You can't ignore either, but the process is not an end in itself.

The latter is more prevalent than you might think. One woman, decrying that practice in the centocracy in which she worked, put it starkly: "Process is our most important product." This story was reported in Vice President Gore's *National Performance Review* report, released in the fall of 1993. In their extensive research the NPR staff found it the widespread practice these days to pay attention to the process—but almost no attention to the results obtained. Accordingly, the NPR report called, in no uncertain terms, for far more attention to *results*—and for measurement and assessment means that will make the results obvious to all involved. (I've emphasized this same point over the years in calling for a *product* and *outputs* orientation in designing the overall management system. You need both. Only a clear-cut definition of the product, and the customer, provides a realistic means of judging the worth of the outputs.)

One must also examine the integration of the various processes if they're to do justice to the product and the customer. I call that larger view of integrated processes a "system," but suit yourself. Webster's says a system is a "set or arrangement of things so related or connected as to form a unity or organic whole." The words aren't important; the concept is. My earlier story about the way we changed the centralized "supply system" in TAC is an example. We worked backward from the internal customers and their needs to look at the entire system—not just at the individual processes. For example, if our fixation had been process improvement, and we had been otherwise committed to maintaining TAC's centralized arrangement, we would have zeroed in on why it took three and a half hours to deliver a part to the flightline. And we would have then taken steps to improve the pickup and delivery process.

Instead, we looked at the problem in subsystem as well as in process terms. Using that broader perspective, we did away entirely with centralized pickup and delivery. We also eliminated other steps and streamlined those that remained to cut cycle times radically. Thus, we changed the entire supply subsystem and all the processes within it—we did not isolate the processes and work on improving them one by one. Moreover, all that was done in concert with a different view of the way to construct the broader management system of which the supply subsystem was an integral part. The moral here is that in looking at "process" matters, many businesses virtually ignore the broader definition and execution cycle of which process is but one part. They compound the problem by also paying little or no attention to their broader management system, which in the final analysis has more influence on the processes than any other factor.

This is aimed squarely at those who are using varied process improvement techniques to tinker with mere patches on flawed and time-consuming processes. Sometimes that's enough. More often, it's not. Therefore, the effect of process changes on the product and the customer must be carefully collected, evaluated, and fed back into the process improvement effort. The faster and more comprehensive the collective feedback, and the less time wasted in taking corrective action, the more responsive the products to changing market dynamics. That seems obvious. But few businesses give it enough emphasis—as their oversight tools reflect.

EFFECTIVE PROCESS IMPROVEMENT DEPENDS ON OVERSIGHT TECHNIQUES WHICH PROVIDE FOCUS, RIGOR, AND EMPHASIS

Besides well-developed means of defining processes, the best companies also have well-structured ways of monitoring them. As an example, John Hudiburg of Florida Power & Light, drawing on what he and his colleagues learned from Japan's Deming Prize–winning companies, developed a *"Seven Steps"* approach to process related problem-solving:

1. What's the problem?
2. Where are we now?
3. What are the root causes?
4. What is needed to improve?
5. What happened from our actions?
6. How do we hold on to the improvement?
7. What is the next item to be addressed?

To make it work, FPL assigned specific responsibility to specific teams, and individuals, for addressing each of the seven. FPL also formed cross-cutting teams, with representation from various structural teams and departments, to look at process issues that involve many teams and departments. That was appropriate because you can't succeed by fixing only one part of a complicated, integrated process. (But that's not all you do organizationally, by any means.) So this seven-step formula was used on process issues confined to a single team, as well as on those that applied to many. It provided rigor to the "process" of monitoring and changing processes throughout the company, and thereby provided impetus to looking at all activity in a disciplined and systematic way. FPL's overall results—and its winning the Deming Prize—speak to the usefulness of the seven-step approach.

The Boeing Company, which deals more in durable products than services, and very complex products at that, has adopted as part of its overall *Continuous Quality Improvement* program a comprehensive ten-step methodology to process evaluation and improvement. These are Boeing's ten steps, somewhat abbreviated:

1. Does it have a name?
2. Does it have an owner who fully accepts the responsibility?
3. Has it—and its boundaries—been defined in writing?
4. Are the involved resources and implementers identified?
5. Are customers identified and required outputs specified?
6. Are suppliers identified and required inputs specified?
7. Is a process flow identified and is each task documented?
8. Are the control points adequate; do they ensure control?
9. Are the customer's measures of success fully incorporated?
10. Is there a formal mechanism for capturing measurements of the process, and is it providing feedback for improvement?

Note how the Boeing approach fits the cycle approach I described earlier—especially the strong customer focus and emphasis on clear definition. Also note the sensitivity to the ownership issue. Boeing ensures a clear-cut internal assignment of authority, achievement responsibility, and accountability. I have found that highly important to the success of these kinds of efforts—as has Boeing. And it works especially well at Boeing because its team-based structure features ownership in all organizational aspects—an important backdrop for process improvement. It's far easier in such a system to identify who has the ball—who is carrying it and who's dropping it. Boeing uses this ten-step methodology very successfully, and handles the larger,

cross-cutting process issues in a manner not unlike that adopted from
the Japanese by Florida Power & Light.

All organizations can productively use such process improvement
methods—with variations to fit their particular needs. However, any
method adopted should encompass the definition of the process and
the installation of a structured approach to optimizing, simplifying,
and otherwise improving that process. The other important element is
to keep it as simple and straightforward as possible. It won't work
unless the employees who must use the system fully understand it. In
balancing simplicity and sophistication, apply that litmus test.

That brings us to the matter of the statistical tools. There's a large
family of them available. They all have their applications, but no
business needs them all. And each business should choose its set
carefully, to fit its individual needs.

THE RIGHT ASSESSMENT TOOLS CAN
SUBSTANTIALLY CONTRIBUTE TO ADDRESSING
PROCESS VARIABILITY AND IMPROVEMENT

Again, much literature on this subject is available, so I'll merely
provide an overview. The tools of statistical analysis to be used depend wholly on the type and complexity of each company's product
mix. That, of course, varies widely by industry and market niche. *Run
charts* which collect and display various elements of actual performance over time—and then compares them to *benchmarks* such as
history, standards, and goals—are useful for almost any business.
Those run charts and their analysis will suffice for the most whose
products involve uncomplicated processes.

Some businesses need more than that, however. And as the processes become more intricate, the tools, too, become increasingly sophisticated. In fact, there's such a variety of statistical tools available
that I use the following chart to address the subject. It by no means
contains them all, and the tools to be selected from the "kit" must
fit the circumstances and needs of each business.

For example, many businesses can make excellent use of Pareto charting. Simply described, Pareto charting is a way of displaying data for analysis purposes in a bar chart arranged in descending order of importance or frequency as you move from left to right along the baseline. The modern techniques of that nature are derived from Vilfredo Pareto, an Italian sociologist and economist, who postulated that a few of the causes account for most of the effect. (His work gave rise to such offshoots as the "80/20 principle," which postulates, among other formulations, that 20 percent of the people cause 80 percent of the problems. There is a long list of these postulates.) The Pareto techniques help to sort out the "significant few" of the various elements that when changed have the most profound effect. Therefore, it's an excellent means of deciding where to place the emphasis in improvement actions in nearly any type of undertaking.

The various applications of *Statistical Quality Control* (SQC) and the closely related *Statistical Process Control* (SPC) also can be extremely beneficial to a wide range of businesses. Both involve ways to measure deviations (variations, if you will) in the processes used in manufacturing materials, parts, and products. There are others that are closely related. For example, many U.S. manufacturing firms are strong advocates of the statistical analysis tools developed by Japan's Genichi Taguchi, specifically including those related to his *Quality*

Loss Function techniques. This genre of statistical tools does not lend itself to brief description. However, it can be characterized. It involves a family of different means of determining the variation from a specified quality norm based on a statistical analysis of the process—and then of using techniques such as probability theory to redefine and further improve the process. These techniques aren't as complicated as they may sound, and they can be extremely useful.

Flow charts, affinity charts, control charts, deployment charts, arrow diagrams, cause-and-effect (Ishikawa) diagrams, checksheets, and the many process-oriented tools in the foregoing "Tool Kit" chart—all these and more have their uses. Obviously it's beyond the scope of this book to explain each, and how it might fit into a particular company's needs. It suffices to understand that they're out there, and that lots of experts are around who can help tailor them to the situation of any business—presuming it needs and wants one or more.

In that regard, modern computers and computer modeling technology make all these tools a good bit more practical and useful (albeit a good bit harder for the average manager to understand) than was so even a decade ago. Also, computer availability at reasonable cost makes assessment and display far easier, whether you're talking about the simplest tools or the most complex. And the perceived complexity shouldn't be a deterrent; as you ascend that ladder of complexity, you can find a good many computer models already available that can be put to use with a minimum of modification to your company's special circumstances. On up the scale of process intricacies you find even more sophisticated computer-based assessment tools, such as *Quality Function Deployment* (QFD). Most researchers credit Genichi Taguchi with development of the first QFD computer model, and its first use to *Mitsubishi*'s Kobe shipyard. Its purpose for Mitsubishi, according to Taguchi, was to help ensure that the "voice of the customer" is fully reflected in all activities from beginning to end. QFD has grown from that to many variants and many applications. Basically, QFD provides an assessment tool for tracking activities and results from cradle to grave—from the requirements stage right on through the many design and production steps to the product's performance in the customer's hands. QFD is designed to provide insight, focus, and coherence to that entire cycle. QFD requires rather complex computer modeling techniques, astute methods of devising the interactive matrices that portray the integration aspects, large data bases, and extensive computer processing capability.

I should have convinced each reader by now that the product mix and business niche determines whether your company should use most, some, or none of these process-oriented analysis tools. Most of these tools were designed for production processes involving durable goods. However, no one should conclude that they have no utility for businesses involved in intellectual products or in services. Since the preponderance of American employees deal in services, not manufacturing, that would be a particularly tragic misreading of the quality management literature. Though they are most associated with manufacturing, variants of these tools can be highly useful in improving the "processes" involved in providing services.

These various tools and techniques have become so closely associated with the quality movement that it's useful here to review their wellsprings. Most researchers trace the origins of this modern family of statistical analysis tools to the *Bell Telephone Laboratories* during and after World War II. And many date those beginnings back to Walter A. Shewhart's *Economic Control of Quality of Manufactured Product*, first published in 1931. Shewhart was among the first to establish a scientific foundation for quality control and techniques for monitoring production process efficiency. He was the guiding spirit in the *Quality Assurance Department* of the Bell Laboratories, and in the 1940s, he and his colleagues created the family of concepts underlying *Statistical Quality Control* (SQC). They also developed related tools such as means of establishing and tracking *Acceptable Quality Level* (AQL). One of Shewhart's other cherished tools, and deservedly so, was the *Plan-Do-Check-Act* cycle (PDCA), later known as the "Shewhart cycle." It provides rigor to the examination, and the control, of both the product and the process.

These techniques provided the basis for the quality control tools W. Edwards Deming and Joseph M. Juran took from the Bell Laboratories to Japan after World War II. Both men continue to be widely revered in Japan for awakening the Japanese to the need for, and the possibilities in, a focus on quality. That included defining a quality product, and then reducing process variability to the point at which that product could be delivered to the customer in a timely and economical manner by avoiding scrap, rework, and wasted motion.

These important contributions, and those of other American quality pioneers like A. V. Feigenbaum, provided the foundation for most modern process-oriented statistical tools. These American wellsprings provide for endless conjecture as to why the tools were embraced and expanded on by the Japanese but largely ignored by Americans. I don't believe you'll find the answer by going back to study those origins, though you might otherwise profit from doing so. Rather, one can best understand it by looking at quality management—and why America is not good at it—in a larger, more holistic context. There are lots of modern management practices other than the statistical tools that America's managers have been slow to adopt. But before turning to that broader subject, a few more observations are in order on the *Process Improvement Tool Kit* I spoke about earlier.

My advice is this: When it comes to "quality management," don't be confused by the jargon, or get lost in the lexicon. It need not be mysterious. Become familiar with these various techniques, even the more sophisticated ones, if they fit your business and product mix. Hire experts to help if need be. However, in most cases you don't need to go very far up the complexity scale in the tools you use. Most processes, at the frontline level, are not all that complicated. For that matter, they're not all that complex in their interaction with the kindred processes that go into the final product. Additionally, most American companies don't do measurement and analysis in any depth at all—of any activity including their processes. Therefore, to leap directly into a bewildering world of advanced statistical techniques can be daunting—and can serve as a barrier to adopting less complex techniques that will suffice for most businesses. Above all, everyone should start.

The best way to start is with the basics. Even simple measurement, analysis, and scoreboarding techniques can yield needed insights and point employees in the right directions. (I find in my travels that most businesses don't use any—at least none that are used regularly and usefully at the frontline.) Also, no matter how adroit you are in determining what needs to be done, you still must address the overarching issue of getting the employees to want to do it—with focus and enthusiasm (a subject usually taken for granted by those who dwell on the tools). As an example, TAC had no shortage of sophisticated process tools and methods when I took over as commander. The U.S. Air Force in that era was as progressive and aggressive as any business in America in adopting the latest "quality" tools and techniques.

Indeed, TAC had paid lots of attention to its "*quality assurance*" concepts and functions. And those functions did a conscientious job of trying to instill quality consciousness and rigorous adherence to quality standards in all the TAC people. Also, TAC had robust "*quality control*" functions in each wing. Those highly capable quality control folks used a variety of inspections and surveys—including "*end process*" and "*over the shoulder*" looks and wall-to-wall "*unit reviews*"—to capture trends and seek out defect-causing behavior before it could create big problems. Therefore, those means also helped determine where extra training was needed. So I fully agree that you must build quality in, not inspect it in. That's precisely what I'm addressing.

Conceptually, that previous set of quality functions, tools, and techniques in TAC was supposed to yield a *do it right the first time* mentality—it wasn't designed just to catch mistakes after they were made. But though they helped, they fell woefully short in instilling the quality mindset—and the level of competence and motivation needed to do it right the first time, every time. What were the missing ingredients? I've talked about them throughout these pages. They involved new organization, new leadership, new empowerment, new ways to instill quality-consciousness, and new incentives to get every employee committed to eliminating defects at the source—and to continuous improvement in every process and every activity.

TAC's quality—and productivity—improved dramatically only when we took those steps. And they far overshadowed the steps we also took to be smarter in our process analysis and improvement actions. In that respect, I'm thoroughly convinced that putting a new twist on those process tools, using even the best of the latest thinking and techniques, would not have done the job. Centralism was strangling incentive as well as precluding ownership, so trying to graft somewhat better techniques onto that system would have availed us little.

This is not to suggest that the process analysis tools mentioned in this section are not of great value, because they definitely are. They're an important part of the picture, but a far cry from being the only part, or even the major part. In fact, some believe that excessive focus on those tools—and an exclusion of the broader management actions required—is a principal reason why the current quality crusade isn't producing much change. There's much to be said for that point of view, so let's take a closer look at the dynamics involved.

THE "QUALITY MANAGEMENT" MOVEMENT IN AMERICA IS SPLINTERED AND IS PRODUCING VARIED RESULTS—SOME QUITE ANEMIC

A good question at this point is whether this new quality crusade, being carried out under a wide variety of names and conceptual frameworks, is doing any good. The short answer is yes, some—but not nearly enough. There are many reasons. For starters, those ignoring it greatly outnumber those embracing it. And most who are embracing it are looking at the issues in a very narrow context—as if it's largely a matter of improving processes. They then shoehorn their minimal changes into their old management practices. As a consequence, they end up not changing much of anything, and certainly don't address the broader ills of their organizations.

In that regard, a few years ago the U.S. Department of Defense asked the *Institute for Defense Analysis* (IDA) to do a wide-ranging analytical survey of businesses throughout the United States that were practicing the new quality management techniques. (IDA is a well-respected and independent think tank highly skilled in doing comprehensive studies.) The IDA study group included in its study sample a large number of firms both inside and outside the defense industry. (At that time the *buzzphrase* used by most industrial firms for describing Japanese-like quality management techniques was "*Concurrent Engineering.*" The "TQM" moniker was to come later.) IDA reported its findings to the DOD in a December 1988 report.

The IDA study group found a consistent pattern in its sample of representative industrial firms. It was so consistent, in fact, that IDA chose to quote extensively from the observations of one of those companies as representative of them all. That was a principal means of articulating the study group's conclusions and recommendations. And the group specifically emphasized the pitfalls to be avoided by any firm adopting quality management techniques. The firm IDA selected as representative of the others had this to say about its own program and the pitfalls it failed to avoid:

> The many improvements and cost savings we have recognized are due mostly to the application of the powerful statistical and quality improvement techniques at the small, local level (for example, a particular machine or manufacturing process). Granted, these have been very important and worthwhile. But the really impressive savings remain largely unrecognized because they result only from improvements of the "larger systems" . . . [which] include policies of the company; training that people receive; actions of management; policies for purchasing parts; barriers between departments; . . . the way employees are evaluated; fostering of teamwork; and so forth. To date, most top managers have failed to comprehend, or at least execute, their critical responsibility. Their verbal "support" is simply not sufficient.
>
>   . . . Most divisions placed too much emphasis on the techniques—SPC, QFD, Design of Experiments, etc.—and not enough emphasis on the critical management philosophy underlying the application of the techniques. This partly explains the lack of top management understanding and involvement. Top management views concurrent engineering as something the lower levels learn and apply. Concurrent engineering is more a philosophy of management than a bag of techniques. Granted, the techniques are crucial to the execution of the philosophy, but without the guiding philosophy the

techniques are not as effectively used at all levels, nor are the great potential improvements fully realized.

If we were to start completely over again, we believe the best approach would be for top management to take whatever time was necessary to learn and understand the principles, philosophy, and some simple tools; understand their responsibility; develop their purpose, direction and plan for implementing the effort company-wide—and then execute the plan with appropriate leadership.

. . . Our company has ushered through continuous "waves" of techniques over the past several years fueling the perception of a coming-and-going fad. . . . People are confused about what they ought to be doing today. . . . We should have focused more on the management philosophy in our initial training, then followed with the techniques.

The IDA study group reinforced that view with an overarching observation applicable to all the companies it studied: "Top management commitment in the form of learning, understanding, and leading the concurrent engineering efforts with a communicated, unwavering purpose and management involvement is absolutely vital to long-term success."

On the matter of the need to change—and the willingness to devote the requisite effort—the IDA report said, "Companies differed in the rate at which they implemented change. Typically, companies that were experiencing the most serious crisis were willing to implement change at a faster rate. Successful companies implemented gradual changes." This is what I earlier dubbed the black-ink barrier to change. The trouble is that gradualism and halfhearted quality management measures don't matter much.

These IDA findings require no further elaboration. And the same observations can be applied with equal validity to the current flurry of activity under the rubric "TQM" and other names. Most of those companies (thankfully not all) are falling into the same pitfalls IDA warned against. It's wise to recall that crusades to achieve greater workplace and product quality are not new to American management. There's been a series of such crusades, such as *Zero Defects* and *Management by Objectives*. As John Betti of Ford said, "Quality commitments and quality programs were not new to our company. In fact, we had a pattern of renewing our commitment every three to five years—bring out the bells and whistles with an occasional new slogan. It changed because we were in a crisis.'' And as John Hudiburg of Florida Power & Light cautions those who are embarking on a new quality management program, ''It's a matter of putting lots of pieces together, in a systematic away, into a *complete management system*.'' FPL earlier had tried to graft a few pieces onto its old system, with negligible effect. I've seen the same in many other companies. So it came as no surprise that IDA found the same results in a large sample of other American businesses.

Admittedly, the content of the current quality crusade is different from that of its predecessors. And the clamor for it is far louder. Nevertheless, I find that many companies that have adopted piecemeal changes are already tiring of the subject. Their top executives are concluding that *''it isn't doing any good.''* Others are noting the same trend. Phil Pifer, a principal of the widely known management consultants McKinsey & Company, commented on the same trend in the January–February 1992 *Harvard Business Review*:

> Increasingly, it appears that too many quality programs are ineffective. In McKinsey's client work, we are seeing a disturbingly large number of companies whose total quality management programs are failing to show signs of meaningful business impact. More and more senior executives privately express reservations or concerns to us about the eventual impact of their quality activities, while still maintaining the public commitment to seeing them through. In a recent McKinsey survey of quality programs, more than half the companies interviewed expressed the view that their quality programs may have stalled or even failed—and such comments were as likely to come from quality professionals as from senior line executives.

Well, what's the problem? Is it all smoke and mirrors? Or does the problem lie in the understanding of what's involved in the application? I'm convinced it's the latter. Most senior managers in such companies have applied piecemeal changes while holding on tightly to their old centralized structure and habits. They simply have not stepped up to the holistic issues involved. They reach out for some of the techniques as a panacea for ills that run far deeper. Thus, it becomes simply one more set of "bells and whistles," as John Betti of Ford so aptly described it.

As many know, after helping Ford turn from losing $4 million a day to America's most profitable automaker during the eighties, Betti agreed to join the government as the top DOD procurement official. He has since rejoined the business world. However, during his stay in the DOD he got to see in action the bewildering variety of quality management programs American companies have adopted—primarily under the name "TQM." The more he saw, the more concerned he became. He shared that concern in a 1990 speech to a chapter of the *American Society of Quality Control*:

> There are many well-intentioned Total Quality Management advocates in our country today. I worry, however, that many of these advocates are doing the concept serious damage as a result of incomplete understanding or misunderstanding. . . . I liken the problem of lack of understanding of Total Quality Management to the story of the seven blind men describing an elephant.
>
> . . . Many, either intentionally or through ignorance, latch onto one or two of TQM's characteristics and define TQM in terms of those characteristics. . . . [For example] individuals and organizations define TQM in terms of employee involvement and cross-functional teams; or statistical process control; or the use of tools such as quality function deployment; design of experiments; Taguchi and other structured problem solving methods. All could be considered an element of TQM, but neither individually nor collectively do they capture the concept of Total Quality Management.
>
> . . . The unfortunate result is that, like the blind men, many in my example are convinced their view of TQM is correct and complete, and cease to pursue any deeper understanding.

That's my experience too. And the problem is compounded because managers can find both the books and the consultants to reinforce their narrow view. Betti continued:

Total Quality Management truly is a cultural change. It involves a change in both the stated and unstated rules which govern the behavior and beliefs of an organization. Adopting new techniques, tools, or programs such as problem solving working groups can be important—but in themselves do not represent cultural change. The critical difference is that unless you modify the stated and unstated rules that govern behavior, you will not affect cultural change. . . . Slogans and simplistic solutions will not help; they will make matters worse. Total Quality Management can make a significant difference, but all of us need to exert the effort to understand it.

To Betti's remarks I say, Amen! He describes the problem—and the narrow orientation of most "TQM" efforts—extremely well.

Betti later received ample indication that his concern was not misplaced when the Navy's A-12 Stealth fighter program blew up in the DOD's face. It was overweight, over cost, over schedule, and over just about everything else. Only weeks after Betti was assured by the top executives of the two companies building the A-12 that the program was in great shape, all the serious problems came tumbling out. The program was in such unsalvageable condition that it was terminated. Lawyers will be arguing for years over who was to blame, and I'm not offering an opinion one way or the other. I will say that in my DOD procurement experience it's usually the case that the top executives of such functionalized organizations (and both were longtime practitioners of the centocracy organizational approach) simply don't know what's going on. They're often misinformed, and even misled, because they have developed no good tools and mechanisms to provide *objective* insight at any level, including at the top. There's a difference between ignorance and deception, but neither is excusable. Both companies now have serious TQM-style management change programs under way.

If quality management is to succeed, it must be far more than a grab bag of statistical methods and tools (as the IDA Report and kindred studies have verified). Those who pursue quality management on that basis are doomed to disappointment. Quality management process improvement tools and techniques are one subject; holistic quality management principles are quite another. However, I readily understand why the nation's managers become confused over whom to listen to and what to do. You can find myriad contradictory ideas about change and how to do it among the nation's host of "experts" who will support virtually anything any company wants to do. And disagreements in that "expert opinion" abound.

THERE ARE WIDE DIFFERENCES OF OPINION REGARDING QUALITY MANAGEMENT, AND HOW TO IMPLEMENT IT, EVEN AMONG THE EXPERTS

Perhaps I was fortunate because I went about doing what I did in the military transformations largely on an intuitive basis (though with lots of practical, hands-on experience and chances to see Centralism's features and failures up close). The management techniques I used turned out later to fit what I saw the Japanese and others practicing, but I didn't know it at the time (because few of them were doing it then). Also, the current avalanche of literature on quality management simply wasn't available then. If you had asked me about *"Deming"* when I went to TAC, the only Deming I knew was a highway truck stop in New Mexico. And I thought of *"Crosby"* as a crooner who loved golf.

However, since joining the business world I've read just about everything I can find on business management and quality matters— hundreds of books old and new. That research has included reading virtually everything written by the *Big Four*: Deming, Juran, Feigenbaum, and Crosby. W. Edwards Deming (*Out of the Crisis*, 1986), Joseph M. Juran (*Juran on Leadership for Quality*, 1989), and Armand V. Feigenbaum (*Total Quality Control*, 1983) all have written extensively on quality matters—the cited books are but samples. Philip B. Crosby (*Let's Talk Quality*, 1989; *Completeness*, 1992) left ITT in 1979 and has been expounding on quality matters and related management issues ever since. I now understand the theories of each of the four, their backgrounds (and how that may have shaped their views), and the place each occupies on the quality advocacy spectrum.

Also, I've heard the varied theories and concoctions on quality management from the scores of academicians and consultants who now populate the advisory landscape.

I no doubt would have benefited, when I was busy running organizations, from what I now know after assimilating all that advice. *But I'm not at all convinced I could have done it any better now than I did then.* Moreover, I haven't read or seen anything since that convinces me there was a better way.

This all leads to two points: First, you don't have to become an expert at statistical and mathematical legerdemain to transform your organization for the better. Second, a background in leadership of large, complex organizations as I have had provides a different perspective than a background in the intricacies of quality control techniques. You will see that leads to areas where I agree and others where I disagree with the nostrums promulgated in the bulk of the current quality management literature. None of this suggests you shouldn't avail yourself of all the knowledge you can acquire on this subject. However, this is the problem you will soon run into: *Whom should I believe*? If you're looking for a single, clear vision on how to go about quality management from these varied sources, you'll look in vain. The widespread differences within the quality advocacy community are well recognized—ranging from mild matters of emphasis to strong disagreement about fundamental principles.

Indeed, some of the latter amount to outright feuds between some of the best-known quality advocates. The open and caustic disagreements between Deming and Juran are but one case in point. *Business Week*, in its 1991 "Quality Issue," addressed that dispute in an excellent article titled "Dueling Pioneers." It covered the rhetorical salvos between the two, and said this regarding Deming's views on Juran: "Still a spry workaholic at 91, Deming has a legendarily caustic temper which flares at the suggestion that Juran's ideas have much merit or staying power. 'I'm not interested in stamping out fires. That's what Juran does.' " The article then turned to Juran's views on Deming: "At 87, Juran is able to give as good as he gets. 'Recognition has become the biggest thing in Deming's life,' he argues. 'But the Deming prize is much more important than he is. . . .' "

And, as reported elsewhere, the Japanese get in the middle of that feud. *Business Week* covered it this way:

> [Juran] too has found his most loyal following in Japan, where he first described his Total Quality Control method in 1954. While Deming's three-year lead there has won him more notice, there's a line of thinking, heavily subscribed to, that Juran's influence has been greater over the years. Once TQC became widely known, "Juran was more important to Japan than Deming," says Junji Noguchi, director of the Japanese Union of Scientists & Engineers (JUSE), which runs the Deming competition. "SQC applies only to technicians," Noguchi adds. "Juran applied quality to everybody, from managers to clerical staff."

These disputes extend far beyond Deming and Juran; one can find differences (and feuds) among most of those who occupy the top rungs in the quality advisory pecking order.

Does any of this matter? It might to historians, but it shouldn't matter to managers contemplating change. That's because the genesis of the ideas is far less relevant than their content, and how well they work in actual practice. However, I find one stark distinction in dissecting the quality management–oriented literature, old and new. That distinction can best be described as the difference between the narrow process focus and a broader holistic focus when it comes to how one should achieve quality orientation and performance throughout the organization—in every nook and cranny.

Given its importance, let's take a close look at the issue. You don't have to choose sides (indeed, you should take from all sides), but you do have to decide what you're going to do. The last thing you need is confusion over that.

THE BROADER DEBATE REGARDING "QUALITY MANAGEMENT" INCLUDES MAJOR DISAGREEMENT OVER THE ROLE PROCESS SHOULD OCCUPY

Further insight into the debate regarding the role *process* should play in a change program comes from the conflicting views surrounding the *Malcolm Baldrige National Quality Award.* It was established by a public law signed by the President in August 1987. Its proponents saw it as a way of mobilizing national attention to greater emphasis on quality. It is awarded by the U.S. Department of Commerce to those who, in the opinion of the evaluators, stand out above all other applicants in their effective implementation of a quality focus and the management mechanisms that go with it. Applicants compete in three different groups—small business, service, and manufacturing—with no more than two awards available in each group, each year. Oversight of the award (and the details of the judging) was left to the *National Institute of Standards and Technology* (NIST). The judging addresses seven separate but related categories worth a total of 1,000 points. Those seven, along with the points to be potentially earned in each category, are:

1. Leadership (100)
2. Information and Analysis (70)
3. Strategic Quality Planning (60)
4. Human Resource Utilization (150)
5. Quality Assurance of Products and Services (140)
6. Quality Results (180)
7. Customer Satisfaction (300)

Within each of the seven categories there are subcategories, and cutting across all of them is a large array of guidelines and benchmarking methods the judges use in their deliberations. The first three winners of the award, in 1988, were *Motorola, Globe Metallurgical,* and *Westinghouse Nuclear Fuel.* Other companies and corporate divisions, ranging in size from the small *Zytec* Corporation of Eden Prairie,

Minnesota, to huge companies like *Federal Express*, have joined the winners' list since.

Though widely praised when it began, the Baldrige Award has attracted increasing criticism—particularly from within the quality advocacy community. Conceptual battle lines have formed regarding the criteria—including the makeup and weighting of the seven categories—and even over the award itself. Some say it helps and others say it hurts America's quality efforts.

The *Harvard Business Review* did its usual first-class job of capturing those disagreements in early 1992. It began in the November–December 1991 issue with an article by Harvard Business School professor David A. Garvin titled "How the Baldrige Award Really Works." The article addressed the growing debate, praised the award, and defended the criteria as being ideally positioned for the present —but still evolving. In its following issue *HBR* collected opinions on the Garvin article (and thus on the Baldrige criteria) from twenty-one individuals with recognized credentials in the field of quality management. *There was widespread disagreement among the respondents.*

I'll remove one, Curt W. Reimann, from the summary of those disagreements because he's the current director of the Baldrige Award. Of the remaining twenty, six were outspokenly against the award itself. Four of the fourteen who supported the award would not support the criteria as they stood; they considered them too flawed to be useful. So only half of these experts voiced support for the Baldrige as it is. Even among those supporters, most offered opinions on how the criteria could be vastly "improved."

The wide range of responses offers further insight. For example, the five respondents from public companies all strongly supported the award and the criteria, as did the two academicians being surveyed. The major criticism—much of it biting—came from the ranks of the twelve consultants whose views were solicited. The most vociferous critic among this latter group was W. Edwards Deming. He completely dismissed the Baldrige Award, and in his response to *HBR* got right to the point: "The Baldrige Award does not codify principles of management of quality. It contains nothing about management of quality. The award is focused purely on results. . . . It transgresses all that I try to teach.''

Several other consultants believed that the award itself is counterproductive to the quality movement. However, Deming's faulting of the criteria for being excessively results-oriented was decidedly the minority view. The others voicing criticism held the contrary view—that the Baldrige criteria primarily are flawed by their lack of attention to results. Also, most argued for additional elements and criteria that would more accurately signal a favorable result. (As one put it, the criteria should be ''closer to overall management excellence.'' Another said it's not enough to just do it, it has to be done right.) Several cited the failure to consider various indicators of success—such as ''financial results''—that would help separate form from substance. Others had their own favored category additions (such as ''Innovation''), or called for greater attention (and weighting) to one or more existing categories.

Phil Crosby is no fan of the criteria either. He said, ''The Baldrige criteria have trivialized the quality crusade, perhaps beyond help.'' He pinpointed his primary objection as follows: ''The criteria are old-fashioned, taken from quality-control practices of two decades ago.'' And he summarized, ''Quality is a serious and difficult business. Like finance, it has to become an integral part of management.'' He's certainly right about that.

Some dislike the criteria for much the same reasons but support the award for ''raising consciousness'' on quality matters. Phil Pifer of McKinsey & Company believes the Baldrige has been ''an unabashed success at generating awareness in total quality.'' On the other hand, Pifer joins those who are critical of the narrow orientation of the criteria. His primary criticism is that ''750 points of a total of 1,000 are devoted to process.'' He believes that puts too much emphasis on ''TQM as a 'check the box' activity, not as a path to sustainable results.'' IDA, of course, reached similar conclusions, as have many others.

If you're to take the right path, and achieve significant and sustainable TQM results, you must pay attention to far more than the processes. That's what Phil Pifer of McKinsey is saying, based on his and his colleagues' observations in scores of companies. And change seekers also must broaden their vision of what is required well beyond some old-fashioned ''quality control practices''—as Phil Crosby forcefully points out. For all these reasons, every manager in America considering the adoption of quality management by any name—or presently in the midst of carrying one out—has a central issue to confront in devising or revising the game plan.

A CENTRAL ISSUE: SHOULD COMPANIES FRAME THEIR QUALITY EFFORTS IN TERMS OF PROCESS IMPROVEMENT OR IN BROADER "SYSTEM" TERMS?

Most of the current TQM literature is centered on quality improvement tools for the processes. Little of it addresses the broader subjects of workplace quality, leadership, and organizational structure and style. (Some of it makes passing reference to these subjects, but makes no material contribution.) To help underscore the point, and to help frame the issue, let's look at some representative samples.

Recently I read an ad for one of the many books coming out on TQM, titled *Excellence in Government: Total Quality Management in the 1990s*. Written by David Carr and Ian Littman, the book is copyrighted by Coopers & Lybrand. (Carr and Littman are consultants with that firm. Both are former government employees with degrees in public administration.) The work is impressively advertised as ''the first comprehensive book on TQM in government.'' Since I know a good bit about the government, and a thing or two about excellence and TQM, I was immediately interested. The book provides good tips on process issues and process improvement. But it falls woefully short in a holistic sense. Following are excerpts, interspersed with my comments, which provide the flavor of the nearly exclusive focus on processes.

> In TQM the basic building block of the system is the process. All other system components revolve around the process. That is why TQM improvement is called ''process improvement.''

This Coopers & Lybrand book is hardly alone in that orientation. Once the authors tie TQM to process—and vice versa—the book goes on to dwell at length on process improvement techniques, with heavy emphasis on the statistical analysis tools. It also discusses the ad hoc, cross-functional organizational arrangements for process focus that are favored in such literature. These excerpts regarding the recommended composition and orientation of the ad hoc "teams" are revealing:

> Usually a team of managers selects the process or issue to receive attention, based on priorities: Which of many processes or issues requires attention now? . . . Improvement teams are temporary groups, operating only until they have completed a project.

My experience is that all the processes should be receiving attention, all the time. This temporary, ad hoc approach to singling out a process "requiring attention" is the "*Code Blue*" approach that I find so curious. I strongly advocate cross-cutting teams to look at special process issues, but to make that the be-all of organizing for process improvement is to miss what's creating the flawed processes in the first place. That approach also ignores the best means of improving all processes all the time—and that's through an organizational arrangement that provides for continuous training, monitoring, ownership, and empowerment. That specifically involves the permanent structure, not just temporary groups—or it won't work. The authors also advance the notion, widely subscribed to in such literature, that the "temporary groups" should have a volunteer flavor:

> Should the members of improvement teams be volunteers or should they be appointed by management? . . . No employee who is truly opposed to the idea should be forced to join a team. . . . A person from outside the process area who has no vested interest in an issue makes the best facilitator. He or she will bring an objective view to team meetings.

As with most who subscribe to this school of thought, this reflects the notion that such teams should be differently constructed than the normal management structure—and constructed of volunteers so that it is further disassociated from that structure. Here we go with another "overlay" that creates additional ambiguity, not clarification regarding authority and accountability. Most are finding to their dismay that you can't make your system work by circumventing it rather than fixing it, or by building competing power centers. The process-oriented fixation on "*facilitators*" also reflects that same temporary, committee-oriented approach to the way all this should work. And the purported "objectivity of outsiders" says little for the critical need to build objectivity in the insiders, rather than fix it by introducing the uninformed and unaccountable into the equation.

Having committeelike groups drawn from the most knowledgeable to provide advice on process repair is fine and dandy. In fact, I strongly recommend it. At its heart, however, the issue isn't whom to make responsible for *pontification*—it's whom to make responsible for *performance*, and how to achieve it through day-to-day teamwork. The process-oriented advocates gloss over the latter—which is the far more compelling need of the two. Moreover, when those "temporary groups" dissolve, as this Coopers & Lybrand book and others like it recommend, the employees carrying out the process often slip right back to their old patterns. I've found that as often as the process methodology itself is flawed, it's the poor execution of it that's the problem. Ad hoc groups can't do much about the latter problem, at least anything that reliably sticks to the organization's ribs when they depart the scene.

All that suggests the need for close and careful integration between such ad hoc groups and the permanent structural groupings that carry out the actual work. It can work harmoniously and effectively. It also can be disruptive. Which it will be depends on involved leadership that ensures an effective blend of the two organizational arrangements. The last thing most of America's organizations need is additional competitive power centers—or further ambiguity regarding responsibility and accountability.

Achieving effective change involves far more than finding creative ways to improve the various processes, one by one, within an organization—the system must be in place to ensure the enthusiastic follow-through, and to create continuous process improvement with everyone involved. You can't wait for the next coming of the *Process Improvement Team* if you're going to be responsive to changing customer needs and wants, or even to ordinary workplace dynamics.

In fairness, the authors acknowledge that companies should alter their "traditional" organization if they are to succeed. However, they portray it as a follow-on, not a primary order of business. And they address it in this fashion:

> Radically altering your structure during the first few years of your TQM initiative is a mistake. . . . Wait until you have some experience, but when you do, do not hesitate to start the transformation. The traditional organizational hierarchy was built for many of the wrong reasons—it will get in the way of your progress.

It sure will get in the way of your progress. Their book doesn't provide reasons for waiting, other than you somehow need experience with these ad hoc arrangements before you can take on the broader issue of organizational transformation. Not only that, it provides no help whatsoever on what's wrong with the "traditional organizational hierarchy," or what one should do to transform it. Finally, if you're searching for ideas regarding leadership, empowerment, and commitment—and the many human system issues that go with those subjects—you won't find them in this C & L book.

Why pick on Coopers & Lybrand? For three reasons: First, the views expressed in this book are representative of those found in the other process-oriented literature—which at the moment is dominating the TQM subject on the bookshelves. Second, Coopers & Lybrand has broad shoulders. The firm's excellence in wide-ranging accounting and consulting activities is well established; it can tolerate some constructive disagreement on this subject (particularly when I conclude that what the authors say is not so much wrong as it is incomplete when it comes to the matter of creating effective TQM). Third, the prestigious *American Management Association* found this book so worthy that it sponsored AMA management seminars, conducted by the two authors, all over the country. So those ideas centered on quality in the processes—and proclaiming that process improvement leads to changes that will transform the entire organization—reach thousands of managers throughout America. And Coopers & Lybrand is one of a host of evangelists who spread this gospel.

Back to the IDA report, and what McKinsey & Company and many others are finding. If this movement is to be a "process improvement" crusade, it won't be with us very long. (America's crusade trash heap stands waiting—it's becoming a real landfill.) In fact, the idea that "these new theories don't work" was a growing refrain around the country as my book was written. If that view isn't altered it will spell a very unfortunate end to the one hope we have to beat the Japanese at the quality and productivity game—and to prosper, not flounder, in the Globalization Age. The stakes are high. That's why I've been unambiguous about my concerns with the process-focused approach. Here's some more evidence of its abundance.

THE WOODS ARE FULL OF ADVOCATES OF THE "PROCESS SCHOOL" OF QUALITY MANAGEMENT: THEIR REPRESENTATIONS ARE VALID; THEY JUST DON'T GO FAR ENOUGH TO PRODUCE SUCCESS

Another of the many cases in point is the *Quality Alert Institute*. QAI is another nationwide consulting firm deeply involved in the quality movement. Like the others, QAI offers its quality management philosophies and methods as the solution for organizations seeking to install a TQM-like management approach. QAI teaches valuable tools and techniques (with a statistical flavor) in a process-related context. Its approach is very similar to others of the "process school" genre. The following excerpts from QAI's promotional literature, along with my comments, provide insight:

> Paradoxically, the most zealous quality improvement crusaders seem almost perversely determined to sabotage their own cause—and America's economic future. Most of today's growing legion of self-proclaimed quality experts deliver nothing whatsoever of value. In-

deed, many have cleverly "reframed" the quality problem to better suit their particular talents and "teaching scripts."

I've noticed the same thing! Presumably QAI is saying that most or all of the others offering opinions on quality improvement are guilty of this—but not the Quality Alert Institute. We're all guilty of that type of thinking, including me. So I stop here not to criticize QAI but to again make the point: *Which church do you attend, and which sermon is appropriate to your circumstances?* The QAI literature expands on its theme in that regard:

> Quality improvement has become an industry of its own; one of our more thriving growth industries. Its most avid customers are executives, upper-level training executives, manufacturing managers, and chief administrators of service organizations charged with the tantalizing but "widow making" responsibility of improving quality and lowering overall costs. Yet many of the "solutions" to their quality problems served up to them in such splendidly expensive packages are either misleading or useless from a practical perspective. Many, of course, are carefully staged, clearly presented, and very provocative. Some are truly inspirational. Few are capable of being put into action. Even fewer are capable of improving quality and lowering cost. In short, the record shows that a large percentage of quality improvement training programs do not get results. Strangely enough, there is a general formula that does produce results.

Not surprisingly, QAI goes on to say that it possesses that general formula. QAI says it derived the concepts underlying its general formula from Deming. Well, almost, but not quite. In that regard its literature says:

> Of late, the word "Demingism" has become "in" with any number of books and articles written about the Deming revolution and the man responsible for it. With due respect to Dr. Deming, most of his methods have been developed and perfected by scores of other statisticians. They've attempted to bring "variation detection" and "variation reduction" methods down-to-earth. Most of these "un-

sung heroes'' have been successful in this attempt. Until now, American management has not been willing to listen.

This is but one of many indications that consulting firms of the QAI persuasion trace their concepts to *"statisticians"*—unsung and otherwise. I again emphasize, however, that if you're interested primarily in your processes, it's consulting firms like QAI you should listen to. They are good at what they do. They can be helpful, so long as you don't decide that they encompass the north, south, east, and west of what productive change is all about.

It also needs to be said that many of those in academia and the consulting profession who wrap themselves in Deming's name and ideas do little to provide amplification of his broader thinking regarding "culture issues" as well as "process issues." For example, one of Deming's famous fourteen points is "institute leadership." Also, some of the other fourteen points—especially those which relate to practices Deming has deemed stupid—include admonitions to stop that particular practice and to *"substitute leadership"* instead. That being so, one could reasonably expect to find lots on leadership in this brand of the literature.

But you don't. That leaves you knowing what not to do, but uncertain about what to do. Just how do you substitute leadership? Why is it important? Where and how is it exercised? By whom? Is there an "old-style leadership" that is best left aside in favor of some new form of collegialism? What form should it take? What do you do to ensure that it creates, rather than stifles, initiative and commitment in the work force? What other dimensions must it have to make it a key to a successful quality management system? Those and related questions are of fundamental importance. You won't find the answers in the literature fixated on the "process" as the be-all of change. Indeed, you find such leadership questions and issues almost completely ignored. And that's but one more indication of an excessively narrow focus.

You need to know what to do as well as what not to do. And leadership is a central issue that can't be blinked away as something everyone will know about when you invoke the term. I can't blame all that on Deming. However, I do worry about it as an all too common thread in the process-oriented brand of the quality management literature—many of whose advocates cite their teaching approach and improvement nostrums as the "Deming way."

W. Edwards Deming is especially admired by the large number of professionals who pursue quality control and assurance as their special professional discipline. That admiration is as deserved as it is understandable. In my experience, those "quality professionals" are knowledgeable and proficient at what they do. But they can't move the elephant very far. That's because they rarely if ever run the place. Even if they know all that should be done, they can't get it done from where they sit. As the IDA study and kindred studies point out, change can only be effective and successful if the *top management* becomes deeply involved—and proactively leads the charge. That's my experience, too. If top management doesn't do exactly that, the effort boils down to a few improved "control" tools and techniques, but beyond that it's largely slogans and atmospherics—and that leads to another empty improvement crusade.

For those seeking more knowledge about the Deming views, I recommend the 1990 book *The Man Who Discovered Quality*, by Andrea Gabor. Sadly, Dr. Deming died on December 20, 1993, at age 93. He deserves great respect. However, neither his notions nor his impact rise to the mythic proportions that many accord to them. I will explain later why that is so. The fact is, his views contradict not only those of Juran but those of many others eminently qualified in this field. Thus, insight into those differing views is important to your own choices. None of that, however, diminishes Deming's secure place in the annals of quality.

Likewise, Joe Juran's contributions over five decades deserve nothing but praise and respect. And the long-standing feud between Juran and Deming should not take away from the ideas or accomplishments of either. Often it's the needs of a particular company that determine which ideas are most appropriate and applicable. If there is "one true religion" when it comes to quality management, I certainly haven't found it. The English novelist Anthony Trollope (1815–1882) was among the first to make the knowing observation that disputes are usually the most heated and rancorous when the actual differences are the smallest. That's seen in politics, philosophy, religion, and almost every sphere of human thought and activity—including the management of human endeavor. Witness the raging debate between the *Bolsheviks* and *Mensheviks* over Communism's form in its early days, as well as the broader and equally angry polemics between the Communists and Socialists for seven decades. And Trollope said about the operation of the principle in religion, "The apostle of Christianity and the infidel can meet without a chance of a quarrel; but it is never safe to bring together two men who differ about a saint or a surplice."

Accordingly, when it comes to devising their quality management initiatives, managers should look not to the narrow differences in the "expert opinion"—heated though the dialogue may be—but rather to the broader issue and decide whom they believe and what they're going to do. My own experience is that you can't narrow the effort down to a few pieces of an overall management system, or to new process improvement methods alone—no matter how impressive and useful those tools and techniques might be. Indeed, there's growing proof that companies can achieve successful change to new, more relevant ways, **only** by doing it in a total system context.

That broader aspect of achieving successful change—through a holistic, humanistic approach—takes the search for wisdom to those who address overall management system issues in informed ways. They are every bit as important as the "quality pioneers" to a complete dialogue. And in more cases than not, they are being brushed aside in the rush to the perceived finish line by those following the process rabbit. That's a big mistake. Let me tell you why.

EFFECTIVE MANAGEMENT CHANGE MUST TAKE INTO ACCOUNT THE ADVICE OF OTHER CONTRIBUTORS TO THE QUALITY MANAGEMENT DIALOGUE

To understand what a TQM-like new system (with the proper foundation) is about in its broad ramifications and techniques, the CEOs and other "management" (at every level in a large organization) need to draw from the thinking of both the process control and holistic management schools of thought. That includes seeking the best wisdom you can find on how to organize and lead, and also on how to build *competence, creativity*, and *commitment* in the entire work force. (That's the essence of leadership. More in chapters 8 and 9.)

There's a lot of such wisdom around. But, for reasons I've provided, you must look beyond the bulk of the literature currently addressing quality management. In that more broadly oriented literature you find those authors who have been espousing change in America's management practices every bit as tirelessly as the "quality pioneers." However, America's managers have been equally resistant to their advice. It's time to listen to both groups.

Turning to others in that broader management thinking, the first name that comes to mind is Peter F. Drucker—a management thinker of extraordinary intellect, insight, and ability to convey management wisdom in understandable terms. Drucker wrote *Innovation and Entrepreneurship: Practice and Principles* (1985); *The Frontiers of Management* (1986); *Managing for the Future* (1992); and some twenty other books on management, economics, and society. His works form an entire bookshelf of wisdom on the human condition and the management of human affairs. No one in American management has contributed so much for so long in the way of wise management counsel. In fact, one temptation in writing a management book is to quote Drucker on every other page. Like Deming's and Juran's, Drucker's counsel has not stuck to the ribs of most CEOs and managers. But whether they listen or not, he's still at it despite advancing years—and his advice remains as cogent and timely as ever.

Writing in the November–December 1991 *Harvard Business Review*, Drucker captured the entire quality management business in a few words: "Defining the task, concentrating work on the task, and defining performance by themselves, these three steps will produce substantial growth in productivity. . . . The fourth step toward working smarter, then, is for management to form a partnership with the people who hold the jobs, the people who are to become more productive." That goes to the heart of the matter. And the partnership is the most important aspect of all. If that doesn't work, nothing else will work well either.

It's widely known in corporate America that Deming went to Japan in the fifties and taught the Japanese useful quality control techniques. It's far less well known that Peter Drucker also made a major early contribution to the current Japanese management style. (Juran's important role, too, is far less well understood.) Peter Drucker's contribution to the Japanese style is largely lost in all the giddiness over process improvement tools and techniques, and statisticians old and new taking bows, but it's relevant to the larger point I'm making here. Drucker explained his own extensive role in advising the Japanese in his 1986 book *The Frontiers of Management*. These excerpts provide the flavor of that advice, and of its extent:

> Three foreigners—all Americans—are thought by the Japanese to be mainly responsible for the economic recovery of their country after World War II and for its emergence as a leading economic power. Edwards Deming taught the Japanese statistical quality control and introduced the "quality circle." Joseph M. Juran taught them how to organize production in the factory and how to train and manage people at work. . . . I am the third of these American teachers. My contribution, or so the Japanese see it, was to educate them about management and marketing. I taught them that people are a resource rather than a cost, and that people therefore have to be managed to take responsibility for their own as well as for the group's objectives and productivity. I taught them that communication has to be upward if it is to work at all. I taught them the importance of structure but also that structure has to follow strategy. I taught them that top management is a function and a responsibility

rather than a rank and a privilege. And I also taught them that the purpose of a business only exists in contemplation of the market.

. . . All these things the Japanese could have learned from my books and they have, indeed, been my most avid readers—some of my management books have sold proportionately many more copies in Japan than they have in the United States. But my real impact in Japan was through the three- to four-week seminars that I ran in Japan every other year from the late 1950s to the mid-1980s for top people in government and business.

. . . I have never slighted techniques in my teaching, writing, and consulting. Techniques are tools; without tools, there is no "practice," only preaching. . . . But central to my writing, my teaching, and my consulting has been the thesis that the modern business enterprise is a human and social organization. Management as a discipline and as a practice deals with human and social values. . . . Only when management succeeds in making the human resources of the organization productive is it able to attain the desired outside objectives and results.

Drucker's point that "*management as a discipline and as a practice deals with human and social values*" deserves repetition and emphasis to highlight the need for your revised approach to be both holistic and humanistic if it is to succeed. The trouble with Centralism is that it largely leaves the "human and social" values aside. Moreover, those human and social aspects are being glossed over in virtually all of the current literature—when they are at the very essence of management, just as Peter Drucker says.

It also should be a matter of special note to managers across America that Deming, Juran, and Drucker *did not* take to Japan a unified management theory that they worked out together in advance. Rather, each contributed a portion of the overall perspective the Japanese found persuasive—and thereby stirred eddies of thought and experimentation. Those eddies, over time, the Japanese turned into the holistic, team-based, quality-oriented system widely used by Japanese companies today (which the Deming Prize winners described to John Hudiburg as "*Policy Deployment*" when he went there to find out why they had been so successful in so many different industries).

The writings of these same three Americans clarify the piece of the puzzle each handed the Japanese—and its distinctiveness from the other pieces. Peter Drucker makes no attempt to describe "SQC" and other statistical tools in any depth, and W. Edwards Deming never described the ins and outs—or the benefits—of organizational decentralization in detail, as Drucker has for many decades. Joe Juran ventures cogently into broader management issues, but not to the extent Drucker does. All three have made important contributions to those who will listen. All make sense. However, none of the three deserves *demigod* status in quality management matters, or sole credit for the Japanese transformation—as far too many accord to Deming. Indeed, to single out any one of the three as the father of quality management, or as the "man who discovered quality," leads one to but one piece of a larger mosaic that comprises the whole story of Japan's success.

Skeptical about these observations? Have a favorite? Reread their books. Listen to the Japanese. In this regard, we shouldn't gloss over the role played by the Japanese themselves in putting these various pieces of advice together into a holistic system—and then spreading it far and wide among their companies and industries. (I later learned that Joe Juran holds this view, too. From his May 24, 1994, speech at the ASQC convention: "Some people believe that had these two Americans [Deming and Juran] not given their lectures, the Japanese quality revolution would not have happened. . . . This belief has no relation to reality. . . . The Japanese quality revolution would have taken place without us. That's why I tell my audience the unsung heroes were the Japanese managers.")

Also, as I've explained, the same conclusions were reached independently by several in this country (and as often as not without input from Deming, Juran, or Drucker). The ideas aren't novel, but they are timeless. And those other leaders put their conclusions—reached however—into aggressive action to create American success stories which rival those of Japan. (See the Motorola story to follow, for one example.) The difference is that the principles at work in those cases have not spread far and wide in our own culture.

The bottom line on the matter is this: America must look on "Quality Management" in much broader terms than the "process school" does—as the Japanese found both necessary and fruitful.

Some who write on these matters, like Phil Crosby, have had considerable hands-on management experience themselves—and thus are moved to discourse on wider aspects of quality management than process improvement alone. For example, though knowledgeable on process improvement methods and tools, Crosby also wrote a book in 1990 devoted solely to leadership and its important role, *Leading: The Art of Becoming an Executive*. Crosby says, "Quality is the result of a carefully constructed culture environment." And he points out that it must be in the *very fabric* of the organization—which doesn't happen without enlightened leadership and the organizational methods that build such leadership. He's right on all counts.

Beginning in the early 1980s, Tom Peters has made major and incisive contributions to the nation's management dialogue. As most know, Peters is the author and coauthor of four best-selling and truly excellent books on management, starting with 1982's *In Search of Excellence*, cowritten with Bob Waterman. *A Passion for Excellence: The Leadership Difference* followed in 1985, with Nancy Austin as coauthor. In 1987 came *Thriving On Chaos*, and in 1992 *Liberation Management*. I commend all four to those who have not yet read them; all contain great wisdom.

In Search of Excellence, in my judgment, deserves a place beside the two or three best management books ever written. That's so in part because it flew directly in the face of the conventional management wisdom of our times. It zeroed in on the purported but unproven efficiency of centralized management, laid bare its serious shortcomings, and positioned it at the root of America's management problems. To illuminate their theme, Peters and Waterman cited numerous companies that were significantly outperforming others in their industries. They do it, the authors found, with a decentralized approach that significantly increases employee focus and commitment—along with curing the many other failings of the centralized approach. The authors also found that dismantling centralization leads to far greater quality, productivity, and profitability.

So *In Search of Excellence* was significantly different from the usual outpouring of management "wisdom" that reaches the bookshelves. It stood out because it systematically questioned the prevailing wisdom—and pointed out how embedded that highly touted centralized approach had become in the American management style. Peters and Waterman say that when they wrote it they expected it to sell a few tens of thousands of copies at most. It sold more than 8 million. Clearly it struck a responsive chord—as well it should have. And its message is even more relevant today, because since 1982, when it was published, the Japanese have shone an unflattering spotlight on the same centralist management policies that the book addressed and discredited.

Peters has augmented his books with countless articles, speeches, and seminars, all on the same general theme. But despite his best efforts, along with those who think as he does, the shopworn conventional wisdom of Centralism remains alive and well in corporate America. In fact, though *In Search of Excellence* sold more than 8 million copies, Peters laments the lack of effect on the *Fortune* 500 companies. He provides numerous anecdotes to back up his lament. The book's message did not get to everyone in the lofty reaches of America's corporate boardrooms, that's for certain. The indifferent continue to greatly outnumber the inspired when it comes to decentralized management in that important segment of the management population. Nonetheless, even there the book's effect was discernible. If nothing more, it made a dent in the self-satisfaction of the centralizers. More importantly, it helped lots of managers to recognize, and to question, the centralized management style. For a while the book even touched off a recognizable management countertrend, in the literature and in actual organizational practices. But then it somehow got lost, or at least most of its themes did.

Ironically, the quality management movement has given managers of the traditional persuasion reasons to set aside the basic issues of centralized versus decentralized management systems. After all, this process quality business is supposed to provide all the improvement magic a business needs. But that's just not so. As processes improve, it cuts out much of the wasted effort and rework, thus enhancing productivity. However, productivity is a far broader matter. And building it leads directly to the issue of management systems. Specifically, it leads to a question of the system that is best at building the motivation and commitment to create far greater quality and productivity. The latter subjects are a specific strength of the writings of Tom Peters. They are a specific weakness of most of the process-oriented literature. Don't believe me? Read more carefully. Often the key message is found between the lines.

Tom Peters pays lots of attention to the human element, and to the issues of attitude, motivation, and commitment. All his books reflect that. He and Bob Waterman, in the pages of *In Search of Excellence*, were the first to draw serious attention to "diseconomies of scale" (the antithesis of what centralization is alleged to provide). Those diseconomies result from centralization—but they are caused by its incompatibility with basic human nature. Peters and Waterman talked about the human "transactions" that make up the lifeblood of any organization. And they pointed out that the complexity of those transactions goes up *geometrically* as the numbers of people involved increase *arithmetically*. My own experience reinforces everything they said on the matter. (In fact, it's those very transaction and scale issues that the team-based, decentralized approach addresses—along with a host of other features of Centralism that are crippling the American management style.)

However, any book that attacks centralization as effectively as *In Search of Excellence* did will excite criticism and derision. If even one of the cited companies faltered, even though it might later spring back, it became front-page news. In many columns and articles the book was seriously mischaracterized—out of either ignorance or maliciousness, or some of both. Tom Peters, in an excellent article for *INC.* magazine's "Coming of Age" issue of April 1989, said this about those criticisms and what *In Search of Excellence* was all about:

> According to popular perception, it was a declaration that all was right with America, a sugary tribute to our largest enterprises. One reporter labeled me "the Dr. Feelgood of American management." . . . [But] *In Search of Excellence* was definitely *not* about American excellence. Rather it was about a few rare pearls in a sea of growing despair. We contended that bureaucracy and narrow, linear thinking were doing us in, that the typical U.S. company had largely forgotten about execution, quality, innovation, and people.

In the same article, Peters addressed the evolution of his own thinking on management matters. And he singled out the abundant evidence he has found that the organizational approach is of overriding importance. He spoke to the spirit and productivity he saw in small teams of individuals—zestfully accomplishing the nearly impossible—while he was in the Navy's *Seabees* out in the field. He then contrasted that with the great bureaucracy, busywork, and wasted effort he saw while serving in the Pentagon in his last two years in the Navy. Working there alongside him were many of the same people whom he had known in the field. So he asked himself the question: "Why did people who were so productive in one setting become such bureaucrats in another?" That created in him, he says, a special curiosity regarding the effect of organizational scale and structure on employee behavior. And he was interested in pursuing that subject when he left the Navy and joined McKinsey & Company as a new Ph.D. Fortunately, he found at McKinsey a managing director who shared his intense interest in the effects of organization on human behavior and business outcomes. So Tom's first McKinsey assignment was associated with those behavioral issues. He explains that his study had just begun when he ran into the "matrix":

> Thus [from complex strategies] was born the matrix, an amazingly complicated organizational structure that had become quite the rage. My erstwhile McKinsey colleague, Allan Kennedy, had a model of one such matrix, which he kept on his desk as a reminder of those days. Called a decision grid, it measured two feet by three feet by six inches . . . [and it] specified the responsibility of every executive in the company for every decision to be made. Nothing was left to chance. It was the ultimate expression of the rational, mechanical approach to giant company administration. . . . My first published article, which appeared in the journal *Business Horizons*, was an out-and-out attack on the silliness of the matrix structure. . . . It was a hard sell back then, and prompted open derision in some circles.

It's still a hard sell. And it gets little attention in current management literature. Moreover, I find in my travels that virtually all managers take its benefits for granted. They simply do not look for its detrimental features or stop to examine why it was adopted in the first place. Consequently, "*matrix management*" remains a key facet of the centralized approach, in large organizations especially, and it continues to do its damage throughout corporate America. It's bad on two main counts. First, it doesn't do what it's designed to do. Second, as an "overlay" (a contrivance) to the centralized structure and its imperfections, it obscures the need to dismantle centralization completely.

Ever since those earliest days as a student of management practices, Tom Peters has been zeroing in on organizational issues—and on the ways in which employees are affected either positively or negatively by organizational scale, structure, and style. Granted, Peters is not the person to provide detailed instruction on Statistical Process Control, Taguchi methods, or the related statistical techniques to analyze your processes. On the other hand, the process school of quality management thinkers are not the ones to tell you about overarching organization, leadership, and human system issues as Tom Peters and Peter Drucker do.

Two notes of special caution: First, don't be taken in by the "process school" that they're describing in toto what the Japanese have done to be so successful. They're not—and the Japanese will tell you that. Second, process-oriented change advocacy comes in many names. "Reengineering" is one example. Sounds new and different, but on examination it's the same narrow process perspective dressed in new jargon. Reengineering processes simply cannot lead the change parade. You must restructure, redefine, and reorient as well as reengineer. Start with the people aspects. Go about change in that context—and alter your processes as a natural successor to the other changes—with everyone's help. Reengineer flawed processes? Yes. But real change involves far more. Thus your own need for a broad perspective on what effective and lasting management change is all about.

Well, is that it—two groups of advisers on management matters? Not at all. There's still a third group—as important as the first two. Every bit as much as the quality management movement needs the statisticians (and their tools and concepts) and those who write knowledgeably on broader matters, it also needs to learn from the successful organizers and leaders themselves. I'll address that matter in chapter 7 in discussing the "system" issues.

THE PROCESS PILLAR IS EXTREMELY IMPORTANT— BUT THERE'S A LOT MORE NEEDED THAN IMPROVING PROCESS SAVVY AND FOCUS

I fully agree with those who contend that quality and the means to achieve it have been ignored for far too long in a majority of American companies. Surveys show that most companies are not even good at defining the product and the customer, much less the specifics of the processes. So it's little wonder they have poor understanding of the process improvement methods and tools now available. But there are many issues to be considered that transcend the highly interesting but comparatively narrow subject of process improvement tools and techniques. I emphasize that I have no wish to come across here as the skunk at the process improvement garden party. All the successes I have had in both the public and private sector depended on improving processes, using techniques similar to those now widely being recommended. However, those successes also were based on a lot more than that, and depended on changes that are barely addressed in that literature. Also, it's a widely observable phenomenon that narrow attention to process issues diverts attention from the broader changes that are required for successful ways for our new days.

It's reassuring that more and more companies are recognizing the need to change their ways. It's far less reassuring that most are seizing on process improvement methodologies as the cure for all their organizational ills. That mindset leads them to jump at the chance to install another "overlay" to their centralized, functionalized organization in the form of councils, committees, and "cross-functional" process improvement teams. In fact, most companies now adopting change have just added the "process committee overlay" to the "matrix overlay"—allowing their cherished precepts of Centralism and functional structure to proceed otherwise undisturbed. I see that frequently, and survey results reported by IDA, McKinsey & Company, and others reveal the same pattern. Unfortunately, that process committee overlay adds even more complexity to organizational relationships that are already too complex. And it further clouds authority, achievement responsibility, and accountability—which badly need clarification, not added confusion.

Fact-finding is important. Consensus-building is important. Sharing quality perspectives is important. Creating a process improvement mindset is important. Committees can be useful in all those respects. However, they should not be seen as paragons of efficiency in getting the actual work done. In one of my many career incarnations I served as senior United States member to the *Military Committee of the United Nations.* Also, as a senior military official, I got lots of close-up and in-depth looks at committees in operation in other forums—such as in the U.S. Congress. Committees are unavoidable in the U.N. and Congress, but in neither place do they serve as models of swift and decisive action or of fixing responsibility. While committees have a definite place in a restructured system, running an organization on a committee basis against fast and agile competition is a recipe for oblivion.

Moreover, surveys reveal that the process committee overlay to the traditionally managed organization is winning limited employee acceptance at best. In fact, there are growing indications it's creating even greater alienation. The employees soon write system revision of that variety off as but one more in the long chain of crusades, all of which involved a new set of bugles and bangles—but no more bucks in their pockets (and no increase in their psychic pay in the form of increased authority either). They can't be fooled by new slogans and innovative ways to hold meetings. They're either organized small, with real authority, or they're not. They're either given a greater voice, or they're not. They either receive a share of any added success they produce, or they don't. No group in America is better at sorting out the difference between mouth and movement than the frontline employees. They've had lots of experience.

The "process" issue is very, very important, or I would not have included it as one of the Five Pillars. However, the nation's cento-cracies can and do adopt these process tools and techniques and still leave the rest of their organizational principles and practices as they are. Adopting these process improvement tools alone doesn't make that much difference. They will, however, make a huge difference when combined with other decentralization and quality-oriented principles put to work in a team-based structure.

I find from extensive interactions with widely varied business audiences that the hardest part of the decentralization concept to grasp is the difference between functions and teams as the organization's building blocks. That's particularly true for lower- and midlevel managers simply because in 90 percent of America's businesses they have never seen teams used in the permanent structural way. Therefore, the TQM principles highlighted in this account will benefit all organizations seeking positive and successful change. They work everywhere.

A CLEAR-CUT EXAMPLE OF CHANGING FROM FUNCTIONS TO TEAMS—AND USE OF A PRODUCT FOCAL POINT FOR PURPOSE AND ACHIEVEMENT

This case involves the maintenance of the many *black boxes* found in a modern fighter aircraft. Those electronics provide the aircraft's brains for complex functions like navigating at very low altitude, advising the pilot of threats, finding targets in the air and on the ground, delivering munitions with pinpoint precision, and all kinds of allied functions. Once we had our flightline maintenance reorganization well under way in TAC, I turned my attention to the supporting maintenance aspects, including the black boxes. Those maintenance elements were centralized and functionalized, as were all the others. So I knew what to look for, and I knew how to fix it. The black boxes are handled behind the flightline in "off-aircraft repair" facilities, which have special equipment and special know-how for complex repair of that nature. Besides the black boxes, this category includes the jet engines, the pilot escape system, and so on.

I began this particular before-and-after saga with the black-box repair facility for the F-15 Eagle fighter wing at Langley Air Force Base, near Newport News, Virginia, on the Chesapeake Bay. TAC headquarters also is there. That made it possible for me to be personally involved as we crafted our new approach. (I had a clear vision of the changes we needed; but, of course, success lies in the details. And as always, it was my practice to learn the many nuances of an activity before embarking on the new architecture.) When I first entered the black-box repair shop there, I was met by the shop supervisor, a senior master sergeant. He was sharp and articulate. And he was very proud of his operation.

Fifty-five people worked there. As our dialogue began, I asked, "Who do they work for?" His answer was, "They all work for me." Little wonder. The shop was organized by function, and in all other respects according to the centralist catechism. As we talked, it became increasingly clear that he busied himself with the glut of administrative detail involved in an effort of that size. There were no teams. There were no leaders, other than him. There were no recognizable goals. And he worked in the managership mode, not the leadership mode. I didn't see any of that as his fault. That's what the centralized system expected of him, and that's what he was doing to the best of his ability.

As I had expected, there were no specific measurements of the outputs of the various work units. And there was no visible linkage with the larger flying mission of the wing. (No overall product perspective in that integrated context.) In fact, the workers at the black-box repair facility were living with a rule, "*first in, first out*," in deciding which black box to repair next. It was like the priority system in a shoe repair shop—never mind that a fighter airplane might be grounded because its radar set was "last in." (The functional arrays of Centralism lead to all kinds of dumb practices like that—you soon find each functional silo doing "its own thing.") As I turned to in-depth discussions with the fifty-five employees, I found them alert and well-intentioned. But they were focused on their own jobs—not their group product—and blissfully unaware of how well their shop was doing in carrying out its responsibilities. Again, that was not their fault. It was the system, and they were but actors in the familiar drama of centralized management. Rather than elaborate further on how it was organized, I'll describe what we did. The Centralism precepts we undid will be obvious.

First, we switched to teams to provide a decentralized perspective and team empowerment—all in a specific product context. By so doing we created focal points of *ownership, objectivity*, and *obligation* that simply do not exist in centralized, functionalized organizations (in part because there are no good hooks to hang them on; in part because no one seems to think it's necessary). With the workers in on the architecture, we restructured the shop organization from a single function of fifty-five people into a team-based structure of eight separate teams. Four teams were formed on each of the two shifts. Each team was given achievement responsibility, authority, and accountability for a specific set of black-boxes. A leader was appointed for each. That was not a layer; the leader had the same hands-on skills as the team members, but also was responsible for team supervision in every sense of the word. That included team training and counseling, and the leader also formally evaluated the team members. Thus, the team leader had real authority, not just cheerleading responsibility. That leader also became the focal point for the team's accountability.

Before, the one and only boss—the senior master sergeant—did all that for everyone. You can imagine how easy it was to be a nonproducer in such a system. I have found that only a decentralized, "organize small" system is good at unearthing the unwilling and the unable. Usually the unwilling merely need motivation, and the unable more training. But it is almost impossible to sort that out when they're all lumped together in an amorphous mass.

Those actions were just the start. We still needed a product orientation, not job orientation, and we needed goals, measurement, comparison, and feedback. So we put up a scoreboard in each team's area. We worked out goals with full team member participation, and then measured against those goals. All were tied to *their* product and its relation to the wing flying mission. The measures of merit we established were those all agreed were highly important. And they were kept as few, and as simple and straightforward, as possible. We provided end-to-end visibility on every black box on the base and on its repair status, along with information on black-box shortages in any of the fighter aircraft. Our data base showed how many replacement parts of that type the flightline needed, on average, per day, and how many spares were available in the system. Because of that new system visibility, and a new sense of authority, the workers themselves changed the previous repair priorities. For example, "first in, first out" quickly was changed to "most needed, first out." Simple change, impressive results. Similar initiatives flowed thereafter as the team members came up with a stream of ideas.

We also kept score on the output of each team, such as the number of boxes repaired per shift by type. Those results were then compared to goals, history, and the data from like teams (both locally and in other TAC F-15 wings). The day and night shift statistics in each shop were also compared. If a repaired box turned out to be bad on installation, we had a simple coding system to trace it to the repair team. Some goals were focused on product quality. Understandably, they took absolute priority over the quantitative measures. That new system provided a feedback mechanism for each team on the quality of its product. If unfavorable patterns emerged, we could address them quickly before they had serious consequences. That fixed a principal weakness in the previous system: an absence of visibility into problem causes and sources. When I later ran into a similar measurement approach at Honda and Toyota I was not surprised at their in-depth, detailed insight.

It's extremely important to see the smoke before the barn burns down. Carrying that metaphor further, the absence of adequate performance insight at all levels means that Centralism's smoke detectors are designed to sense only major conflagrations. Moreover, they don't tell you with accuracy where the fire originates. I've seen many such organizations that have become adept at firefighting. They should be; they get lots of practice. On the other hand, I've seen few that are good at fire prevention in the sense of detecting shoddy performance early and eradicating it. In TAC, our new focal points and scoreboarding techniques provided all the smoke detectors we needed for incipient fires. We saw fewer and fewer as the other positive aspects of our reorganization took hold.

Clearly, you need to be sure that you use the system and the system doesn't use you. In that respect, you need to be alert to the "incentive" such a system provides—to a few—to fudge the numbers to look good. That, of course, can set off an escalating contest to manipulate the facts. Those are not reasons to rule out such a measurement system, but reasons to design and operate the system so that it will operate accurately, honestly, and productively. That reality doesn't impede the Japanese from improvement by such means, and it didn't impede us in TAC either. Indeed, I've found it far easier to cope with those human impulses than it is to operate in the dark, and to manage by intuition about what's going on at both micro and macro levels. I've heard it said this way: "In God we trust; all others bring data." I put it differently: "I trust you to want to get better and to tell the truth so you can—and the data helps us recognize where and how we can—together. Where you need help, holler."

None of our measurement and comparison in TAC was done in an outright competitive context. It was merely a way of providing visibility and objectivity for each team to judge its own product by relevant *benchmarks*. The feedback went to the workers directly, not through managers. It was a case of *their* product, *their* outputs, *their* obligation, and *their* rewards for achievement. And they looked on it that way. Intervention seldom was needed. Facts speak loudly for themselves, and the system became largely self-correcting. Moreover, it provided ownership. Each team now had overall product responsibility for keeping aircraft shortages from happening—not just the "job" of fixing the next part to show up in the repair line. They now had wall-to-wall visibility into, and authority over, the product cycle from beginning to end, not lifeless chunks of it. That provided a focus, a dynamism, and a sense of obligation to their activities that had been missing before. More people were exercising leadership down where the problems arose. Thus, we had more and better leadership.

As a direct consequence, productivity in that Langley black-box repair facility improved 30 percent in that first year, and kept climbing. Quality also greatly improved. That success pattern was repeated in the scores of off-aircraft repair facilities throughout TAC. In fact, the improvement statistics in our jet engine shops were even more remarkable. The same team-based approach was applied in all cases, and it worked everywhere. The workers liked the new system, and reflected new enthusiasm for their activities. That was an objective as well as subjective assessment—our reenlistment rates quickly climbed, and improved by 136 percent. When you cut the turnover rate, and the turnover training costs, by more than half it's a telling indicator of satisfaction with the system, and of its cost efficiency as well. The supervisors also liked the new system better. They also had more authority and latitude—and everyone likes to coach a winning team.

This black-box story is but one of many that made up the overall TAC transformation. The principles applied were the same in all cases. Variations on the theme were developed to fit the particular activity involved; also, variations were encouraged to fit special circumstances at different locations. This was not *"one size fits all,"* the battle cry of Centralism. However, there was an overriding *human system theme*. And we didn't allow people to use the old "we're unique" excuse to invent different laws of human nature—or to opt out of the changes.

Our commitment to the decentralized, leadership approach was complete and unwavering. But we were flexible, and we got everyone involved in the architecture so as to make it everyone's system. That produced greater commitment, which in turn produced significant improvement in every organizational element. I am convinced, from the TAC experience and many others before and since, that we could not have achieved anywhere near these results by simply improving our process savvy. That's a part of it, but substantial improvement takes far more than that.

THE PROCESS PILLAR IS OF FUNDAMENTAL IMPORTANCE. NO NEW SYSTEM WILL SUCCEED WITHOUT IT—BUT IT CANNOT STAND ALONE

The Process Pillar is but one of Five Pillars, and it depends on the others to carry out its important role in supporting a holistic, humanistic system. You can't build success on a single pillar.

The Japanese don't try. In fact, no one yet has pulled that off—though many continue to give it their best shot. The bottom line is this: It's high time to broaden the quality dialogue well beyond the matter of process. If we don't, this particular quality crusade, like its predecessors, will end up not mattering much, and America's competitiveness will further erode.

For expressing that strongly held view I fully expect counterfire from those of the statistics-based, process school of quality management. But that's OK. I flew 280 fighter combat missions in two wars, and I've been fired at before. I'm not looking for a war. And I'm not looking to further divide the quality community into opposing camps. However, this issue is of such central importance that I feel obliged to address it, and to do so as unambiguously as I know how. There's room for lots of different views. But advice that focuses excessively on one aspect to the exclusion (and the detriment) of all the others must be challenged.

So we come down to the pivotal question of what quality management is to be based on. Here is where the most important split of all divides expert opinion. It's pivotal because 95 percent of businesses need broad systemic changes—not patchwork changes that leave the traditional style basically untouched. It's also my experience that the readiness of managers to adopt the decentralized approach is greatly enhanced by an understanding of Centralism's features and failings—and of how their own management system is being affected by that old-time religion. In that spirit, chapter 7 addresses why change must involve the entire system, not a few pieces of it. It also explains the history of Centralism, why it's so destructive to quality and productivity, and further explains why process committee overlays and other contrivances to make Centralism work won't get the job done.

TQM Involves the Entire System, Not Pieces of It

IT'S THE SYSTEM THAT COUNTS,
NOT PIECES HERE AND THERE

As John Hudiburg, creator of the Florida Power & Light success story, points out, you can't graft a few new pieces onto your old management system and expect it to produce effective quality management. Hudiburg knows; they tried that at FPL, and it didn't work. The lesson he learned by studying the Japanese, he says, is that "quality improvement teams, and, indeed all of the other parts of a TQM system are each well worth doing in their own rights. . . . But it is all of them working together in a systematic way that produces the dramatic results companies really want. Anyone interested in quality management must consider it as a complete management system." For the TQM principles to work together *systematically*, you must build the entire management system on them. You can't use a few pieces of those principles or apply them to a few pieces of the organization and hope to succeed, as many have now found out.

Accordingly, this chapter examines the systemic influences that the centralized and decentralized approaches—and their contrasting principles—bring to an organization. And to shine that spotlight as brightly as possible, I provide an in-depth look at Centralism's features and failings. A good way to start on those overall system issues is to turn to the third group of important contributors to the quality management dialogue: the *successful* organizers and leaders themselves. No dialogue on how to improve American management is complete without them.

TO IMPROVE THEIR SYSTEM, AND THEIR COMPETITIVENESS, MANAGERS ALSO NEED TO LEARN FROM THE SUCCESSFUL ORGANIZERS AND LEADERS

Their theories and convictions result not from theoretical musings but from proof in practice. Considering the views of those proven achievers helps drive an even greater wedge between centralization and decentralization as a guiding organizational principle. Unfortunately, most who have done it surpassingly well themselves don't write books and articles. However, others increasingly are looking for such successful exemplars, and writing on the perspectives and the principles that created their successes. That's all good. Alas, however, you're still left with the very real problem of sorting out those books from the many that continue to preach the old-time centralized management religion, albeit in new dress and new jargon.

Some, a few, do express themselves. Take, for example, Lee Iacocca's two books, *Iacocca* (1982) and *Talking Straight* (1988), on his dramatic rescue of the floundering Chrysler Corporation. Both are full of useful tips on bringing about organizational change. Others thought so too. *Iacocca* sold 6.5 million copies; *Talking Straight* was a big best-seller as well. His second book, written several years after the first, contained some interesting insight into the further evolution of Iacocca's management philosophy. One assumes Iacocca had ample reason to be smug and self-satisfied with the techniques he had used originally, since Chrysler already had been saved from the ashheap, and had recovered strongly. Not so, however. Among other passages in *Talking Straight*, I found two to be most revealing and relevant to the system issues I'm addressing in this chapter.

The first: We appointed a brand manager for product and a brand manager for marketing, and we told them: "You two are going to be like Siamese twins. Live with each other. Get together day and night." Turned out, the idea was a fiasco. How did I find out? Because in a lot of the skip meetings [communicating several layers deep], people told me it wasn't working. I heard the same things over and over again. There should be one guy, not two. Also, the current two weren't able to get access to the company's resources early enough to have real responsibility. They were stuck on the outside like cheerleaders. That's how I discovered that we had to take the system apart and give the brand managers genuine power.

The second: Last year [1987] I decided to reorganize Chrysler. . . . I came to the conclusion that I wasn't using all my people to their fullest potential. I was deep in talent, but it was arranged in such a monolithic way that I couldn't get second-level people into the flow of things. . . . [So] I decided to make a number of my second-tier people more accountable. At the same time, I wanted to deploy them so they'd be closer to the marketplace. . . . And so I divvied up the company into manageable pieces and told these executives to go play the game to the hilt. It's now their show. Make it or break it.

That Lee Iacocca continued to unearth such Centralism style management practices hurting the "New Chrysler" shows how deeply embedded those practices had become in the Chrysler management style—and how much they were taken for granted as ideal. It's also interesting to note what Iacocca substituted for those flawed practices. He decentralized, eliminated the "two boss" ambiguity, and made the delegated authority real, not illusionary. (Being "stuck on the outside like a cheerleader" just doesn't hack it.) Chrysler's crisper lines of authority also provide much easier means of affixing and tracking accountability. And track you must if you're to continue to improve. Iacocca explained that need as follows: "Let's say you've done a good job of delegating. Even if the people to whom you've assigned responsibilities are top-notch, you must let them know that you remember what you gave them and you're keeping track, for everyone's sake."

Chrysler's problems in this regard certainly were not and are not unique. What makes Chrysler and Iacocca different is that they faced up to them. Most senior managers in American business still have not—their devotion to Centralism precepts and practices continues unabated. Some might quarrel with my using Chrysler as an example. However, it is incontestable that Chrysler is much, much better than it was, and is getting better in all ways, including product quality. Moreover, Chrysler has done an excellent job of holding market share since Iacocca's arrival. And that's in contrast to the General Motors performance, where one finds less energetic commitment to replacing the flawed management practices of old.

America's managers also can learn much from other successful business leaders, such as Robert W. Galvin of *Motorola*. If there was an all-time, *All-American Team* for management, Bob Galvin rightfully would be among the very first selected. That's because he understood and practiced *quality management* for decades before it became a popular subject and before anyone had any reason to study the Japanese. He didn't learn it from anyone else; he helped invent it. As a result of Galvin's great insight into the issues of management style and process quality, the Motorola of today reflects the benefits of a smooth blending of those two imperatives into a holistic, humanistic approach. (Frank Shrontz used Motorola as one of the models for his transformation of the Boeing management structure and style. Many others have similarly benefited by going to school on Bob Galvin's management philosophies and techniques.) All that makes the Motorola quality management story richly instructive.

THE MOTOROLA STORY: CHANGING TO A SUCCESSFUL "QUALITY MANAGEMENT SYSTEM" WHEN FEW WERE EVEN DISCUSSING THE SUBJECT

Motorola is a U.S. based, global company. Headquartered in Schaumburg, Illinois, outside Chicago, it has operating elements in eleven U.S. states and seventeen foreign countries. With a total of 105,000 employees, Motorola's business strategy focuses on four interrelated electronic product lines: communications, components, computing, and control. Its sales at the turn of the decade were above $11 billion, continuing a healthy growth rate. By way of comparison, annual sales were less than $3 billion at the beginning of the eighties. The balance sheet is strong in all other respects, including a low debt-to-equity ratio and a positive net profit pattern. (You must look hard among the *Fortune* 500 to find more impressive figures, and the eighties did not treat many in that august group kindly at all.)

Motorola is the largest semiconductor manufacturer in North America, and it is thriving in product areas that play into the face of Japan's special strengths in the global marketplace (the Japanese strengths in electronic products being well documented, and visible in nearly every American home). Despite that, Motorola has more than held its own—indeed, it has prospered—in that bitterly competitive market. Like General Electric, it is flourishing, not floundering from globalization: As evidence, 1990 non-U.S. revenues were 44 percent of total revenues, up dramatically from 24 percent in 1985. Motorola has even succeeded in cracking the Japanese market with several of its product lines. It also has extensive sales elsewhere in the Orient. That shows, if still more proof is needed, that Japanese companies are not invincible for those that use a quality management system that's as strong, or stronger, than theirs.

The leader who established the vision, the overarching principles, and the management style that produced Motorola's sustained success is Robert W. Galvin. He served as CEO of Motorola for thirty-one years, from 1959 until 1990, when he turned the reins over to George Fisher. (As this was written Galvin continued to serve as chairman of the board's executive committee.) Bob Galvin's leadership and Motorola's success story are inseparable. Motorola was doing well but not spectacularly in the fifties and early sixties in its primary market of radio products, especially car radios. The company was growing at a 15 percent clip—which most CEOs would gladly settle for. But there was no *black-ink barrier* in Bob Galvin's mind. He saw stagnation lying ahead on that path—and an entirely new company future through a major change in Motorola's emphasis, both in products and in the way it managed its people.

On the product side, he decided that Motorola's future lay in a wholesale commitment to microelectronics and semiconductors. Nothing about Motorola's position in that marketplace gave any reason for confidence. Other U.S. and foreign companies had a big lead in the technology, and Motorola would have to start almost from ground zero. Undaunted, Galvin laid out a ten-year plan to make Motorola the leader in the industry. The engine of Galvin's "catch-up and surpass" machine was to be far greater employee involvement and commitment through a completely different style of management. In time it was called Motorola's *Participative Management Program*—and from its very outset Galvin used it as the vehicle for a total reworking of the corporate culture and organizational approach. It was a wide-ranging program that changed the entire management system. The premise behind it was uncomplicated: If Motorola could build greater employee motivation, and do it better than the competition, it could overtake and surpass the others despite their head start. A simple premise—but making it happen was the challenge.

I won't detail all that Galvin did; others have written comprehensively on the subject. However, elaboration on a few of the techniques he used—way back before most were even thinking about quality management—is useful, since those principles and practices work equally well today. As a cornerstone, Galvin established the character and culture of the company he wished Motorola to be. He based the new "Motorola culture" on "respect for the dignity of the individual, and uncompromising integrity in everything we do." As Motorola's leaders see it: "The result is a thriving company that constantly transforms itself while adhering to beliefs that are not subject to change."

Part of that new culture was a far more intense focus on the customer. Galvin called Motorola's "fundamental objective" nothing less than "total customer satisfaction," and he used that intense customer focus as the pivot for all other elements of the Motorola character, culture, and climate. He also realized he might as well not start if he could not get the full support and involvement of every Motorola employee. To mobilize that support, he carried out a massive decentralization of the Motorola organization, providing new empowerment and ownership throughout. He also significantly flattened the organization and instituted a ''team concept'' approach that was radically different from the way Motorola had been organized and managed.

Galvin simultaneously laid the groundwork for a new incentive compensation system which would involve all employees and give each a *clear stake in the outcome*. As a consequence, Motorola has long been unique among America's industrial firms in having an incentive bonus system that reaches every one of its thousands of employees. It's not just eyewash—it allows employees to increase their salaries by as much as 40 percent, depending on team and individual accomplishments. That's exceedingly rare in corporate America, even now. Lots of incentive compensation programs for managers, almost none for workers. Creating an entirely new level of employee focus and commitment from those measures, Bob Galvin also took vigorous action to improve communications throughout the company—downward, upward, and laterally. And by establishing coordination committees operating within the team concept, he brought about far better mutual support.

As in all successful quality management programs, Galvin also gave far more emphasis—and committed far more resources—to training. *''Motorola University''* was established, with a university culture to go along with it, to ensure adequate training at all levels to ''nurture the creative skills.'' Reflecting that strong training emphasis, Motorola has had a long-standing commitment to provide at least one week of *formal* training for every employee, every year. Where needs suggest, they provide much more than that. That's but one element of a training approach that goes well beyond that found in most *Fortune* 500 firms. (Again, the training pattern found in the most successful companies is quite consistent—and quite different from that found in most businesses.) Currently, about 40 percent of that training is specifically dedicated to the subjects of quality improvement and cutting cycle times.

Motorola knows what it does better than others, and sticks to it with tenacity—and with the mechanisms and investments that promote continuous renewal and rejuvenation. Also, Motorola puts its money where its mouth is, spending over three-quarters of a billion dollars annually on research and development. That ratio of R&D

expenditure to total sales rivals the most aggressive Japanese companies.

Well, that's fine, but how about all this process improvement business? Motorola has long been a leader in that as well, and it has never stopped to rest on its laurels. The Motorola people talk all that jargon and apply the latest concepts along with the best of them. Particular sensitivity is paid to the need to keep the tools and methods fully understandable to the employees who must use them. As a reflection of its emphasis and its leadership in this area, a few years ago Motorola committed itself to *"Six Sigma"* quality, and is vigorously pursuing it in all of its product lines. "Sigma" in this case is a statistical term used to describe how close a product comes to meeting its quality goal. One sigma means 68 percent of products are acceptable; three sigma means 99.7 percent, and six sigma means one is achieving process perfection 99.9999997 percent of the time. Translated, *that's only 3.4 defects per million.* And that ranks right up there with the defect standards the best Japanese companies are able to meet. As this was written, Motorola was well above the five-sigma level and closing in on its six-sigma goal.

As another example of its long-standing holistic view of quality management, Motorola has extended this same focus to its *nonmanufacturing* areas. George Fisher, who replaced Galvin as CEO, has explained how they generalized their process methodology and extended it to those nonmanufacturing areas through a program they call *Six Steps to Six Sigma.* Those steps are:

1. Determine what your product is.
2. Determine who the customer is for that product.
3. Identify the suppliers you need for your product.
4. Map out the process you must use in putting it together.
5. Examine that process to eliminate errors and wasted steps.
6. Establish measurement means to feed continuous improvement.

Note the similarity with the techniques cited earlier that are used in other outstanding businesses. And those first two steps (determine the product and the customer) are especially relevant for the non-manufacturing areas, where those two items traditionally have been most overlooked. In short, Motorola understands that reducing process variability in its manufactured goods is of critical importance—but that improvement there tackles only one portion of building a world-class organization. Beyond that, its policies and practices reflect full understanding that all those process improvement tools and techniques really won't matter much unless the employees are fired up about doing it right. Many of the companies panting passionately over the new process improvement tools are leaving that aspect aside. Motorola does not. In fact, that's the heart of its system.

This is why I describe Bob Galvin as having understood and applied the holistic approach to quality management steadfastly and progressively for more than thirty years. The extraordinary similarity between Motorola's principles and practices and those now in use by Honda and Toyota proves nothing more than the right quality management approach works equally well for everyone smart enough to adopt it.

The Motorola story also helps to emphasize that success in improving quality and productivity involves changes to the entire system, not some tinkering on the edges.

No matter how much one jawbones from the top, managers won't give up the system they know for no system at all. That's why admonitions to *"just let go"* are not only superficial, they're meaningless to those raised in a centralized system. They just aren't going to do that. Instead, they must be coaxed and conditioned into a far more decentralized system—but a system nonetheless. That new system must include a change to management tools that suit the empowerment concepts and control needs of decentralization. Those tools are far different from those used for centralized management. *So you can't just use the old habits in a new way. You have to change the old habits.* Or, as Ron Riedasch said in telling how Boeing's Corinth, Texas plant successfully changed to a decentralized system, "We had to rethink the issues and create new touchstones."

Why can't you find more Motorolas and Boeings—and their team-based, decentralized management style—among American companies? Because the principles of Centralism have such a strong grip on the American management style. And, as Boeing's Riedasch also points out, you can't develop the new touchstones without understanding the old habits. In that spirit, let's take a closer look at Centralism, why America adopted it, and why it fails.

THE AMERICAN MANAGEMENT STYLE WON'T CHANGE UNTIL MANAGERS COME TO GRIPS WITH THE FEATURES AND FAILINGS OF CENTRALISM

It's appropriate to expand on this subject because Centralism and its precepts have become so common and so traditional they're not readily recognized for what they are. I've also found if that conditioning is not understood and confronted, companies won't even consider the change to a decentralized system. Or if they do, they can't make it work because, much as GM has, they hold on to most of their old centralist ideas and methods, and that cancels out even their best-intentioned efforts at decentralization. Also, I've found in every organization I've helped to move from worst to first, in both the public and the private sector, that the managers could only appreciate in retrospect how damaging their previous centralized management style had been.

To gain better understanding of the centralist concepts and what's wrong with them let's look at their massive failure in the Soviet Union. The USSR was the world's prime and most devoted practitioner of Centralism for three-quarters of the twentieth century, and its citizens have paid a terrible price for the experience. So there's no better place to look at the features and failings of Centralism. And there's also no better way to draw lessons applicable to America's business future.

THE FORMER SOVIET UNION—A COMMONWEALTH
OF BASKET-CASE COUNTRIES FROM SEVENTY-FOUR
YEARS OF COMMUNISM AND CENTRALISM

Mikhail Gorbachev deserves great credit, if for no other reason than for keeping the Red Army in the barracks while Eastern Europe exercised its pent-up urge to break free of the yoke of Communism. But his contributions go well beyond that. He brought starkly into question all the guiding principles on which the Soviet system was based. In his heyday of introducing this profound change, Gorbachev was fond of telling people that his generation was composed of "the children of the Twentieth Party Congress." That was the Communist Party Congress at which First Secretary Nikita Khrushchev first exposed and condemned the crimes of Stalin. And, as Gorbachev was wont to explain, you can't condemn the man without condemning the system.

Gorbachev also was quick to admit that the process of globalization played a major role in cracking open the closed Soviet society. He often expressed his conviction that a closed society is an anachronism in a global society. Enter *glasnost* and *perestroika*, along with the issues of determining where they would lead, and how fast. And, as the *Iron Curtain* came down along with the Berlin Wall, the contradictions and failings of Communism (and Centralism) were finally exposed for all the world to see. And it saw that the USSR not only had faulty political and management stratagems at work, but had papered them over for so long by shielding the society from the glare of comparison. It all finally came apart at the seams.

As everyone by now knows, nothing has ever worked well in the countries of the former Soviet Union. Construction quickly starts crumbling and coming apart. Most families share their apartment with another family, or two. Worker apathy has been and remains rampant. A favorite saying was, "They pretend to pay us, and we pretend to work." Housewives still stand in line to get a paper authorizing them to stand in another line, just as they've done for years. Soviet agriculture employed some 25 percent of the overall labor force. They couldn't feed themselves. In the decentralized American agricultural sector the comparable figure is 3.5 percent of the work force. And American agriculture doesn't know what to do with its surpluses.

The formal dissolution of the Soviet Union in December 1991 did not automatically change any of that for the better. So the former Soviets are left with the questions, *What will? And when?* The answers aren't easy. They involve, for them, a vision not yet developed and a path never before traveled. Indeed, the great majority of the citizens of the former USSR appear abundantly clear on what they want to get away from. They and their leaders are far less clear about what they want to go to—except in the broadest "market economy" terms. And the reorientation obviously is slowed by years of Centralism conditioning and the continuing devotion by many to "socialist principles." Even Gorbachev, during all the years of *glasnost* and *perestroika*, as dramatic as his initiatives were, still tried to carry water on both shoulders. His book *Perestroika* helps establish that from the very start Gorbachev was out to reorient, not dismantle their system. He hoped to create a "democratic" form of Communism— one with a human face. (Still guided, however, by many of the underlying socialist—and centralist—philosophies.) He had a change of heart after the abortive coup in August 1991. However, by then events were well beyond his control.

I cite this to illustrate the complexities of changing the mindsets of managers conditioned all their lives to the merits of Centralism as a powerful adjunct to autocratic Communism. It is not condemning Gorbachev to point out the confusion surrounding the dismantling of the Soviet Union as a political entity. Confusion was inevitable, and resolution won't come soon. The former Soviets will need a much clearer vision of how to carry out the needed changes than has been demonstrated to date. And facing up to that need will be painful, involving as it does the renunciation of political and management principles long embedded in every phase of Soviet life. Those old ideas will not yield easily, no matter the superficial appearances that they no longer are operative in the body politic or in the leadership mindset. Appearances, and sweeping pronouncements, can be deceiving (just as with organizational change in companies). Watch the changes in their management philosophies to judge their future success.

CENTRALISM STIFLES THE BREADTH OF MENTAL OUTLOOK AND CREATIVE IMAGINATION— DECENTRALIZATION NOURISHES THEM

That dramatic transformation is still unfolding, and the results to come are cloudy and uncertain. The abortive coup against Gorbachev in August 1991 and the bloody face-off in October 1993 between the Yeltsin government and the "Parliamentarians" reflected some of the deep divisions within Soviet society, which will not soon be resolved. And the new genre of populist politicians will have to deliver far more than free elections. They also must find the courage and the vision to overcome the vestiges of Centralism—and to replace it, root and branch, with a system that unleashes the work ethic of their people. Communism is dead. Centralism is not dead. And it's not clear how they will replace it. Bromides regarding a "market economy" form the opening line of the opening paragraph of a very thick book that is yet to be written by their actions. Their past will linger—and will not be easy to overcome. Among others, Mikhail Gorbachev understands that very well. He perhaps put it best when he said not long before the USSR's demise:

> The Soviet Union is in a spiritual decline. We have had to pay for this by seriously lagging behind, and will be paying for it for a long time to come. . . . We were one of the last to realize that in the age of information science, the most valuable asset is knowledge—the breadth of mental outlook and creative imagination.

Those are the right touchstones: *breadth of mental outlook* and *creative imagination*. All former Soviet citizens will indeed be paying for a long time for their leaders' having ignored the former and suppressed the latter. They would have spared themselves, and much of the world, all the anguish that has come from their flawed thinking had they listened not to Lenin but to another Russian, Leo Tolstoy. Tolstoy clearly had radically different ideas from Lenin on the very nature of mankind. In his monumental work *War and Peace*, written in the latter half of the nineteenth century, Tolstoy said this:

> All men's instincts, all their impulses in life, are only efforts to increase their freedom. Wealth and poverty, health and disease, labor and leisure, culture and ignorance, repletion and hunger, virtue and vice, are all only terms for greater or lesser degrees of freedom.

There is ample evidence that the centralized way of organizing and managing frustrates the elementary quest for freedom Tolstoy describes so eloquently. Lenin's approach to Communism and Centralism stifled the expression of that freedom, in both political and managerial terms. It was thus doomed to fail—but not before it had ravaged every society it touched. A look at East Germany amplifies that point.

THE DIFFERENCE IN THE TWO GERMANYS—A CASE STUDY IN MANAGEMENT STYLES

There's a lot to learn from the dissolution of Communism in Eastern Europe as well as in the USSR. Unfortunately, the management lessons are obscure to most in our country, buried as they are under the sea of rhetoric related to the collapse of the political ideology. They are there nonetheless. Consider the difference between East and West Germany when the reunification process began. West Germany had one of the strongest economies on earth. East Germany's was as feeble as West Germany's was strong; its currency was worthless and its products unmarketable. Worker apathy was as rampant as in the Soviet Union. And the fabled Teutonic thoroughness and attention to detail had disappeared.

That raises the question how such a dramatic difference could develop between workers from the homogeneous German culture. After all, the rift developed despite common origins, traditions, work ethic, and language. Why such a difference when both started from identical starting points after World War II? The quick answer, of course, is Communism, and the effects on East Germany of forty-four years within its grip. On that all could agree. That leaves, however, two questions: Which aspect of Communism? And is that aspect somehow unique to Communism, and of little relevance to non-Communist societies?

The answers are to be found in the centralist management features of the overall Communist dogma. Those features, and the structural arrangements that go with them, were installed courtesy of the Red Army along with the broader panoply of Marxist-Leninist concepts. Even though Centralism and Communism entered East Germany together, they did not leave together. The concepts of Centralism will linger, as will the damage they cause, even though Communism there has become a historical footnote. In that sense, the management lessons emerging from the two Germanys have relevance to the American experience, and to American businesses.

COMMUNISM AND MANAGEMENT CENTRALISM ARE COMPANION PIECES—BUT ARE TWO SEPARATE CONCEPTS

There's little question that Communism is closely linked conceptually with management Centralism. There's also little question that it has depended on that centralization of power and decision-making to sustain its other features. It's not true, however, that management Centralism depends upon Communism, or that it is to be found only in Communist societies. It is a separate concept, and a separate phenomenon of our times. The Communist variant of management Centralism goes much further, to be sure, than the variant found in democratic societies. The market-based economies and private ownership in Western democracies make an essential difference in the scope and application of the centralization concepts. However, that alone does not set aside Centralism's common roots, and common features, wherever they're applied.

In that regard, we know that Lenin, besides being mesmerized by the philosophical ruminations of Karl Marx, also was influenced by the management notions of Frederick W. Taylor (1856–1915). Taylor set forth his *Scientific Management* theories at the turn of the century. His time-motion studies on workers loading pig iron onto railway cars in the late 1800s, and, separately, his studies on the best "techniques of shoveling" received lots of attention at that time. He spread his notions through various papers he published and lectures, and a 1911 book, *The Principles of Scientific Management*, which was a compilation of his papers and lecture notes. Taylor's techniques for studying work flow and output were not terribly "scientific" by today's standards, but they were for that era. And they can reasonably be described as among the forerunners of what today we call "process analysis."

But that was not to be Taylor's main impact. His lasting influence instead came from his notions on how work should be managed. He believed workers always would malinger, and produce far less work than they were capable of performing, unless they were closely supervised. He believed the amount of "piecework" they would produce could be substantially increased if they were closely supervised by "functional foremen" who would ensure the workers conformed to established piecework standards. He also believed all the work should be closely monitored by "inspectors." Further, he believed the organization required a "planning department" that was totally separate from the "working department." As he espoused it, *"All possible brain work should be removed from the shop floor*, and centered in the planning and laying out department." (Emphasis added.) Another of the keys, he said, was to "Give each workman each day in advance a definite task, with detailed written instructions, and an exact time allowance for each element of the work."

Taylor's ideas attracted lots of disciples in the United States and abroad. And Vladimir Ilyich Lenin, who led the successful November 1917 Bolshevik revolution, was captivated by Taylor's ideas. Indeed, Lenin said in *Pravda* in 1918, "We should try out every scientific and progressive suggestion of the Taylor system." Lenin took those ideas and embedded them in the Communist system. He no doubt did so because their centralist themes—and their absolute disdain for workers' ability to manage their own work—fit well with his vision of how to manage an entire society.

Marx was not a humanist, though he fancied himself to be. Taylor was not a humanist, and didn't pretend to be. Lenin was not a humanist, and didn't know how to be. Their thinking, markedly devoid of a fundamental understanding of human nature, is what Lenin ennobled into a system that gave rise to autocratic thugs like Stalin, Khrushchev, and Brezhnev. Communism provides only one such example over the course of human history.

It therefore would be a mistake to isolate Communism as some unique form of philosophical cancer, not seen before and not to be seen again. Autocracy continues to thrive in many countries around the globe (and also in organizations large and small). History is full of such isms, and we have hardly seen the last of them. The point? Just this: *Worker commitment is inversely proportional to the degree of management centralization.* So if your system depends on such centralization, commitment is sure to be a casualty.

I raise the issue to emphasize that we should not place the former Soviet Union and Eastern Europe on one pole of centralized management extremes and place the United States on the other pole. We have reason to be proud of our democratic political system. No one has invented one that's any better. We have no reason to paint American management in the same colors. Some is quite good; most is not. Thus, the case of the former Soviet bloc has important application to the American experience. Those same contrasts are at work here between organizations that are centralized and decentralized, because the basic dynamics are the same.

Fortunately, that transition from the centralist orientation in America is not nearly so difficult to contemplate or carry out as it will be in the former Soviet bloc. We have more decentralized models, and fewer practical obstacles. However, that affection for Centralism must be overcome here as well. Bosses need to take a critical look at their entire management system. They must decide, as the ex-Soviets must, that they will have less control of people and more control of events. That's not a contradiction in terms. I'm convinced I had far more control of TAC on the day I left it than the day I took over, despite the massive decentralization. Actually **we** had the control. TAC ran far better because more people were exercising control, including people at the lowest levels. Decentralization, empowerment, and ownership created great improvement in our control of *events, products*, and *outcomes*. That, in the final analysis, is what organizational control is all about.

These comparisons between Centralism Communist-style and Centralism American-style may seem excessive to some, but I consider them relevant and instructive, in part because of my mounting concern over widespread insensitivity to the lessons to be learned in our own society—and the scant attention the *human spirit* receives in the management structures and techniques employed in so many American businesses.

This is not an attempt to tar all forms of Centralism with the same brush. Rather, I want to shine a spotlight on its underlying precepts and the damage they cause—everywhere. It's a point of considerable importance because the *comparative advantage* of management approaches is playing an increasingly pivotal role in sorting out the global winners and losers. That brings us back to Centralism American-style, which in turn leads to a discussion of the "matrix management" variation of centralized management. That variation spread rapidly beginning in the sixties during America's rage for Centralism. Understanding the matrix management approach—its notions and nostrums—helps you understand how the precepts of Centralism got another strong push—and thus were able to insinuate themselves more securely into the warp and woof of the American style.

MATRIX MANAGEMENT: UNDERSTANDING ITS CONNECTION TO THE CENTRALIZED APPROACH, AND WHY IT DOESN'T HELP MATTERS

Over the years several contrivances—organizational "overlays" —have been devised to make the centralized, functionalized organizational approach work more interactively and responsively. None have done the job, because all fail to address the core issues of Centralism. One such overlay is the *matrix* approach, which swept across America's centralized organizations in the sixties and seventies. Understanding the thinking behind that *matrix management* movement is a key to understanding the ills of Centralism—because it was believed to be a cure for some of the most grievous of those ills. It hasn't been, but that's what makes the story so relevant. Understanding the thinking underlying matrixing also provides clues as to why so many organizations devoutly practicing Centralism will stoutly deny that they do.

The organizational theorists who have championed the matrixing approach candidly label it an organizational *overlay*. And that's what it is. The idea is that the basic organizational structure—to which the matrix arrangement is applied—is to remain centralized and functionalized. Despite its widespread use in America, you'll will find little mention of matrixing in current management literature. It simply has become an embedded and customary part of the traditional centralized management style. (I briefly explained its role in chapter 2 in discussing the General Motors addiction to the centralized approach.) Since it's infrequently studied and mentioned these days, let's take a look at what it is, where it came from, and why it doesn't work.

Matrix management is based on the premise that you can preserve the vertical, functional flow of authority that the centralizers demand and yet address the obvious need for efficient horizontal interaction, all at the same time. That is done, under the matrix approach, by the "assignment" of the employees in two ways. First, each is assigned to a specific function with a functional boss. That's the preferred organizational model, and the way, Centralism says, to construct the building blocks. That boss has the solid line on the organizational chart—the *real* boss. The very same employee is then assigned, in a matrixed arrangement, to a project pulling together the various disciplines under a different "boss." The power of that second boss is ill defined. However, the responsibility is clear, if not the authority. That responsibility is to pull everything together for project (read integrated product) success. Thus, the "matrix" is formed at the intersection of job know-how and job performance. And the know-how side is given the real *clout* when it comes to authority. As the centralizers see it, the functional chief can ensure the employee's qualifications in the functional specialty. The inability to witness actual job performance is considered a matter of minor consequence. However, that ignores a simple truth: *How employees feel is even more important than what they know in determining job performance.* Know-how, once acquired, does not quickly slip away. On the other hand, motivation, once acquired, needs continuing sustenance and reinforcement. Seems obvious, but not to many.

The "assignment" to a second boss purports to solve the get-the-job-done issues, but creates ambiguity in the flow of authority—and makes a muddle of accountability. However, its proponents claimed, and still claim, that it will outperform any other approach. (The empirical evidence refutes that claim, but it persists nevertheless.) Because the issues are not widely understood, let's look at its use in a neighborhood supermarket. It's far from the best or most prevalent example, but it helps bring the issues down to earth. It also illustrates that small as well as large organizations must decide how to handle the matrixing issue.

Let's say the supermarket has two shifts, and look at the night shift. There are groups of employees with specific job specialties, such as cashiers, stock clerks, and meat-cutters. Each needs adequate know-how in his or her specialty. However, each also needs a strong measure of motivation to provide friendly and responsive customer service. That sets the stage for the matrix arrangement. Under the function-oriented approach to the flow of authority, the night cashiers work for a head cashier. The meat-cutters have their own meat-cutter boss, as do the other specialties. That gives the night manager, who is responsible for quality service, the unenviable task of heading up the coalition without any real authority. And the functional bosses are not around to get an adequate sense of job performance—whether it's efficient or inefficient, cooperative or uncooperative, curt or courteous. I'm assuming here that the bosses in each case work the day shift. In my experience, that's a safe bet.

As you increase the size and scope of an organization, the bosses become separated from their employees in the functional silos by distance and by immersion in paperwork, as well as by working different hours. When we switch from this straightforward example to a business with complex products and processes, the matrix management arrangements become far more complicated as well. And the issue of their efficiency becomes far more serious. When everyone who you supervise actually works for someone else, it's far more difficult to deal with lackluster performance than in the small, more intimate setting of a supermarket. Indeed, lackluster performance often becomes intractable. (GM and many others can tell you all about that.) As Casey Stengel once said, "It's easy to find the players. It's getting them to play well together that's the hard part."

A LOOK AT THE WELLSPRINGS OF MATRIX MANAGEMENT, ITS CONCEPTUAL UNDERPINNINGS, AND ITS STAUNCH DEFENDERS

The origins of the matrix arrangement and its accompanying management concepts can be traced to the early sixties. Matrix management entered the American management bloodstream as an answer to centralization's contradictions and inflexibility, and rapidly became all the rage throughout the business community. Today it remains in widespread use in America's large industrial companies. Beyond that, variants of it can be found almost everywhere because it fits the other precepts of Centralism so perfectly. Insight into how it all started, and the reasoning behind it, is available from the writings of its champions over the nearly three decades of its life span.

Representative of that literature is an article distributed in the summer of 1977 by the respected American Management Association, titled "The Human Side of the Matrix." The article the AMA found so persuasive had three authors: Paul R. Lawrence, Professor of Organizational Behavior at the Harvard Graduate School of Business Administration, along with Stanley M. Davis of Columbia, and Harvey F. Kolodny of the University of Toronto.

The authors captured the genesis of matrix management in this way: "Matrix management gained acceptance in the space age of the late 1960's. In fact . . . in the early 1970's it almost seemed to be a fad." It sure was a fad. And it still is. The article extolled the effectiveness of the matrixing approach, with "flexibility" as the centerpiece. The authors also addressed the inescapable issue of the authority flow. They framed it as an issue of power "balancing":

> Matrix managers share "common" subordinates. . . . Dual command structures, administrative and technical, maintain a "reasonable" balance of power between the two arms of the matrix. . . . In a [matrixed] functional organization, managers have authority over the objectives of their function, the selection of individuals, the priorities assigned to different tasks, the assignment of subordinates to different tasks and projects, the evaluation of progress on projects, the evaluation of subordinates' performance, and decisions on subordinate pay and promotions. . . . Much of the function is self-contained.

I leave it to the reader's imagination what tiny shred of "authority" is left to the project leader. The article went on:

> Matrix organization is more than matrix structure. It must also be reinforced by matrix systems such as dual control and evaluation systems . . . Matrix organizations assign dual command responsibilities to functional departments [marketing, production, engineering, and so on] and to product/market departments. The former are oriented to specialized resources while the latter focus on outputs.

What businesses have long been learning, the hard way, is that you need *everyone* focused on the product and the outputs. Therefore, being "oriented to specialized resources" is just another way of describing the input rather than output orientation that is rampant in centralized systems. The authors were not insensitive to the problems the dual command structure presents. In one place they used the phrase "fiendishly difficult" in describing the complexity of the resulting dynamics. However, they also cited what they saw as advantageous aspects of the dual command arrangement:

> The two arms of a matrix organization are . . . of equal power and
> importance. . . . The perceptive matrix organization manager is
> aware that subordinates have other voices to attend to, other masters
> to please. Orders that seem irrational or unfair can more easily be
> circumvented under the protection of the other boss, than they can
> in a single chain of command. . . . [Therefore] More care must be
> given to making clear the logic and importance of a directive.

The consequences of a subtle circumvention of orders are altogether obvious. Not the least is that the boss being circumvented
believes that the organization is headed one way, when in fact it's
headed another. Thus, the ambiguity in the split authority flow creates
organizational confusion, and Homeric breakdowns in communication. It also produces poor discipline and coherence, and distrust
among the players. Regarding increased supervisor sensitivity, I agree
that great sensitivity is needed, even vital. I believe deeply in persuasion, not bluster and bombast. However, that persuasion must rest on
a base of *authority* so that with all said and done, decisions can be
made, understood, and carried out faithfully and rigorously. I also
strongly advocate an interactive process, with extensive employee involvement. But that doesn't mean creating a debating society in which
bosses with conflicting views argue for acceptance based on the logic
of each argument as seen by the subordinate(s). That turns the whole
notion of authority, and accountability, on its head. Also, the disagreements between the two bosses usually involve subtleties in emphasis, priorities, and the like. That's more common than outright
internecine warfare between the two. But over time it's just as corrosive to organizational coherence and employee motivation.

The authors repeatedly commented on the matrix arrangement's
many complexities, and tied its effective operation to centralized
power at the top. For example:

> One of the several paradoxes of the matrix approach is that it re-
> quires a strong, unified command at the top, to ensure a balance of
> power at the next level down. In some senses this is the benevolent
> dictator.

The Centralism principles all fit together. Matrix management is a family member in good standing. The article also provided insight into when it started and how it spread:

Not too many years ago few managers in our classrooms had heard of matrix organization and today [1977] nearly half of them raise their hands when asked whether they work in a matrix organization.

It kept spreading, and spreading. The authors then ventured a prediction on the future of the matrix arrangement as an overlay on the vertical structure:

We believe that in the future matrix organizations will become almost commonplace and that managers will speak less of the difficulties of the matrix structure and will take more of its advantages almost for granted.

They proved to be prescient on both counts. Matrix management did become commonplace. And scores of managers came to take its advantages for granted.

These same three professors also wrote a book in 1977, *Matrix*, which elaborates on these themes. There you can find a fuller description of the overlay features of matrix management, which the authors found in both temporary and permanent forms in the practitioner companies they had studied in depth. They also discussed the many variations on how such matrices are put to work, including as many as four separate phases—with each consisting of increasingly complex matrix arrays. And they described having seen "matrices that move well beyond dual command to three and even four simultaneous lines of command." (I have seen the same thing. They're even worse.) Significantly, the authors never questioned, in either the book or the article, the wisdom of using vertical functional silos as a means of separating the authority over functions from that over projects. Only they know why. However, one passage in their book provides insight into their probable reasoning:

We see matrix, then, as being able to take advantage of the two orientations that dominate its structural arrangements. On the one hand, the scale economies of large organizations can be achieved, and on the other, the sensitivity, flexibility, and adaptability of small innovative teams is realized. The benefits of standardization are coupled with the capacity to respond to change—a way to have your cake and eat it too.

That was the thinking of the times. That's still the thinking in most business circles. Yet the track record shows that the functional arrangement does not produce the sensitivity, flexibility, and adaptability of which they spoke. Also, my experience has been that the functionalized, centralized approach produces far more diseconomies of scale than economies, no matter how cleverly you provide matrices to help resolve its many contradictions and detrimental effects. If you want the benefits of organizing small, you must organize small—and from the bottom up, not the top down. Overlays and other contrivances just don't do the trick. They may help, but not nearly enough. Worse yet, they provide lots of ambiguity and material for debate on the relative merits of centralization and decentralization. Therefore, the matrix approach clouds the issues—and helps perpetuate the centralized style. In one passage the authors acknowledged the firm grip the traditional, vertical arrangement can exert:

> The structure in most traditional forms of organization rarely changes. The patterns of political power, authority, and status and the investments in seniority and security are all bound up with a hierarchy that carefully guards career paths and maintains entrenched positions. Resistance to change is everywhere in vertically structured organizations.

It was true then; it's true now. Here is another example where the authors saw the matrix arrangement as a way of ameliorating the observed shortcomings of the vertical, function-oriented structure. But it simply has not measured up to that daunting task. However, the authors, like most others then and now, saw those shortcomings as a necessary evil in maintaining control. In fact, it has long been considered a "contradiction in terms" in American management circles —even the most enlightened—that decentralization could improve control. The authors reflected the same conviction among other places in this passage:

> Structures are intended to channel people's behavior in desired ways. . . . In the traditional pyramids . . . the structure was either centralized, and there wasn't enough freedom, or they were decentralized, and there wasn't enough control.

This widespread perception that decentralization and control are mutually exclusive was a principal ingredient in the notion of retaining the "traditional pyramid" but to ameliorate its many shortcomings with the matrix overlay. It has not worked as hoped. Nor can it, because it finesses rather than confronts the fundamental issues of authority. But those who feared loss of control seized on it as the only feasible action for organizational change from their standpoint —albeit that it was complicated and contradictory in operation. In that regard, the authors themselves, in passing, foresaw the day when more than overlaying the vertical structural arrangement would be required. Although they were not sure when, they said this:

> Assuming the matrix survives all these critical times, there may occur one final passage: knowing when to discard the matrix. Many organizations may never reach this point, and certainly no date can be fixed in its regard. But it is just as important to recognize an idea whose time has passed, as one whose time has just arrived.

To that I say Amen. And the time is now. There are signs everywhere that we need new management for new times, and a need to abandon the centralized approach itself rather than continue to overlay it to try to make it work. The authors could have challenged the wisdom of that kind of structure and style in the first place—but they did not. Such an inquiry could have produced serious questions and a thorough analysis regarding the precepts of Centralism that underlay the entire scheme.

Nor did the authors comment on the impact of the matrix management methods on the workers, though they had lots to say about the psychological impact on the managers. That no doubt was deliberate, since their subject was the management of the managers. However, that's the tendency I find so worrisome. Management in the final analysis must create worker motivation and commitment, or it won't create much of anything else. Therefore, any management book worthy of the name should have that as a pivotal issue, not give it short shrift.

In fairness, these three learned professors did not invent *matrix management*; they simply studied it and commented on it as they saw it spreading rapidly through the business world. I have reviewed their perspectives on the matrix management fad primarily to explain when this variation erupted onto the management scene, and what the thinking was that gave it its big push, so that you can understand its contribution to the staying power of Centralism.

Let's sum it up: *"Matrix Management"* is a blueprint for organizational confusion, which in some of its variations approaches anarchy. It does so in an altogether appropriate quest—the quest for more effective internetting of effort. But the clouded authority and accountability, and the continued dominance of the top-down, functional structure in decision-making and ownership, washes out almost all its beneficial effects. While good people can make it work—after a fashion—that doesn't mean it's the best approach. The best approach is not to organize in the centralized manner in the first place. There's a better way to internet and integrate the organization.

Is this a part of the past that deserves to stay buried? No, not in the least, because it's not past. The matrix arrangement, which shores up the centralized organizational approach, is still with us; it can be found all over the place. It hangs on for the same reasons that the vertical, functional arrangement stoutly resists change—defended by those protecting their turf. In protecting their "political power, authority, and status," its legions of staunch defenders will hotly defend its merits at the drop of a hat, particularly in certain businesses. For example, in industrial firms that build complex, cyclical products, the technical specialists feel deeply about "a functional home to go back to'' when projects conclude. Arguments also are advanced that you often need ''a third of an engineer on three different projects,'' and that you always need to move people around to meet shifting requirements. Those arguments then assert that functional alignment is the only logical answer. Indeed, that's one of the oldest *canards* defending centralization and functional czars.

The same issues are worked more successfully by breaking up those functional silos. In large organizations a small functional remnant can sometimes productively be retained—part of the top of the old functional silo—for arranging companywide recruitment and training for that particular discipline. However, the people who make up that remnant emphatically should have no voice whatsoever in the chain of authority. *They should be supporters, not czars.* The authority should be vested in those with multidisciplinary *product* responsibility, not functional responsibility. Even where a team remains of a single functional discipline—for adequate reasons that I explained earlier—that team should report through a product or project chain of authority, not a functional chain. For example, Honda has its ''engineers'' mixed in as required throughout the manufacturing organization. This alternative to the matrixing arrangement is exactly what I used in curing a large, troubled government procurement organization. And I've seen the same change produce equally beneficial results in lots of companies. (More to come on how to go about that different way.)

Why can't the centralizers see that the functional flow of authority hurts and hampers the organization? Because the catechism of Centralism takes job performance for granted. And that dehumanized view lends itself to enchantment with Centralism's precepts—and insensitivity to the ''feel'' part of a very complex performance equation. The champions of Centralism would profit from another piece of Yogi Berra's wisdom. He once said about baseball: ''This game is ninety percent mental, and the other half is physical.'' As Yogi suggests, the key is attitude. Enter the *human spirit*; exit approaches that dehumanize and demotivate—such as the centralized approach. But getting it to exit is a serious problem. In fact, over the years a few have warned what it would do to stifle an organization's quality and productivity. But they have been ignored. Since we must keep trying, and we may find more receptivity now, let's turn to one of the more prescient of those warnings.

THERE HAVE BEEN WARNINGS OF THE MANY PROBLEMS WITH THE CENTRALIZED, FUNCTIONALIZED, MATRIXED APPROACH—BUT THEY HAVE GONE UNHEEDED IN EVEN THE MOST ASTUTE MANAGEMENT CIRCLES

In reading countless articles and hundreds of books on management philosophies and techniques, I have encountered very few that discuss organizational structures (alongside styles) in any depth. Most give the matter glancing treatment, if that. One exception is Henry Mintzberg's *The Structuring of Organizations* (Prentice-Hall, 1979). It provides a veritable *tour d'horizon* of various organizational structures, and the policies underlying them, complete with extensive references to other authors and real-world events. Mintzberg, a professor of management at McGill University in Montreal, received his Ph.D. from the MIT Sloan School in 1968, and describes devoting his academic life from the very start to studying the theory of management policy. (Mintzberg continues to be a prolific and insightful commentator on management matters.)

His 1979 book on the structuring of organizations is chock-full of insight into management structures and their effect on employee motivation and performance. For our purposes, I call special attention to the chapters on *structural configurations*. Mintzberg chose to place them in five separate configurations: *Simple Structure, Machine Bureaucracy, Professional Bureaucracy, Divisionalized Form*, and *Adhocracy*. Given that the book was written in 1979, Henry Mintzberg observed correctly that the last, adhocracy—was the structural form that most businesses in North America had adopted. Without going into needless detail, adhocracy as Mintzberg described it is the centralized, functionalized, matrixed structure I have described in these pages. As I said, it became all the rage, starting in the sixties.

Mintzberg warned those who would listen about adhocracy's

many deficiencies. But reservations such as his were drowned out in the widespread cacophony of support—including from throughout the academic community. Let's take a look at Mintzberg's perceptive observations.

Unlike most in the business and academic communities, Mintzberg was not persuaded that adhocracy was the best answer. He saw some merit in it; back in 1979 when his book on structures was written, almost everyone did. But he also perceived its critical flaws. He described it accurately, for example, as "a tendency to group the specialists in functional units for housekeeping purposes but to deploy them in small market-based project teams to do their work." And he observed:

> [Adhocracy] is the most complex structure of the five. . . . It is [also] the newest of the five, the one about which we know the least. . . . Of all the structural configurations, Adhocracy shows the least reverence for the classical principles of management, especially unity of command. . . . Managers abound in the Adhocracy—functional managers, integrating managers, project managers.

Besides its irreverence for the classical management principles, this matrixing approach has not provided a workable substitute for them, especially for *unity of command*. Indeed, that's one of its most serious flaws. Also, Mintzberg is right about "managers" abounding in the adhocracy. In fact, they keep bumping into one another. And they form their own private *ecosystem*, which spits out lots of rules and reams of paper—which most often detracts from rather than contributes to the work going on at the frontline level. Mintzberg also saw that pervasive efforts to *formalize employee behavior* would be a natural consequence of leaving the functional hierarchies standing in this structural configuration. (And they remained every bit as common to adhocracy as they did to other centralized approaches—indeed, they proliferated.) He assessed that matter this way:

> Performance control is a key design parameter in market-based structures. But what happens in functional structures? Functional

work flows sequentially or reciprocally across them. This means that distinct organizational goals cannot easily be identified with any one unit. So aside from budgets and the like to control their expenditures, performance control systems cannot really cope with the interdependencies of functional units. . . . In other words, something other than a performance control system must be found to coordinate the work in the functional structure. . . . Direct supervision effected through the superstructure and standardization of work processes effected through behavior formalization emerge as key mechanisms to coordinate work in functional structures. They are preferred because they are the tightest available coordinating mechanisms.

That sums it up well. I've made the same point in the earlier chapters. Surveys show that where you have excessive behavior formalization as the principal management tool you get alienation and apathy, not motivation and initiative. Mintzberg also saw other problems affecting employee cooperation with the adhocracy configuration, as well as with its organizational efficiency:

Structures this fluid tend to be highly competitive and at times ruthless—breeding grounds for all kinds of political forces. The French have a graphic expression for this: *un panier de crabes*—a bucket of crabs, all clawing at each other to get up, or out. Take for example, the matrix structure, what it does is establish an adversary system, thereby institutionalizing organizational conflict. . . . Adhocracy is simply not an efficient structure. . . . Adhocracy is not competent at doing ordinary things. . . . The root of its inefficiency is the Adhocracy's high cost of communication.

Mintzberg saw problems where most did not, and these are but examples of his insights. Another of his insightful observations addressed the newness of the adhocracy configuration versus its widespread popularity:

Adhocracy is new. And every new structure, because it solves problems the old ones could not, attracts a dedicated following—one enamored with its advantages and blind to its problems. With this kind of support, time is required to bring its issues into focus—time to live with the structure and learn about its weaknesses as well as its strengths. Especially in the case of a structure as complex as the Adhocracy.

The evidence is in. Adhocracy has lots of weaknesses—and very few strengths. Or at least the strengths aren't apparent because they are overwhelmed by the weaknesses.

Mintzberg deserves high praise for his perceptiveness in issuing these caveats about the widespread enthusiasm for the adhocracy arrangement. While Mintzberg called this structural configuration adhocracy, which served his purposes well, the companies that adopted it continued to operate as *centocracies* as well as *adhocracies*. In fact, they became even greater centocracies than they had been before. The U.S. Air Force and General Motors serve as cases in point—and there are countless others. And the flexibility and efficiency that adhocracy was alleged to provide failed to show up for work. Also, the precepts of Centralism now had even more legitimacy than before—along with new legions of devout advocates. Thus, the adhocracy structural model—with its alleged management magic—provided an ideal rationale for perpetuating the centralized, managership approach.

(In the same way, most are now seizing on process improvement "magic" as an excuse to do the same thing. The evidence is in on that also. We now know that the alleged process magic isn't doing all that much for its practitioners either, at least not as long as they use it as but another centocracy overlay.)

"Centocracy" is my term here. That's what I have continually encountered in the public and private sectors. That's what GE was before Jack Welch went to work on it. The same term can accurately describe Boeing before Frank Shrontz's *Continuous Quality Improvement* restructuring initiatives broke up that centrocracy and tore down its functional walls. Alas, these few success stories aside, America has far more centocracies than anything else. There's an element of good news in that, though: That's why there is such enormous *potential* for constructive change in the American management style—and in the nation's competitive posture.

It may be useful to summarize in simple language to complement the scholarly observations of Henry Mintzberg. Knowing the alternative to adhocracy, here's how I look at that traditional organizational structure in down-to-earth terms: Let's face it. It's an old model. Time to stop taking it to the garage for new paint jobs, and instead get busy trading it in. This book is devoted to showing shoppers what the new model looks like. Believe me, it gets far more productivity to the gallon! Also, your neighbors—and your competitors—will be far more envious when you make the switch. Newfound affluence has a way of doing that. Happiness is your competitors disappearing in your rearview mirror. I've been able to enjoy that a lot. But most have not. They continue to putt-putt along with the old ways. So let's examine the many reasons the traditional style remains so stubbornly resistant to change. Knowing the resistance patterns and the roadblocks is important to transformation strategy.

HOW THE CENTRALIZED, MANAGERSHIP APPROACH PERPETUATES ITSELF

The idea that Centralism produces the greatest efficiency just won't go away. After all, its merits were preached by our business schools for several decades. Also, it's perpetuated by those attracted to the idea of banding together as *birds of a feather*. Many believe it is only natural that all engineers should report to a chief engineer, or that the procurement people should operate in their own procurement cocoon, or that other disciplines should have their own hierarchical functional silos. And they can give you abundant rationale for that— largely related to the nuances of their specialty, not to the dynamics of an integrated effort with other specialties.

Also, most such specialists, regardless of type, see the functional arrangement as their only path to higher pay and greater responsibility. They prefer a system in which they are judged by "their own kind." And most cherish the ability to climb the ladder in their functional silo without taking on bullet-biting responsibility for a specific product. That, of course, requires orchestrating the skills of many specialties. In my experience, most specialists see their strengths in terms of their technical education and expertise, not their managerial skills. Alas, far too many are justified in their technical preoccupation, because the system has never asked them to develop leadership skills. That's not their fault. It's the way the traditional, centralized system has worked, and they have grown accustomed to it. I have found that while they initially will resist change, they're some of the strongest proponents of the team-based organization once it's in place. The leadership skills they need to make the decentralized system work can be rapidly learned. Some say leadership can't be taught, but they're wrong. I've done it, and seen it done, far too often to have any doubt about it.

I emphasize here that many small companies—that have no such engineers and specialists—also are highly centralized. Centralization has little to do with overall size. Some megacorporations successfully operate on a decentralized basis, while very small organizations, of, say, twenty-five people, are highly centralized and functionalized. There are several reasons for that. First, the managers of organizations large and small are products of the same era, and have been greatly influenced by the same management theories. Second, the authoritarian approach comes much more naturally to most managers than the more complex business of consensus-building and sensitivity to the human system aspects. Third, many midsized companies are centralized because the CEO has never made the transition from an owner-operator mindset to that of president and CEO. That step involves moving from management by *presence*—hands-on, do this, do that—to management by *principles* through the medium of distributed authority. Those same influences apply to the *middle managers* running the departments, divisions, and companies within the nation's corporations. Also, everyone in a centralized organization gets conditioned to standing around and waiting for orders to come from on high. Having been steeped in a centralized, conformance-oriented system, it takes a while for them to grasp decentralized authority enthusiastically, and to share it with others to magnify its power and effectiveness.

A few refuse to make that transition. However, the great majority will, and they will make it gladly once they're sure the empowerment and ownership are real and not empty slogans. I know they will, because I've put that matter to lots of tests in both the public and the private sector. As a way of demonstrating that entrenched centralist attitudes can be changed, even in the most die-hard setting, I turn now to another example. It demonstrates the advantages that flow from replacing the centralized, managership approach root and branch—including the functionalism and matrixing arrangements on which it feeds. It's a story of still another organization that listened to the siren song of Centralism to become an entrenched centocracy —and how we moved it from the bottom of the heap to the top by changing its management system, structure, and style.

The story begins on my return from Europe, when I was given still another of the stiff tests to which I have put the principles of *Five Pillar TQM*. In this case, the challenge was to turn around a highly troubled government procurement agency, the *Electronic Systems Division* outside Boston. ESD annually bought $6 billion worth of high-tech electronics at that time, ranging from computers to communications to specialized aircraft, for Air Force and other DOD agencies. ESD also managed major programs for several friendly foreign nations. Those programs included the design and procurement of nationwide communications systems.

I was given very short notice to go to ESD and take over. The previous ESD commander had been summarily fired because of dissatisfaction at very high governmental levels with the organization's many problems. (He had been there only four months himself, and had inherited all the problems, so that was a reflection of the depth of the problems and not so far as I was concerned on him.) All I knew about ESD before I took over came from the numerous *scathing* stories about its deficiencies which my new bosses along the chain of command told me—from the secretary of defense himself on down.

Also, I was completely new to the research, development, and acquisition business. So I was being asked to learn it and change it at the same time. I later learned my reputation as a troubleshooter had overridden concern in many circles due to my inexperience in that particular business. (The previously mentioned General Dave

Jones, then Air Force Chief, was the one with the guts to send me there—despite the naysayers.) Believe me, that lack of experience also occurred to me. But I was eager to give it my best shot, and I went with no preconceptions except one: that the right TQM style principles work in any setting involving human endeavor—adapted, of course, to the setting and circumstances. That again proved to be correct.

THE TURNAROUND OF A FAILING GOVERNMENT PROCUREMENT AGENCY—THE DECENTRALIZED APPROACH AT WORK IN A HIGH-TECH SETTING

As with the Madrid wing turnaround, I present this story through the eyes of another observer rather than ask you to take my word for the scope of the change and how it was carried out. To that end, I asked Bob Doane to provide his perspective on the principles we put to work in ESD with my arrival. As ESD's senior technician for many years he saw the full range of management approaches—not only within ESD, but also in the business world. His high-level responsibilities there have allowed extensive interaction with a wide array of this country's manufacturing and services companies. He's seen good ones and bad ones, and was obliged to delve into why the bad ones were bad. So he has ample background as an informed and insightful observer on management matters. As a retiree he has no masters to please. Beyond that, he's a free spirit with a well-earned reputation in the government procurement community for telling it like it is. Here is Bob Doane's account of what we did to improve the fortunes of ESD:

> I recently retired from the U.S. government Senior Executive Service after thirty-eight years in government research, development and acquisition, including thirty years at ESD outside Boston. Twenty-six were in a supergrade capacity. For the last fifteen years I was ESD's senior civilian employee, and I also served as the division's technical director. The point of covering that experience is

to place in perspective my enormous respect for the unique abilities of Bill Creech as a leader.

Bill came to ESD as the new commander on short notice after no less than the secretary of defense himself decided we needed new leadership. The secretary was enormously dissatisfied with how some of our programs were being managed, and made no bones about it. Bill came to us from the operational side of the Air Force where his reputation was well established, but he was a "rookie" in our business. Quite frankly we expected the worst.

He said on arrival that he was "just a fighter pilot," and that he would need our help since it would take him awhile to learn the ropes. It was mind-boggling how quickly he captured the essence of our business and started making improvements. He began by asking questions about our programs—technical, business management, financial. There seemed no end to his interests or talents. He said that he wanted to be where "the action is," and that, we found, was everywhere. His imprint was all over the place, yet he gave each of us even more authority and latitude than we had before.

At that time I was the "Deputy Commander for Command and Management Systems." Our programs spanned the gamut of command and control systems, and were highly technical. We had our own special jargon and "mumbo jumbo" that allowed us to operate in our own little cocoon secure from outside kibitzing. He cracked that code in a hurry! It wasn't long before he was talking like one of us—compiler, higher order language, assembly code, and the rest—and he brought his own special brand of insight to our program challenges. We soon welcomed his involvement. We knew that when we needed his help we had an informed and sympathetic ear, and a leader who believed in tackling problems aggressively but with a reasoned and thoughtful approach.

He raised our standards significantly. All the facilities took on new standards of professionalism. He preached pride and professionalism, and he showed that those were not empty phrases. We soon were feeling a lot better about ourselves, and the plaudits soon started rolling in on the way we were doing things.

After he was secure in his knowledge of the division, and with the counsel which he constantly sought from others like myself, he started restructuring the way we were organized. As an example, one of his enduring legacies was to change our "matrix structure." He placed full authority in the hands of individual system project leaders rather than with the chieftains of functional specialties as it had been in the past. This placed clearer focus on each project, and its product, and resulted in far more responsive and informed decision-making throughout the organization.

He bored into the core of our command and control business, and was particularly masterful in assessing deficiencies and correcting them. He also introduced a wide array of initiatives to improve program management within ESD and the defense industry. These included "total cost caps," "unchanging program baselines," and a host of new measures to improve equipment quality. For example, under his leadership we had the government's first major program with both a "design to cost" to control growth and a "reliability improvement warranty" to ensure that the product would perform in the field as advertised. He constantly spoke of "unleashing our creativity," and that's what he did.

Our reputation quickly turned around. Rather than worrying about the way ESD was managing we were assigned several new major programs, of the type that would have been assigned elsewhere in bygone years. Perhaps the greatest plaudit of all to our newfound image and expertise was that bright young Air Force engineers of all grades started asking to come to ESD. Before it had been a place to avoid.

In all my years there I never saw a better leader or manager than Bill Creech. It was particularly amazing how his leadership concepts reached all elements of the organization—and how much they brought out the best in all of us. Although we were skeptical when he came in, he listened, he learned, he assessed and he acted—and he made a major turnaround in ESD that paid large dividends in more successful programs and far better combat capability. I have often told others over the years that Bill Creech produced ESD's finest hours. In the process, he conclusively demonstrated that the right principles can vastly improve even something as bureaucratic and as complicated as U.S. government procurement.

This ESD transformation story sets the stage for the points I will make about leadership, and leadership styles, in chapters 8 and 9. In that respect, it's worth reflecting on one aspect of Bob Doane's narrative. In one place he said: "His imprint was all over the place, yet he gave each of us even more authority and latitude than we had before." In another place he said, "Bill Creech produced ESD's finest hours.'' But actually I didn't produce them. All the people at ESD did. My contribution was the principles.

True as that observation is, it is not meant to diminish the important role of the top boss. Indeed, it starts there. To create organizational success the boss must build a system that, among other TQM principles to be applied, provides widespread empowerment and non-interference from the top. However, the top boss also must stay involved and informed. That's necessary to keep the decentralized empowerment going, and to resist the ever-present tendency of lower-level managers to recentralize. The boss also must know when and where to intrude to head off incipient problems before they can grow to disasters. It is striking that balance between involvement and intrusion that's important. Some characterize the notion underlying that balance as *"Nose In, Fingers Out,"* or *"NIFO."* By whatever name, those at the lower levels quickly perceive how you are striking that balance, and whether their own empowerment is real or fanciful. It's not difficult or complicated so long as you base your actions on trust and respect until the scoreboard and other measurements show that intrusion is required. Even then, if that intrusion is thoughtful, helpful, and clearly warranted—not capricious—it is ordinarily welcomed, and will not be read by other leaders as a threat to their empowerment. Thus, this ESD story amplifies an important point: *Detailed personal involvement by the topmost leader and widespread empowerment of others are complementary, not mutually exclusive.* Those who look on it otherwise are making a serious mistake.

I raise the subject because many management books advise that the key to decentralization is to "just let go," or "just get out of their way." That advice is well intended but stops well short of describing the actual need. It assumes that some form of lower-level leadership and coherent, focused effort will emerge magically on its own once one stops "managing." That's simply not the case. The need is for better integration of effort, not even more separation between managers and workers. Leaders indeed should get *out of the way*, but they also must help *find the way, show the way, and pave the way*. Therefore, extensive involvement by the leaders is essential, in ways I will further describe in the chapters that follow.

I'm staying away from personal war stories in these pages, though fighter pilots have an abundant supply. However, I am including these stories of my personal involvement in organizational turnarounds for two reasons. First, they add texture and credibility to my representations on *how to organize* and *how to lead*. That, after all, is the purpose of the book. Second, they give insight into the issues involved, how to recognize them, and how to approach them. As I said in chapter 1, the management principles I espouse derive their principal merit from having been honed and proved in what Teddy Roosevelt termed the *"floor of the arena"* (not from some lofty philosophical perch above the fray). And, as Dizzy Dean used to say, ''If you done it, it ain't bragging.'' Finally, as I've stated repeatedly, it was the switch to TQM management that created these successes— the organizations involved stayed changed for the better after I left the scene.

The challenge to transform ESD was as daunting a leadership mission as I have undertaken. As Bob Doane said, I was a *rookie* in their business. Also, I was an *outsider* if there ever was one. Consequently, in most ESD circles there was downright hostility when I arrived. To further complicate matters, they were highly miffed over the aspersions being cast—they thought unfairly—on their own abilities, an attitude that was aggravated by the firing of one of their own as the commander. That makes for a rather stern test of any change in the management approach. What won them over to the new approach was persuasion, not bombast—and, even more so, *results*. Nothing speaks louder than powerful, irrefutable indications that you are getting far better all the time. And we were; and it showed.

I'm convinced their acceptance also was helped by their being fully involved. They had a strong voice in our architecture of change as well as in its implementation. The key for me was the principles, selling their worth, and getting everyone to enthusiastically apply them—not ordering change. A second key was in fitting those principles to the setting and circumstances. I'm pleased that the principles were so successful at ESD, just as they had been for me in previous settings. The many systems we improved as a result of our new TQM orientation all performed with distinction in the Gulf War. And that's what the *business of our business* at ESD was all about.

So attitudes can be changed, even where Centralism has been the order of the day for decades. Granted, centralist conditioning creates strong resistance to change. Fortunately, in my experience such resistance melts away as it becomes clear that the employees are more empowered and enthusiastic, and as the organization becomes more successful. It's a rare individual, after all, who does not prefer a winning team to a losing one. So conditioning need not be a lasting barrier to change. However, that barrier of resistance will not come down on its own. Business leaders must take it down. To add further weight to this discussion of Centralism's origins and effects—and the great difference you get in results from the two management styles —let's examine some decentralized management success stories in other cultures. Language and customs vary; human nature doesn't.

THERE ARE ABUNDANT EXAMPLES IN OTHER COUNTRIES OF THE POWER OF ORGANIZING SMALL TO WIN BIG—THE PRINCIPLES WORK EVERYWHERE

BTR, plc, headquartered in Vincent Square, London, England, is its country's fastest-growing and most successful industrial conglomerate. At the end of the eighties BTR's revenues stood at some $13 billion. Its overall worth was pegged in 1992 as $17.2 billion. BTR employs more than 100,000 employees in some sixty decentralized subsidiaries in forty different countries. BTR came into the world as *British Tire and Rubber*, but sold off most of those holdings and now is into products ranging from women's apparel to plastics, to oil, to heavy construction. And with the acquisition of *Dunlop*, an American firm, BTR is back in the tire business also. Its companies are found in such far-flung places as Australia, India, Japan, South Africa, Taiwan, the United States, Zimbabwe, and several Western European countries. At the end of the decade its growth pattern in earnings per share averaged a whopping 30 percent a year, and it had steadily increased its profits over twenty-one straight years. Its management successes have been nothing short of spectacular—and it follows the decentralized, leadership style of management.

Let me give some quick examples of the management philosophy that has served BTR so well. Managing Director John Cahill (who recently left BTR to head up struggling British Aerospace) put BTR's decentralized philosophy to me this way: "The secret to running a company this big is to have a noninterfering system. There is an inverse ratio between corporate management attention and meeting your plan." One of the many BTR company presidents said to me, "Our performance is measured exclusively on how we perform. If we perform to the objectives we receive very little or no interference" (a view echoed by the others).

Cahill explains BTR's measurement and tracking approach: "The reporting system takes you through the P&L account, the cash account, et cetera—but it is far more than that. It also takes you through all of the key ratios that you need to be sure the business is on course." I mentioned earlier the periodic "zero-based reviews" BTR conducts on the business of the business of each of its subsidiaries— why each is in it and how it's doing. That attention to competitive *situation awareness* is one of BTR's great strengths. A company president of a recently acquired BTR subsidiary summed up BTR's approach this way, "I have been in this business for over twenty years and I never saw anything like BTR's reporting system. The system highlights all the key output variables." BTR's chief financial officer characterizes it in these terms: "The reporting system is an operating tool *for* the operating managers. It is most comprehensive, and provides an overall feel of how the company is working. Using it, one can quickly identify drifts and changes, and then hone in on that aspect." Enough said.

A good part of BTR's successful growth formula in addition to impressive internal growth has been to acquire struggling companies and transform them into winners (some seventeen major acquisitions during the eighties). John Cahill summarizes how they succeed in that:

> We are successful in taking over poorly performing companies because our new people quickly discover that we are all on the same team, all with the same objectives, and that we take decisions very quickly. They find that in BTR we have a single purpose. . . . We

use the same managers that we inherited, and we succeed by a change in their approach. Of course our plans and our management approach are all premised on the need for a relationship with our customers that stand the test of time.

BTR also emphasizes the entrepreneurial leadership spirit at all levels—in fact, that's what makes its management system and style work so well. In that respect, after I had given a speech to 125 BTR company leaders from around the world on the decentralized approach—including the theme that the first duty of a leader is to create more leaders—John Cahill followed up my advice by restating the BTR philosophy in that same respect: "Creating good leaders below you does not push you out, it pushes you up. Until you've created a leader in your organization capable of easily assuming your job, and for someone to easily assume their job, then you are not promotable." Again, enough said. Cahill also speaks eloquently about the need for recognition and reward—at all levels. When Cahill left BTR to pursue other management challenges, he was replaced by Alan Jackson, an Australian, who had been well groomed for the position. So the BTR beat goes on. For example, even in the face of the worldwide economic recession of the early nineties, BTR's net worth rose substantially. BTR's long-running success provides still more proof of the merit of the decentralized approach.

In my international travels, I have run across many others that fit the same mold. Coles Myer, Ltd., of Tooronga, Victoria in Australia, is the largest retailer in Australasia and the twelfth-largest retailer in the world. The company operates more than 1,600 retail outlets, with a focus on department stores, discount stores, food stores, and specialty shops. It has become Australia's largest corporation, with a staff of more than 163,000 employees. Coles Myer is another sterling example of how a company can grow big by staying agile and flexible through a decentralized, "organize small" approach—and through enlightened policies that build strong customer focus, and commitment in all the employees to serving those customers well. Growing big it is. Growing fast it is. For example, profits over the ten years of the eighties more than quintupled (521 percent), with a 58 percent average growth rate. During the same period sales grew fourfold, from just over $3 billion to nearly $12 billion. Coles Myer pulls that off by avoiding the various afflictions of "megadisease" that affect so many corporations as they grow large, unwieldy, and bureaucratic— and by staying in close touch with their employees and customers.

Coles Myer, much like Wal-Mart, makes a virtual religion out of *quality, reliability, service, and value to the customer.* And it stays on the cutting edge of improvements in retailing. It was one of the first retailing giants anywhere in the world to offer debit card service to its customers at the checkout counter—a faster, more convenient way to pay than the credit card approach. Also, not surprisingly, Coles Myer's leaders, from chairman and CEO B. E. Quinn on down, say their devoutly practiced policy of "decentralization of management functions" is the foundation of their success. Don't tell Coles Myer about the vicissitudes of globalization; the firm welcomes them. For example, it expanded near the end of the decade into New Zealand, and has been equally successful there.

I could also point out the extraordinary success of another Australian company, *National Mutual,* headquartered in Melbourne and specializing in financial services of various kinds, including insurance. Like most of the best companies, National Mutual sees the changes sweeping the global economy as full of opportunity, not of challenges and despair. (The firm already has subsidiaries in Ireland, Hong Kong, the United Kingdom, and the United States and sees globalization as a way to expand much farther and faster.) I won't bother to explain National Mutual's management philosophy; you already know what it is or I wouldn't be invoking the company's name.

Canada's *Bombardier, Inc.,* headquartered in Montreal, is still another example of the power of decentralization in building commitment in employees and customers. Looking for success measures? In a five-year period nearing the end of the eighties its sales tripled and profits went up by a factor of ten. That brought its revenues to $2 billion—by 1992 they reached $3.5 billion. Thus Bombardier is an instructive model precisely because it started small and has been tenaciously successful in a bitterly competitive business: Aerospace. The Bombardier management approach? As you would suspect: "Decentralized organization, people orientation, and commitment to ethics and service.'' Laurent Beaudoin, chairman and CEO, says Bombardier uses ''decentralized and multidivisional management,'' and he emphasizes:

> Our company has been built on some core values and beliefs. These values must continue to inspire and guide our management and employees. . . . While a company's strength may be measured in financial terms, its level of dynamism and its prospects for the future can only be measured by the caliber of its men and women. . . . Bombardier owes its success to the pride, the professionalism, the entrepreneurship, the commitment, the dedicated efforts, and the team spirit of all its employees.

Success flows only from that—in all companies. These stories from England, Australia, and Canada provide still more proof that sound management principles transcend national, cultural, and company boundaries. The common denominator is human nature, the common accelerator is the human spirit, and decentralization unleashes the human spirit. How much more proof do America's managers need?

VIRTUALLY ALL CENTOCRACIES LIKE TO TALK THESE DAYS ABOUT CHANGE AND DECENTRALIZATION. BUT THEY WON'T COME TO GRIPS WITH CENTRALISM—SO THEY CHANGE AND IMPROVE LITTLE

For at least a decade there has hardly been a centocracy—at least in the *Fortune* 500—that hasn't bragged about the big ''changes'' it's making to fit our turbulent and trying times. Despite the big talk, most have done little that has had any real impact on their Centralism-oriented management systems. That's largely because, like GM, centocracies just don't get it when it comes to what's causing their management system problems. I explained in chapter 2 how Roger

Smith hyped to the heavens GM's 1984 reorganization as a "massive decentralization." It was hardly that. Breaking into two centrocratic pieces did little to confront or change GM's centralist ways, and the downward slide continued. That pattern of supposed change is quite common.

Of late, we have more and more centocracies getting all steamed up over "teams" and believing they have the idea down pat. However, it's virtually always the *cross-functional, committeelike* kind they adopt—which leaves their centralized system and style otherwise undisturbed. Sometimes the slight changes they make at the same time create enough improvement to convince them they've done all that's needed. But then new problems gather, and they tack on a few more changes.

Perhaps one of the most illuminating cases of the halting steps in the metamorphosis of a long-standing centocracy is the *Xerox Corporation*. In fact, it's a metaphor for the way every such centocracy changes grudgingly—unless someone grabs it by the horns and takes it all the way to a decentralized, leadership approach. A bit of history reveals the various stages in the Xerox transformation—nearly always responding to outside pressures. Xerox had always done just fine—swimmingly, in fact—until the Japanese entered its principal market of office copiers. (Many still call a copier a "Xerox machine," and people still talk about "Xeroxing" a copy. That's because Xerox had the market largely to itself.)

When the Japanese entered the copier market in a big way, Xerox found, to its shock, that the Japanese companies were selling copiers in the United States for considerably less than Xerox's production costs. At first, Xerox thought they were "dumping." But then Xerox executives had the good sense to go to Japan and see for themselves (using the good offices of Fuji, Xerox's joint venture partner in Japan). To put it in a nutshell, they found that the Japanese just did it a lot better than Xerox did in all respects: quality, cost efficiency, market value, and all the rest. The dominant Xerox domestic market share was cut by more than half, and its return on assets shrank from the glory days to well under 10 percent.

All that was finally enough to spur Xerox into making a number of changes. Without reprising all of them here, they were enough to recapture some of that lost market share (but far from all). As one example of its changes, Xerox formed *Quality Improvement Teams* (cross-functional, of course, in keeping with the current gospel that one doesn't have to disturb the basic organizational structure as long as they get the quality process religion). Xerox also placed a great deal more emphasis on formal training in all elements of the corporation, and at every level. These varied improvements, made under David T. Kearns when he was chairman, led Xerox to apply for and win the *Malcolm Baldrige National Quality Award*. All of this garnered considerable praise for Xerox and its leaders in the national business press, and even from the MIT Commission on Industrial Productivity, which cited the Xerox improvement in these respects in its report *Made in America*. Through it all, however, Xerox remained a centocracy.

Inevitably, problems returned. New products were not being developed as fast or as skillfully as the intense Japanese competition demanded. And an excursion into financial services and insurance as a diversification measure became a big financial drain on the corporate treasury. For these and a variety of other reasons, Xerox in the early nineties found its earnings dropping and problems growing. That set a challenging stage for a new chairman and CEO, Paul Allaire, who took over on the retirement of David Kearns. The obvious question confronting Allaire was how to fix the growing host of Xerox problems. New ways or more of the old?

The answer, according to Allaire, is at long last to break up the centocracy that Xerox has been for all of its corporate life, stoutly adhering to it even when the Japanese kept putting the writing on the wall for Xerox along with the rest of corporate America. Allaire says his new initiatives involve far more than a reorganization—that they involve a complete redesign of the entire ''organizational architecture.'' He freely admits that throughout all its earlier travails Xerox had retained the ''structure, practices and values of a classic big company,'' including an ''extremely functional organization'' and a ''staff-driven'' management system. He goes on to explain the classic problems that stem from that organizational arrangement: bloated staffs, passivity at the lower levels, poor coordination, and so on. I've described those results in detail, so I won't amplify; Xerox simply fit the familiar pattern of recurring problems that encumber all centocracies. Why did it take Paul Allaire to recognize the management system and organization as the key to fixing those problems? The answer is conditioning. Managers bred in the Centralism era look but do not see, at least most of them don't. With that by way of background, let's turn to the changed view at Xerox.

Paul Allaire's new "architecture" for the Xerox management system calls for decentralization into nine independent business divisions organized to provide specific products to specific markets, each with full P&L authority and responsibility. Not only that, but each division is to be decentralized into "*Business Teams,*" each oriented to a specific niche in the marketplace. And within those various business teams the frontline workers are to be formed into "*Self-managed Work Teams.*" In a very real sense Allaire is going from the centralized organizational model to the decentralized model. At least it appears that way. Clearly Allaire has homed in properly on the *Product* and *Team* aspects of building a successful decentralized system. And note that this time around they are to be real-life structural teams, not the ad hoc Quality Improvement Teams Xerox previously had grafted onto its centocratic system and structure. It remains to be seen, however, how well Xerox understands and is prepared to include the *Outputs* and *Leadership* elements of the decentralized model as I used it and as the Japanese practice it. Without that, the old managership habits will stifle the results Xerox seeks.

I like what Paul Allaire is saying—because it contains much of what I've heard from the most successful CEOs using the decentralized approach as I have described it. In a wide-ranging interview in the *Harvard Business Review* of September–October 1992, Allaire explained the new Xerox management system rationale: "In a sense we have turned the traditional vertically organized structure on its side. At one end is technology, and we have retained an integrated corporate research and technology organization. At the other end is the customer. [And] Between those two poles are the new business divisions." He explained the many advantages in that arrangement, including: "A big advantage of this structure is that it is remarkably easy to adapt. When we see new markets emerge or new technologies that don't fit into our current structure, we can simply add another business team or even a whole new division." He also explained that this organization provides a "total business focus, something the narrow functional organization does not provide."

With these words and his other descriptions of his new approach, Allaire comes very close to describing the restructured TAC, or Honda, or Toyota. As the Japanese and I might put it: Welcome to the club! And though the Japanese won't say it, because they don't necessarily welcome their competitors waking up to what's been wrong, I'll say it: *What took Xerox so long?* I know the answer, though. It's that Xerox had long embraced the precepts and style of Centralism—along with almost everyone else in corporate America. And Allaire made a telling comment to *HBR* in that regard. He said his Xerox search team couldn't find a model anyplace of how to do it, even though it searched far and wide. In fact, all Xerox found in rummaging through corporate America was what Allaire described as "a few pockets of organizational innovation" in several big companies. But the search team could find no overall model. That's no surprise. While they can be found in America, it's certainly not easy—they're few and far between.

Why is that so? David Kearns, previous Xerox CEO, helps us understand. Kearns said in a 1994 PBS interview: "We made lots of changes, but each time we didn't go nearly far enough. And we did that time after time." Xerox, thought to be in the forefront of change, actually was not. Xerox is not unique. Most businesses aren't budging at all from the old ways. Others talk big about change (and change some—like Xerox did), but fall way short of the total changes needed in these new times.

Is the new organizational arrangement a guarantee that Xerox will now succeed? No, it isn't, because Centralism dies hard. The challenge will be to make the decentralized approach stick—and to convert the managerial conditioning from decades of exposure to the hallowed Centralism concepts to the principles of decentralized leadership instead. Xerox would profit by studying Boeing's experience:

Xerox also will need to create leadership at all levels. The techniques I will describe in chapters 8 and 9 will be of help in that respect. Old centocratic habits will die, and when they do it gives rise to a new spirit of ownership and commitment at all levels. More delay in the switch Xerox is making is a luxury most simply can't afford.

It's appropriate to add a final word on the Xerox story for the lessons it holds for businesses all over America. In his account in *HBR* Allaire also said the Xerox search team couldn't even find a good theory on how to do what it hopes to do. That, according to Allaire, is to install a team-based, product-based, quality-oriented, decentralized management system (and structure) to replace the centralized, functionalized, staff-driven system of old. I agree with him on the difficulty of finding a good theory on that. You can find pieces—a sort of design-it-yourself kit—but they contain glaring theoretical omissions. For example, current literature is largely silent on how to use permanent structural teams (as the Japanese do), and it's even more silent on how to create distributed, bottom-up leadership —on which effective decentralization depends. I, too, looked but did not find a comprehensive and proven theory. That's why I wrote this book.

This trend of *lots of mouth but little movement* in the present quality crusade is also clearly visible in Europe. The TQM movement spread there from the U.S., and the E.F.Q.M (European Foundation for Quality Management) has established a European Quality Award. Patterned after Baldrige, it has similar categories, judging, and the rest. But they've also extended that appreciably with their "ISO 9000" approach—a series of manuals setting forth what companies must do to pass a complicated certification process—with triennial follow-on audits. (ISO 9000 has spread to 70 countries, largely because ISO certification is necessary to sell products in Europe.) Has it all worked out? Depends on your point of view. The major accounting firm Deloitte-Touche did a 1994 survey of all the ISO 9000 certified companies, world-wide. A whopping 91 percent of them said that it had helped their "documentation" and "quality awareness" but that they saw no other notable results. And a bare 9% said that using the ISO 9000 principles had resulted in any discernible change in their productivity and/or efficiency.

Moral: It can't just be a process-centered drill, with the people issues (and thus management issues) left aside. But finding that stubborn resistance to real change permeates Europe as well as the U.S. is no comfort. That's because some around the world do see the message of what's wrong—and are changing in the right ways. Others will join. Where do you stand?

Admittedly, finding the proper formula is not a simple undertaking, given the huge variety of notions and nostrums loose today on the management scene. (And given the large number of centocracies posturing in new garb but old habits.) The big challenge will be to ensure that the overall change effort in American companies doesn't continue to get sidetracked by the "process school" of thinking—leading to more ineffectual grafts on the nation's centocracies. I fervently hope it won't turn out that way. America is running out of time. And the challenge of changing the old ways to the new is a thorny one. Tolstoy left us this wisdom in that regard:

> I know that most men, including those at ease with problems of the greatest complexity, can seldom accept even the simplest and most obvious truth if it be such as would oblige them to admit the falsity of conclusions which they have delighted in explaining to colleagues, which they have proudly taught to others, and which they have woven, thread by thread, into the fabric of their lives.

That beautifully describes the biggest hurdle. But it can be overcome. All it takes is gumption, guts, and fortitude.

This chapter has explained why TQM must involve the entire system, not just a few pieces. I now turn to the *Leadership Pillar*. TQM can't stand without it. The next three chapters explain why, and why managership is TQM's natural enemy.

8

Leadership: It's a Must, and It's Not Managership

THE LEADERSHIP CONCEPT—A CASUALTY OF THE MANAGERSHIP AGE

Let's again state the management axioms that establish the critical importance of distributed leadership to successful TQM:

> *Product is the focal point for organization purpose and achievement. Quality in the product is impossible without quality in the process. Quality in the process is impossible without the right organization. The right organization is meaningless without the proper leadership.*

Centralization breeds and nurtures managership. In fact, it depends on it. You can't run on autopilot with people down below charting new directions and taking new initiatives. Decentralization breeds and nurtures leadership. And each depends on the other. You need leadership to be successful, but you won't have it unless you empower people to exercise it. I spoke earlier of those who are convinced they have adopted *quality management* but have done no more than put patches on their old centralized system. Predictably, those superficial changes do little to create the initiative, innovation, and ingenuity that come only through humanistic practices and proactive leadership—at all levels.

I wish to make it clear that when I invoke the word "leadership" in contrast to "managership" I'm not talking about the merit of one management *term* versus another. That's an insignificant part of it. Instead I'm drawing a distinction between one management *practice* and another. And in pointing out the preference in the American management culture for managing, not leading, I wish to draw attention to the questionable worth of sticking to that preference. It has been with us for most of the twentieth century, changing somewhat in form but not in substance in the century's second half. The evidence says that preference for an abstract form of "managing" is no longer valid—that it must change.

I've now had extensive exposure to management practices that cut across all kinds and sizes of businesses and industries. Unfailingly I've found that executives of every company like to think their company is different. In minor ways, every company is. In major ways, it's not. What I see instead of differences is an amazing degree of consistency in the American management culture, and the patterns and practices of that culture. The jargon is the same (the management jargon, not the jargon of the particular profession). The titles are the same. We have CEO, COO, CFO, executive VP, senior VP, general manager, and the like. The lexicon for drawing distinctions between groups also is the same. We have blue-collar and white-collar, salaried and hourly, exempt and nonexempt, management and labor, and so on. Management gets incentive pay, and labor doesn't. And on and on. There are all kinds of such indicators of the differences we have sanctified, and the policies we have dignified, in the way these various groups are treated within our culture. Taken in the aggregate, these terms and practices—and the management pattern—are consistent from company to company. Indeed, that's the underlying contributor to our collective shortcomings. And it is that culture that must be substantially altered if our competitive posture is to change for the better.

In this *potpourri* of terms "Leader" and "leading" long ago dropped out of the American management lexicon. "Manager" and "managing" gained cachet in theory—and nearly exclusive status in practice. That's what the American management culture believes in, that's what it expects, and that's what it teaches. So when the Japanese come along and call their frontline employees *associates*, the American management culture heaves a collective yawn. In effect, it says, "So what?" The "so what" is that the language reflects the patterns and habits. The Japanese call frontline employees associates because their management philosophy is to treat them as such. And they do so, in the ways I have described.

The Japanese companies also call the supervisors of their teams *leaders*. That's because they expect them to do some real leading, and they train them accordingly. Most U.S. companies don't even organize by teams, and wouldn't think of "leaders" at that low a level if they did. Indeed, the majority of American managers raised in the Centralism era think of leadership as something that starts at the top and trickles down from there—but not very far. And the Japanese show us, every day, the "so what" of their own focus on *leading* from the very bottom to the top. The fact that the words "leader" and "leading" have made a minor comeback of late in the management literature is merely the exception that proves the rule. Let's examine the issues.

A MAJOR BAR TO THE REPLACEMENT OF MANAGERSHIP BY LEADERSHIP IS THAT THE MANAGERSHIP CONCEPT HAS PERMEATED OUR CULTURE

That we long have prized managing over leading is one of our biggest national problems. And the nation's business schools have been the catalysts—or at least fellow travelers—in perpetuating that preference. Indeed, in most circles it became the dreaded "L-word" —an out-of-date and out-of-style term unworthy of inclusion in a "more modern" and "more sensitive" approach to management. In like manner, the nation's literature fell silent, with some minor exceptions, on vital subjects like human dynamics, practices that stir the human spirit, and the need for shaping attitudes to create employee commitment and common purpose. In this managership catechism an important question emerges. If the ''managers'' were not to be responsible for proactively and positively influencing frontline employees' attitudes in the rage for Centralism, who was? The answer, I have found—in centocracy after centocracy—is no one at all. Managing, Centralism-style, somehow ascended to a loftier plane—a sterile plane—above the messy, contradictory, and often thorny business of affecting employees' beliefs about their work, their managers, and their stake in the outcome.

You cannot have leadership unless you believe in it. I am convinced that had we not decentralized TAC I could have preached leadership loudly and incessantly and it would have had little effect. The system simply wouldn't have allowed it to flourish even if I had done everything possible to nurture it. There's a vast difference between exhortation and empowerment. You must do more than talk about it; you must change the organization *conceptually* and *structurally* to bring leadership alive at all levels.

Principles flow from the top down; decisions flow from the bottom up. That implies the need to have leadership operating from the very bottom of the organization. Obviously, some decisions can only be made at the very top—but they should be rare exceptions, not the rule. And they should deal with major resource decisions and new directions, not day-to-day management. The leaders at the top should chart the course, not constantly steer the ship.

The Malcolm Baldrige National Quality Award criteria allocate only 100 of 1,000 total points to leadership, just one reflection of that traditional view. I would despair over that except for my elation that leadership made the Baldrige list at all. That's progress! Nevertheless, I believe that if those administering the Baldrige award looked on leadership as I do they would realize that you must look for its presence *everywhere* in the organization. And that should make it a prime category worthy of far more than a 10 percent share in the quality management formula. Said another way, if it isn't widespread and working effectively, then the quality management scheme in that company simply is not working—no matter how much the company is dutifully "filling the squares" to impress both themselves and the evaluators. This is less an attempt to quibble over how many Baldrige points leadership should be worth than to suggest that the smart business leader will make it a pass-fail item on his or her organizational effectiveness checklist. It's that important to the success of everything else the organization does.

MORE ARE QUESTIONING OUR TRADITIONAL PRACTICES, SO THERE IS REASON FOR HOPE

More and more are speaking out on the subject of our past (and current) practices versus our problems and needs. As one example, *Business Week* in November 1988 published numerous outstanding articles that took a hard look at our business schools and their contributions to our current dilemmas. Some articles addressed our Master of Business Administration (MBA) graduates and how they have been performing as a consequence of how they have been taught. The following excerpts provide the flavor of the observations in those articles.

Thomas Nourse, a San Diego investment adviser, compared the cash flow performance of three groups of industrial companies: those run by CEOs with MBAs, those run by CEOs with technical or industry-specific educations, and Japanese companies. The MBAs did the worst job of all. The dean of the MIT Sloan School of Management, Lester Thurow, mused: "I get a deep feeling of unease about what we're doing. If our business schools are so good, why are our American companies doing so badly?"

From a sampling of MBAs themselves: A Wharton graduate commented, "At no time in two years did any of my classes discuss organized labor, the role of government and business in society, the causes and possible solutions of the trade deficit, American industrial decline, or any other issue that can't be solved in 80 minutes." A Duke graduate: "My lasting regret is that I spent $40,000 to learn useless tools . . . I can crunch numbers to death, but I didn't learn anything about managing, motivating, and leading people.'' A Columbia graduate: ''I and most of my classmates graduated with virtually no knowledge of manufacturing or operations. But we all learned a hell of a lot about portfolio hedging strategies that have nothing to do with management.'' These student critics are fortunate in recognizing that their management education had key omissions. Most don't recognize that and will not take steps to acquire the knowledge elsewhere.

Most companies have not recognized the problem either, or taken steps to fill the void. Certainly there's an embryonic trend among major corporations to adopt leadership training programs, but such corporations remain notable exceptions. So let's not lay the blame on the academicians alone. It is, after all, a problem that must be solved by senior business leaders themselves. Jack Welch of GE, Frank Shrontz of Boeing, and others of the nation's best business leaders are not wasting their time affixing blame or looking for outside saviors. They're taking the aggressive steps necessary to meet their own challenges in this respect.

It's to be hoped that the business schools will change their education of America's future generations of managers to include more on human dynamics and leadership skills. Indeed, those subjects clearly are staging a comeback in academic and business circles. More books are showing up these days on leadership. Many are quite good; a few are excellent. Two of the latter are books by Warren Bennis of the University of Southern California School of Business Administration, *Leaders* (1985), cowritten with Burt Nanus, and *On Becoming a Leader* (1989). Bennis's findings and insights are especially valid because they were not cooked up in ivory-tower isolation. They were reached through extensive interviews with business leaders across the country.

The MIT Commission on Industrial Productivity also zeroed in on the leadership aspect in its investigation of America's eroding competitiveness. In its 1989 report *Made in America*, after discussing the effectiveness of using teams, the commission observed, ''Setting up the right organization is only half the battle. IBM, Hewlett-

Packard, Ford and other firms who have pioneered in these approaches stressed that it is also essential to have a strong project
manager who is capable of unifying the functions of the various team
members.'' The report expands on that leadership theme.

All of this is good. Over time, it should help convince businesses
practicing Centralism to change. As always, though, some of the concepts emerging in the management literature under the rubric of leadership are seriously off the mark. For example, the learned professor
who holds the ''*Leadership Chair*'' at one of our nation's most prestigious schools was interviewed at length a couple of years ago in a
leading business magazine. He held forth on a philosophy of leadership as an activity that is best carried out *without* leaders. His theme
was that you do need leadership—but not through leaders. He explained that exercising leadership through leaders merely ''makes
people dependent.'' While he made some worthwhile corollary points
about getting everyone involved, he implied that such involvement
by the workers depends wholly on leader passivity. It doesn't. In fact,
it's the other way around. It's managership, not leadership, that breeds
apathy, disincentive, and dependency. There's lots of evidence of that,
for those who are willing to look.

In an aside to the reader, the interviewer said the professor admits
he has limited knowledge of how businesses actually work. If he's
going to teach leadership, it might not be a bad thing to go out and
find out about that—as Warren Bennis has. Even so, this professor
at least used the word, lifting leadership out of business school pur-
gatory. Most academicians have not even done that, as the comments
from MBAs and others illustrate. That's a serious problem; I have yet
to see a top-notch organization, public or private, that didn't have the
benefit of strong leadership.

In fact, the more I see the more convinced I become of how vital
it is. *There are no poor outfits, just poor leaders.* I've seen too many
turnarounds to have doubts about that. I've also seen too many organizations fail because of poor leadership to doubt that it works the
other way around. I'm talking here, as I've made clear, about the kind
of leadership, *exercised through leaders*, that makes people independent, not dependent—and thereby turns everyone else into ''lead-

ers'' through far greater empowerment and involvement. Thus, creating leadership depends on the widest feasible distribution of *responsibility*—along with the *authority* and *accountability* that must accompany it if it is to work.

It also involves development of the proper leadership traits and attitudes. Leaders must be taught, and can be taught. And they must be taught how to motivate those who work for them—and to accept *personal responsibility* for building common purpose and organization success. In contrasting the centralized and decentralized approaches in chapter 1, I tied managership to the former and leadership to the latter. There's a very good reason—and empirical basis—for doing that.

LEADERSHIP VERSUS MANAGERSHIP: THERE ARE CRITICAL DIFFERENCES

I am convinced that *leader, leadership*, and *leading* did not drop out of the business (and business school) lexicon for so long because those words are working synonyms for *manager, managership*, and *managing*. Rather, they dropped out of usage because they are *not* synonymous. Indeed, they are the flagwords of an approach that Centralism does its best to avoid. Even your friendly dictionary spells out those differences—at least the conceptual distinctions between the two families of terms. The fact is that it is not leaders and leadership that have been in demand. It's managers and managership that fit the other precepts of Centralism. Although I phrase this as a binary distinction for emphasis, leading and managing can be complementary, but they are separate concepts. And using the terms interchangably, as many do, should not mask the fact they are separate, involving different patterns of supervisory outlook and behavior.

Leading involves determining the right things to do. It involves creating the favorable organizational dynamics to get people to commit themselves, energetically and enthusiastically, to bringing those right things about. Leading involves vision and principles. It involves influencing employee mindset and motivation. It involves creating a positive culture and harmonious climate. It involves creating ownership and empowerment in pursuit of the shared vision and common purpose. So leadership is hardly the sole province of the top leaders. And it most definitely is not the centralist business of just telling employees what to do, how to do it, and when to do it.

The concept of leadership has animation, dynamism, and a strong proactive, not reactive, flavor. That's what is usually missing when supervisors look on their jobs as simply directing the activities of people rather than influencing the *attitudes* and activities of people. To achieve the latter I have always looked for supervisors who had the blend of skills, or could be readily trained in them, that would fit anyone's definition of both leading and managing. Admittedly, it's not enough to be just an energizer and a cheerleader. On the other hand, it's surely not enough to be just a beancounter, a paper shuffler, and a kibitzer. So my purpose in drawing these distinctions is not to build a firebreak between the two, but to expand their combined dimensions. I have seen again and again how Centralism takes the leadership aspect out of the supervisor's job title. It does so not only in the conceptual sense but also by setting up a management system (and organizational structure) that provides no room for leadership at the lower levels. It's the oxygen of empowerment, and a supporting system and structure, that makes leadership at all levels thrive.

Therefore, it's important for those considering change to recognize the difference in the two mindsets. The *manager* mindset is both consistent and persistent in centralized, traditionally managed organizations. It's consistent because it's a *natural by-product* of the management system, not the product of chance from organization to organization, or manager to manager. And it's persistent because once established, the system feeds on itself to thwart attempts to change.

In contrast, it's the *leadership* approach and mindset that I brought to organizations so structured and so oriented. Where I succeeded, they in turn succeeded. Moreover, it's the *leadership* approach that one finds in the very best companies in the United States and abroad. And the marked distinctions between the two flow from radically different notions of how one can best manage human endeavor. Thus, an understanding of those distinctions is central to a TQM transformation strategy. Here's my list.

MANAGERSHIP AND LEADERSHIP FEATURE DIFFERENT MINDSETS

- Leaders shape the outputs.
  Managers chase the inputs.

- Leaders focus on group products.
  Managers focus on individual jobs.

- Leaders encourage new ideas.
  Managers enforce the old ideas.

- Leaders stimulate right things.
  Managers monitor for wrong things.

- Leaders thrive on tough competition.
  Managers talk little of competition.

- Leaders prize comparison with others.
  Managers see scant need for comparison.

- Leaders think of involvement programs.
  Managers think of suggestion programs.

- Leaders empower others to make decisions.
  Managers tightly control the decision process.

- Leaders see leading as animate and proactive.
  Managers see managing as inanimate and reactive.

- Leaders think of a dynamic, caring human system.
  Managers think of a business following a script.

- Leaders think of improving initiative and innovation.
  Managers think of improving compliance and conformance.

- Leaders shape organization character, culture, and climate. Managers assume that's neither a big deal—nor their job.

To boil it down to four: *Leaders provide the vision; managers carry it out. Leaders make it better; managers make it run. Leaders make it happen; managers hope it happens. Leaders create more leaders; managers create more managers.*

In setting forth these differences, I'm not suggesting that every manager in a centralized organization fits an exact profile. And I'm not suggesting that the above distinctions describe all Centralism managerial conditioning with certainty. I am suggesting that, over time, the centralized approach forces managers into these kinds of thought and behavioral patterns. Therefore, these distinctions, stark though they are, provide markers of what to look for and address if one is to change successfully from the traditional ways.

Leaders, properly trained and properly empowered (it takes both), contribute in other ways as well. Leaders address the constant race between *inspiration* and *indolence*—and add to the inspiration. Leaders understand that quiet *persuasion* and *persistence* are far more effective than *bluster* and *bombast*. They praise the messengers not shoot them. Leaders understand that *motivation* and *alienation* are at opposite poles and that they grow or shrink in inverse proportion. Therefore, leaders build commitment through policies that increase motivation and decrease alienation. And leaders constantly probe for evidence of each. That requires involvement and sensitivity. It also requires trust, openness, and unfettered communication—not aloof, Olympian managerial detachment, as is so common in centralized organizations.

Beyond all those important elements, leaders understand that the way to win starts with the will to win—and that instilling both is leadership business. In that pursuit, leaders understand that fervor feeds on opinions—and opinions feed on presumed facts. So they influence those opinions by getting the actual facts out for everyone's benefit. They combat misinformation, and disinformation, with the *straight skinny*. They understand that it's *objectivity* that keeps misdirected subjectivity under control. Uninformed opinions and misplaced fervor thrive in an information vacuum because there's no counterforce at work. Yet most companies and managers pay scant attention to the need to keep employees well informed—or to seek their opinions. They simply don't invoke the four most important words in any management system: "*What do you think?*"

Please note the connection in all of these to the *human spirit*, and to the operation of the *human system*—the subsystem that matters above all others. And this list is merely representative. In most cases it's not that managers, long conditioned to the centralist way of managing, deliberately choose the "mushroom principle" of "keeping subordinates in the dark, and feeding them lots of fertilizer." The problem is more subtle than that, but every bit as damaging. The centralized system, ignoring as it does the human system factors, simply does not condition managers to the value of keeping employees informed on and involved in key company issues. Thus, the insensitivity, even indifference, of those managers to the need to create motivation proactively is not at all surprising.

IT'S LEADERSHIP THAT'S NEEDED TO BUILD MOTIVATION; IT GETS LITTLE OR NO ATTENTION UNDER THE MANAGERSHIP APPROACH

Leadership and motivation go together. If motivation were a given, or were unimportant, managership would do just fine. But poll after poll shows that motivation makes a critical difference—and it always has. Just looking at our own society yields abundant proof of that. We look in one direction and we see extraordinary achievement. We look in another and see plants closing and growing concern about America's future. If we're willing to look, we also see what a dramatic difference motivation makes. We live in a society in which fewer and fewer people read a newspaper or are reliably informed on current issues that directly affect their own well-being. Functional illiteracy is one of our biggest problems.

College entrance scores are either flat or falling, and we stack up poorly against other industrialized societies in knowledge testing in a wide array of subjects from geography to mathematics. For example, in test results released in February 1992, we fared poorly vis-à-vis all other major nations in math and science testing. And it's not our spending on education; we rank at or near the top on that. Korea, for example, devotes 4.5 percent of its GNP to education; the United States devotes 7.5 percent. But it didn't show up in the students' knowledge. Korea finished first in both math and science testing. The United States finished no higher than thirteenth in either. So we have to look deeper. And when we look we find a difference in standards, expectations, and motivation. As one American teacher put it in discussing these results on CNN, "We keep moving toward making our schools a good place for kids that are not motivated—so we keep moving in the wrong direction."

Since motivation plays such an important role in the workplace as well as in our schools, I am perplexed by those in our society, particularly those in managerial positions, who pay so little attention to that transcendent issue. Far too many detach themselves from the way their management system affects their employees. By the way they organize, and by their actions, they reflect the view that employees work as well under one management system as another. (Or if they don't, they should!)

There's a better way than the traditional way to build commitment and motivation throughout the organization. It's by use of an organizational model based on *Teams, Outputs, Product,* and *Leadership.* Successful TQM involves far more than delegating a bit more authority while otherwise clinging to the old ways; it's not only a matter of creating agile organizational building blocks, it's also one of distributing authority—and in chapter 1 I posed these questions: *How wide? How deep? How much? How is it being done? Where is the authority—and accountability—vested? Who is being empowered?* The best answers have been touched on in the intervening chapters. What the lessons from those varied business failures and successes add up to is this: The team-based approach is the ideal way to ensure that real empowerment reaches the frontline—and that it gets exercised in a focused and responsible way. I have described earlier the important role played by the *Product*, not *Job* element of this model, and I now turn to the other two elements of that model: *Teams* and *Outputs*. I will describe the key roles they play, and explain why including those elements in the decentralized model is essential in a shift from managership to leadership. Let's begin with teams and emphasize what they bring to successful system revisions.

STRUCTURAL TEAMS PROVIDE THE BEST MEANS OF DISTRIBUTING AUTHORITY AND ACCOUNTABILITY; THUS THEY FACILITATE LEADERSHIP THAT OPERATES BOTTOM UP AS WELL AS TOP DOWN

The Venn diagram below shows the interactions and interdependencies between teams and other important system ingredients. All those ingredients are vital to success. Here's why: I've yet to see a centocracy that's good at getting leadership operating from the bottom to the top, no matter how much it uses the word "empowerment" in its annual report. The organization simply doesn't lend itself to that because it's geared to the principles of Centralism. And, there's ample evidence that you cannot simultaneously serve diametrically opposed

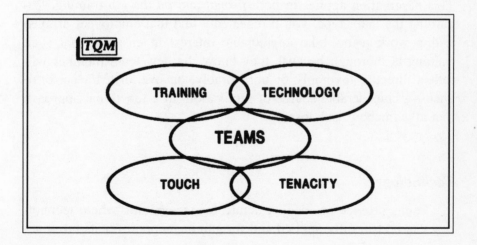

management concepts. It creates confusion, not cohesion, and adds to existing alienation as employees see a continuing difference between *what management says and what it does*. On the other hand, the decentralized, leadership approach—using as it does the team-based structure—is ideal for getting the leadership to every employee on the frontline in a way that he or she can understand, support, and enthusiastically exercise. Thus, teams serve as the *hook* for the decentralized leadership concepts, as the *focal point* for productivity and quality, and as the *fulcrum* for these other important elements of TQM success. Let's look briefly at each of the four and address why a team-based structure works in harmony with each one.

Training

Many studies on training (including those carried out by the MIT Commission on Industrial Productivity and the Commission on the Skills of the American Work Force) reveal that companies that use the team-based structure stand out among U.S. businesses in the success of their approach to training. Those companies turn out to be much more attuned to training needs, for individuals and teams. They also are far more aggressive in devoting the necessary effort and resources to that training than the traditionally managed companies. This observation applies to both *formal* and *on-the-job* training. Regarding the latter type, you'll repeatedly find that employees arrayed within work teams take appreciable interest in ensuring that such training is thorough because they know the new team member will reflect directly, favorably or unfavorably, on overall team performance—a considerable source of motivation. In a functional approach that all somehow gets lost.

Technology

Teams provide an ideal structure for recognizing where technology can be fruitfully applied and for gaining support for its introduction into the work equation. In fact, experience shows that employees arrayed in *Integrated Work Teams* begin taking a different view—a more positive and proactive view—regarding the application of new technological advances to their team endeavors. They're more inclined to view technology—including robotics—as a friend rather than an enemy thanks to their own quest for team product improvement. They also are much more likely to take the initiative in devising ways in which technology can be applied. I've noted that positive transition in thinking in many different settings.

Tenacity

This is my shorthand for *backbone, chutzpah, determination, endurance, fortitude, guts, grit, spunk, stamina, pluck, persistence*, and *perseverance*. I've never associated tenacity with functions (except in protecting their functional turf). On the other hand, I have repeatedly seen tenacity infusing the spirit of a team. (If, that is, the team is given a charter, adequate authority, and a stake in the outcome.) The "front and rear" analogy applies here also. Try to win a battle sometime when those at the rear have *tenacity* but those at the front don't. Any responsible military leader will tell you, don't even bother to try. But that's what America's centocracies try to do every day. Inspired "tigers" at the front are needed every bit as much, or more, as armchair tigers at the rear. And if those at the front are indifferent, not inspired—lacking motivation and tenacity because of the way they're being "managed"—then forget success. Unless, that is, you're fortunate enough to be pitted only against those still mired in the same centralist insensitivities to organizational and leadership dynamics. If so, your luck will soon run out—because more and more are catching on to why that style must be abandoned. Thus, you need to be among the first, not the last, to abandon it.

Touch

I'm talking about good touch with the product, good touch with the customer; the touch that comes from intense involvement and insight; the touch that comes from in-depth understanding of what creates worker frustration and fulfillment; the touch that flows from leadership sensitivity and awareness; the overall organizational touch that flows from shared values and common purposes. And touch is even more than that. It's the finding and fixing of organizational elements that are out of touch. In other words, it's being in touch with the out-of-touch. There should be no doubt about the importance of touch. In fact, *high touch* is needed every bit as much as *high tech* if American businesses are to succeed in the nineties and beyond.

Teams provide the basis for the right kind of touch in all these respects. I've explained, for example, how the team approach puts the employees in touch with their product, not just their job. It also puts them in touch with the processes that must be properly focused and quality oriented if the product is to turn out well. Especially, it puts them in touch with one another in a team endeavor, as well as with the other teams with which they integrate, interface, and interact. Finally, the team approach fosters excellent touch, and continuing touch, among and between all organizational layers. That's of special importance to collective commitment.

The team-based approach helps in all these ways. It's the ideal way to distribute the leadership to ensure that it reaches *everyone* in the organization and provides the means for all to participate in the exercise of leadership. Perhaps that can be done in other ways, but I have yet to see it in the centocratic approach. And the consistency of the best companies in using teams, not functions, and the consistency of the beneficial results, suggest that if there is a better way it has yet to be found—by the Japanese or anyone else. I will have more to say on teams in chapter 11—on how to form them, charter them, and support them. Before that, though, let's turn to the *Outputs* element of the decentralized, leadership model—and examine how it interacts with the *Product* and *Team* aspects of the model in ways that nourish leadership.

A SUPERVISORY FOCUS ON OUTPUTS, NOT INPUTS, IS A KEY TO EFFECTIVE DECENTRALIZATION, AND IMPROVES CONTROL

In chapter 7 I presented evidence that it's the widespread view in the American management culture that decentralization means loss of control. There's an accompanying reluctance even to consider a decentralized system. That's conditioning. It's as Ron Riedasch explained in discussing how they struggled at Boeing Corinth before changing that prior conditioning: "It was as if you had lost your anchor." In that regard, I vibrate as much or more to the need for discipline, coherence, and control as any manager in America. It started early. When you have your fanny strapped to a high-performance fighter doing rolls, loops, and high-G turns with wingmen three feet or less away, you have a certain *vested interest* in coherence and control. And when you're in combat, with your own life and those of your compatriots in peril if you lose coherence and control, that need is unmistakably obvious. I also vibrated to that need when I was a wing commander, and in every other assignment including the most senior leadership positions. *But that rules decentralization in, not out.*

For example, what you saw in action in the USAF portion of the Gulf War air campaign was a highly decentralized management system. However, you also saw a vivid example of coherence and control within those scores of flights of fighters. And one could set the *second hand* of their watch by how closely to the scheduled time they were hitting their targets. The story was the same in the ground activities to generate those combat sorties. Therefore, please don't class me among those who the centralizers claim "don't understand why you have to maintain control"—a criticism quick to their tongues. I just use different ways to achieve it. So let's set aside that old notion (and old fear) and attack another of Centralism's sacred tenets by explaining how decentralization can *improve* control, not diminish it.

That's where the *Outputs* element of the decentralized model comes into play. A change to an outputs focus is essential because it inhibits micromanagement on the one hand, and on the other serves as the focal point for other conceptual elements of a decentralized system. As the Venn diagram on the following page suggests, changing the supervisory and employee focus to *Outputs* has a very positive effect on *Objectivity*; enables real, not illusionary, *Ownership*; creates the desired sense of *Obligation* in the decentralized "owners"; and thereby provides the overall *Orientation* by which the entire management system operates.

This *Outputs* theme in the interactive model is important because changing the supervisory focus to outputs, not inputs, is a key to making decentralization acceptable to managers, and also is the key to making it work. The issue of control, which I find uppermost in managers' minds as they consider decentralization, cannot be glossed over. Indeed, it's the single largest stumbling block preventing more widespread acceptance of decentralization and the team approach. Thus its importance. Let's examine the various aspects of what the outputs focus and this synergy of "O's" provide. The place to start is with the ways to measure, to provide objectivity. Frankly, centralized organizations couldn't use the outputs focus in this manner if they wanted to (and they don't) because they don't measure and compare in ways that lend themselves to these applications. And that's one of their most serious deficiencies.

PROPER MEASUREMENT SYSTEMS ARE ESSENTIAL. YOU MUST KEEP SCORE, ASSESS, AND PROVIDE FEEDBACK TO ALL OF THE EMPLOYEES

When I first started in supervisory positions I was told there are two basic management questions: *What's the plan*? and *Who's in charge*? The more responsibilities I accrued the more I realized the wisdom of that observation. When things went wrong it almost always was because the plan was poor or the execution faulty because of poor leadership, or some combination of the two. But increasingly I came to realize there are not two but three basic management questions. The third is, *Compared to what*? Without meaningful compar-

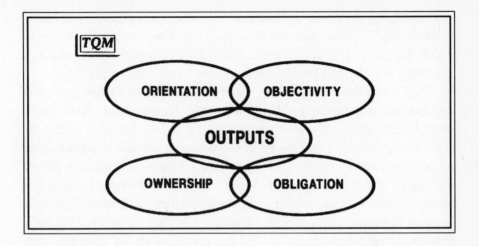

ison, people in all walks of life are simply not objective about their strengths and weaknesses. They tend to magnify the former, downplay the latter, and overdramatize their standing and accomplishments. If there were no football games in the NFL and you polled the teams, at least three-fourths of them would contend they were the best. That eventually gets sorted out, and placed in perspective, on the field of competition. But businesses that do not provide measurement and comparison, and most don't, can count on their planning being faulty and their leadership misdirected, because neither is formulated in the harsh light of objective reality.

On that subject, Marcus Aurelius, noble Roman and Stoic philosopher, said this in *Meditations*, Book IX: "Facts stand wholly outside our gates; they are what they are, and no more; they know nothing about themselves. What is it then, that pronounces the judgment? Our own guide and ruler, Reason." But you can't apply the reason without the facts, and most companies, for reasons of their own choosing, don't collect facts and analyze them. That's a big mistake. And Johann von Goethe, in his *Maxims and Reflections* (1833), pointed out the danger of ignoring an objective and energetic search for errors: "The most fruitful lesson is the conquest of one's own error. Whoever refuses to admit error may be a great scholar, but he is not a great learner. Whoever is ashamed of error will struggle against recognizing and admitting it, which means that he struggles against his greatest inward gain.'' Those are words to live by. You can't pull the facts inside the gates, and derive those fruitful lessons, without measuring, assessing results, and providing feedback to all employees.

That's what we did in TAC (and what I did in earlier and subsequent transformations). That's what the Japanese do. And that's what Boeing does. It's also what a lot of others are now doing. It boils down to this: *You can't tell the winners without a scoreboard, or tell the losers either.* And without a scoreboard neither winners nor losers will know which they are. No one will know how to get better, either. In that regard, I strongly believe a leader's greatest nemesis is human subjectivity. I quickly add that it can be a leader's greatest ally—when marshaled in the proper way. In all cases, the greater the *objectivity* of everyone in the organization—based on ample data, facts, and surveys and not on supposition—the better off you are. And it's not only for Goethe's persuasive reasons of recognizing and correcting error; it gets the competitive juices flowing.

It's also how you wean the supervisory orientation away from micromanagement. That turns the doers at all levels into *thinkers* and *doers*, and makes even the frontline level a part of the *management*. None of that implies anyone should become indifferent to the inputs. Quite the contrary. You get everyone worrying about their adequacy and timeliness, not just the senior managers. It does mean, however, that one must reorient the supervisory focus if decentralization is to work. And one of the first things to address is the rules.

We did that in TAC. I called in working-level groups from operations, maintenance, supply, and the various other field activities. I then put them in a room with all the regulations that pertained to their activities and told them to get rid of at least half of them—and even more if they thought appropriate. *It was a labor of love.* There was a mountain of regulations because centralizers always add rules as they go along in the futile effort to *force* compliance. I then set up a system for periodic zero-based reviews of the regulations to screen out even more. Also, if commanders at lower levels added any rules, a copy came to my office for my personal attention. Most centralizers want those below them to tighten the screws, not loosen them, so this was a big change in the culture. If I detected even a hint of "CYA" in the rule, or thought it patently unnecessary, I picked up the phone and reasoned with the rule writer. Normally I practiced a hands-off style. But I have found that you have to work *hard* at keeping organizations decentralized.

As you would expect, when we cut way back on the various rules it was extremely popular with those at the frontline. However, I readily confess it was not a universally popular move at the upper levels of TAC. Most exulted; some worried. And some voiced their concern in no uncertain terms. For example, one of the TAC numbered Air Force commanders (group president in corporate terms) expressed the views of many when he told me, "After all, those rules are there for a reason. They are saving us from our past mistakes." My reply was "They also are saving us from our future accomplishments." In fairness, all the senior officials along with everyone else at lower levels had long been sensitized to—and constantly berated about—the need to maintain control through the rules. That's what Centralism preaches. And that attitude was particularly applicable to flying safety.

WE IMPROVED TAC'S FLYING SAFETY RATE 275 PERCENT BY SUBSTITUTING DISTRIBUTED LEADERSHIP FOR CENTRALIZED MANAGERSHIP

When I took over TAC it was averaging one fighter crash every 13,000 flying hours. (It's a challenging and dangerous business.) Based on past experience, the conventional wisdom was that if the flying rules were relaxed the least bit, or the risk factor increased, that accident rate would worsen dramatically. Like the other aspects of the conventional Centralism wisdom, I decided to stand that view on its head. So, as in every other area, we cut way back on the rules that applied to flying operations and loosened the ones we retained. Not only that, but we greatly increased the training realism. Two examples of those changes set the overall tone.

First, in bygone years, indulging in practice aerial combat—dogfighting—with other units and other services had been ruled out. The "fangs" of the competing pilots come out in that kind of aerial dogfighting. Because pride gets involved, unless the pilots exercise strong self-discipline and excellent technique, the aircraft will be flown beyond its limits—and once a heavy, swept-wing fighter goes out of control it nearly always crashes. For those reasons, this kind of training had caused lots of accidents in the past. Thus, such training, though valuable, had become strictly forbidden. Believing that was shortsighted and unnecessary, we allowed such dogfighting—in fact, we encouraged it. We even provided special funding to wings so they could deploy to the bases of other units and services to carry it out. The money came from the significant savings we generated elsewhere.

Second, we dropped the minimum altitude for low-altitude navigation missions from 500 feet to 100 feet. (Considering human reaction time, that's attention-getting low when you're traveling at more than 600 miles an hour—10 miles a minute—over rolling, even mountainous terrain.) That and a combination of other increases in training realism raised the overall risk factor by a factor of three, at least. This was to be a noble experiment: relying on greater leadership latitude and professionalism at the frontline level instead of the rule-mongering and stifling managership from above that were the trademarks of Centralism. I believed that those at the lowest level, if given more latitude and responsibility, could and would train more realistically with no increase in accidents. Not only that, I was convinced that if we improved their professionalism by that means we could actually bring our accident rate down significantly. So how did we do?

At the time I left TAC the accident rate had been reduced from one crash every 13,000 hours to one crash every 50,000 hours—a 275 percent improvement. All achieved in the face of greatly increased realism, and far fewer rules. Moreover, that improvement had been in place for four years by the time I left. In fact, by reducing the accident rate so dramatically, during my stay at TAC we saved 133 fighter aircraft—a savings of $1.6 billion in replacement cost avoidance—and saved the lives of 104 air crews. This is but one example. Every aspect of safety improved, along with our quality and productivity, as the power of the decentralized, leadership approach kicked in.

However, prior conditioning to Centralism doesn't give up easily. It's Air Force practice that every time a fighter accident happens an accident board is convened, headed by a full Colonel. The board carefully examines the facts and then briefs the top commander (such as at TAC) on its conclusions and recommendations. Nine times out of ten the board would recommend several new restrictive rules. Nine times out of ten I turned them all down. That trend of the boards recommending new rules and my turning them down became so common that I often wryly observed to TAC's senior officers that it had fallen to us to save TAC (including its improved combat proficiency and increased savings) from its accident boards. Most of the morals of the story are obvious, but three are worth emphasizing. First, the best way to achieve coherence and control is through leadership, not rules and managership. Second, you have to work at keeping decentralization going because of the prior conditioning of generations of our managers. Third, it takes some guts to be a decentralizer, but the payoff is large.

All games need rules. All playing fields need boundaries. And nothing in the above story suggests that I, or anyone else in TAC, tolerated any foolishness or cavalier use of the taxpayers' equipment. We applied a simple rule: *A mistake is not a crime, and a crime is not a mistake.* Everyone soon learned to honor the difference, and also to honor the fact that we were as good as our word on both counts. However, if the rules are too strict, or the boundaries too narrow, forget initiative, ingenuity, and innovation. And forget employee motivation. When the system is overly restrictive the employees revert to the narrow *job* orientation and again begin doing just enough to get by. Moreover, the centralist focus on holding everyone, not the individuals, vaguely accountable produces people who spite the system by testing it to and beyond its limits. Thus, Centralism produces accidents, not eliminates them.

As you provide far greater trust and latitude, you should also keep track of how things are going. You then share the results for the benefit of one and all. With authority comes accountability, but with authority also comes pride of ownership and breathing room for creativity and innovation. That's where measurement comes in.

WHAT DO YOU MEASURE? THE "PERS" OF PRODUCTIVITY AND QUALITY—IN COMPARISON TO GOALS, HISTORY, AND LIKE ACTIVITIES

So much for the underlying philosophy, but how do you do it? First match an activity in product terms with a specific group of employees. Then work out straightforward ways to measure vis-à-vis goals. One technique is to measure the *"pers."* Sales per employee, widgets per shift, defects per parts produced, customer complaints per department per week, and the like—oriented to both quantitative and qualitative measures of merit. You don't want a lot of them. A few will usually get the job done. Why "pers"? For comparison. A story told about golfer Lloyd Mangrum makes the point. Mangrum, not unlike Arnold Palmer, was known to spray his shots around the golf course—but then somehow recover to get the ball into the hole at par or below. So he was usually high on the *Leader board* at the end of a tournament. During one such tournament an opponent grumbled, "Mangrum, I never see you as we go from tee to green, you're always out in the bushes, but I'm down to you by six shots. And you do that all the time." Mangrum smiled sweetly and replied, "What is this we're playing: How? or How many?"

Empowered employees who are provided insight into the "how many" will soon come up with innovative ways to improve the "how." Since employee attitudes are the key, the measurements should be kept as simple and as relevant as possible. W. Bruce Chew of Harvard, an expert on factory productivity in North America, Europe, and Japan, has set forth his "No-Nonsense Guide to Measuring

Productivity.'' Chew's advice is: ''Don't sacrifice function for form.''
He explains further:

> A multifactor index to track productivity gives managers a conven-
> ient scorecard to answer the question, ''How are we doing?'' But
> an index can play this role only if managers and workers understand
> it, which may require certain compromises in mathematical elegance
> and accuracy. . . . When the primary goal is to influence behavior,
> the simpler the better must be the rule. If the people who use an
> index can't understand it at a gut level, it probably will not affect
> their decisions and priorities.

To that I say, Amen. The measurement system must not only be
simple and understandable, but it must be primarily designed for the
employees who are actually doing the work.

The results also are used, of course, by supervisors on up the chain
for insights into outputs and trends. But supervisors are to use these
results for intrusion if (and only if) required. So you should get the
frontline employees in on the design. To every possible extent make
it *their* system—measuring *their* product, *their* outputs, and *their*
quality, and providing *their* rewards for outstanding achievement.
They'll take it from there. At the same time, methods must be established for free-flowing communication between and within all levels
of the organization—communications that will effectively, openly,
and honestly address all matters related to common purpose and common perspectives. Such unfettered communication is a distinguishing
feature of all the best companies I've seen. Given its overriding importance, let's look at the matter of communication flow in some
detail—top-down, bottom-up, interpersonal, and interdepartmental.
That's the organization's bloodstream. If that isn't in good shape the
organization isn't either.

FREE-FLOWING, UNGARBLED COMMUNICATION IS IMPORTANT TO EVERY ORGANIZATION—BUT IS STILTED IN MOST. AND IT IS VASTLY IMPROVED BY AN INTERACTIVE STYLE AND SEAMLESS STRUCTURE

Communication is at best an imperfect art. George Bernard Shaw captured the principal problem with this short sentence: "The greatest problem in communication is the illusion that it has been accomplished." That illusion is particularly rampant where there is not a good feedback loop. There are communication breakdowns every day, everywhere.

Henry Mintzberg wrote about that very problem in his book *The Structuring of Organizations*, and he gave a classic example of the imperfections that show up in the communication process. The story emerged from World War I:

> Word-of-mouth communication along the trenches in the British sector during a period when the field telephone was out of order is reputed to have resulted in the message "Send reinforcements, we are going to advance" from the front line being relayed to headquarters as "Send three-and-fourpence; we are going to a dance."

Such communication breakdowns also occur when the "field telephone" is *in* order. In fact, the much-cited "fog of war" is primarily due to the imperfection of communication. We're far better at it now than in World War I, but it remains an art that we probably won't ever master completely. If it's left alone, you can depend on it being bad.

One of the cardinal rules in effective communication is to be sure you're saying what you mean to say in the first place. Often that's not the case. Sometimes the differences are subtle, sometimes they're blatant; either way they can cause problems. A classic example is where the first word somehow gets lost in the admonition, "*Cease fire!*" And often what is said conveys a different message than that intended. Here are some amusing examples of not getting it quite right. Notice in an Acapulco hotel: "The manager has personally passed all the water served here." Sign in a Bucharest hotel lobby: "The lift is being fixed for the next day. During that time we regret that you will be unbearable." An Austrian ski resort advised its guests: "Not to preambulate the corridors in the hours of repose in the boots of ascension." A dry cleaner in Bangkok boasted: "Drop your trousers here for best results." A Paris hotel sign said: "Please leave your values at the desk." A Tokyo hotel topped that with this sign: "You are invited to take advantage of the chambermaid." In a booklet on the room air conditioner another Japanese hotel offered this sage advice: "Cooles and Heates: If you want just condition of warm in your room, please control yourself."

Obviously they didn't quite get the desired message across. And not all the cases are as amusing, and as innocuous, as these. With regard to the example from the Japanese product information booklet, such errors once were typical of the booklets accompanying Japanese products. Almost always they were good for a chuckle or two. But the Japanese changed that along with everything else in their continuous quest for quality in all things at all times. Compare the owner's manual of a Japanese car with that of an American car. You'll find it just as good; in fact, more often than not you'll find that the manual for the Japanese car is clearer, crisper, and easier to understand. And the Japanese are doing that in a host of foreign languages. How? By making it important, by paying attention, and by reaching out for the right kind of talented help. In a phrase, they work hard at it. Therein lies the secret to effective communication: The harder you work at it, the better it gets.

It's been said that interpersonal communication gets so badly garbled at times because when people talk, many different messages are involved. In fact, there are at least seven.

1. *What you mean to say.*
2. *What you actually say.*
3. *What the other person hears.*
4. *What the person hears in light of what they want to hear.*
5. *What the person hears in the light of their experience.*

6.   *What the other person says you said, and then does about it.*
7.   *What you think the other person said—about what you said.*

So breakdowns and misunderstandings occur constantly. In fact, they're inevitable. The more serious question is: How long will they persist, and continue to be passed along to others? That raises the key matter of whether the organization has continuous and multiple loops of information. I'm talking here of robust, unfettered communication loops—operating vertically *and* horizontally across *all* organizational "boundaries"—that allow the misunderstandings of today to be corrected by the communication of tomorrow.

Centocracies are particularly weak in this respect, for all the reasons I've given. Communication in centralized, functionalized organizations flows from the top down, and through the functional silos—just as it is designed and expected to flow. Consequently, communications upward are stilted and imperfect, as are the lateral communications between the functional silos. In that respect, I've already discussed the two distinct loops that develop in centocracies between the managers and the workers.

Sometimes the most important upward communication of all is *silence.* It can tell you what you need to know even more forcefully than heated words. Leaders also must learn to "listen" to the message that resides in actions and behavior. These actions often speak of dissatisfaction and divergent purpose more loudly than words can. Frontline employees also speak in body language, sometimes loudly and forcefully. But you have to see it to "hear" it. And if you don't go to the front a lot, you won't. Besides "listening" to individuals and the various groups in that way, many years ago I decided that perhaps the most vital aspect of proactive leadership is to stay constantly tuned to the *"Organization Language."*

ORGANIZATION LANGUAGE: EVERY ORGANIZATION HAS ONE—AND IT REFLECTS THE ORGANIZATION'S PRINCIPLES AS THEY'RE PRACTICED

It's no mystery to anyone that the language used in an organization is one signal of its policies and practices. To repeat one example, those who call their frontline workers associates are signaling their adoption of a different management philosophy than those using more traditional terms. Indeed, an organization's vocabulary, taken in its entirety, provides lots of clues regarding the system, structure, and style that are in use. Moreover, beyond the terms and descriptors there is a fuller dialogue that I call *organization language*. When one learns to listen to it with extended antennae and sharp ears it provides great insight into the management system principles that are actually at work. Accordingly, it's a valuable tool of proactive leadership—a means of determining what's working and what's not when it comes to the principles the organization *believes* it is practicing.

Let me explain how I learned to listen to the organization language—what was being said and not being said—for those very purposes. When I was a captain leading the *Skyblazer* aerobatic team in Europe, a new four-star general took over as commander of Air Forces Europe. News of his fearsome temper and harsh ways soon spread throughout the command. When displeased, it was said, he would throw a tantrum—including pitching his eyeglasses against the wall of his office or conference room. Soon everyone was calling him "Friendly Frank" behind his back—because he most assuredly wasn't. After a couple of years he left Europe and took over as commander of TAC shortly before I also came back to the United States, to TAC, and to the "Top Gun School" in Nevada. Same behavior on his part, same stories, same results.

My point in telling the story is to focus on the poor results. The fact is, his displays of rhetorical firepower had absolutely no effect down at the frontline where I was. He bullied and berated all those around him, but the only reverberations that reached us were related to his behavior, not his policies. Moreover, in the four years I served in those two commands under him I never met the man. And I had high-profile jobs in both. He never once visited either of the two bases where I was stationed—and each was the premier base of that command. We heard he traveled a lot, but it certainly wasn't to the front of his own organization! The moral is this: He had absolutely no effect on the organization's policies or on our behavior at the front. In essence, he was a nonevent in the life and language of the organization. I derived a powerful leadership lesson from that.

This lesson on organization language was reinforced when I was later selected as executive aide to the TAC commander who followed "Friendly Frank." He traveled much more, and to the frontline bases. I traveled with him. A familiar pattern emerged when we visited bases. Upon arrival, the general would get into the front seat of the car alongside the wing commander, and I would sit in the back. The general always started out by asking, "How's everything going, Colonel?" The answer, invariably, was some version of this: "Just great, General. This is the best wing in TAC. No problems here of any kind." The pattern was so predictable that I came to say to myself each time I heard it, *Either he's fibbing about no problems or he doesn't know any better, and either is inexcusable.* But I didn't blame the wing commanders. I blamed the fact that the system wasn't geared to creating effective communication *up.* That TAC commander was much more effective than his predecessor, particularly in communicating *down.* But I thought then, and later confirmed, that there was still much to do to improve the upward communication and the objectivity of the appraisals—at all levels.

Accordingly, when I later became TAC's commander we emphasized scorekeeping and objectivity. Every wing commander knew I was interested in the wing's problems—which every organization has and will always have—and it was no reflection on the wing that it had them. The only bad reflection came if wing leaders weren't seeking problems out, or were ignoring them or glossing over them. That's why openness and honesty are critical to continuous improvement and organizational health. It's also why organization language—and the art of affecting it and listening to it—is both a means and a result of effective leadership. The decentralized organizational model goes a long way toward curing the classic organizational ills in communication, but you still must work hard at it. I made up and used twenty-five reminders to myself on how to help make communication boundaryless, honest, and unstilted. They reminded me of the keys to making it a language of purpose, not protest, between front and rear:

1. Speak the language of trust, not of mistrust.
2. Don't confuse fancy words with profound ideas.
3. Don't harangue the many as the message for the few.
4. Reward the messengers of bad tidings, not shoot them.
5. Listen intently to the dissenting view; it may be right.
6. Keep all the language goals-directed—not rules-directed.
7. Talk in numbers as well as in words to crystallize purpose.
8. On key issues communicate several layers deep.
9. If the policy is important, put it in writing—concisely.
10. Listen for the echoes to learn if it's all getting through.
11. Follow up to ensure there is full comprehension throughout.
12. Remove all barriers to upward communication.
13. Be candid, and tell it like it is—without fear or favor.
14. Get all possible facts before expounding on the conclusions.
15. Get out the straight skinny—to combat misinterpretations.
16. Don't overhype or advertise. Let actions speak the words.
17. Praising the winners has more power than criticizing losers.
18. Credibility depends on flexibility, not mindless consistency.
19. Knowledge is power when widely shared, not withheld.
20. Feel free to admit you don't know, but you do want to learn.
21. The best opening sentence of all is: What do you think?
22. Listening, Hearing, Caring are the keys to making it thrive.
23. Provide the means and the incentives that will make it work.
24. Go where you need to go. Spend whatever is needed.
25. Treat the communications grid as an electrical grid. Any node failures leave people in the dark. Fill the vacuums. Find the reason they're there. Fix the grid.

Further, I might summarize the importance of effective communications to effective leadership this way:

- Though communication is an art, there's also a science to it. Companies that apply the science are far better at the art.
- There's a language of common purpose and one of divergent purpose. Stay closely tuned to which is being spoken.
- If what the rear stands for is not reflected by words and actions at the front, you're not communicating. If the front's language is not spoken at the rear, you're in even more trouble.

I also told leaders this: *If you always look up to the troops at the front—as you should—you'll never talk down to them.*

In short, leaders need to stay closely attuned to the *organization language*. It is telling them what the organization is thinking, feeling, and doing. *Effective* communication depends on the means and methods to make it free-flowing—and also depends on the leadership positively affecting the thinking, feeling, and doing. That can't be done with adequate effectiveness unless employees at all levels are sharing common information about what's going on. Therefore, the need is not only for caring, proactive leadership and free-flowing communication, but also for effective means of information gathering and distribution that provide the insight for enlightened choices and decisions. Many companies are weak in all these respects. Progress in such organizations remains anemic because they don't know how, when, and where to give it the needed boost. Let me provide an example from my business travels. This involves a well-intentioned company that professed to have adopted all of the "TQM" techniques but still was missing those tools of enlightened leadership. The story is illustrative. You can find the problem almost everywhere.

CONTINUAL PROGRESS: THAT'S HOW YOU JUDGE HOW EVERYTHING IS WORKING, BUT MOST COMPANIES DON'T HAVE GOOD ASSESSMENT TOOLS

In mid-1991 I was asked to give a speech on quality management to 110 top executives of a *Fortune* 500 corporation. The corporation professed to adhere to a decentralized organizational philosophy. (That no doubt was why they asked me to speak.) It also, in the recent past, had adopted what its executives perceived as a vigorous quality management program. They, like so many others, had named their program "TQM." Since I had seen TQM programs of all shapes and descriptions, I was interested to know the details of theirs. So as part of my speech preparation I met with the corporation's insider *quality guru* so he could explain it. He did a good job. He covered the operation of the firm's *quality councils* and *quality committees*. He also explained how the corporation was using cross-cutting, cross-functional teams to seek out and improve flawed processes. After explaining all that in great depth, he added, "So we're proud of our TQM program. Everyone has taken it to heart, and it's been implemented in all of our many companies and divisions. But to be honest with you, we've been in it two years now, and I don't know whether it's doing any good or not." I almost fell off my chair. Had I not been so long conditioned to similar stories I probably would have.

In following up, I found that the corporation had essentially no means to measure progress by other than the financial bottom line. (And it was varying little, but with all kinds of variations in the conditions that were influencing it.) Such a lack of detailed insight was not at all surprising to me. It's a condition that affects most American companies, even those that have embraced some—they believe all—of the new quality management techniques. At least the corporation in question is trying to come to grips with the forces of change. Most are not. So my intention is not to criticize them, but rather to point out that you must have ways to measure progress throughout. Otherwise you *"don't know whether it's doing any good or not"* when you take actions to improve. And you don't know where to make midcourse corrections, either.

Again, I emphasize these are not new ideas. I've read here and there that using *"benchmarking techniques"* to acquire such insight was an invention of the eighties. That's nonsense. I was using benchmarking for comparison (in the full sense of the modern term) decades earlier. And so, I have discovered since, were lots of others. But that was all lost in the general cacophony supporting Centralism. In fact, years before benchmarking became a buzzword in this nation's new quality lexicon, Peter Drucker was advising his readers, "If you want it, measure it. If you can't measure it, forget it."

Another hot phrase in the quality management literature these days is *"continuous improvement."* It's a good phrase, and a good concept. However, progress has many dimensions and thus requires many ways to measure it. In that respect, most businesses keep reasonable track of the various inputs, such as labor hours, inventories, and the like. And most also measure outputs—but only in macro terms such as sales, shipments, and the financial results. While such tools are important, they are wholly inadequate for detailed analysis of progress on other important aspects of organizational activity—at every level. Tom Peters caught the spirit of that greater need in his outstanding 1987 book *Thriving on Chaos*: "I have become a fanatic about quantifying—but a new sort of quantifying. I insist upon quantifying the 'soft stuff'—quality, customer linkups, innovation, organizational structure, people involvement." I put that same philosophy to excellent work in lots of settings over the years. You see the same in the Japanese companies.

Progress is what any management system should be all about. If companies don't know whether they're making progress, and where they are and where they aren't, their management system is not a system at all. That brings us to the matter of *information technology*, and how it is being underused in nearly all companies. When used imaginatively it facilitates decentralized leadership, enlightened decisions, common perspectives, and common purpose.

LEADERSHIP IS EASIER THAN EVER BEFORE BECAUSE THE TOOLS OF LEADERSHIP ARE BETTER THAN EVER —BUT TRADITIONALLY MANAGED COMPANIES DON'T PUT THEM TO WORK IN THAT WAY

Today we are acquiring more detailed knowledge about more phenomena all the time, and at an accelerating pace. Along with that new knowledge come new opportunities and complexities in its application. As one of the results both professional specialization and product specialization are proliferating. We see a new array of product and professional "niches" with each passing five years, and subspecialties now abound within old specialties. The trend is particularly discernible in medicine. From the general practitioner and general surgeon "specialties" at the beginning of this century we now have twenty-five physician specialties and fifty-six subspecialties with accredited training programs. The *Journal of the American Medical Association* reports that thirty-five of those subspecialties (well over half) became recognized in just the past five years. As one physician, a top AMA official, explained the trend, "Specialization is very important. It has to continue because it is the byproduct of advances in medical knowledge." He went on to express, however, his worry that the trend is leading "towards doctors who specialize in the left elbow alone." That, he opined, is bad for medicine. How far it will go no one knows for sure. But it undoubtedly will fractionate even further.

Similar trends can be observed in the other professions, perhaps not as dramatic but there nonetheless. Some cite these trends in contending that a generalist style of leadership is becoming more and more difficult, if not impossible and irrelevant. That adds fuel to the flames of Centralism, already burning brightly, with the same sort of strained "functional specialization" arguments I set up and knocked down in chapter 7. Those arguments have no more validity now than they did in the past, but they add to the stubborn resistance to a change from managership to leadership.

And they're wrong. Leadership is needed more than ever. As knowledge and attendant complexity grows, the more important, not less important, core values become. Also, complexity calls for even more efficient operation of the human system in every organization, regardless of its type. And we know, from countless cases, that the human system does not work harmoniously or efficiently without enlightened, involved leadership—at all levels—that can pull the various disciplines together into an integrated product effort. Can physicians operate independently or in a functional silo? Sure they can, and they do. But try to run a hospital that way. Or try to build an automobile, or another durable product, or provide a complex service that way. It simply doesn't work. At least, it doesn't work well enough in the face of intensifying competition brought on by globalization.

The premise that leadership is now much more difficult is wrong as well. Leadership is far easier than ever before, not harder. It's far easier (because the tools are available) to provide overall purpose and coherence while at the same time widely distributing authority for agility, responsiveness, and effectiveness at all levels. The best companies, including the Japanese companies, prove it. With such tools we can acquire, aggregate, analyze, assimilate, and disseminate timely management information in more efficient and creative ways than ever before. However, those leadership tools aren't being used in most businesses.

Lester Thurow, dean of the MIT Sloan School of Management, says in that regard, "I would no sooner go back to a typewriter than I would to pencil and paper. I think there's a mystery here. Why do we have all these wondrous things and productivity gains aren't showing up?" Excellent question. Unraveling that mystery (and relegating it to the past) starts with the issue of management styles and goes on to the issue of management tools. Those two subjects go together, and Tom Peters helps us understand why they do. In a 1989 article in Marriott's *Portfolio* magazine he addressed that very subject:

> To understand information's role, consider that a hierarchical organization is nothing more than an information processing machine. . . . Losers leave the essence of age-old hierarchical organization alone and layer modern information-technology systems on top of the traditional scheme. Additional sluggishness usually occurs. The key is using state-of-the-art information technology as a decentralizing tool, to substitute for hierarchy and to boost fully empowered and unencumbered workers.

As usual, Peters is on target. To follow that advice companies must get over two hurdles. The first is a conceptual one—the conviction that information technology can and must be used to facilitate decentralization. Most companies, particularly traditionally managed ones, can't marshal the enthusiasm to get over that first hurdle. The second hurdle rises from a lack of comprehension of the tools available and the way they might be put to work. As a result, these tools are not put to good use by more than a few companies. Yet there's no need to stand around scratching your head over how to start. You don't have to be a Ph.D. in computer technology or mathematics to go about it, as I explained in chapter 6. A simple rule applies: *It can't be that hard, people do it.* The controlling issue is making up one's mind to do it. Once that decision is taken, employees throughout the business are easily trained on its application.

THE USE OF MODERN INFORMATION TECHNOLOGY TO PROVIDE AWARENESS, VISIBILITY, AND FOCUS IS AN IMPORTANT PART OF TQM. THAT ISN'T WIDELY RECOGNIZED—AND IT ISN'T WIDELY USED FOR THAT

Paul A. Strassmann is one of the country's most learned and experienced authorities on information technology. He was the chief computer executive at General Foods, Kraft, and Xerox, and then began his own consultancy business in New Canaan, Connecticut. (He recently helped the DOD develop new uses of information technology to provide better insight into its far-flung operations, and provide greater coherence as well.) Paul Strassmann has written extensively on this complex subject including a 1985 book, *Information Payoff: The Transformation of Work in the Electronic Age.* He explains how companies improve through the appropriate and imaginative use of information technology—and about what's right as well as what's wrong. Among his many cogent observations, these caught my eye:

- Automate only after you simplify.
- You cannot measure what is not defined.
- **Effectiveness is a matter of team performance.**

- Without productivity goals business has no direction.
- Without productivity measurements business has no control.
- Without strong leadership little success can be expected.

He explains that by leadership he also specifically means "a strong sense of purpose and a vision that the leader articulates about how the results to be obtained from the technology relate to the purposes of the business." He has a way of getting to the crux of the matter.

Obviously you need to make sure you use the information system and the system doesn't use you. And Strassmann cautions, "Big information systems failures arise from an imperceptible drift towards chaos. Unless continuous action is taken to the contrary, all information systems tend toward disorder." I've seen the same, often. However, it's a very manageable problem. Also, most companies are now dealing with a dearth of data, not with a data deluge, particularly when it comes to the applications I'm discussing in this book. Therefore, the need to control the system before it controls you is no reason for reluctance to use the tools that can provide for enlightened leadership at all levels.

In his extensive other writings, Strassmann points out that "the [information] technologies flatten hierarchies." That's based on empirical evidence. In studying sixty different companies he found that the top performers got that way by spending more than twice as much on information systems than their competitors—and they had an average of four management layers as compared to eight in their poorly performing rivals. That provides additional proof that those astute enough to organize small and flat also are the most astute at using information technology to network the elements together. And that permits even more streamlining.

A relevant question at this point is: Should the management information system be operated on a centralized or decentralized basis? Strassmann says:

I find the most practical way of resolving the disputes between the big computer centralists and the microcomputer autonomy-seekers is not to listen too much to technical arguments but to follow the maxim that system design should follow organizational design. If the chief executive really believes in decentralization of authority, then distributing the responsibilities for systems management is in order, and vice versa.

That's the right point to make. Information systems indeed can be adapted to any organizational structure and style. However, the decentralized way—the "organize small" way—holds the key to unlocking workplace potential for abundant other reasons.

Let me add my own cautionary note: The centralizers seize on every new development as a means of defending the continued validity of their preferred management approach (just as they have in using the specialization trend argument). They've seized on this issue, too. You can now hear rumblings from those of a "centralist management persuasion" joining voices with those of a "computer centralist persuasion" to argue that modern information technology is perfectly suited to the precepts of Centralism, and that the two form a great partnership in producing economies of scale, economies of effort, lower costs, etc. (You know the rest of the litany.) Thus, they've found another reason—and another "overlay"—to perpetuate the disastrous centralist style.

Paul Strassmann also confirms that information system technology is simply not being put to fully effective use in most companies. Some of the abundant evidence comes from a comprehensive study of the combination of "Management Productivity and Information Technology." Conducted by the Massachusetts-based *Strategic Planning Institute*, under Paul Strassmann's direction, the five-year project gathered and analyzed data on 292 manufacturing cases. Among the findings was the revelation that "operations" receives a minuscule share of information technology dollars. The report explained it this way:

Who in Management spends all the computer money? It is concentrated in Administration and Sales & Marketing. During the five years of our study Manufacturing, Distribution, Field Sales, and R&D activities did not show any appreciable gains in information technology costs. The only heavily automated Operations function is in administrative processing.

That drives home the principal point to be made here, so there's no need to go into the study's many other important findings. The scant use of information technology to track and improve "operations-related" activities is verified by other studies.

The fact is, almost all companies that use information technology use it exclusively for administrative matters, personnel matters, inventory matters, and financial matters. But using it to track performance, quality, and productivity in a detailed way—as we did in TAC and as the Japanese do—is rare. This is now changing somewhat, but with glacial slowness. Tom Peters, in a 1990 article in *Business Watch* titled "Nine Steps to Speeding Up Your Operations," provided this advice on the matter:

> Become a pioneer in the application of information technology, both inside and outside the firm. Inside the firm you have to link everyone together, across levels and functional barriers. All information must be available to virtually everybody in the organization. . . . The biggest problem is that you have to start now. You won't have time to catch up later. Many companies are waiting for industry standards to evolve. But that's not the point. About 95 percent of the issues related to application of information technology are power and organization issues, not technology issues.

Outstanding observations, outstanding advice. Not many companies look on it that way. But the best companies do.

Jack Welch of GE says, "For me, good communication is simply everyone having the same set of facts. When everyone has the same facts, they can get involved in shaping the plans for their components." Boeing also is highly attuned to these issues, and is a leader in the use of information technology to make every aspect of its operations better. For example, in its *Commercial Airplane Company* Boeing has developed and installed a *Quality Improvement Project Sharing System* (QIPSS) that contains information on improvements throughout Commercial Airplane's activities. The whole idea is to share the information on improvements, and to have that collective wisdom readily available to all. The QIPSS system nets together more than 1,500 Boeing teams, helping make each one better. I have already written, in chapter 3, about the great benefits GE and Boeing have garnered from their team-based management approaches—as well as from imaginative use of information technology to net those teams together and to create continuous improvement.

Boeing also is working (with IBM) on ways to use a "paperless design" in its next generation of airliners. Computer-based technology has progressed to the point at which that's an achievable goal: To design the plane, eliminate the classic physical mockup always used before, and go right to the shop floor and build it—all without paper. In fact, three dimensional computer software programs, such as "CATIA" (Computer-Aided Three Dimensional Interactive Application), already are taking most of the guesswork and *cut-and-try* out of product design, for even the most sophisticated products. It does so by allowing designers and engineers to "see" final designs —with tolerances of thousandths of an inch—and to manipulate and revise those designs, all on a computer screen.

A big step toward the "paperless design" of an airplane has already been taken. The Air Force's new F-22 Stealth air superiority fighter was designed on desktop workstations linked between the involved companies (Lockheed, Boeing, and General Dynamics). Each company was responsible for one-third of the airplane structure. When it came time to put together all those pieces—built in three different locations by three different companies—they all mated together *perfectly*. One senior engineer captured the import of that, and the great difference from the past, with this observation: "We can now throw away the ball-peen hammers we always have used to pound on the mockup pieces to make them fit when we first put the mockup together." The engineering drawing board couldn't produce enough precision to avoid cut-and-try. Information and data processing technology do. It's a veritable revolution in engineering efficiency and in eliminating design problems at their source to create far greater product coherence and efficiency.

The point of including this insight into the evolving information technology is just this: On the one hand, we have extraordinary benefits flowing from the use of computer-based information systems; on the other, we have barely scratched the surface in using information technology for distributed leadership and the networking of small, agile, focused organizational elements. We're also painfully slow in using it to get rid of the sea of paper that currently swamps our management systems. Many say the Medicare system is strangling in paper. Medicare is not alone. In fact, most of the exchanges within the nation's centocracies are paperful and purposeless. In other words, the traditional American management style has got it backward.

We employed computer networking in TAC to aid our new organizational network featuring distributed leadership through product-oriented teams. Computer networking also was a key to decentralizing the supply system—and to improving its efficiency and responsiveness. By thinking small, and using information technology to facilitate the "organize small" approach, we made that important supply subsystem far more purposeful and paperless, simultaneously. A 65 percent reduction in paperwork and speeding up parts delivery from several hours to only eight minutes are impressive productivity improvements in anyone's ballgame. That's but one example of the great productivity power that resides in the imaginative use of information technology as a *decentralizing tool*. Despite such examples, and there are many around, it remains to be seen how many will heed Tom Peters's sage advice to "*become a pioneer.*" So far it's not exactly the *Great Oklahoma Land Rush*. It needs to be. To the victors go the spoils.

In my own business travels I find the same correlation that Paul Strassmann's studies and others like them have found. The companies that make the fullest and most imaginative use of information technology—in a "think small," "think wide" context—are leaders in their industry. Wal-Mart serves as a graphic example. Some think of Wal-Mart's success as coming solely from price discounting and Sam Walton's extraordinary feel for the marketplace and rapport with frontline employees. That was a big part of it, but it was a lot more than that. Wal-Mart grew big in Bentonville, Arkansas, by thinking small, wide, and modern when it came to use of information technology.

All Wal-Mart stores are netted into a companywide satellite communications system for the rapid movement of information. And Wal-Mart has a management information system as sophisticated and effective as you'll find. Computer-based, with a decentralized theme, it nets together all of Wal-Mart's stores and other company facilities and activities (including a huge warehousing and trucking system). The system is geared to knowing what's going on in all aspects of "operations," to sharing successful practices, to keeping inventory moving swiftly, and to gaining the other *edges* that separate winners from losers in the wholesale-retail business (or in any business, for that matter). Sam Walton gave us a perfect example of how to turn a percent or two on the dollar into billions. The *competitive edge* is a delicate as well as critical matter, and he understood that surpassingly well.

Instructively, Wal-Mart designed its system, and uses it, to *decentralize* authority and to get *leadership* operating from the bottom up. Bob Martin, senior vice president for corporate information systems, explains the Wal-Mart approach, and its underlying rationale, this way:

> Our corporate culture is to continue to push decision making ever further down in the corporation. Our management style is grass-roots—no heavy hands from the upper echelon. All our people are encouraged to become entrepreneurs. This means we have to provide information at all levels. The personal computer lets people get just the information they want, just when they want it, in the specific format they want. . . . Our view of technology never has been to replace people but to support what our people do. Our technology has to match how they think and the way they work.

It can't be said better. That's precisely how the best companies think—and how they go about it.

A glowing example of an industry leader with great moxie regarding information technology is *American Airlines*. Perhaps no company in America can lay a stronger claim to being the nation's leader in its innovative application—American uses it to shape everything the company does. AA's *SABRE* (Semi-Automated Business

Reservation Environment) system is the travel industry's most sophisticated and largest data system. Much has been written about the advantages American has gained from this system. For example, by providing it to travel agencies throughout the country, American brought them into the SABRE "family"—and made it far easier for them to book travel on American. But SABRE does more than that. American also uses it to work out flight schedules, made increasingly complex by the need for smooth and timely transfers at its hubs (and American is the best in the industry at that), and to track maintenance actions and parts, as well as a host of other details affecting almost every aspect of its overall operation. SABRE also provides the management overview information that is vital to timely and informed decisions by the leaders at all levels.

That American's innovative and hard-charging chairman and CEO, Robert L. Crandall, and AA's senior management team have been out in front of everyone in the imaginative use of information technology is one of the principal reasons for American's great comparative success in a highly competitive industry. One who helps put that aspect into clear focus is Donald Burr, founder of *People Express Airlines*. As most recall, People Express burst on the management scene like a meteor and attracted reams of favorable comment, only to fizzle out. Don Burr's sensitivity to "people systems" and imaginative policies to motivate employees were widely reported on, and justifiably so. When People Express failed, many thought the problem centered on that aspect.

Burr thought differently. He said this in an *INC.* interview in April 1989:

There were people who were pessimistic about people systems. Some say, "Well, People Express may have been interesting, but the evidence is that it doesn't work." The reason People Express didn't roll on had nothing to do with its people systems. What happened had everything to do with information technology and nothing to do with people systems. The airline business happens to be the first industry to have been transformed by information technology.

Burr provided more insight in the February 1989 *Business Week*, in a cover story titled "The Frenzied Skies": "I heard Crandall talking about a high-tech airline in 1983–84 but I didn't know he was talking about computers. . . . They took my margin away and I couldn't survive." In other words, American had the vision regarding the pervasive use of information technology and its SABRE system—and People Express had neither and thus no way to compete. In the same interview, Burr went on to make this prediction: "There are going to be dozens of industries that will be transformed by the ability to manipulate information in a really lethal way." Burr is absolutely right. That's happening in America, but not widely, and far too slowly.

Bob Crandall is not letting American rest on its laurels in this regard. Constantly attuned to the need for renewal and rejuvenation to stay ahead of the competition, American has spent over $150 million to install an even larger, more advanced information system called *InterAAct*. Its purpose is to make the corporate data bases available to *everyone* in the company—vastly improving communication, coordination and decision-making at all levels. American's information guru explains its advantages this way: "Before InterAAct we were all slaves to telephone tag and the delays inherent in internal company mail. . . . Now we can be more efficient about administrative tasks, so we can spend more time with people instead of paper. Our highest priority is to get everybody to be leaders." Enough said.

The astuteness of Crandall's leadership at American shows itself in other ways. For example, Crandall is a great believer in the use of performance measurement, comparison, and feedback to employees, and American was the carrier that convinced the Department of Transportation (DOT) to start publishing comparative data regarding on-time arrivals and baggage handling. The fact that all U.S. airlines have substantially improved in both since that program started is another powerful endorsement of the beneficial effect of measurement and feedback on employee performance, especially when done in a comparative context. Crandall has also suggested that the DOT publish comparative data on the maintenance spending and quality of each carrier; thus far to stoic DOT silence. This shows that Crandall, like all good leaders, doesn't shrink from comparison with others. In fact, he prizes it.

Deregulation has had a profound effect on the airline industry, and most carriers have fared poorly. Witness the woes of Braniff, Eastern, Frontier, Midway, and Pan Am (all now defunct) and those struggling with bankruptcy (America West, Continental, and TWA). In that intensely competitive environment in which many have failed, American Airlines has grown dramatically. Indeed, it more than doubled in size between 1983 and 1990—a remarkable rate of expansion given the environment. As this was being written *all* the airlines were struggling financially. Their problems were compounded by those in bankruptcy protection selling seats at a loss, forcing the others to follow suit. In an industry where *price is king* that's a formidable challenge, even for the best. Nevertheless, there's no question that all of American's stakeholders have profited greatly from the caliber of the AA leadership under Crandall's tutelage—which has turned American into the country's best airline *by far*. Given my background, it stands to reason I know what to look for in making such a judgment. (And I travel on all the airlines extensively.) As another measure of merit, in Crandall's first nine years at the helm, the price of American's stock increased eightfold. Not bad in a troubled and turbulent industry!

I emphasize it starts from a philosophy of leadership not managership throughout the organization. The creative use of information technology is simply the way to feed and facilitate that leadership—and to create the *hustle* by everyone that makes quality happen. Thus, American Airlines provides still more proof that paying the price for an effective information system is a value issue, not a cost issue. Indeed, the highest cost of all comes from incomplete knowledge, fragmentary situation awareness, and poorly informed employees. One could get by with that in the old days, but not anymore.

I also emphasize that the first step is to organize small and to get the leadership going from bottom to top. To do that one need not have as a precondition a highly sophisticated computer network. In other words, you need not get the cart before the horse (or buy an exceedingly expensive cart) to make *Five Pillar TQM* work. It is within the financial reach of all businesses to acquire the kind of information system that is adequate to their particular circumstances. In fact, you can't afford *not* to have it. The moral is this: Be a pioneer. Use information technology to aid the switch from managership to leadership. Otherwise, expect lots of bad news in this age of hard-nosed global competition.

WHEN THE VISION INCLUDES THE POWER OF THE HUMAN SPIRIT—AND THE MANAGEMENT SYSTEM IS BASED ON IT—SUCCESS ENSUES

Mostly I've provided examples of companies that have changed their vision of the best way to organize and lead—and then decentralized their way to success. Let's now turn to a couple of companies that have applied the right vision and decentralization principles from the moment of their founding. The company that deserves to be mentioned first in that respect is *Federal Express*. FedEx is a well-known modern success story—and it has succeeded in the face of the "cultural handicaps" that others are blaming their failings on. The story has been adequately told by others. It's enough to say that I have unbounded admiration for founder Fred Smith and what he has achieved by thinking big about what FedEx can achieve—and thinking small about how to achieve it. Fred Smith also is among the mere handful of savvy corporate executives who make highly imaginative use of information technology, especially to make proactive leadership work from the bottom up. And he has proved himself a master at taking the time, wasted steps, and spotty quality out of every single process—in fact, he built FedEx on the principle of doing just that. As a result, Federal Express is a richly deserved winner of the *Malcolm Baldrige National Quality Award*. Its success story is inseparable from the story of Fred Smith's vision of how to go about it, and the skill and tenacity with which he carried it out. He did it right, right from the start.

I have primarily cited large, well-known companies in offering examples because they have identity and resonance with the reader. However, I've run across fully as many small companies that serve as exemplary role models. Let's look at one that started out with the right principles many years ago—and stuck to them in growing from a mere gleam in the eye to a half-billion-dollar corporation. The *Dynatech Corporation* is hardly a household name in America. But its story is relevant because it's another example of the power of the decentralized approach. And its great success further proves the "organize small" approach is the right way to go.

Dynatech, headquartered in Burlington, Massachusetts, was founded in 1959 by two MIT professors, Warren M. Rohsenow and J. P. Barger. From the very outset they established the Dynatech management and growth philosophy on the interlocking themes of *Technology, Decentralization*, and *Diversity*. (Warren Rohsenow, after decades as chairman and CEO, now serves as honorary chairman. Cofounder J. P. Barger took over as chairman and CEO.) The strong commitment of Rohsenow and Barger to the decentralized approach, in an unwavering way from the very start, has paid huge dividends to Dynatech's stakeholders. For example, Dynatech has enjoyed eighty consecutive quarters—twenty years—of consistent profitability, and an impressive degree of growth. The ten years from 1982 to 1992 alone tell the story of the effectiveness of its decentralized style. In 1982 Dynatech's annual revenues were $99 million. Its 1992 revenues topped $500 million, bringing it into *Fortune* 500 country. Annual sales growth during that period averaged 19 percent, and cash flow increases averaged 16.5 percent.

Dynatech's current product lines fall into three categories: communications, medical and environmental, and specialty products—all with a high-tech, electronics flavor. (For example, chances are the moving clouds you see in your nightly TV weathercast, or the impressive computer-driven graphics you see during an NFL football game, came from one of Dynatech's many product lines—it is the market leader in that field.) So, how has Dynatech done it all? Rohsenow and Barger say it was due to their faith in decentralization and empowerment even when that "wasn't the popular way to go." Each of the companies has its own distinct identity, ownership of its profit-

and-loss fortunes, and the autonomy it takes to be *"fast, fluid*, and *flexible."*

Claude Olier, Group VP for The Data Communications Group, puts it this way: "People are really in charge of their operations and are committed and accountable for results. There is a risk leaving people with large autonomy. But results provide freedom." Dynatech has also established mechanisms and incentives for networking within and between the companies. On that Olier says, "Each company should know what the others are doing to prevent reinventing the wheel two or three times."

And yes, Dynatech uses measurement and scoreboarding to keep track of what's going on. Terry Kelly, President of the Video Group, summarizes the Dynatech corporate philosophy this way: "There is no conceivable way that we could be as effective as we are in all these varied technology niches, in all these locations, unless we were completely decentralized with a high degree of autonomy—yet with all of it woven together in a common fabric." Clearly, not many of the *Fortune* 500 agree with that; that's why so many of them are struggling in the turmoil of globalization.

One of many indications of Dynatech's devout adherence to decentralized principles—woven tightly into its corporate character and culture—is that within the corporation there are 125 separate employee benefit plans at the various operating locations. The conventional Centralism wisdom is that Dynatech should have only one, and that it would recognize significant "economies of scale" and "great buying power" if it had but one. Rohsenow and Barger are not insensitive to those potential "savings." They just happen to believe that it makes much more sense to let each company adjust as it sees fit to its own market niche and special challenges. This is hardly the best example of Dynatech's decentralization and empowerment philosophy in action, but it's a particularly telling one because few American corporations of its size would do it that way. In fact, Dynatech's leaders believe it's because they have gone counter to the conventional management philosophy that they've been so hugely successful over so many years.

Currently Dynatech has six product groups containing seventy-one diverse companies in the United States and fourteen foreign countries ranging from Japan to Germany, Sweden to Hong Kong. The corporate staff is extremely small, and corporate headquarters doesn't meddle in any way unless one of its companies loses its way—almost always by forgetting the importance of the decentralized approach. Warren Rohsenow confirms that as Dynatech's biggest challenge over the years: the firm has been hurt several times by too little decentralization, but almost never by too much. Thus, the Dynatech experience further verifies that without top-down decentralized management beliefs, devoutly practiced and constantly reinforced, organizations do two predictable things: *They tend toward centralization and away from quality.* Dynatech's experience is but one more indication those two tendencies go hand in hand.

NO MATTER HOW GOOD THE MANAGEMENT SYSTEM, OR ITS SUCCESS RECORD, IT MUST BE ADAPTED TO CHANGING CONDITIONS

Rockwell, long one of the nation's premier and most successful corporations, serves as an instructive case in point. Its accomplishments in high-technology platforms to operate in air and space are unrivaled by any other manufacturer in the world. It has built an entire family of superb fighter aircraft over the years, which performed with distinction in the country's armed conflicts. Rockwell took America to the moon in its Apollo spacecraft and brought all the astronauts home safely—and now is making new space ventures possible with its "Space Shuttle." It has long been known also for the reliability and durability of its systems. (The unfortunate *Challenger* disaster owed to design and management inadequacies of the manufacturer of the solid rocket booster and of one NASA division, not to Rockwell.)

The Rockwell product mix is not confined to aerospace products. In fact, its largest segment by far is electronics, accounting for half of Rockwell's annual revenues of $12 billion at the turn of the decade. Automotive products provide 20 percent of sales, and the Allen-

Bradley Industrial Automation business has long been on the cutting edge of "factory of the future" technology. As this was being written, Rockwell had paid dividends to shareholders for forty-four consecutive years.

When Donald R. Beall, the astute, hard-charging chairman and CEO, took over Rockwell's reins in 1988 he recognized that the corporation, as successful as it had been, faced immense new challenges calling for new ways. So Beall set out to significantly streamline and delayer the organization. He started by eliminating the layer he previously had occupied as president and COO, and went on from there. His reorganization addressed the horizontal as well as the vertical by creating "flexible and entrepreneurial" business units. And he installed a *Total Quality Management* program even before the DOD called for one. That TQM program is one of the most imaginative, vigorous, and effective in corporate America, a notable exception to the rule.

In line with Don Beall's decentralized operating philosophy, each of the major groups names its own TQM program as it sees fit, and each is free to have variations fitting its own circumstances. However, Beall has made it crystal clear that Rockwell-style TQM will be far more than slogans—that it "requires evaluating, integrating, and changing organizational structure, reward systems, technology, management systems, processes, and other systems as required." He also emphasizes that each variant *"must be designed to encourage a high degree of employee participation while fostering a commitment to total quality and customer satisfaction."* At Rockwell, they fully understand the *sine qua non* of effective TQM.

Does Don Beall believe in leadership, not managership? You bet. In fact, he has come to call the entire Rockwell management approach *"Leadership Performance."* As he puts it, "The people of Rockwell understand that competitive excellence requires rising above parity, developing the full potential of our businesses by reaching for what we call 'Leadership Performance.' " (And Rockwell has established a school in the California mountains to teach leaders at all levels what that leadership philosophy must entail to be successful.)

Here is but one example of the philosophy in action: The Rockwell Automotive business decided to enter an entirely new product line, building transmissions for heavy-duty trucks. This was no simple undertaking as its competitors were highly experienced and well entrenched. Rockwell's Laurinburg, North Carolina, plant was structured to take on and surpass that competition using the company's TQM principles. As Beall describes the approach, "The workers there have been provided with great participation in decision making and great responsibility for results." Rockwell also is doing all it can to make the plant operate on a "paperless" basis. And the work force is organized into "*Self-Managed Work Teams*" that have responsibility for every facet of manufacture of the transmissions. Every employee is salaried, and there is only one job title: "*Production Technician.*" Is it working? Since its entry into the business in 1989 more than 600 fleets have purchased the Rockwell transmissions, and customer satisfaction is high as evidenced by many second and third purchases.

Rockwell has a related "*Continuous Process Improvement*" program in all its companies and divisions—and sends the leaders at the various levels to "CPI boot camp" to learn all about it. As one example of its beneficial results, the Rockwell "Avionics factory" reduced production cycle time from 265 days to 77. In short, these TQM principles work well at Rockwell just like everywhere else. Also, Rockwell adds proof they must be vigorously championed from the very top of the organization. Thanks to Don Beall's imaginative applications of the TQM principles, Rockwell has managed the downturn in defense spending as well as or better than any firm in America with a very large percentage of defense work in its product mix. In fact, shareowners' equity per common share has continued to climb despite the falloff in defense contracts, as has the size of Rockwell's dividends. That's because proactive distributed leadership is at work everywhere, day-in and day-out.

That, of course, is a common theme in the success stories I have recounted throughout these pages. First, these stories tell us that there must be strong leadership at the top. Second, they tell us that top management must be committed to distributing the authority throughout the organization—so that leadership can be exercised at the cutting edge, where it counts the most. And that requires change from the traditional ways. The old cliché goes: *You can't teach an old dog new tricks.* Don't you believe it! I've found, and have cited many examples, that the *old dogs* are some of the very best at the *new tricks*—and the most enthusiastic about carrying them out—when top management builds those new tricks fully into the company's management system and style. Let me coin a new adage that is all too true however: *You can teach a new dog old tricks.* The nation's centocracies prove that every day.

In his epic book *The Art of War*, Sun Tzu explained the overarching importance of strategy and style with these words: "A victorious Army seeks its victories before seeking battle. An Army destined to defeat fights in the hope of winning." Despite the truth of that timeless admonition, the nation's centocracies fight on—in the hope of winning. That's a hope that looks more forlorn with each passing year. In 1991 a staggering 103 of the *Fortune* 500 companies lost money—a full 20 percent. (And most assuredly they didn't make it to the *Fortune* 500 with such dismal outcomes.) The fortunes of those 103 have not noticeably improved since. Not only that, but at least half the others in that august *Fortune* 500 group are struggling to hold their heads above water. Put more bluntly, a great many are in trouble, that trouble is growing, and more businesses join their ranks all the time.

As this trouble mounts, more and more of America's managers are beginning to question the old "vision"—but are failing to come to grips with it. As Yul Brynner said, in prancing and pontificating as the *King of Siam* across a Broadway stage: *There are times I almost think I am not sure of what I absolutely know. Very often find confusion in conclusion I concluded long ago.* We need America's managers to reach that same new belief—it's the first step in giving up the old ways.

Vision? We've had no shortage of it—but far more often than not, it has been the wrong vision. Moreover, most of it has been carried out without heed to a *"law"* that I use on the matter of vision. It says: *A leader's vision has power only to the extent it is shared by those who are asked to carry it out.* Once one understands that, it's difficult to fathom why America fell so hard for the idea, and remains so affixed to it, that the managers must share and support the vision but not the workers. That's bad application of a management vision no matter what its other redeeming features.

In the dark and early days of the Civil War, filled with gloomy news, Lincoln said this to the United States Congress: "The question recurs—Can we do better? The dogmas of the quiet past are inadequate to the stormy present. The occasion is piled high with difficulty, and we must rise to the occasion. As our case is new, so we must think anew, and act anew." I recall those words here because the question does recur. Indeed, it is with us again today—in full force. As the "globalized economy" case is new, so we must think anew, and act anew, just as Abraham Lincoln advised us in leading the way to a new plateau in our thinking—and in our nation's heritage.

I've given many reasons in this and earlier chapters why we must think and act anew, what that new acting should entail, and why the *Leadership Pillar* is indispensable. Chapter 9 delves further into this surpassingly important subject. It addresses what form leadership must take to be effective and how to make it flourish from front to rear.

Creating Organizational Leadership and Competence

THE LEADERSHIP MAKES ALL THE DIFFERENCE—ALWAYS

After observing leadership in action in a large variety of public- and private-sector settings over many years, these are the conclusions that have emerged:

> *There are no poor outfits, just poor leaders. Often it's because they're poorly informed. Often it's because they're wrongly motivated. Often it's because they use flawed principles—and outdated techniques.* Always *it's because they've been poorly prepared. Leadership is learned. Leaders must create more leaders. Success in that shapes everything else.*

There's a well-traveled adage that says: *Lead by example.* (Meaning positive example, of course.) However, it's important to note that every supervisor in every organization leads by example, regardless of the organizational approach and leadership style. That's inescapable. The only questions are whether the example is negative or positive, how much so, and in what ways. That unavoidably leads to the issue of the leadership qualities the organization chooses to prize, teach, and otherwise encourage. Organizations that don't have a set of such qualities are overlooking the important fact that behavior is learned. Numerous studies show the influence of supervisors' qualities and behavior in shaping the attitudes of their subordinates. Nearly all employees continually strive to adapt to their workplace surroundings and to the expectations of their supervisors and peers. So copycat behavior is a fact of life, either a fortunate or unfortunate one depending on the example that is set. That seems obvious. However, it doesn't receive enough attention in most organizations.

I've seen too many organizations reflect the principles and behavioral style of the boss to have any doubt about the matter. And I've frequently seen employee behavior and performance swing markedly back and forth as leaders change—even between positive and negative extremes. Therefore, it's important that the top leader decide what leadership style he or she believes appropriate for his or her organization and its circumstances. (That's for the principles of leadership they espouse, not to try to make everyone a clone of themselves.) Positive, constructive behavioral patterns are important in leaders from the frontline level all the way up. The best companies don't take chances in this regard. They groom their leaders with those realities of human nature in mind. Therefore, no management book worth its salt should fail to address the issue of leadership—and the qualities that produce the right kind of leadership. When all is said and done, that's what "management" is all about.

The leadership effect receiving the most press and attention in management books is where a new leader takes an organization from rags to riches, failure to success. However, I've seen enough of the reverse effect when a new leader takes over, a negative influence which takes the organization down, to have any doubt about the importance of the leadership dynamics. And I've also observed how quickly a new leader can affect those dynamics in an organization. In that respect, TAC, due to its size and many operating locations in the United States and abroad, served as an excellent "laboratory" in which to observe those leadership dynamics at work as leaders changed over. There were many such opportunities, because the leadership mobility in the Air Force is much more rapid than in the business world. That's caused by people transferring, getting promoted, or simply being moved aside after a period to give others the chance to lead.

In watching those changeover results closely, *I never saw a new leader fail to have an effect*. Usually it was good, but sometimes it was bad. I found that leadership failures usually fit one of three basic patterns, and in looking at troubled businesses I've noted the same patterns. The first of the three involves the aloof and detached boss who simply doesn't know what's going on and whose employees don't know what he or she stands for. These bosses confuse managing their in box with leading people. They don't get involved, so they're not informed and aware, and they have no good basis on which to shape the organizational dynamics. Sometimes they pay lots of attention to external events, but almost none to internal events. Some call that the "happen back" school of leadership. They sit at their desk, wait for something to happen, and then they happen back at it. Leadership must be proactive, not reactive. That's what separates it from managership. And proactive leadership depends upon detailed involvement and awareness.

The second of the three patterns involves those who practice rule through terror. Their leadership tools are threats, bombast, and intimidation. (And I've encountered as many or more in the business world as I did in the military.) They shoot the messenger, second-guess decisions right and left, and end up alienating everyone. They also affect the subordinate leaders within the organization in one of two undesirable ways. First, many are fearful of exercising any leadership themselves because they know they will be "chewed out" on the flimsiest pretext. The second effect is even worse: Subordinate leaders become clones of the threatening, bombastic boss. They mirror that behavior and magnify the detrimental effect.

As an example of the intimidator effect, I've seen an entire outfit turn bad in a hurry when a new wing commander chose to "lead" through intimidation. I've worked for a few bosses like that myself, and they became my role models—of what *not* to do. That intimidator approach is always a loser. Everyone below the boss becomes frightened to take any initiative, and communication dries up completely. Therefore, the intimidators are no better informed than the detached bosses in failure pattern one. As a result, they huff and puff over the wrong things, and yell and scream at the wrong people. That's an exercise in futility—and a sure way to ruin an organization.

The third pattern is at the opposite extreme. That's the type of boss who is all over the place, but "running for office" and glad-handing, not probing, understanding, and setting new directions where necessary. This boss's personality craves the affection of everyone. In pursuit of that desire, he or she has a kind word for everyone, and a word of counseling for no one. Such bosses confuse leniency with leadership. As with the other two types of leaders they are poorly informed, for two basic reasons. First, they don't dig to find out what's going on. Second, employees soon learn it's no use telling them what's going on; they won't do anything about it anyway. Bosses like this are in the good news business, not the bad news business. They don't turn an organization bad as fast as an intimidator or the aloof boss, but it still ends up at the bottom of the pile.

The leaders do make the difference. However, that's a plus, not a minus; otherwise we would have no good way to mobilize human endeavor in pursuit of group goals. Reinforcing my belief regarding the criticality of the leadership dynamics, when a TAC organization of any size turned bad and counseling didn't fix it, I knew we could correct the situation by sending in a proven leader. And there was not a single case in which the new leader did not rapidly turn matters around. The turnarounds I've studied in the business world—and helped to create—fit the same pattern. So it boils down to this: *There are no poor outfits, just poor leaders.*

Yes, leadership is essential—and it's not managership. But you won't have leadership without the freedom to exercise it. And you can't get it by sloganeering; it depends on structure and system changes that provide the oxygen of empowerment. Only then will it flourish at every level. And that, in turn, will make the organization flourish. (If, that is, the *right kind* of leadership qualities are at work.) All this brings us to the matter of the leadership qualities—the right kinds—that are important to building the organizational character, culture, and climate that ensure success.

(I use the word "qualities" here to stand for the beliefs that shape an individual's attitudes, principles, and actions. I am not addressing the way those "qualities" may have been shaped by nature or nurture, nor do I suggest by the use of the term that leaders are born not made. In fact, I believe the opposite to be true.)

I've already addressed in some depth the organizational approach that frees the leadership to operate. Here, then, I speak to the nature of that leadership. Clearly, there isn't a single list of leadership qualities that's right for every organization. Also, setting forth only one such list can hardly encompass the different needs at different supervisory levels; or, for that matter, the leadership style that's appropriate in widely disparate types of organizations. My coverage of the subject, therefore, is designed to be representative and thought-provoking, not inflexibly prescriptive for every organization. I've seen the worth of these leadership qualities proven in many different settings, and by many different leaders. I emphasize that each organization must address the matter in its own way, and decide on the qualities that best fit its challenges. I commend these for consideration.

THE LEADERSHIP QUALITIES THAT MATTER MOST— BECAUSE OF THEIR EXTENSIVE EFFECT ON THE ORGANIZATION AND ALL THE EMPLOYEES

There are six I have found to be of the greatest importance: *courage, confidence, savvy, maturity, integrity*, and *desire*. They interact, one with the other. Indeed, that's what makes each of the six, and all of the six, so important. Here, based on my experience and observation, is a summary of the role each plays in shaping a leader's behavior, and through those leaders the behavioral patterns throughout the organization:

1. *Courage.* As most know, General George C. Marshall was the senior U.S. Army general throughout World War II, and later served as the secretary of state who crafted the *Marshall Plan* to help a ravaged postwar Europe to recover. After the war, General Marshall was asked, based on his vast experience, what leadership quality he

prized over all others. Was it insight, intelligence, dedication, aggressiveness, honesty, compassion? General Marshall thought for a moment and said, "It's courage. Because all else depends on that." He explained that he wasn't talking about the kind of courage it takes to attack an enemy airfield or a pillbox stronghold, that kind of courage, he said, was in plentiful supply. He meant instead courage in interpersonal relationships and in adherence to principle. That brand of courage includes the courage to follow your convictions, but also the courage to change your mind, the courage to say, "I don't know, but I'll find out"; the courage to admit that neither you nor the organization you lead is perfect—or ever will be; the courage to keep learning, not resting on your laurels; the courage to place principle over prejudice, and over expediency. All should keep in mind General Marshall's admonition placing courage foremost among leadership qualities. All else does depend on that.

2. *Confidence*. It goes with courage. Doing great things always starts with the belief that you can. So leaders need the tenacity that flows from confidence, not the timidity of doubt. But there's a vast difference between *confidence* and *arrogance*. The confident leader recognizes his or her need to keep growing and learning. The arrogant leader knows it all, so there's nothing else to grow toward. The confident leader listens to others intently and is not threatened by criticism or the need to change policies that aren't working. In fact, the confident leader continually seeks them out. The confident leader is patient, and quietly but unambiguously counsels those needing it. The arrogant leader pontificates and blusters.

The confident leader doesn't fear showing his or her human side. Such leaders ask lots of "dumb" questions, at every level, so they will be more aware. The arrogant leaders bluff it. Asking a dumb question exposes shortcomings in knowledge they're not prepared to admit or display. John Wooden addresses that matter best. He's the legendary coach who built the amazing UCLA college basketball dynasty, capturing ten NCAA collegiate championships in twelve years. So there's every good reason to listen to him regarding what goes into creating an organization's success. He says about successful leadership, "It's what you learn after you know it all that counts." Not all understand that, or take steps to apply the principle. And that makes life very difficult for the organizations the arrogant leaders encumber with their incomplete knowledge and narrow views.

Some leaders build confidence in their subordinates; others drain it away. You want the first kind; you can't afford the second. Organizations should prize confidence and work hard to build it. Where they find arrogance, either lessons in humility or traveling instructions are in order. If it's confidence the organization reflects, based on the example of its leadership, the need for continuous improvement is taken for granted. If it's arrogance, forget improvement. Look to the leadership behavior to spot the difference—and to foretell success.

3. *Savvy*. It's more than knowledge and more than intelligence. It's a practical blend of the two. So the word is chosen deliberately. Webster's says savvy means *"Understanding, Know-how. Shrewd, Discerning."* It's certainly more than IQ. Intelligence obviously is important. But it's pragmatic, down-to-earth intelligence that an organization should look for in its leaders. It's intelligence grounded in reality as well as in theory, in empirical evidence as well as in abstractions. I've known people with towering IQs who couldn't manage a three-car funeral. The reason? They weren't savvy about what makes people tick, and by extension what makes organizations tick. And they weren't about to go find out. Such people know a lot about what they see in books; they know almost nothing about what they see in people. So they know an awful lot about an awful little when it comes to effective management. The savvy are smart enough to recognize what they're dumb about, and take steps to fill in the blanks. And being savvy about people as well as about processes is a requirement at every level. That need grows, not dissipates, as one reaches ever higher levels in the organization. This especially means acquiring the savvy that comes from staying in touch with the people down where the work gets done.

4. *Maturity*. I'm speaking here of emotional maturity, not age and not experience. Some have it at twenty. Others never have it. We've all seen the emotionally immature in action: temper tantrums, loss of emotional control. Figuratively speaking, *they pound on their high chair with their cereal spoon about anything and everything*. Raving

and ranting, so much a part of the American leadership style of old, is seriously out of date. I've seen my share of those old-timers in the military, and read about them in business. Many had towering reputations in that regard—but not with me. I thought it was foolish and totally unnecessary, besides being inexcusably abusive of people. It's not a minor issue. I've seen the emotionally immature in action at every level, even today, including at the top of some very large pyramids in both the public and the private sector.

Leaders need to be trained so they do not confuse inspiration with intimidation, or being tough with being mean, or exercising control with their own loss of it. Why should any organization want someone in a position to exert control over 10, 100, 1,000, or 10,000 others when they can't control themselves? Invariably, the emotionally immature are ineffective—though they fancy themselves the opposite—because that immaturity shows itself in other more subtle but equally damaging ways. Not the least of those are snap judgments and bullheaded obstinacy. That immature kind of leadership behavior is terribly damaging to employee morale and commitment. Accordingly, I have always considered it a pass or fail item for remaining a supervisor. And I made certain everyone knew that from my actions as well as my words.

None of that means leaders shouldn't be tough-minded, make tough choices, and even be tough in handling individuals when required. But that should be reasoned and reasonable behavior, targeted at the specific issue or individual; it never calls for impulsiveness, outbursts, or attacking the dignity of any employee at any level. Employees *always* know the difference between reasoned judgment and emotional behavior. For years they accepted such immature behavior from bosses, largely because it was so prevalent that they had little choice. But now they find ways to get even, and that's to be expected. So organizations simply can't afford it; it's too damaging. That's why maturity is high on the list of leadership qualities.

5. *Integrity*. It goes with the first four. Indeed, it's that combination of courage, confidence, savvy, and maturity that removes the need to pose as being perfect. To establish organizational character, leaders must reflect integrity and honesty in all their actions, and

demand the same from others. Shading the truth, hiding the truth, or manufacturing facts to look good are all forms of cowardice. As such, they are extremely corrosive to an organization's health. When employees see their boss exercise dishonesty they follow suit, including in their dealings with their boss. Effective communication breaks down completely. To overcome that, supervisors at all levels must be conditioned not to fear sharing bad news, and not to feel threatened by others' knowing what's going on. Virtually all can be taught that. But it takes an effort, because most don't want their bosses skipping levels to acquire information. They want to control the facts, not let them speak for themselves. They also are closemouthed with employees below them. They treat knowledge as power, believing the less they share it, the greater its benefit to them. You can't build a seamless leadership network that way.

Fortunately, ethical and confident behavior can be learned as readily as unethical and fearful behavior. But it needs to come from the top down—by example, by teaching, and by insistence. There's simply no doubt which kind of character in an organization produces the greatest employee loyalty, satisfaction, quality, and productivity. It's so important that in the organizations I led, a conscious integrity violation of shading or suppressing information at any level was cause for prompt dismissal as a supervisor. It's that critical to successful human system dynamics. Organizations can't correct the bad by pretending it's good. But pretending is what some do. And an honest, open organization depends entirely on the example of the leaders— along with the emphasis those leaders place on integrity in word and deed.

6. *Desire.* The last quality of the six is the desire to lead—for the right reason. The other qualities depend on that as heavily as they do on courage, because only desire to lead brings them into play. The right reason? To make life better for others, not for oneself. That's what sustains the best leaders, and makes them go the extra mile and work unceasingly to make the organization succeed. Shortly after World War II was over General Dwight D. Eisenhower was asked what special leadership quality he looked for in deciding whom to promote among all the generals who worked for him during the war

(a related but somewhat different question than that asked General Marshall). "Ike" replied immediately, "*Selflessness.* That's because I know he'll be working the organization's problems, and not his own problems."

That, no doubt, is why Eisenhower had such high regard for Omar Bradley. Bradley was widely revered as the "*GI's General,*" precisely because he not only was selfless but also went out of his way to stay in touch with the GIs' feelings and frustrations, and their hopes and needs. How many of America's corporate leaders are viewed as the "*Worker's CEO*" by those on the frontline? Far too few I fear. Some say military leadership and business leadership are different. That's not so. The objectives are different in many respects (and similar in others), but the need to achieve successful results through people is common to both. The most successful leaders, military or civilian, are good with people, and they provide the people-oriented leadership example for the entire organization. (And those only good with ideas are not the ones you want in charge.) The late Sam Walton of Wal-Mart is one illustrative model of a business leader with conceptual *and* people-oriented leadership skills. He was, without doubt, a *Worker's CEO.* He understood fully the importance of staying in touch with the attitudes and activities at the frontline, and in tailoring the company's practices accordingly. In fact, he worked hard at that and was renowned for doing so. His success speaks for itself. Many business managers, particularly at senior levels, are just "headquarters animals," who can relate to almost everything the organization does except with the frontline troops that do the work—so they don't even try. That's bad news.

The strong desire to be the leader who "*makes it better*" for others fuels determination that translates into extra effort and concern. It also generates a can-do spirit when the going gets toughest and the frustrations highest. When the leaders are primarily working for the prestige, pay, and perks that come with greater responsibility, they can't resist the temptation to start enjoying them—even at the expense of effort needed to make the organization better. That's not hard to spot.

I have also found that those who desire to lead for the right reason have the greatest empathy with those who work for them, and they build the needed rapport between the various layers of the organization. They are comfortable around people because they like people and are secure in the knowledge they are working in the best interests of everyone. So when I visited organizations in the field I looked for the *comfort and rapport index* between the leaders at the various levels and the frontline workers. When the leaders had aspired to their leadership responsibilities for the right reason, I found a strong comfort and rapport index. When they were self-engrossed and merely going through self-serving motions to get promoted, I found no such comfort and rapport with the frontline people. I find the business world no different. It's one of the important markers of the *right stuff* in leadership qualities.

How do you find the leaders who have the desire to lead for the right reason, and the dogged determination and work ethic that goes with it? In my experience, they give *and then some*. Ask them to do a job, they do it—and then some. Ask them to be better informed, they become so—and then some. Ask them to make a sacrifice of their personal aspirations, they make it—and then some. Ask them to tackle a problem, they tackle it—and then some. Ask them to handle a tough decision, and they handle it—and then some, without fear or favor, even at the expense of their personal popularity. They're running to make the organization and all its people better off, not running for office or for self-aggrandizement.

Such leaders, drawing on courage and confidence, get involved in the problems, helping in the solution where needed and appropriate. None of the "*that's your problem*" approach for them; and they don't credit others with all the organization's problems and themselves with all its successes. They are in the bad news business as well as the good news business, and everyone knows it. These leaders trust people until there is clear evidence that such trust is unjustified, and in those cases they take action to fix that specific problem, not translate it into distrust of everybody. They praise in public and condemn or counsel in private. More than that, they're always aware of the need to accentuate each employee's dignity, not tear it down.

Some cynics say you won't find that kind of leadership these days.

That's nonsense. It's all over the place, just waiting for the example and the chance. If any of this "and then some" business sounds corny in today's increasingly materialistic world, it's time to get corny. *The more complex the world becomes, the more important core values become.* It's when the organization's leaders stray from those core values for convoluted reasons—and to pursue personal agendas—that the organization runs into trouble. This brings us to the matter of loyalty. Often its importance is overlooked. Even more often it takes the wrong form and produces hurtful, not helpful, results. What goes around comes around.

LOYALTY IS AN ISSUE OF MANY DIMENSIONS, AND THERE ARE RIGHT KINDS AND WRONG KINDS

The kind of leadership I espouse here, I have found, builds loyalty throughout the organization. It builds loyalty down and loyalty up. It does so because it produces leaders *who are loyal to the right principles and the right people.* That's an important distinction because the loyalty practiced by some is more an abuse of the principle than a proper use of it. As one example, a leader of any organization of any size sooner or later runs into the need to move someone aside because he or she just isn't getting it done. There are legions of managers who, not infrequently, "carry" such an inept subordinate manager long past the time when further counseling simply can't help. Those managers usually rationalize this forgiving approach on the basis of "loyalty," as in "I feel great loyalty to him; he's worked hard for this organization and he's trying his best." That's the "good old Joe" syndrome.

Good old Joe (or good old Jane) deserves every opportunity to change. Good old Joe does not deserve a lifetime pass to exercise incompetence in an important job. The leader's loyalty should be directed toward the 7, or 70, or 7,000 who work for Joe. A lot of people who make excuses for the good old Joes of the world are primarily being loyal to themselves. Joe usually is a friend, even a crony, and they don't want to be disliked if they take forthright action to move Joe aside as they should. Those leaders desire to lead for the wrong reason; their cronies or their personal popularity take priority over the good of the organization. Protecting cronies ruins many fine organizations. I didn't practice it or tolerate it.

The loyalty principle often is also misapplied in dealing with problem-makers at the frontline level. Overlooking such behavior is not being loyal to all employees, as some would have it; it's being disloyal to the vast majority who are doing it right. When leaders allow even a small percentage of habitual troublemakers to continue making mischief or sowing dissension out of misguided and misplaced "loyalty to everyone," it doesn't reduce productivity by an equivalent amount, say 5 percent; it reduces it by 30 percent or more, because of the effect of the negative behavior on the attitude and performance of the other employees. Surveys prove that. (Chapter 10 will say more on the matter in the overall context of reducing alienation and creating strong commitment.)

It's not a minor issue; I've seen organizations become hotbeds of alienation because of a moral copout on the part of the senior leader that results in a culture where virtually anything goes. That was one of the main reasons for the myriad problems in the GM plant in Fremont, California, which led to the plant's closing before Toyota came in and cleaned up Fremont's act. "*Anything goes*" was replaced by "*anyone goes*" who would not choose to meet Toyota's standards. And the plant became far happier, healthier, and more productive as a result. The union is the last to profit, indeed the first to lose, when it protects such troublemakers just because they wear the union badge. Fremont's but one example that proves the point.

I discussed this subject at length with a senior Japanese business leader. He said, "We Japanese pride ourselves—and we are well known—for working hard to provide job security for our employees." Then he added, "However, we're not afraid to fire somebody when that's justified." That readiness, he said, gives them a "large advantage" over competing American firms that have "lost control over that." He went on to say, "They allow the bad apples to spoil the barrel; we don't." There's truth in what he says. Clearly, you need a fair "due process" procedure in deciding to remove someone. But making a job a sinecure and essentially the worker's "property," regardless of performance and behavior, is what worked so brilliantly in the Soviet Union! I'm pro-worker in these matters, but we had better all start being pro-productivity, or we'll all be out of a job. Ask the many who are finding that out to their dismay.

The same misguided application of the loyalty principle can be found in many policies, specifically those which benefit the few, not the many. That's also where the *double standards* come from that can be found in all kinds of organizations, large and small. The workers almost always get the short end of the stick in the double standards precisely because they are developed with the few (the managers), not the many (the workers), in mind. Loyalty is an issue of many dimensions. When leaders practice the right kind of loyalty to their employees, they get the right kind in return. When they practice the wrong kind, they get none in return—at least none from the frontline employees. Organizations and their leaders should continually evaluate their policies and practices in that light—and take steps to ensure that the loyalty principle is operating in the right way.

Courage, confidence, savvy, maturity, integrity, and *desire*—these, I have found, are the qualities essential to leadership success, and thereby to an organization's success. Some will find other qualities they prize conspicuous by their absence. I'm not excluding any by offering these. (I will emphasize that "charisma" doesn't make my list. I've seen a wide variety of personal styles prove effective, so long as the principles are right. Many great leaders I've observed in action are low-key, and I've seen my share of charismatic snake-oil salesmen. Look for character, not charisma.) I've found that these six generate the other needed qualities, and produce the most positive impact on the leaders at lower levels, and through them a constructive influence on the entire human system of the organization. For these reasons, the attitudes and principles the leaders exemplify, at every level, provide the major determinant of success. That's where the competence of the organization—and its cohesion—begin. And that's also where they end if the leadership is not exemplary and constructive.

Some will read these observations on leadership qualities as blinding glimpses of the obvious. Others will read them as utopian and hopelessly out of date. Still others will profit from them (at least by being reminded of their importance). Contrary to the representations of many, leaders are made not born. And organizations that put their mind to it can build such leaders and leadership. *To receive the fruits of leadership you must address the roots of leadership.*

ASTUTE, DISTRIBUTED LEADERSHIP DEPENDS ON FOCUSED TRAINING AND EMPOWERMENT TO EXERCISE AUTHORITY—YOU MUST HAVE BOTH

Many assert that leadership skills cannot be conveyed through instruction. That's hogwash. The centralizers love that argument. It helps them perpetuate the old-time religion. I wasn't born with the ability to lead. I learned how to lead flights and sections in air combat. I learned how, at a tender age, to lead a constantly on-the-road aerobatic organization in a responsible and mature way. I learned how to enter a lion's den of government procurement and bring about positive change. I learned how to transform a sprawling organization of 180,000 people. Also, I learned how to teach proactive, transformational leadership methods to others—one accomplishes nothing alone.

And I learned what leadership is all about from others. I did so by study and observation, and by synthesizing lessons my bosses provided along the way. Some of those lessons were negative. You can learn from those, too. However, most of my bosses provided positive lessons, particularly two of the thirty-one I served under in going from buck private to four-star general. Those two were especially effective because they went out of their way to teach leadership principles and skills. Those two bosses also were far and away the most productive of the entire lot in building a successful organization, and they provided by far the most empowerment to their subordinates. As a result, they produced a raft of good leaders who applied the same principles elsewhere with great success.

Inspired by their example, I spent a lot of time creating more leaders through teaching and empowerment. By way of brief example, at TAC we conducted comprehensive classroom sessions for those in line to take on greater responsibilities. We did not assume that they would understand how to operate successfully at a higher level of responsibility just because they had done well at lower ones. All should keep in mind the *Peter Principle*, which says that everyone eventually gets promoted to their "*level of incompetence.*" That needn't happen, not if they continue to be prepared properly.

Those training sessions included TAC's most senior leaders. We called the sessions for both incumbents and aspirants "*CLASS*"—an acronym which stood for *Commanders' Leadership, Awareness, and Sensitivity Seminar.* (The emphasis being that without the latter two you don't have effective leadership.) It lasted a full week, four times a year. I conducted virtually all the sessions myself.

We also took pains and the time to teach the senior leaders *the things they didn't know*. A centralized system provides a very narrow education in its functional silos. For example, most of those with the greatest potential for senior responsibility in a "fly and fight" organization knew a lot about operations, but very little about activities like maintenance, supply, and base support. The same is true in large, traditionally managed corporations. For example, those who grow up in manufacturing have little understanding of marketing, financial, and other corporate functional activities—and vice versa.

So we conducted periodic two-week courses to provide the lieutenant colonels and above *throughout* that large command with the neglected parts of their education. The courses covered all kinds of maintenance, engineering, supply, support, and financial issues. I participated heavily, conducting several of the classes myself. That demonstrated I had taken initiative over the years to educate myself on those various support matters, and sent a signal that the attendees were expected to do no less. That training paid big dividends in building our new culture, and our success. Some say the top boss is too busy for that sort of thing. Nonsense. *That's where it all starts.*

GROOMING OF THE LEADERSHIP SHOULD BE A
CONSTANT PREOCCUPATION OF
THE ORGANIZATION

I also spent a large amount of time in the selection, training, and grooming of the most senior leaders. (The more time I spent on that, I found, the less time I spent cleaning up after the ill prepared.) Those at the rank of colonel and above whom we saw as having the potential for the most senior positions were groomed by moving them from job to job, and by making the jobs as diverse as possible. I've seen this same approach work effectively in business. Most of what we do in the management business is not rocket science, though some would have you believe it is. It's really a case of the human science; and some are good at that, some are not. Those who are can take jobs with which they are unfamiliar and soon start making positive contributions. As a result of that approach to grooming, it came as no surprise to me later when the TAC people started dominating the Air Force's senior leadership positions. Their broad-based grooming gave them an appreciable advantage, and it showed in the promotion lists.

What do I see in the business community? Mostly, the same traditional approach of narrow education and grooming even for those who clearly are candidates for the most demanding positions in the organization. That widespread practice is the key reason the "Executive Search" firms are some of the busiest companies in America. Since most companies simply don't groom and train their leaders well, they see no good option but to proselytize and fill top positions by raiding other companies of their talent. That approach, by definition, provides no net increase in talent across the business universe. Many companies also operate on the flawed theory that *you can't do it unless you've done it before*. Therefore, when they need a key executive they look at the ones they've groomed themselves, conclude that the prospects are bleak, and call in the executive search specialist to find someone from outside. Frankly, a lot of those searches are more like beauty contests than in-depth inquiries into skills and principles. Sometimes it works out, sometimes it doesn't. The safest way is to groom one's own. And companies adopting a team-based structure in a holistic TQM system will find new means and methods of grooming leaders, at all levels, that they never had before.

Again, I'm convinced leaders are made, not born. *Nurture* can overcome *nature* in nearly all cases, given the right training. Admittedly, not everyone has the qualifications and desire to be a leader. But the woods are full of those who do have the ability, drive, and desire to make excellent leaders. And it has nothing to do with race or gender. The successes at ESD and TAC were based on being color-blind and gender-blind when it came to promotions and leadership opportunities.

For example, women comprised some 15 percent of the Air Force (and TAC) as I was departing TAC for the private sector, yet more than 35 percent of TAC's fighter squadron *Aircraft Maintenance Units* had women in place as the AMU commanders. (AMUs are commanded by a captain and comprise roughly 250 technicians of various kinds, as described in chapter 4.) That wouldn't have happened if we had had some subtle discrimination at work against women in leadership positions. That is not an unknown phenomenon in our society, particularly in so-called nontraditional fields such as aircraft maintenance.

The women also were every bit as good as aircraft crew chiefs on the flightline, as repair technicians, and in supervisory positions both above and below AMU commander. Air Force women flocked to aircraft maintenance as a means of proving themselves, and that they certainly did. Some were spectacularly good; a few failed. But those percentages were comparable to those of their male counterparts in all respects. In all these cases, actual performance proved more powerfully than speeches on equitability that our strenuous efforts to be color-blind and gender-blind added to our success, not subtracted from it.

The issue is relevant to this discussion because the doors aren't open to that level of opportunity in many businesses. That is going to have to change, if for no other reason than the changing makeup of the American work force. The demographic trends are clear. By the year 2001 less than one-fifth of the entering work force will be male Caucasians. So, for those companies not already dealing with this issue in constructive ways, it's time to start devising ways to include all five-fifths of the work force when it comes to training, grooming, and opportunity.

Beyond creating the leaders with the right qualities and instincts, there's the matter of creating the organization's competence. That goes hand in hand with the quality of the leadership; organizational competence obviously doesn't happen on its own. It comes from proactive, aware leaders who pay close attention to the training provided to *each employee at every level*. Unfortunately, surveys show that training is another of the weaknesses in the American management style. It's especially weak as contrasted with the frequency, scope, and depth of training carried out by our international competitors, including the Japanese. When further judged in the light of the poor preparation provided by the nation's education system—which involves problems of long standing that won't soon be resolved—it is even more seriously deficient.

AMERICA'S EDUCATION SYSTEM AND BUSINESS TRAINING SYSTEMS WORK IN CONCERT TO PRODUCE THE NATION'S COMPETENCE— BUT NEITHER IS VERY GOOD BY INTERNATIONAL STANDARDS

Yogi Berra said, *If you don't know what you're doing, you keep making the wrong mistakes.* A look at the training approach common to the American management style shows that this is not understood in most companies, or at least they don't act on it. Clearly, situation awareness must include assessing internal training needs. And you've got to know what you're up against in terms of the competition, and the earlier education of your employees.

In that respect, American companies start with a competitive handicap because the student education we are providing isn't very good, comparatively speaking. And its deficiencies can only be rectified, if ever, once those students reach the businesses in which they will work. The statistics on America's education system are sobering. They show that we spend more on education than other industrialized countries, but come in last in achievement testing. For many in our society, the system is not just weak—it is failing them. Surveys show:

- Only 75 percent of Americans have a high school education.
- Some 700,000 high school students drop out each year.
- Some 1 million each year graduate functionally illiterate.
- 27 million Americans of working age are at best semiliterate.
- Some one in eight Americans can't read at all, in any language.

Inescapably, this all shows up in the workplace. For example, The *National Association of Manufacturers* in November 1991 announced the results of a survey it had commissioned of 400 companies. It showed that manufacturers in all regions of the United States are unable to find enough skilled workers to meet demands. At the same time, those companies reject five candidates for each one they hire. The report said almost two in three companies surveyed found that the applicants ''simply are not ready to work, lacking the motivation and/or general skills needed to be productive employees.'' The survey said some one-third of the companies find that most of their rejections are related to applicants' poor reading and writing skills. As one reflection of what is causing that, James M. Howell, president of a Boston-based economic consulting firm, reveals that four of every ten students drop out of Boston's schools, and of the six who do manage to graduate, three will be functionally illiterate. NYNEX, the AT&T spin-off that provides telecommunications for New York state and contiguous areas, finds it necessary to reject eighteen of twenty job applicants because of educational deficiencies.

When we look to the future, with the accelerating demands of technology and globalization, the picture grows still darker. The Department of Labor has estimated that over the next decade some 38 percent of the new entrants to the work force will be required to read at high competency levels—and only 5 percent will have the needed skills. Even most high school graduates test in reading comprehension skills at eighth-grade levels, or below. Comprehension levels are not only low, they are getting no better. The Department of Education recently reported that 79 percent of Americans ages twenty-one to twenty-five cannot understand the main argument in a long newspaper editorial. Newspaper readership is down significantly. Moreover, a recent survey shows the average age of the readership nationally has risen from twenty-seven to forty-two, and continues to climb. As a related concern, a review of TV viewing habits by age group shows that we—particularly young adults—are growing ever more likely to seek entertainment rather than knowledge in our TV viewing preferences. While we can't blame all that on our education system, it plays a part.

Surveys also show these problems extend to our brightest and most industrious students (industrious in comparative terms) due to a lack of motivation on their part, and little demand for them to excel by parents and educators. Paul Krouse, publisher of the *Who's Who Among American High School Students*, speaks out on this motivation problem, and says his polling shows a "wide gap between reality and perception" in those students regarding how much they will earn, and how soon. In fact, 81 percent of those teens expect to do better than their parents financially. However, they don't directly connect how hard they study, or the rigor of their courses, to those expected outcomes. (Other surveys show that students increasingly are falling prey to that *"we're entitled"* mindset.) Krouse also says, "Students are not being challenged and motivated enough. I think these brightest students are telling us this curriculum is way too soft. I think the expectations from schools, teachers, curriculum directors, etc., are way too low. And there's probably insufficient involvement of their parents, in terms of expectations of their children, as well as their schools."

The problem, stated in simplest terms, is that our schools have found ways to calibrate classroom instruction to a lowest common denominator, and educators and parents are doing little or nothing to correct it. Also, American children spend a good bit less time in the classroom than is the case with our international competitors. For example, Japanese kids go to school 210 days a year, American kids 180 days a year. We have a huge national problem on our hands— at least when our educational approach is matched against the demands of the Globalization Age. Despite that, we continue to act as if we're insulated and isolated and have a natural birthright to be first in everything. Unfortunately, there are no signs of improvement on the horizon. Lots of talk, but no action.

As one bright spot, our system of advanced education arguably is the best in the world. We provide more advanced education in our colleges, per capita, than any other country. The colleges must deal, however, with the educational preparation of the students who reach their doors, and deficiencies there pull the college standards down as well. Also, the courses many students pursue are of little relevance to the challenges they will meet in the rough-and-tumble business world. Many seek refuge in "basket-weaving" degrees, and an unhealthy percentage try their best to avoid the education they're paying lots of money to get by studying just enough to get by. For those and associated reasons, we simply are not producing the skilled professionals global economic competition demands.

As one oft-cited example, though we have more lawyers than the rest of the world combined, we continue to produce at least eight lawyers for every engineer. (No surprise in that; they're going where the money is, and that's where it is.) So while we're stoking the fires of the most litigious society on earth, others are gearing themselves to provide us with our products and take our money in return. (Japan produces ten engineers for every lawyer.) I've already covered the gaps in the education of our MBAs, especially as they relate to the human system and leadership aspects of "managing." So our system of advanced education isn't broke. But it needs a lot of fine-tuning if it's to contribute as it must to America's competitiveness in a changing, challenging world.

What can America's managers do about this picture? Not much. We must be realistic. America's education system has proved stubbornly resistant to change. And we continue to ignore the problem by ignoring the facts. For example, we wring our hands over flat or falling SAT scores when they're coming from some of our best students—those who hope to go on to college. We currently have no means of measuring, on a nationwide comparative basis, the level of educational achievement of those who don't take the SAT tests. Common sense says such measurement would reveal similar trends, if not worse.

There are solutions that would help the dropout problem, but we're not pursuing them. As one example, Germany has a vocational apprenticeship training program, more than a century old, that's the best in the world. Students work for about half the week as apprentices and spend the other half in school. Many knowledgeable observers credit that system with Germany's economic strength and the quality of its products, particularly in manufacturing and related high-tech areas. There is even competition among companies, and regions, to offer the best apprenticeship programs. And they are pervasive: A 1982 sampling by the German government found that 59 percent of all employees in Germany had graduated from one of 380 two- to four-year apprentice programs. The goal is to increase that to 65 percent of all workers by the year 2000. Sweden also has such an apprentice system, and it, too, excels in high-tech products. We treat every student the same. Why? Largely because we've always done it that way. Would an apprenticeship system work in America? Why not? It's difficult to envision it working more poorly than the one we have now.

Reform proposals such as nationwide testing in every grade, merit pay for teachers, and curricular changes to place more emphasis on the three Rs and the sciences are loudly shouted down by almost all the educators within the system. Old habits die hard, even among educators. That's particularly so when they see their job security threatened by innovation. They have, after all, prepared themselves diligently over many years for the system and the subjects as they exist today. The parents of America, products of the system, are not agitating for change either. A few are, but they appear to be outnumbered nationwide by those campaigning to save the whales.

Certainly, there's no groundswell for change. As a result, the elected school boards, which theoretically manage the system, end up tinkering on the periphery of its major problems. If the school boards don't get exercised and organize themselves for change in some reasonably consistent way across the land, don't expect change. Given that those school boards are committees, and there are thousands of them, my advice is not to hold your breath waiting for them to act.

In any event, America's managers cannot count on changes in the nation's education system. It's a societal problem that won't be easily or quickly solved. However, America's managers can attune themselves to the need for more training to make up for those educational deficiencies, and act accordingly. This picture is not new, and given those deficiencies, you'd think American business training would have become some of the best and most comprehensive in the world. That's not the case. Taken collectively, it's as bad as—or even worse than—the education system. However, *that can be fixed*. The problem is brought on by individual decisions of business leaders. Thus, entirely different reasons, and circumstances, are involved than those that make the education system so resistant to change. Let's look at what's wrong with the American approach to training to discern how it might be fixed.

We simply don't train as much as our overseas competitors, especially Germany, the Scandinavian countries, Japan, and other countries of the Pacific Rim. Surveys of businesses across America reveal:

- Only 60 percent train managers.
- Only 50 percent train technical workers.
- Only 18 percent train blue-collar workers.
- Formal training benefits only one in ten workers.
- Less than 50 percent of businesses do any formal training at all.
- America spends less than 25 percent of what Japan spends per worker.

In late 1991 the *American Society for Training and Development* estimated that 42 percent of the American work force—some 49.5 million workers—need training immediately to be able to do their jobs properly. That may be overstated, but not by much, especially when you factor in the intensifying competition. In fact, the more you look, the more disturbing the picture. In June 1990 a thirty-four-member *Commission on the Skills of the American Work Force* published troubling findings from a year of surveys and study of America's training practices. The commission conducted more than 2,000 interviews at more than 550 companies and agencies in the United States, Germany, Sweden, Denmark, Ireland, Japan, and Singapore. It was led by Bill Brock and Ray Marshall, labor secretaries under Presidents Reagan and Carter. The commission warned, "A majority of U.S. workers could face lifetimes of low-paying jobs and America will lose its global economic race unless drastic changes are made in training average workers."

The commission called on business, schools, and government to overhaul the "haphazard, incoherent and bureaucratic system" of job training now in operation. Only 18 percent of the managers polled worry about the shortage of skilled workers, reflecting widespread insensitivity to intensifying competition and the possibilities of improved output through training. Less than 30 percent of those surveyed are planning special programs for women, immigrants, and minority youth, who "will make up 85 percent of new workers."

The commission surveys also revealed that less than 10 percent of U.S. companies are reorganizing their work force into the team-based approach the Japanese use so successfully. So here is still another survey showing that well over 90 percent of American businesses continue using the traditional approach.

On spending patterns, the commission calculated that businesses in America collectively spend only $30 billion annually on formal training. That's a pittance when measured as a percentage of payroll. It's also a drop in the bucket for a $5.5-trillion annual GDP. To make matters worse, the commission found that fully $27 billion of the $30 billion is being spent by only 5 percent of all U.S. companies. Cumulative spending is so low, the commission estimated, that if American businesses would set aside just 1 percent of payroll for formal training it would bring about a dramatic increase in workers' skills and national competitiveness. A mere 1 percent outlay would make it substantially better. That's a troubling indictment of our spending practices now.

What's the moral in all of this for America's managers? Let others rail and rant about the education system. (Maybe someday such criticism will do some good, but don't look for help in the near term.) Business leaders—at every level in every company—should instead devote their energies to improving the training approach in their own organizations. Training has always been important. Globalization makes it even more important. And the new competitive challenges must be met against a background of these national educational shortcomings as well as ever growing job complexity. Indeed, experience already shows that those who do not face up to their training needs will find the new global game of economic hardball very unforgiving. It's again useful to note that the Japanese view training, including formal training, as a *value* issue, not a *cost* issue. They're right about that. Many other companies in many other countries prove that also. In the United States, Motorola is one of them. So the good news that comes with the bad news is that greatly expanded training—frequent, focused, formal—pays for itself many times over. Pay the price or pay the piper.

TRAINING MUST BE TAILORED TO ENSURE COMPETENCE IN ALL AREAS—BY TEACHING PRINCIPLES AS WELL AS METHODS, AND BY FORMAL TRAINING AS WELL AS ON-THE-JOB TRAINING

Comprehensive and highly focused training was a big part of TAC's success story. Many people have heard about TAC's large-scale training for combat operations, such as the realistic *Red Flag* training programs in the Nevada desert against replicated Soviet-built combat equipment—ground and air. And *Red Flag* is but part of a much larger program. We also devised comprehensive *Blue Flag, Black Flag, Green Flag, Gold Flag, Copper Flag, Silver Flag*, and *Checkered Flag* training programs. Never mind what each stands for; it's enough to know that they cover every phase of combat involvement (the business of TAC's business), including deployment, bed-down, sortie generation, resupply, air base defense, all types of combat support, and command and control of the forces. That training was extremely valuable—even invaluable—to America's performance in the Gulf War.

However, I wish to emphasize here a different type of training in TAC to which we also gave great attention and emphasis. That is the basic skills training to get the same kind of work accomplished that's done in varied kinds of businesses across America. Air bases are in effect small cities on which you find a cross section of employee skills. So a major part of our new focus was to increase substantially that broad-based skill training, and at all levels. That stepped-up training incorporated principles as well as methods, and team-bonding techniques as well as individual skills.

To make it happen, we opened a *"University"* on every TAC base. There we provided additional training to those coming out of the formal Air Force technical schools. Though these schools did a good job, we found that the graduates needed even more training and providing it on a *formal* classroom basis was highly cost-effective because it cut down dramatically on mistakes and rework. Also, we established new courses for first-level supervisors that included detailed instruction in leadership skills and the principles of quality management. In fact, all those courses devoted lots of time to quality, everyone's role in its pursuit, and ways to improving the processes to achieve it.

I was not surprised later to find the best companies doing the same. Certainly the Japanese do. As you move around a Japanese automobile plant you're struck by the amount of training going on (formal classroom training, not the on-the-job training you see in all plants). At the time I visited it, the Honda Accord plant at Marysville, Ohio, Honda was giving *six weeks* of formal training to its frontline team leaders—yes, six weeks to every single one of those who supervised some four to twelve employees. The Japanese president of Honda America, Yuki Yoshino, explained that the normal practice is to provide those team leaders "only three weeks of formal training" each year. (Even three weeks would blow the hats off most of America's corporate beancounters.) Yoshino explained that Honda had been in business at Marysville sufficient time for team leaders' getting promoted to create large turnover—thus the longer period was appropriate. Scott Whitlock, the Marysville plant manager, emphasized that devoting time, money, and effort to frontline team leader training makes sense because the caliber of the leadership there determines Honda's success. (That's true for any organization, but not all understand it.)

Since the Japanese management principles are so similar, you see the same strong commitment to training at Toyota's plants. In fact, at NUMMI that's how Toyota keeps the former GM manager's offices busy. And the noteworthy enthusiasm for their work, the quality mindset, and the high productivity you see in those plants clearly is influenced by that extensive training. Incidentally, Japan does not have an apprentice system like that of Germany or Sweden, and they don't use the American system either. Japanese workers are trained in each company's own training institute, or in government-sponsored schools. And they train them for months, not the days common in American companies. One simply cannot achieve high levels of competence, or of cooperation and commitment, without ample formal training.

It's the leader's responsibility to build the competence and motivation within the organization. In the best companies they also participate in the teaching. Some of America's most successful business leaders show how important that is. Andrew S. Grove, the imaginative chairman and CEO of the *Intel Corporation*, the Santa Clara, California, manufacturer of microprocessors and computer memory devices, says, in that respect:

Training is, quite simply, one of the highest leverage activities a manager can perform. . . . Most managers seem to feel that training employees is a job that should be left to others, perhaps to training specialists. I, on the other hand, strongly believe that the manager should do it himself. . . . A manager generally has two ways to raise the level of individual performance of his subordinates; by increasing motivation, the desire of each person to do his job well, and by increasing individual capability, which is where training comes in.

It is generally accepted that motivating employees is a key task for all managers. . . . Why shouldn't the same be true for the other principal means at a manager's disposal for increasing output? . . . You yourself should instruct your direct subordinates and perhaps the next few ranks below them. Your subordinates should do the same thing, and the supervisors at every level below them as well.

The dramatic growth and continuing success of Intel make it wise to listen to what Grove has to say. (The overall principles he applies were set forth in his outstanding 1983 book, *High Output Management.*) I agree completely on who should be responsible for the training, and who should carry it out. This doesn't mean, however, that companies should not reach outside for help if that's useful, all needs considered. There's certainly no shortage of such training help available; in fact, there are more than 3,000 private training and consulting firms to choose from.

Many of those firms are excellent at what they do. But there are lots of them, so you must choose carefully. In that respect, I have one special piece of advice. If the business leaders aren't prepared to do it all, the one thing they simply should not "outsource" is determining the *kind of training* they need to provide. The organization's leaders must determine that, and then find firms that offer services and courses to fit those special needs. Let's go back to what the Institute of Defense Analysis discovered about the pitfalls of implementing a quality management system. The company IDA singled out as representative said this about its program—after explaining why that program had been largely unsuccessful: "If we were to start completely over again, we believe the best approach would be for top management to take whatever time was necessary to learn and understand the principles and philosophy . . . understand their responsibility, develop their purpose, direction and plan for implementing the effort companywide; and then execute the plan with appropriate leadership." That's the only way it works.

I see no need for despair when it comes to competitiveness, either on an individual company or a national basis—if we train better than we do now, that is. It's not the raw material. Americans are actually getting better, not worse. People get confused about that because the critics confuse weaknesses in the job performance in America with character weaknesses in the American worker. Some see a widely proclaimed *erosion in the American work ethic* as a sign of our times that's irreversible. I agree there's been an erosion, but I emphatically disagree that it can't be reversed. *It's the managers who are failing the workers, not the other way around.*

For example, contrary to current conventional wisdom, I found that the young Americans entering the Air Force over the years consistently were brighter, more mature, more conscientious, and harderworking than those who had entered only five to ten years before. Let me say that again. *They just kept getting better in all those respects.* Don't attribute that to the effect of the all-volunteer force; we've had that in the DOD since 1973. For that matter, the Air Force always has been made up of volunteers, not draftees, since it became a separate service in 1947. My colleagues in senior leadership positions in the Air Force thought the same way I did, and still do. As I wrote this I polled a number of them still serving in high positions. Every single one confirmed it still holds true.

It's also true, however, that those new entrants, in most cases, are not well prepared by the rigor or content of their high school curricula. That was and is a special problem, and training programs must take up that slack. So, judging by the Air Force, which is a microcosm of society at large, the work ethic is *alive and well* in America. (Provided, of course, that you don't turn the employees from committed to alienated with dumb management practices.) If you don't believe those entering the Air Force have just kept getting better than those that went before, you should see them in action. But they need training, to begin with and as careers unfold. The leadership must provide the training, and the training the leadership. That's what organizational competence and renewal are about. The rest is background music. *Fail in that and you fail in everything.*

The record shows that training is still another case—like the quality mindset—in which the American management style concentrates on the seen, not the unseen, costs—and is maladroit at sorting value from cost. To solve that, companies must replace the customary cost obsession with the uncustomary value orientation. And that, in turn, depends on each company's addressing and eliminating the *bean-counter mentality* that's rampant in the traditionally managed organizations.

THOSE WHO TAKE THE INANIMATE VIEW OF MANAGING HUMAN ENDEAVOR ARE GUILTY OF A BEANCOUNTER MENTALITY

Companies using the traditional centralized managership style are not strong on either evaluating or building motivation. That's because, surveys show, they fail to factor into their decisions how fundamentally their success is shaped by human factors. Those who think of management issues in such inanimate and dehumanized terms are called by many, including me, the *beancounters*. Once, after a speech in which I had talked about such a beancounter attitude and its effects, I was asked by a questioner to explain more fully what I meant by the term. A baseball metaphor popped into my head as the question was asked, and I answered this way:

> Perhaps I can best amplify my view of the beancounter mentality with a baseball metaphor. I believe we would all agree that one of the great acts of celebration in baseball is when a player hits a home run, circles the bases with his fist in the air, and is greeted at home plate by his enthusiastic teammates. Let's suppose we pose this question: If we changed the rule so circling the bases is neither necessary nor condoned after a home run is hit, would baseball be fundamentally changed? The leaders would say yes, and therefore they would be very strongly against it. The beancounters would say no, it has not been changed. In fact, based on what I have seen of the beancounter mentality in action, they would welcome such a change. Their basis, applying their usual reasoning, would be: (1) the outcome is still the same, (2) it saves time, eliminates an unnecessary step, and speeds up the game, and, (3) it saves the player's energy which he can more productively use later in the contest! In other words, they do not factor into their deliberations the important

role played by the human spirit, and how critical that is in creating desire, motivation, enthusiasm—and stellar performance. In so doing they ignore the basic issues of human nature that make leadership, and its motivational and inspirational aspects, so fundamental to success.

Please don't conclude that I use the word beancounter to relate to accountants, or others who keep track and keep score. My use of the word has nothing to do with one's profession or job. You can find beancounters in almost any job, at any level, in any endeavor. Very often they are in charge. They simply don't pay attention to the human aspects of their undertaking except in the most cursory way. For that very reason, Centralism glitters in the abstract but fails in practice. If we could somehow resurrect Lenin and show him what has happened to his grand dream of the perfect way to run a society, he might even agree. (On second thought, centralizers always believe the flaws are in the execution, not in the principles. Let's just take him out of his mausoleum and plant him six feet under along with his ruinous ideas.) So much for the beancounters, and their sterile view of human endeavor. My advice is to change their thinking. But let's not blame them. Let's blame the way they've been taught and tolerated in the Centralism era. Change that, and those who know the cost of everything and the value of nothing will simply fade away.

Given the importance of motivation, let's turn to the matter of *involvement* and start with how to merge the rear with the front to foster common values, perspectives, and purpose among one and all.

THE IMPORTANCE OF A SEAMLESS ORGANIZATION— CREATING COMMON PERSPECTIVES AND COMMON PURPOSE

The right leadership ethic calls for more involvement, not less. True, it calls for less intrusion by several orders of magnitude in the day-to-day management and decision processes. In those elements of overall management the "managers" turned "leaders" need to butt out far more, and butt in far less. However, *far greater* leadership involvement and dynamism are called for in the shaping of the organizational structure and organizational dynamics. What is needed is highly involved leaders—leaders who are not micromanaging but who are creating leadership thinking and involvement *by everyone*, and eliciting stronger motivation and commitment *from everyone*. Jack Welch of GE has framed this issue in an excellent way:

> The word manager has too often come to be synonymous with control—cold, uncaring, button-down, passionless. I never associate passion with the word manager, and I've never seen a good leader without it. The world of the 90's and beyond will not belong to ''managers'' or those who can make the numbers dance, as we used to say, or are conversant with all the businessese and jargon we use when we want to sound smart. The world will belong to passionate, driven leaders, people who not only *have* enormous amounts of energy but who can energize those whom they lead.

That's the long and short of it. And, to do that right, leaders must stay in close touch and in tune with those they lead. However, not many of America's senior managers, raised in the Centralism era, think that way. The common managership approach, particularly at the very top echelons of a centocracy, is to remain ''above'' all that goes on at the frontline level.

Here's one example of that thinking. The chairman and CEO of one of America's largest corporations retired a couple of years ago. In an interview at that time in a leading business magazine, he explained his management style. He said that he had well over 100,000 people who ''worked for him,'' and he added that he had not the ''slightest idea what those people do, or are supposed to do—that isn't my worry.'' Even being long conditioned to such centralist thinking, I still had to go over that three times to make sure I hadn't read it wrong. But the whole interview left no doubt that he said what he meant, and meant what he said. Suppose that on the eve of Desert Storm, Lieutenant General Chuck Horner had said, ''I have tens of thousands of people who work for me to be used in this air campaign, and I have not the slightest idea what any of them do.'' The criticism would still be ringing in our ears, and he would have been summarily packed off to the funny farm. If General Norman Schwarzkopf had said anything remotely similar the nation would have had apoplexy out of concern for its sons and daughters, and properly so.

Yet a comment like this from one of the nation's key CEOs passed without criticism—or any particular notice. Why? We've become conditioned to such thinking. At its worst it represents the *Lord of the Manor* mentality. (I'm in my castle, and the drawbridge is *up*. Keep me posted on how the serfs are doing in the fields, but don't bother me with the details of how they do it.) However, that's not the widespread reason for such detachment (though it's by no means rare). This CEO probably was simply demonstrating that he had reached the ultimate aim of functionalism as zealously practiced by the centocracies. He had the big box at the top of the matrix, and as a functionary his functions were therefore well defined and understood—board meetings, handling the financial analysts, dabbling in the strategic planning, and the like. Many if not most of the centocracy devotees who saw the interview no doubt silently applauded his thinking. Likely they even couched their support in terms of ''appropriate delegation.'' But that view overlooks perhaps the most important principle of proactive leadership: You go to the front not to issue instructions, but to gain insight and perspective. That cannot be delegated. The best leaders know that.

That's why I went to the front a lot. And I knew that I set the example. If I was aloof, the leaders below me would be also. In like manner, I took steps to be sure the TAC staff—department heads and staffers alike—were out in the field as much as I was. I told each of them, repeatedly, that they got their report card based on what people told me in the field. The policy was that we were supporters, not sovereigns, and that to do our job right required personal interaction, not insulated management of an in box and a telephone from the rear.

We used still another technique—an innovation I used earlier in the two fighter wings. I called it *immersion*—a particularly intense form of involvement to be used periodically by the wing leaders to gain even greater frontline insight. All the wing leaders (read company) were asked to periodically *immerse* themselves totally, with no distracting influences, in the hour-to-hour frontline work activity for enough time to see all the victories and vexations going on there.

One element of the overall program involved the full-colonel *chiefs of maintenance* in each wing. They were asked to immerse themselves for two weeks at a stretch, at least once each four months. One week of the two was on the night shift. Immersion meant being out of their offices the *entire* period. It meant working alongside crew chiefs on the flightline, alongside repair technicians in the repair shops, and alongside weapons loaders in their intricate tasks. It meant getting a deeper understanding of the demands made on those various skills. It meant understanding fully the *environment* in which the frontline did its work. Above all it meant getting to understand and empathize with the people themselves. At the end of each immersion period, each of the chiefs of maintenance (in TAC about fifty all told) wrote me a letter outlining the insights they had acquired. All also provided their recommendations for changes in TAC's procedures.

Let me mention two examples, of many, of worthwhile productivity steps we took from recommendations growing out of those immersion periods and the insights they yielded. First, we launched a program to greatly improve night lighting in all the TAC maintenance work areas, on the ramp and in the hangars. Productivity rose greatly on the night shift. It wasn't that the lighting had been terrible, it was that it needed to be far better. Second, we did away entirely with the third maintenance shift. (I immersed myself in the third shift to check that one out.) Conventional wisdom said there was no way we could do without it. When we did away with it, and placed those people on the two main shifts, productivity from the same work force shot up. Wonder why? Work the graveyard shift for a couple of weeks.

We had similar programs for all the senior wing leaders, including wing commanders. Again, all wrote me letters outlining their observations and recommendations. I gained all sorts of insights from those letters, and I also learned a lot about the letter writers. The insights were invaluable (on what we were doing right as well as wrong). Often a single observation was enough to kick off a different approach that contributed significantly to our continual improvement across the command. It's my strong belief that in-depth insight into all organizational elements is the foundation for nonintrusive management. It's when leaders do not understand the challenges—and the real problems and issues—that they intrude with direction that adds to the problem rather than to the solution. Such ill-conceived direction conditions the human system to operate all the more haltingly and inefficiently, and further widens the gap between the rear and the front.

The applicability of such *immersion* programs to the business world is obvious. However, it's rarely used. In fact, it's big news when *McDonald's* and *Kentucky Fried Chicken* institute programs in which executives go down and man the frontline battle stations for even a day or so. You hear about a few such programs. The *Hyatt Hotel* chain has a program of frontline immersion for its executives, for example. But such programs are rare.

Some predicted in TAC that the frontline employees wouldn't like *immersion* when we kicked it off. Quite the contrary—they welcomed the chance to sound off about their problems and challenges. In these days of instant communications, you need never be out of touch with "headquarters." But leaders, especially senior ones, can't get a proper feel for problems and perspectives at the front by telephone or fax. Involvement, immersion, interaction—call it what you will. American management doesn't do enough of it.

As an aside, many in the nation's host of centocracies who have become slaves to the "paper trap" and their in box—as well as the little schedule card their secretary hands them each morning—can't conceive of taking the time for such immersion. Yet they give not a thought to taking off for vacations, sometimes extended ones. I always had time for such matters, even when I was a four-star general. And if an important and particularly thorny issue arose, even if it was one of many, I thought nothing of isolating myself for days, or a week or more, and working on nothing but that single problem until I understood it well enough to solve it. I went wherever necessary and spent whatever time was required to acquire that insight. From my perspective I was charting the course and looking way ahead for the reefs and the icebergs, not constantly steering the ship. It worked well. And no one missed my absence from the daily give-and-take. If anyone had, it would have meant I had done a very poor job of pushing authority downward to the fullest feasible extent. It wasn't that I shied from work; I relished it. However, I knew the more I became a slave to my desk and in box the less well I would do my job.

As a related principle, from the time I was a wing commander on—when the size of the organization tempted me toward insulation—I kept a list in my desk drawer of the places I hadn't recently been and the activities I didn't well understand. I won't soon forget the first time I visited the sewage disposal plant at the fighter base outside Madrid. The Spanish civilian who ran it was thunderstruck. He had been there sixteen years, and he had never seen anyone higher than a first lieutenant. I also invited him to attend our expanded staff meetings, held every two weeks. I had no reason to suspect we had trouble at the sewage disposal plant, but I didn't want any either— and I wanted him to know he *mattered.* He was one of many I referred to as representing the *"pearls and diamonds."* No one called them the "cats and dogs," at least not around me. Tom Peters, writing in *A Passion for Excellence* about that style and its salutary effect on TAC productivity, said, "General Creech motivated, celebrated, and virtually canonized the typically unsung support people." I did indeed work very hard at that, and asked everyone else to do the same. I had a reason. My strong belief in that came from my several years at the bottom of the pile. I never once forgot that the need to matter has no relation to where people stand in the pecking order. That human need is important to everyone at every level.

WHY LEADERSHIP? BECAUSE WITHOUT IT— AT ALL LEVELS—THERE IS NO TOTAL QUALITY MANAGEMENT

If anything can go wrong, invariably it will. Nearly all will recognize that as the best known of "Murphy's Laws." And it proved itself in Murphy's own case. That's because no one thought to take

down his full name and address! Murphy provided several other
"laws" of the real world that remind us that human endeavor rarely
proceeds smoothly and serenely:

- Nothing is as simple as it first seems.
- Nature always sides with the hidden flaw.
- Left to themselves, things always go from bad to worse.
- If everything seems to be going well, you have obviously over-
  looked something.

Another purveyor of management "laws," one C. Northcote Parkinson, reminded us that:

- Managers prefer to multiply subordinates, not rivals.
- There need be little or no relationship between the work to be
  done and the size of the staff to which it is assigned.
- Work expands so as to fill the time available for its completion.

Parkinson's third point reminds me of the *Von Stauffenberg Principle*.
During the last of my two tours in Germany I was told about it by
the chief of the German Air Force, Gunther Rall. Many will remember, when reminded, that Count von Stauffenberg was the German
army general who tried to bring World War II to an end by killing
Adolf Hitler with a bomb in a briefcase placed under a table in Hitler's underground bunker. Due to a fluke the briefcase was moved
elsewhere under the table, and Hitler survived the blast. Von Stauffenberg, and his coconspirators, paid with their lives. Even more trag-
ically, the death and suffering of millions continued as WWII dragged
on and on. What is less well known about Von Stauffenberg is that
he was a well-respected personnel specialist in the Wehrmacht. After
seeing human nature in action in many different settings (including
on a Prussian General Staff noted for its no-nonsense efficiency), he
set forth his Von Stauffenberg Principle: *Any bureaucratic entity of
forty or more people can stay busy ten hours a day, six days a week,
with no inputs and no outputs.* Anyone who has been in the management business very long should appreciate Von Stauffenberg's sage

observation. Parkinson makes the same basic point: that work is generated to fill the time and number of people available to do it, without any obvious connection to real-world needs.

Parkinson's other timeless admonition, that "managers prefer to multiply subordinates" (irrespective of the organization's actual needs), brings another World War II story to mind. It was after the victory over Japan in August 1945—an abrupt surrender that found no plans in place for demobilization. The system coped as best it could, and started shipping troops home in wholesale numbers to await discharge. The story is told that at Lincoln Air Field, Nebraska, such troops were stacked up in the barracks with nothing to do. So the colonel in charge of the base decided to farm the problem out. Accordingly, he called in a young major, a hotshot, can-do fighter pilot with a chest full of ribbons, and told him, "I want you to take these fifty people and keep them busy. Idle hands are the devil's workshop, and they're sitting around with nothing to do. I don't care what you do with them, just keep them busy. Report back to me in two weeks and by that time we should have discharge instructions." The major saluted smartly and went off to corral the fifty people. In a week, he was back. The colonel said, "I thought I told you two weeks." And the major replied, "I need more people."

While these stories, and the "laws" of Murphy and Parkinson, are served up in whimsical fashion, they convey a serious message. It's altogether true that if anything can go wrong, invariably it will. It will, that is, unless there are concerned people exercising involvement and leadership to ensure that it doesn't. It's also true that left to themselves, things always go from bad to worse. That's why they can't be left to themselves. So running an organization on a remote, impersonalized basis—in the centralized style—just doesn't hack it. Those who can mobilize the necessary effort to make things go right are too far removed from the action to make a difference where it counts and when it counts. Given that, we might take the liberty of adding two new "laws" to Murphy's list:

- *The fewer the people who care whether it goes right or wrong, the greater the certainty it will go wrong.*

• *The less the authority vested in those closest to the problem, the more the problem lingers and spreads.*

That pretty well sums up what's wrong with the centralized, managership approach. These tendencies thrive in a centralized hothouse. And while they never go completely away, they're far less rampant and lasting in organizations structured on the decentralized, leadership model. So if you want to keep the laws we received from Murphy and Parkinson from biting you where it hurts the most, it's a very good idea to start worrying about leadership. What people feel is important. That provides motivation. What people know is important. That provides competence. And, as Andy Grove of Intel points out, creating motivation and competence are the twin means of forging success. Leaders must build both. It won't come from without. And it won't come from sterile managership either.

In that regard, I've explained how "leader" and "leading" fell out of the management (and management school) lexicon, and have yet to make any substantial comeback. In fact, that built-in bias is so strong that even when centralists use a term other than "manager" they use some euphemism for it that makes the concept even fuzzier when it comes to the important matters of authority and accountability. A case in point is the term "*facilitator*." You can't read a book on quality management these days without running into it again and again—it's all the rage. Indeed, the term and the concept are deeply embedded in the process school of thinking mentioned in chapter 6. More than anything, you need leaders and leadership, not some pale substitute for both. Let's look at the difference.

FACILITATING VERSUS LEADING—WHICH IS IT TO BE, AND WHEN

The term "facilitator" is the preferred title of the "process school" of quality management for those who head up the cross-functional "process improvement" committees (which they euphemistically call "teams"). I have no problem with the term "facilitator" used in that "overlay" committee context. Those "improvement committee" sessions, after all, are meant to be free-floating forums unencumbered by people pulling rank or position to shape or constrain the discussion unduly. So its use is OK there, though I still prefer "leader," even for a group such as that. But that's not the main problem. The problem is that "facilitator" as a term (and concept) is taking on a life of its own, and finding its way into other applications in the structure of organizations.

As an illustration of the point, in a recent seminar I conducted for another *Fortune* 500 company (not heretofore mentioned), that very subject came up. In one of our interchanges an executive said, "Well, we've formed some permanent structural teams and they seem to be beginning to work, but we don't have team leaders. We call them facilitators. When we started out by calling them leaders they couldn't resist telling people everything to do." My response was they were working on the right problem, but in the wrong way. You fix that problem by educating the team leaders to stay away from that type of autocratic micromanagement. But you don't fix it by using a eu-phemism that blurs the lines of authority and accountability. That's precisely what is wrong with the managership approach. And new names, "facilitator" or any other, won't change that.

No matter how you slice it, a team without a leader is a *committee*. And a team without a leader, a plan, and specific goals is the *lost patrol*. It is important to keep in mind the three basic management questions: *What's the plan? Who's in charge? Compared to what?* Facilitators don't lead, they facilitate. I believe I understand what both facilitating and leading are all about. And there's a big difference between the two. In fact, I'm at a loss to understand the arguments for the use of "facilitators" in a structural management context, so much so that every time I hear the word I think of spectators going to a *Thunderbird* airshow and then hearing the narrator announce "Flying the left wing today is So-and-so, flying the right wing is So-and-so, flying the slot position is So-and-so, and flying the facilitator's position is . . ." At that point, if they're smart, they would grab their companions and say, *"We're outta here—it's not safe to stay!"* Such concern should arise from the expectation that the team had some tangible, proactive leadership—both to put the team together diligently and then in the air—and a form of leadership that goes well beyond anyone's idea of facilitating.

The Japanese populate their companies with *leaders*. So I wish all those who populate theirs with *facilitators* lots of luck. They're going to need it. You simply will not create the right kind of leadership by avoiding the subject. I recognize that's been the popular way, under the *mistaken* assumption that leaders create problems, not solutions. They won't if they're trained properly and empowered properly, as the best companies prove every day. And here, of course, I'm speaking of the enlightened, caring leadership that is based on full recognition of the profound difference between *ordering* people and *persuading* them to make good things happen in an organization. It's appropriate to address that as we prepare to leave the subject of leadership because that also is misunderstood by many—especially those long conditioned to Centralism.

More than once after a speech I have had some close variation of this question that came on one occasion:

I had heard about your successes in turnarounds and in improving productivity in the military. But what you said about needing leadership at all levels surprised me. I thought that since people in the military have to do what they're told, and you're a four-star general, then it's simple—you just tell them to do better and they have no choice but to do better.

In answering the question, which was presented in all seriousness, I made the following points: All workers have a choice, including those in the military. You can order compliance, but you can't order initiative, enthusiasm, and creativity. *The power of resistance can always overcome the power of direction.* That's what leads to creative incompetence as an art form practiced the world over by those who are not motivated and committed. In fact, you can count on it from the alienated. It's the worst kind of incompetence of all because it is the purest form of squandered potential. I said that if it was as simple as ordering people to do better, then every other general in every other command could have done as well as TAC, but they did not and could not until they changed their approach to replicate that of TAC. I also explained it's those very issues that proactive leadership must address.

In a nutshell, it's the caliber of the leadership that sorts out the winners from the losers. Every organization has leadership at work, whether it's called that or not. It just isn't very good in those organizations that don't believe in it—because they shy from the actions that will bring it alive and allow it to flourish. Also, when the decentralized culture is firmly established, the *Five Pillar* system will perpetuate itself—and resist efforts of the centralizers to change it back to the old-time religion.

ADAPTING TO CONSTANT CHANGE REQUIRES MATCHING ORGANIZATIONAL CHANGES—CARRIED OUT ACCORDING TO SOUND TQM PRINCIPLES

It's been said that the only thing that doesn't change is change itself. That's never been more true than in the modern era. And organizations must be flexible enough to adapt to those new circumstances. Clearly, no one can come up with one organizational "school solution" that fits all future circumstances. But sound principles allow organizations to be continuously remolded to fit changing circumstances and new challenges without departing from those basic principles. Motorola's top executives say that need is to create a *culture* that results in "a thriving company that constantly transforms itself while adhering to beliefs that are not subject to change." Motorola has made that work for a long time now.

In that respect, it was never expected that TAC would hunker down and rest on its laurels, and it has not. In fact, continuing refinement and improvement are among the key litmus tests of any new system. They are also telling indicators of whether all the principles have been fully embedded in the organization's fabric, and have created advocates who will perpetuate and further strengthen those TQM principles and methods. TAC passed those litmus tests with flying colors. It didn't skip a beat when I left—it just kept getting better, and it still is. In that light, let's take a quick look at the TAC of today and see how it is responding to recent world changes.

As all know, the end of the 1980s saw a dramatic change in the circumstances facing the U.S. military coincident with the collapse of the Soviet Union. Those developments obviously called for reevaluation not only of old strategy but also of previous organizational approaches as the DOD began a major downsizing. The Air Force responded with a major realignment. On June 1, 1992, the name of Tactical Air Command (TAC) was changed to Air Combat Command (ACC), coincident with the merger of Strategic Air Command's (SAC's) combat assets—its bombers and ICBMs—into the combat assets of TAC. The merger of SAC into TAC was sensible because the changing world situation has brought about not only a reduction in the sizes of both but also a convergence of the "business" that each is in.

This is why: The collapse of the Soviet Union is speeding the disappearance of the boundary between "general war" (massive nuclear exchange) and "limited war" (tailored, flexible, conventional response). The other boundaries between strategic and tactical airpower had disappeared far earlier. Therefore, when the need was removed to have SAC's bombers sit constantly poised on fast-reaction alert with nuclear weapons for general war (and thank God for that), the opportunity arose to merge SAC into TAC and make all the combat airpower seamless. That is what the formation of Air Combat Command does.

Two management lessons are involved. First, the Air Force action in this instance reflects an organization eager to change with altered circumstances, a critical need for an organization if it is to remain world-class in these changing times. Second, there are appropriate and inappropriate types of consolidation (as I discussed earlier). This is the right kind—the useful kind. That's so because while Air Combat Command will be much bigger than TAC or SAC standing alone, there is no intent to "organize big" *within* the new ACC. To do so would be to revisit the troubled past, not stay attuned to the "organize small" needs of today. The ACC commander will see to it that it's the "organize small" approach.

General John Michael Loh became TAC commander in March 1991 and then became ACC commander coincident with its establishment in mid-1992. (TAC headquarters at Langley AFB, Virginia, became ACC headquarters.) Mike Loh was one of TAC's best of the best, emerging from the extensive grooming process. He is as devoted a foe of Centralism as I am. He's seen TAC at work before and after our decentralization and quality initiatives—and fully subscribes to all aspects of the new TQM approach. Mike Loh said this in an interview in April 1991 as he took command of TAC:

> One of the most dominant characteristics a leader must portray in these times is a sense of vision. A vision of where he or she wants that organization to go and what that organization should be thought of. A good leader sets goals, measures progress and rewards performance. He or she tries to give everyone a stake in the mission of the organization and its outcome. That's the role of leadership.

Recently, in a speech delivered to defense industry executives gathered in San Diego, Loh expounded on the issue of TQM:

> The fact is, people all over the world look for the same thing in the products they buy—quality. Quality is meeting the customer's expectations—and quality is the result of effective leadership. In other words the route to reaping the rewards TQM promises to bring is not primarily through Total Quality Management. It is through leadership that inspires people to do the things Total Quality Management suggests. Leadership is often the forgotten dimension. Quality didn't begin in the Tactical Air Command as a management initiative. It began as the leadership style of a former commander, Bill Creech.

General Loh put his finger on the problems with much of what passes for TQM these days. The reason most TQM programs are floundering is that TQM is being treated as another management initiative and not as a pervasive change in the leadership style. Loh understood that fully, as does his 1995 successor—General Joe Ralston. In fact, Ralston served in many key jobs in TAC (now ACC) throughout this revolution, including 3 years as my own full-colonel Executive Officer. And he's as fully a believer in the Five Pillar decentralized approach as I am.

The same holds true for General Merrill A. McPeak, who served as Air Force Chief of Staff (1980–1984). Tony McPeak played a large role in developing the TAC culture as its deputy for plans. As the Air Force chief he led the charge in the design and implementation of the massive Air Force reconfiguration—of which the new ACC is a part—as a timely response to the radically changed world circumstances. In this entire reorganization process McPeak made it clear, repeatedly and in numerous forums, that *to consolidate is not to centralize*—and that he would have no part of the latter. And the same holds true for McPeak's successor, General Ron Fogelman—still another product of the TAC grooming system. Ron Fogelman is clearly—and repeatedly—on record that he champions the decentralized, leadership approach we introduced in 1978, and that there's no chance the Air Force will return to the Centralism practices of the past.

Organizations must adapt to changing circumstances; they're foolish if they don't. But they should, like the Air Force, apply the new principles, not revisit the flawed Centralism of the past. In that spirit, this is an appropriate place to turn to the subject of *vision*. It's most important, and often misunderstood.

THERE HAS BEEN NO SHORTAGE OF "VISION" ON HOW TO MANAGE HUMAN ENDEAVOR—BUT MOST OF IT HAS BEEN WRONG

One of the longest-running clichés attached to the subject of management is that top managers or leaders must have "vision"—implying that some have it and some don't and that if you have it it's of the positive, future-oriented, workable, and successful type. If only that were true. A wag once said, "It isn't ignorance that causes the problems in the world, it's what people know beyond a shadow of a doubt that just isn't so." In 1880, Edison said, "The phonograph is not of any commercial value." Grover Cleveland said in 1905, "Sensible women do not want the vote." Tris Speaker advised in 1921, "Babe Ruth made a big mistake to give up pitching." And Harry Warner said in 1927, "Who the hell wants to hear actors talk?" We have seen many such examples over history of profound but profoundly clouded vision—even by the "experts." The point is, there's plenty of vision around; there always has been. But that doesn't mean it hasn't been wrong as often as it has been right.

Tojo and the other Japanese warlords of World War II had a flawed vision of how to bring about the *"Greater Asia Co-Prosperity Sphere."* Among other blind spots, it overlooked the fact that when people are kicked they are very likely to kick back—harder than you might ever imagine. But some imagined that very result, though they were not calling the shots at the very top. In fact, Admiral Yamamoto is reported to have said as the ebullient reports came from the Japanese pilots regarding the scope of the damage on an unprepared Pearl Harbor, "We have awakened a sleeping giant." Indeed they had— and that was the end of that particular vision of how to ensure the future prosperity of Japan. Some now say, with caustic irony, that since the Japanese couldn't get Hawaii by bombing it, they are buying it—and with *our* money. That's too uncomfortably close to the truth to contain much humor, even gallows humor. And the American giant sleeps on.

We now have a modern example to add to the list of a vision that didn't quite work out. Saddam Hussein, a legend in his own mind, long has seen himself as an expert in military matters and a consummate strategist. He even built a war memorial in Baghdad after the Iran-Iraq war based on a pair of huge hands which "molded Iraq's glorious victory" (Saddam's hands, of course). After occupying Kuwait, Saddam said any U.S. effort to dislodge him would be futile: "The United States relies on the Air Force, and the Air Force has never been the decisive factor in the history of war." But when the shooting had died down and a senior Iraqi general was asked at surrender talks why the Iraqi army had totally collapsed, he gave a simple answer: "*The airplanes.*" So much for vision of the wrong kind—and of the right kind on our part.

The Air Force used quality, precision, and professionalism to get into the *absolute* business, not the *almost* business. Every company in America can do the same. But it takes proactive leadership, not reactive managership. And you won't get it throughout the organization unless you believe in it and organize for it. *Five Pillar TQM* does that.

The primary point here is that we've always been up to our necks in vision—and visionaries—about the best way to conduct warfare, as well as the best way to manage human endeavor. However, often those visions have not been practical, workable, or successful. Regarding management, that's primarily because the visionaries have not taken into adequate account the critically decisive matter of how the human spirit will be affected in carrying out the vision. Marx, Engels, and Lenin had no shortage of far-seeing vision. History proves that it was fatally flawed. Frederick Winslow Taylor had ample far-seeing vision, too. It hasn't worked either. Yet Taylor has served as the Pied Piper of Centralism for too many of America's managers for too long—whether they know it or not. (More in chapter 12.)

THE MOST SUCCESSFUL ORGANIZATIONS, WORLDWIDE, USE LEADERSHIP—NOT MANAGERSHIP —TO CREATE THEIR SUCCESS

All the best organizations I have encountered—public or private, in the United States or abroad—believe deeply in leadership as the principal means of making the right things happen. They do not shrink from the use of the term, or from the concept, or from what the concept entails. And they do not shrink from establishing leaders, with clear responsibility, commensurate authority, and unambiguous accountability at *all levels* from the very lowest to the very highest. That is the indispensable ingredient for success. There is no other way.

The change in approach, therefore, involves a shift in style, focus, and emphasis, not an abdication from involvement or an abrogation of responsibility. After decentralizing TAC I didn't put a sign on my desk that said *"Gone Fishin'."* Neither has Jack Welch at GE. And if other corporate giants had achieved anything like GE's remarkable transformation under Welch's leadership, we wouldn't be wringing our hands over America's competitiveness. In that regard, Welch has capsulized his approach into six rules for success:

1. Don't manage, lead.
2. Face reality as it is, not as it was or as you wish it to be.
3. Be candid with everyone.
4. Change before you have to.
5. If you don't have a competitive advantage, don't compete.
6. Control your own destiny, or someone else will.

Those are outstanding rules. They should be heeded by every manager in America. And the most important of the six is "Don't manage, lead." That's where it all starts. Without that none of the other good things happens. Alas, most *Fortune* 500 companies saw their fortunes erode during the eighties, not prosper. So they would benefit by studying what GE has done, as well as the other models presented in these pages.

Let's now turn to more human system issues and center on employee commitment. I'm talking here about the degree of commitment flowing from the satisfaction of the employees with the organization, its principles, its policies, its practices, and their own role within it. Commitment obviously comes in weak and strong varieties. And the management system shapes it for better or worse.

There's ample evidence that commitment heads the casualty list produced by America's traditional management style. The problem can be fixed, but not with new slogans. For those reasons *commitment* is critical to an organization's success—and is the indispensable Fifth Pillar. The other pillars support it, it supports them. Chapter 10 provides more clues to what's wrong with employee commitment in the American workplace—and how the troublesome lack of it can be fixed.

Commitment: TQM Builds It, and It Creates Success

A BRIEF OVERVIEW OF THE ISSUE OF EMPLOYEE COMMITMENT

An organization not only has a head; it also has a heart. And the size of the heart depends upon the size of employee commitment to its ideals and goals. Organizational vitality from the bottom up must be built. And it doesn't happen with halfhearted employee support of where the head wants to go. Centocracies don't take that fundamental principle into account. You simply don't find commitment on the list of centralist precepts. That very omission has made the Communists a vanishing species, and Centralism does its damage everywhere. Thus, commitment must not only be on the list, but at the head of the list.

Let's start with some relevant quotations. Vince Lombardi: "The quality of a person's life is in direct proportion to their commitment to excellence, regardless of their chosen field of endeavor." Mario Andretti: "Desire is the key to motivation. It is the commitment to an unrelenting pursuit of your goal that will enable you to attain the success you seek." Napoleon Hill: "The starting point of all achievement is desire. Keep this constantly in mind. Weak desires bring weak results, just as a small amount of fire makes a small amount of heat." Abraham Lincoln: "Things may come to those who wait, but only the things left by those who hustle.'' Walter Lippmann: ''Ignore what a man desires and you ignore the very source of his power.'' And, on the day the first atomic bomb was detonated on a barren plain in New Mexico, Albert Einstein said, ''Everything in the world has changed except for our thinking.'' These are the themes of this chapter.

It is very difficult—no, virtually impossible—to achieve the loftier goals that globalization demands unless the employees at each level, bottom to top, perceive continuous improvement as a benefit and become committed to the goals that produce it. Accordingly, let's look at surveys that reveal the current state of desire and commitment in the American work force. They don't paint a reassuring picture. And they raise the question of why employee commitment—particularly at the frontline—became the conspicuously missing ingredient in the American management style, and what can be done about it.

YOU CAN'T BUILD GREATER QUALITY AND PRODUCTIVITY WITHOUT THE COMMITMENT TO MAKE IT HAPPEN—AND THAT'S HARD TO FIND

We know that organizational practices and policies directly affect the attitudes of the employees within that organization—and by extension their level of desire and commitment. Therefore, an overarching look at the state of employee attitudes in America can provide useful insight into the worth of this nation's traditional management style. When measured in terms of the employee attitudes it is creating, it's not worth much, and it cries out for change. Employee commitment is a largely neglected realm of American management, and within it lies the key to our competitiveness in a rapidly changing world. Said simply, globalization is busy eliminating the comparative advantage we once enjoyed. Therefore, it's time to build a new one, on a new basis. It's an entirely new war—with new realities, new challenges, and new rules—and we need fired-up and competent troops to fight it. The raw material is there; in fact it's potentially better than ever (just as it was in the Air Force when we tapped into that potential with a new approach). So it's our thinking about how to create desire, motivation, and commitment that needs changing.

Doubtful? Consider these results from a variety of relevant polls and surveys:

- In separate pollings of a large representative sample of three separate groups, workers, executives, and the general public, an extraordinary degree of agreement exists on what the growing problems are. (Agreement regarding solutions is a different matter.) For example, some two-thirds of each group believe that "people do not work as hard as they did ten years ago." And approximately three-fourths of each group believe that when compared to ten years ago: (1) people have less pride in their work, (2) workmanship is worse, and (3) job motivation is not as strong.
- From 1966 to 1980 Lou Harris conducted an annual poll in conjunction with ABC News on "Feelings of Alienation." Alienation has grown dramatically since this survey began in 1966 and in virtually every sampled "job satisfaction" category. In fact, in that fifteen-year period the Lou Harris/ABC "Alienation Index," synthesizing all poll results, rose from 29 to 58. It's worse now. Employee alienation has continued to grow throughout the eighties and early nineties, according to numerous other polls and samplings.
- In 1966 only 9 percent of American workers "felt left out of things." Using the same polling techniques, by the mid-1980s that number was nearly 50 percent of all workers—and growing.

   (I didn't look for polls with a sixties benchmark, but it's interesting that these samplings provide a good benchmark on the level of alienation at that time. The new brand of matrixed Centralism promulgated in that same period—promoted as a cure for America's management woes—didn't quite do the trick. This is just more evidence of that.)
- A recent Harris poll asked, "What action could your company take to improve overall productivity?" It listed various catego-

ries of actions polling large samples of both "executives" and "workers." Here are the results in the five categories sampled:

—*Better tools?* Yes, said 67 percent of executives. Less than half that number of workers—and less than a third of the total —listed that as a source of greater productivity.

—*Better communication?* Of the executives polled, 40 percent agreed this would improve productivity. A seemingly consistent 42 percent of workers agreed that it's an important category. (But other poll results show that the communication between the groups is very poor now, suggesting that it has a critical effect on productivity. Moreover, the poll question wasn't structured to get at how much they like what they're hearing, or what they want to hear. And if only 40 percent of executives think better communication improves productivity, how about the other 60 percent?)

—*Pay for it?* Nearly 50 percent of each group agreed this could play a positive role. (But, as I will show later, only a handful of American companies thus far have implemented any kind of pay-performance, pay-productivity linkage.)

—*More say in decisions?* Only 16 percent of executives saw this as a productivity issue. More than twice as many workers did.

—*Less pressure on the job?* A bare 3 percent of executives agreed. Nine times as many workers, per capita, agreed that this would make a positive contribution to productivity. (I assume the other 97 percent of executives view worker perceptions of undue pressure as no big deal when it comes to productivity. They're wrong about that.)

With further regard to the issue of pressure on the job, a 1992 survey conducted for the *Northwestern National Life Insurance Company* disclosed that 46 percent of workers say their jobs are highly stressful, which is double the percentage cited in a 1985 *National Health Interview* survey. Also, 34 percent said they had thought seriously of quitting their jobs in the last year because of workplace stress. And 14 percent did quit or change their jobs for that reason.

In the same survey some 70 percent of workers said job stress caused frequent health problems and made them less productive. What did they say was the principal contributor? The head analyst says the research shows that ''little personal control on the job was the single largest cause of burnout.''

(I have emphasized throughout these pages ways to place more control in the hands of those frontline workers—and to profit greatly from it. In that respect, a recent Gallup Poll asked, ''If workers are involved in decisions, will they do a better job by working harder?'' The answer from 84 percent of America's workers was yes. Experience shows they mean what they say.)

These and similar surveys also reveal that frontline workers have little respect for their employers, and that they express their disaffection in a variety of ways. As one illustration, in a 1989 Harris poll, 87 percent of workers said ''ethics'' are very important—but only 38 percent said their boss was ethical. Other surveys show that two-thirds of employees have a low opinion of their bosses. Granted, business isn't a *popularity contest*. However, there's growing proof that our traditional style has turned into an *unpopularity contest*. And from a variety of other nationwide surveys we see ample evidence of the damage this is causing to attitude, desire, motivation, and commitment. For example, 50 percent say they ''don't put any more effort into their job than is required to hold on to it''; 52 percent believe ''working hard doesn't lead to a better job''; 60 percent admit they ''don't work as hard as they used to''; and 77 percent say they're ''not working as hard as they could.''

MOST AMERICAN EMPLOYEES SEE LITTLE MERIT IN WORKING HARDER

The workers themselves explain that a principal reason for their lack of enthusiasm for higher productivity is the lack of incentive to work harder. Indeed, 73 percent say their own job effort has declined ''because coworkers get the same pay increases and rewards regardless of how hard they work.'' It's no big surprise they feel that way. That's a specialty of the centocracies. Even if you're an *eager beaver* when you join most companies, it doesn't take long to get the message. And if you don't get it on your own, the other workers will make sure you do. Thus, we have negative peer pressure. It comes from the dispirited and disenchanted who have learned there is no payoff from working harder than anyone else, in peer acceptance or anything else. That's why I have emphasized the need to get the peer pressure working in positive directions, and from the growing ranks of the committed, not the uncommitted.

With regard to the value of compensation as a motivational tool, 72 percent of America's employees don't see any link between performance and pay. And 87 percent of union members see no such link. These numbers come from an in-depth survey by the *Wyatt Company*, a nationally known compensation consulting firm. Other surveys provide confirmation that some three-quarters of frontline workers don't see any link between their pay and their performance. (This widely held belief comes as no surprise either. Our traditional compensation practices can yield no other plausible result.)

On the hopeful side—the potential side—75 percent say they "*could be* significantly more effective than they presently are.'' So there's no mystery in their own minds why they aren't working harder. They keep telling us, every chance they get, that they're out of the loop—in communications, in involvement, and in sharing success. Little wonder they do. In at least eight American companies out of ten, they are. And they keep telling us that they could and would work harder if the policies and practices were to change to include them. Guess what? That's the "magic formula'' the best companies use. And their success proves that the employees are as good as their word.

So all these fissures between management and labor take their toll where it counts most—in diminished employee job satisfaction and skepticism, even outright rejection of the idea that increased productivity brings any personal benefit. Widespread samples taken by a variety of polling organizations disclose that a majority of frontline employees see no benefit to themselves *whatsoever* when productivity improves. And many see a negative result. They believe increased productivity only means harder work for the same pay. They also believe it means more layoffs and downward pressures on their wages as more workers compete for fewer jobs. And it's not changing for the better. For example, a nationwide Harris poll in 1991 showed that an overwhelming 91 percent of frontline employees do not believe that "workers are a major beneficiary when productivity improves." It's not a matter of rocket science to deduce the difficulties involved in improving productivity when the great bulk of the American work force sees no personal advantage in doing so.

These surveys speak loudly for themselves—and they don't portend success if we continue on our present course of tenaciously adhering to outworn management practices and policies. And it's worth highlighting two special aspects of these surveys regarding attitude and commitment. The first is the amazing degree of consistency from industry to industry, and from poll to poll—as reported by a variety of polling organizations. Ponder for a moment on what is creating such consistency from industry to industry. Some vociferously deny there's a traditional American management style. They should look again.

The second common and disturbing thread in these surveys is that American employee attitudes about their employers are getting worse, not better as the years roll by. That's why America is in trouble. The Globalization Age demands greater productivity, but even in the face of all this evidence, we can't seem to figure out the way to get it. We keep working at the fringes of the problem and debating endlessly over peripheral issues. Meanwhile, our management style rolls on— placid in its presumed superiority. So it's high time to recognize this bottom line: *We cannot substantially improve productivity when the preponderance of America's workers simply see no benefit in it to themselves.*

NEGATIVE ATTITUDES AND LACKLUSTER COMMITMENT ARE BEING GENERATED BY THE TRADITIONAL AMERICAN MANAGEMENT STYLE

The traditional management style has created those attitudes, so they have ample reason for existing. And they can be changed. Unfortunately, I find very few company executives who believe *their* employees think and behave that way. In fact, if you poll business managers across the country regarding their own organizations, you wonder where in the world all these statistics regarding negative employee attitudes and growing frustration come from. It's another sad commentary on our management style, but all too true, that most managers are out of touch with the feelings and frustrations at the front of their organization. In fact, it's a centocracy trademark to distance the senior managers from such attitudes at the front. And those senior managers take refuge from the negative attitudes and alienation to be found there by rarely, if ever, going there. (Polls show that. Employees say that.) That aloof style and the management system approach that creates it has to change before those frontline attitudes will change. Also, unless the employees perceive that productivity and quality improvements *will benefit them*, directly and tangibly, you can forget the company's productivity improvement plan. It won't work because it lacks the principal ingredient.

In my own travels I make it a point, every chance I can, to talk to frontline employees. I find the single largest source of frustration is that they would like to make more of a contribution than they do now—if the practices were changed so they could. Here are comments I encounter frequently:

- *"Ask my opinion? No one ever does. But I give it to them anyway, I just don't do it verbally."*
- *"No one around here seems to care. We just do our thing."*
- *"They keep telling me we have to do more with less. I recall them telling me that many times before. From what I've seen*

around here we do less with less, not more. So they're going to have to tell me how we do that, not just that we should.''

- *"Everyone in this company gets paid to do a job. I guess they're all important in one way or another. But when they divvy up the profits, nothing at all goes to the folks who, when it comes down to it, produced those profits. Why should I work harder so managers can get fat bonuses? What's in it for me?"*
- *"OK, I'll become committed. To what?"*
- *"I want to do a good job. I really do. But the system doesn't let me."*

I'm convinced most do indeed want to do a good job. That's the very source of the substantial untapped potential which the best companies prove beyond doubt is there. But to tap it the management system in traditionally managed businesses must be reoriented toward frontline inclusion, not exclusion.

In that regard, Tom Watson, Sr., who along with Tom Watson, Jr., led IBM to a level of overall corporate success second to none in this century, was renowned for exhorting the IBM employees as follows: *"Put your hearts in the business, and the business in your hearts."* Good advice. And for a long time, IBM made it work. However, recently IBM has found that the old practices, good for their times, no longer suffice. (I addressed why earlier.) In that respect, I believe corporate America now needs a slightly revised version of Tom Watson's admonition. That revision is this: *If you will put the business in their hearts, they will put their hearts in the business.* And putting the business in their hearts involves changing the practices of today that are taking it out of their hearts. Look at the differences the traditional American management style draws between managers and workers in virtually every organizational activity—from information flow, to partaking in "management decisions," to the matter of sharing success. Therein lie the clues to changing commitment from negative to positive.

To begin that discussion, let's take the matter of sharing success, and examine the compensation policies most widely used in America. Again, repeated polls show that some 75 percent of frontline employees see no link between their performance and their pay. Surveys also show that frontline employees find it difficult to rationalize why the managers share in the organization's success but they do not. Compensation policy is not the only source of employee frustration —or the only source of improvement in employee commitment. However, a look at our long-standing practices shows they bear little relevance to today's needs.

The best companies prove that making compensation policies more inclusionary of the frontline employees is one important means of building a new spirit of commitment, and a new spirit of partnership among all organizational levels. It is only one of the many issues to be addressed, but it is by no means the easiest. In my speaking and advisory activities I find it the most contentious issue of all— and the most resistant to change—for most of the nation's managers. Simply put, it's the hot button of all hot buttons when it comes to accepting the need for change in current policies. Therefore, I've learned to tread gently in that minefield of opposition, lest my overall message be lost in the highly charged issue of who gets paid what, and why. Accordingly, I explore before each speech where the mines are strewn, and whether the top management is involved in removing them or leaving them in place. It's indicative of the overall mindset on this matter that seven out of ten speech sponsors say, "Leave it alone."

That's fine with me, because each company needs to address the matter in its own way, and there is no one "school solution" applicable to all. However, no book on change should get by without addressing the subject. It's a major cause of frontline employees' estrangement from the management system they work within; the surveys leave little doubt about that. Let's see whether we can discern where those deeply entrenched managerial beliefs and biases regarding compensation come from.

A SHARE IN THE SUCCESS CREATES COMMITMENT TO BUILDING IT—AMERICA'S TRADITIONAL COMPENSATION POLICIES OVERLOOK THAT

The idea of linking pay to performance, and providing "incentive pay" in that regard, is hardly a new one in American management. It goes back at least as far as certain management pioneers early in this century, such as Pierre S. Du Pont, famous for the company that bears his name and for helping to rescue General Motors in 1920. In instituting an incentive compensation program for his company, his stated purpose was "to align the interests of the managers with those of the owners." In this same regard, Maryann Keller, writing in *Rude Awakening* about GM's trials and tribulations, cited Alfred Sloan's establishment of an incentive bonus program in GM's early days. She quoted Sloan on his reason for doing so: "The interests of the corporation and its stockholders are best served by making key employees partners in the company's prosperity." Keller went on to disclose that "the [GM] bonus incentive, which included a broader base— some sixteen thousand workers—in Sloan's day, has today been narrowed to include only an elite four thousand." (And that's in a GM that's far, far larger than it was in Alfred Sloan's day.)

This same trend was reflected across the American business landscape. Nearly all American companies sooner or later adopted pay-performance linkage for their managers. However, a mere handful did so for the workers. That's still the case today—and it's but one more piece of evidence of the staying power of Centralism-oriented management thinking. A look at current statistics is instructive. In late 1990, KPMG Peat Marwick published the results of three broad-based executive compensation studies. They showed that performance-based *annual* incentives for managers are now used in nearly all major U.S. companies. In fact, the Peat Marwick surveys revealed that such incentives are found in 84 percent of America's industrial firms and 89 percent of its service companies. In addition, a *long-term* incentive plan is in effect for management in 98 percent of industrials, 96 percent of financial services, and 89 percent of service companies. (They include stock options and other means of developing personal equity from company success.) It appears the American management style has the notion down pat that—at least when it comes to managers—there is a need for a clear-cut pay-performance link. Thus, American companies are virtually unanimous on the need for a *stake in the outcome* if they are to ensure a committed performance from the managers.

There is, however, no such mindset when it comes to the frontline workers. For example, a 1989 *Conference Board* study of more than 450 companies revealed that only 11 percent of those surveyed companies had a profit-sharing plan. A mere 8 percent had a bonus system that reaches all employees in one form or another, and only 3 percent of companies were found to be using "Group Productivity Incentives."

In the same context, the *William M. Mercer, Inc.*, compensation advisory company, citing a *1991/92 Compensation Planning Survey National Summary* resulting from data gathered from some 3,100 companies, reported as follows on what it termed "*nontraditional practices.*" (As you will see from the results, there was a very good reason to call them nontraditional.) "*Gainsharing,*" the current buzz-word for wider forms of incentive compensation reaching all employees, was found in only 7 percent of American companies. And 90 percent of those not doing it said they had no plans to adopt it. Regarding "*Small Group Incentives*" (achievement bonuses), only 10 percent use any variant of that now, and 87 percent of the remainder said they are not considering it. Other surveys show that only 8 percent of American companies use any variant of "*Pay-for-Skill*"—an incentive for workers to increase their job knowledge and productivity.

Still another form of reward that can create employee incentive (and focus) is "*Earned Time Off.*" Time off is given as a reward for productivity and quality achievements against specific goals. To work well, it has to be a case of all involved minding both "*P's & Q's,*" not just a quantity game. Evidence shows that earned time off rewards, structured properly, can greatly improve productivity and quality. Thus it can help make money, not cost money, in the long run.

And we're not talking about a lot of time off here; even a small amount has a big impact. I know; I've used the technique very effectively to drive up attention to the P's & Q's and drive down waste and cost. (You can't offer bonuses in the government, or I would have used that in selective ways as well.) I emphasize here that *Earned Time Off* is not necessarily desirable or practical for every business, but the technique can be highly effective for many. Still, the aforementioned William Mercer survey found that only 10 percent of America's companies now use any variant of earned time off, and 97 percent of companies not using it are not considering it.

I've seen the effectiveness of all these techniques in practice, separately and in various combinations, depending on the company circumstances. I emphasize that not all involve added compensation— but all do involve added recognition and *psychic pay* for achievement. Notwithstanding their proven effectiveness, few U.S. companies use them, either singularly or in combination. The Mercer and other surveys confirm that between 90 percent and 95 percent of American companies disdain the use of any of them. And a nearly insignificant number of those disdainful companies are even contemplating using them. Again, some vociferously deny there is a traditional American management style. They should look closer and reconsider.

Though resistance to sharing success with frontline workers is deeply rooted in the traditional American management style, there is no doubt in the minds of most people—managers and workers alike —that incentive compensation and reward can provide strong impetus to work harder and smarter. A few years ago there was an interesting national debate over the issue of tipping versus a set service fee in the nation's restaurants. A widespread survey revealed that 19 percent of respondents favored a set service fee and 77 percent favored the tip system practiced now. At the gut level, there is little doubt that we Americans, of all stripes, understand "merit pay" and its benefit in focusing attention and enhancing performance. Rosabeth Moss Kanter of Harvard, writing in her 1989 book, *When Giants Learn to Dance* (an excellent, well-reasoned treatise on the need for a new American management style which she calls *Post-entrepreneurial*) said this on pay and performance:

Most Americans share the assumption that pay should reflect worth, and pay increases should be based primarily on performance. Social psychologists have devoted considerable energy to studying the values people hold with respect to the distribution of rewards, and "merit" or performance emerges again and again as number one. The "equity" principle that people should get what they "deserve" based on their contributions wins out over competing principles like "equality"—to each the same. There is a strongly held belief that performance-based reward is not only fairer, but also encourages higher levels of productivity, as people learn that they will get back more if they put more in.

We Americans do believe in that. But alas, there's little evidence that America's managers have taken it to heart. Most frontline employees simply don't get back more when they put more in. That's what they keep telling us.

In this same respect, in mid-1990, while still the USSR president and riding atop the *perestroika* tiger, Mikhail Gorbachev said this in a speech in Sverdlovsk: "Talent must be stimulated. The country will not manage without it. Should we fail to break out of this foolish system of wage leveling, we will ruin everything that is alive in our people. The nation will suffocate." He was right, but his warning came far too late. The suffocation already had occurred. Remember that Soviet joke, "They pretend to pay us, and we pretend to work"? There's an American version of the same thought that legitimately could be voiced: *They pretend to pay us for extra productivity, and we pretend to work harder to provide it.* (An old military expression also comes to mind: *Theirs is not to reason why, theirs is but to do or die.* That hasn't worked, not for a long time now, and its functional equivalent doesn't work in the business world either.)

Barriers to change in America's traditional compensation policies abound. Many managers believe the "workers" already are too highly compensated for what they produce, and are unsympathetic to any notion of bonuses or incentive pays. These managers often cite "runaway costs of benefits," such as health care, driving labor costs to the point at which their companies are increasingly "noncompetitive." However, most have never tried those techniques, as the surveys starkly reveal. And such reasoning has been used for decades now to rule out frontline inclusion in the sharing of success. It goes beyond incentive pays. For example, *Business Week* in its December 17, 1990, issue published a retrospective on how "managers" and "blue-collar workers" had fared in "wage and salary increases" over the eighties. The workers lost ground, inflation considered. Managers fared well. When *will* the time arrive to rework our compensation policies to form a better and more productive partnership?

In fairness, because of long conditioning, opposition to change in traditional compensation methods also comes from the ranks of the employees, particularly unionized employees. In fact, a curious alliance has formed between some of the nation's unions and the managers of unionized companies in rejecting ideas of a pay-performance link, or incentive compensation bonuses for workers as well as managers. While curious, it is understandable given the history of compensation and how they perceive their gains have been achieved—largely through confrontation, not cooperation.

This facet of the problem notwithstanding, most employees in most companies welcome such a change in compensation policies. Nearly everyone can readily recognize the benefits of having a direct stake in the outcome. Moreover, the companies using such inclusionary compensation policies find them every bit as popular with the workers, and as effective, as they have long been with the managers. They also find that it gives their frontline employees a different perspective regarding "profit" and their stake in it. Because they have long been out of the loop, it is well documented that the vast majority of employees have incorrect, even negative views regarding profit. They consistently and dramatically overestimate the levels of profit within their own and other companies in their industry. Company balance sheets are almost impossible for them to decipher (they're not alone in that), and most companies don't go out of their way to bring those numbers down to earth and educate employees in understandable ways on what the profits are and where they go. It's little wonder, then, that while the profits are a matter of fundamental importance to the frontline employees—and to their compensation levels and job security—hardly any of them look on it that way.

As a related matter, most employees measure their compensation in terms of their *take-home pay*—largely taking the view that their "benefits" (and the related costs, including costs for their company-funded health care and retirement) are outside the pale of their "compensation." Only one in twenty considers the company's matching contribution in Social Security taxes part of their own compensation. That even extends to matching contributions in 401K plans and the like, where the focus is on what the employee pays in, not on what the company pays to match it. Many companies have successfully demonstrated that those widespread perspectives regarding "company profit" and "personal compensation" can be significantly and positively altered. However, these companies are the exceptions.

Any manager who believes this is not an appropriate matter for employee education, with all the plain facts on the table, is badly underestimating the negative influence of current perspectives. The traditional American style perpetuates those negative and indifferent attitudes by failing to address them seriously, and by exclusionary treatment that provides no employee interest one way or the other in operating margins, profit, and company labor costs in a competitiveness context (unless the company is on the verge of complete failure and their jobs are clearly threatened; by then it's usually too late).

Quality, productivity, and, yes, profitability need to be the business of everyone in the organization—and a matter of intense interest to everyone, not just to the managers. That would seem to be axiomatic. But it's not. I'm constantly perplexed by those who read surveys on employee attitudes in these respects and do not question why we've built a Centralism-oriented management system that shunts such important attitudinal matters to the side. That can be changed, too. But it will not be changed until companies recognize that it is indeed *theirs to reason why*. In fact, experience shows that when employees are brought into the partnership and fully share in all the reasons and reasoning, it greatly contributes to their own reasonableness, to their trust, and to their commitment. Why do we persist in underestimating the frontline workers in this respect? Old beliefs. Old policies. Old suspicions. Old wounds. And, it seems not too strong or unfair to say, a long tradition of perpetuating a two-class system in the workplace. Americans have not been alone in that. But we've been very slow to recognize it for what it is, and to question why it's the way it is. So let's turn to that.

CREATING A SEAMLESS NETWORK OF LEADERSHIP AND COMMITMENT—ELIMINATING THE GAP BETWEEN "MANAGEMENT" AND "LABOR"

One of the most damaging results of the centralized, managership approach—deeply rooted in the precepts of Centralism—is a two-class system in which executives and managers participate in one loop of information and reward—reserved to themselves—and workers participate in quite another. Those two classes, snuggled within their separate loops, inevitably become out of touch with one another. Each develops its own values and perspectives, notions and emotions. The gap between the two widens, and distrust and alienation grow. That's not idle speculation. The surveys I have quoted—and they are only representative—consistently reveal the widely divergent values and perspectives between management and labor, American-style. That's particularly serious because a strong sense of common purpose simply cannot be created in a system that perpetuates two separate classes. No one benefits in such a system, but those practices are deeply entrenched.

Earlier I spoke of an *Eastern Airlines Syndrome*—in which management and labor find reasons to fight to the death. As this was being written, another such titanic struggle was going on at *Caterpillar*. In fact, if we were to plot potential sites of labor conflicts on a map of the United States (as the Pentagon does on a map of the world to track potential trouble spots) we would have a veritable thicket of markers. I also referred earlier to the different "classifications" that dignify the two-class system. American employees understand—indeed, they support—a system in which some make more than others in salaries and bonuses, scaled reasonably to position, responsibility, and talent. What they cannot understand, and do not support, is a system in which the management enjoys *all* the perks, the bonuses, and other rewards of success.

They resent the stark cleavage between management and labor—American-style. The managers have positions; they have jobs. The managers get salaries; they get wages. The managers don't punch time clocks; they do. They are assured overtime pay for working extra long because they are nonexempts—and it takes, they believe, the existing *labor legislation* to keep management from hosing them on that, too. The managers get bonuses; they don't. Indeed, most front-line workers perceive the American workplace as divided into *blue-collar, white-collar*, and *suits*—with accompanying social order distinctions and isolation of one group from another. Our vocabulary matches our practices.

I'm certainly not suggesting that we turn the entire American management culture inside out, and upside down, and find a modern *Robespierre* to march all managers off to the guillotine. I would be the last to suggest we don't need leaders, or don't need clearly to identify those responsible for creating coherence and cohesion everywhere in the organization. I am, however, strongly suggesting that America's companies need to pay far more attention to those long-standing practices—and the apathy and alienation in the work force that result. I first raised this issue in chapter 2 with respect to Japanese practices. Many have cataloged the techniques the Japanese use, so I won't elaborate on that. However, I do believe it's useful to point out the startling irony that the Japanese, not the Americans, have taken vigorous action to eliminate the bulk of those two-class practices—and effectively to span the gap between management and labor.

The irony? Simply this: America prides itself on being the most democratic society of all. The Japanese, on the other hand, historically have prized and practiced autocratic control. To this very day the Japanese have one of the most class-conscious societies on earth. Even a cursory study of their history reveals that aspect of their culture, which reaches back thousands of years. Further evidence comes from the many cultural artifacts of those autocratic and class-conscious notions found in current Japanese society. The Japanese language is imbued with all manner of class-oriented stratifications and subtleties. Similarly, the Japanese manner of paying deference, as reflected by the many ritualized nuances in the vigor and manner of their bowing, and in who bows to whom, reflects even now a level of class-consciousness Americans stoutly reject.

As another example from their history, in the Japanese military of World War II it was the right of every person of higher rank to strike anyone junior in rank—if, in the superior's sole judgment, that subordinate needed to be disciplined. It was the duty of the one on the receiving end of the blows to suffer that treatment silently and stoically. Such class-conscious attitudes and practices are a far cry from the practices in Japanese companies today. You can't find such managerial attitudes and behavior, or anything resembling them, at Honda or Toyota, or in the other Japanese companies I have studied. Nor did I find two distinct and separate classes. Instead I found employees at all levels who communicate freely and openly with one another, from bottom to top. I also found widespread involvement, shared goals, healthy interactions, and a common language of purpose.

The bottom-to-top interfaces are not perfect in Japanese companies, or at Honda or Toyota in the United States. However, they are dramatically better than those to be seen in most American companies. Also, I found both Honda and Toyota doing all possible, from the top down, to ensure that perspectives and values are *not* developing along two separate tracks. There's little question they're succeeding in significantly spanning if not eliminating that classic gap in communications, perceptions, and trust—and doing so with American employees. That's not by accident. Their decentralized, leadership approach and team-based structure are designed to do precisely that. It makes no sense to call frontline employees associates unless you're going to treat them as such. And they do. The positive employee attitudes, and performance, speak eloquently to their success with these inclusionary techniques. (A reminder here: It's not only the Japanese who practice and prove that. They have no corner on good ideas.)

THE JAPANESE HAVE OVERCOME THEIR PRIOR CONDITIONING TO CHANGE FROM AUTOCRATIC MANAGERSHIP TO DECENTRALIZED LEADERSHIP— AMERICA NEEDS TO DO NO LESS

To accomplish that change in their management style they altered their historic autocratic conditioning—at least so far as it applies to the workplace. And they did it because it was in their economic interest to do so. If nothing else, the Japanese are pragmatic—particularly on business matters. They realized that to make *"Policy Deployment"* work they had to create harmonious and cooperative interaction among all layers of the organization and between all its elements. To make it happen, they adopted practices designed to eliminate the barriers between managers and workers that a two-class system inevitably creates in any society, our own included. Recognition spread of the value of that approach as more and more Japanese companies saw it work in the hands of others. Indeed, it spread so pervasively through their various networks that it's now a central aspect of modern-day Japanese management—and is among its most recognizable features.

Many accuse the Japanese of being the world's most accomplished *copycats*. That distinction is overdrawn; however, I'm not sure the Japanese are offended by it. A willingness to learn from others is a strength, not a weakness. None of us came into this world with full-blown concepts and conditioning. We all learn from others. But some learn lots and some learn little. A willingness to learn from others, and a readiness to adapt to changing circumstances, help set the best companies apart. Indeed, that's how the Japanese made the transition from shoddy to superb products.

Like it or not, the two-class aspects of the traditional American management style must change. The best companies prove that when they are changed it enhances employee morale, motivation, and commitment—and thereby quality and productivity. There were a lot of reasons why a two-class system evolved in the American business culture, with its walls and its plethora of coping mechanisms by both management and labor based on isolation and confrontation rather than integration and cooperation. However, we can't let it continue. Globalization won't let us. As Abraham Lincoln so aptly observed in another context, *A house divided against itself cannot stand*. The management must take the lead, and labor must be willing to change also. Citing the sins of the past as the excuse for today's behavior, by either side, drowns out what needs to be done to cope with a far more challenging future. So let's look at how we shake off the practices—and the shackles—of the past.

OLD HABITS DIE HARD—BOTH LABOR AND MANAGEMENT HAVE BUILT BATTLEMENTS OVER THE YEARS ON BOTH SIDES OF THE DIVIDE

Obviously, those battlements must come down if a new, more productive partnership is to be formed. Largely erected in our minds, they nonetheless produce all sorts of tangible results. They weren't put up overnight, and they won't come down overnight. But they will come down; there is ample proof of that. Trouble is, most companies haven't initiated new thinking and new practices to take them down. And that leaves the employees, particularly some unionized employees, as alienated and ready to take to the barricades as ever (perhaps more so as our problems mount, their pay and job security come under greater pressure, and they revert to old habits in response).

From the time the team-based approach first staged its *reappearance* on the management scene in the eighties, surfacing primarily in terms of "Japanese" management practices, it has been opposed by many of America's major unions. Critics like Mike Parker and Jane Slaughter, former auto workers and UAW members, voiced the concerns of many in their 1988 book *Choosing Sides: Unions and the Team Concept*. They declared that work teams are inevitably used by management as a union-busting device and aren't good for workers anytime, anywhere. There was no ambiguity about their position—

they trashed the team concept in a variety of imaginative ways. In fact, one of their formulations was to call it "management-by-stress."

There are lots of other reflections of that bias. In the July 10, 1989, *Business Week*, an insightful article titled "The Payoff from Teamwork" quoted John Brodie, president of United Paperworkers Local 448: "What the company wants is for us to work like the Japanese. Everybody go out and do jumping jacks in the morning and kiss each other when they go home at night. You work as a team, rat on each other, and lose control of your destiny. That's not going to work in this country." *Business Week* also pointed out that even union presidents who favor such forms of "employee involvement" often cannot overcome strong opposition at the local level. The article cited support by the national president of the United Steelworkers and then cited the opposition of many of the union locals. For example, Mike Mezo, president of USW Local 1010 forcefully stated his view of the matter: "We don't think there's any benefit to cooperation. No way will we ever take part."

That dim view of the team concept also is held at the top of some of the nation's most powerful unions. In the fall of 1990 George Kourpias, president of the 740,000-member International Association of Machinists, issued a "White Paper" to every IAM local instructing the membership to stoutly resist any team concept approach being promoted by management. In his cover letter to all union officers, Kourpias wrote, "Government and industry are engaged in a serious effort to undermine our collective bargaining rights by promoting 'team concept' programs under the guise of labor-management co-operation. These programs by their very nature interfere with our duty to protect the interests of all bargaining-unit members." He said some workers might find it attractive because it calls for "employee involvement and teamwork," but that "upon closer examination it is actually a top-down, executive-directed, communication, command and control system intent on achieving efficiency and cost cutting by eliminating rework, scrap, waste, and inspection, and it has very little to do with meaningful worker participation." Talk about an enthusiastic reception! The team concept has not been warmly received in some union circles—to say the least.

Consistent with this reasoning, the concept has had a rocky passage among United Auto Workers. A few years ago members of UAW Local 645 in Van Nuys, California, ousted the leader of that local for advocating support of it. The GM plant at Van Nuys is now closed. Is there a moral there? You bet there is.

The critics say the Japanese management style is callous and insensitive to workers' welfare. Some of the Japanese transplant auto plants in the United States are unionized and some are not. Those unionized have yet to go out on strike. The UAW has had no success in organizing those that are not. If the Japanese approach is so bad, why isn't it showing up in worker dissatisfaction? Why are management-labor relations better there than in the Big Three plants, which still have lots of bickering, even walkouts? The old way is supposed to be vastly superior to the new "Japanese" way according to the critics. Where's the proof?

In June 1992, Owen Bieber, United Auto Workers president, in his speech to the annual UAW convention threatened the U.S. Big Three automakers with an industrywide strike. He said, "Do not forget it takes two to make peace, but only one to make war." He also said, "Do not forget that in the consumer-driven retail competitive markets in which you sell your products you are especially vulnerable to lost production and to lost sales." (He's sure right about that. But, on sober reflection, so are the UAW's workers.) This, of course, was primarily triggered by GM's continued downsizing and massive closings of more plants.

Then, in August 1992, 2,400 workers in the UAW local at a GM metal parts fabricating plant in Lordstown, Ohio, walked out over "job security" issues, immediately idling nine other GM plants dependent on "*just-in-time*" supply from Lordstown. After ten days of intensive negotiations, the strike was settled when GM made sufficient concessions to placate the disgruntled Lordstown workers. The settlement included restoring 240 jobs GM had planned to cut, filling 150 vacancies, and adding 140 new jobs. GM also promised not to "outsource" the work performed at Lordstown. The UAW workers involved obviously looked on that as a victory, reinforcing the belief that the traditional ways are the most productive ways of dealing with GM.

Trouble is, this puts even more pressure on GM to consider two obvious solutions: (1) drop just-in-time in favor of the old practice of thirty to sixty days' stockage of the various components, a costly proposition, or (2) move more work away from in-house suppliers to outside competitive sources (notwithstanding temporary agreements). Using that approach, they can develop two sources so that labor strife in one won't idle the entire GM production empire, and so that GM can enjoy the benefits of continuing competition on quality and value. (This technique has long been used in the aerospace industry, for both reasons.) When you're losing money hand over fist, those are nearly irresistible alternatives. So it's much too early to say whether this was a real victory, or whether, over the longer run, it simply makes it more likely that Lordstown one day will join the list of closed GM plants. The trends unfortunately suggest it may be the latter.

Indeed, the current pattern in most large corporations is to edge away from "one-of-a-kind" in-house suppliers in favor of outside vendors so that the corporation can enjoy those benefits of competition. *Vertical integration* (using in-house sources for virtually all components) was once all the rage, and GM has long been an avid practitioner. However, it has seriously fallen out of favor because, over time, many of those in-house suppliers simply have become noncompetitive in terms of quality and value. (I'm not suggesting that Lordstown is noncompetitive, because I haven't the data to study the matter, but that's the general pattern. And if GM is running true to form it doesn't have the data either, and the workers at Lordstown are in the dark regarding how they stack up in a competitiveness context.)

An increasingly favored alternative to the old-time vertical integration, unfortunately, is for U.S. companies to close supplier plants here and open them in other countries with lower overall labor costs (or at least develop sources there). The examples are abundant and growing. In 1992 GM closed a plant in the United States in favor of acquiring the same components from a GM plant in Canada, and all kinds of plants are springing up in Mexico along the U.S. border— the so-called *maquiladoras*. Other jobs are migrating as far away as Bangladesh as new sources are developed abroad to replace previous sources in the United States. The net result in all cases is the same:

bad news for the nation's workers, and for the nation itself. Greater quality and productivity in the American work force are the most obvious answer. All the other glib answers fall afoul of the *Law of Competitive Advantage*, and no one in the United States will ever be able to repeal it. It's an inescapable consequence—and an unrelenting reality—of a globalized economy.

This doesn't mean the prospects must remain bleak—that is, if we manage better and forge a better work-force partnership. Some corporations, trying to respond in a balanced way, are approaching this dilemma by having their in-house suppliers compete against outside suppliers. So long as in-house productivity, quality, and value hold up, they win. Otherwise, they lose. Sounds callous, but consider the alternatives: The more a company (GM, for example) perpetuates favored in-house sources regardless of productivity, when others are enjoying the benefits of competitive pressures in driving value up and costs down, the less competitive that company becomes compared to those already beating up on it in the marketplace. The day may come when striking for *job security* will be a contradiction in terms. In fact, there's a strong case that it had better come soon; otherwise, troubled companies (like GM, but there are many on the list) enter a self-perpetuating and self-destructive cycle of union retaliation for downsizing, through strikes or other manifestations of alienation. That, of course, simply adds to the host of problems necessitating the downsizing in the first place.

It's sobering to contemplate the growing list of such companies —centocracies all. I again emphasize that the burden of bringing about that day of harmony and identicality of purpose between management and labor rests on the leaders of both the companies and the unions. Neither side can do it on its own. However, it's abundantly clear that it won't have a chance of happening unless the company management takes the initiative to bring it about. And the unions must respond in a positive and constructive manner, not with more invective. The confrontational methods worked in the old days; that's why they're still with us. They won't work now, at least not for much longer. The new realities of globalization are not to be denied; the only question is when and how we will face up to them.

For example, with all its other problems, the last thing GM needs right now is a major strike, which would merely contribute to its downward spiral. When the UAW met for its convention in the summer of 1992 its membership was down a startling 43 percent since 1979. That was not because union members were dropping out; it was because they had lost their jobs to layoffs and closures. That provides sobering food for thought for all concerned. A continuing decline in auto worker jobs, on the scale of the past fifteen years, will prove a major catastrophe for the American economy and for all the related industries and workers.

THE TRENDS IN THE JAPANESE INCURSION SHOW EVEN MORE CAUSE FOR CONCERN—AND FOR DECIDING THAT IT IS TIME TO CHANGE

We should all worry about the disturbing trends, and we should worry about our country even more—because we don't appear to be getting the message. The message is clear to me, and the auto industry trends serve as a warning to us all. In 1960 the Big Three accounted for 97 percent of domestic passenger car production; only 3 percent was foreign, with one-third of that Volkswagen. By 1989, U.S. firms had only 67 percent of the same domestic market, with the greatest loss coming in the eighties. Also, the loss rate was accelerating. Had it not been for Japanese voluntary restraint, due to repeated pleadings by the U.S. government, the Japanese proportion would have been far higher.

Toyota, Honda, and the other Japanese automobile producers (eight in all) continue to open dealerships and transplant plants all over North America, including significant expansion in Canada. There's little question why. *Maclean's*, the Canadian news magazine, commented at length on that expansion and the reasons behind it in its April 15, 1991, issue. One of a series of articles in that issue cited the results of a "Five-year, $5.8 million study of the automotive industry by researchers at the Massachusetts Institute of Technology

(MIT).'' Among the MIT study findings reported by *Maclean's* were these:

> GM, Ford, and Chrysler each took an average of 24.9 hours of labor to produce a car. By contrast, Japanese car makers needed only 20.9 hours per vehicle at one of their North American plants, and 16.8 hours at one of their factories in Japan. The main reason for the difference, the study found, is that companies like Toyota and Honda have abandoned the traditional mass-production system and switched to a more efficient method.

Less than one decade after they started building automobiles outside Asia, the Japanese now own or jointly operate ten North American plants, with more on the way. This has been a successful strategy for the Japanese because it helps blunt the controversy regarding the huge trade deficit between Japan and America. At the beginning of the nineties, autos and auto parts were contributing upwards of 70 percent of that deficit. So ways to duck the voluntary restraints on imports are most attractive to the Japanese.

These transplant factories do create American jobs, or at least transfer them from American to Japanese companies as market share shifts. But that's not enough reason to root for Honda over GM, Ford, and Chrysler. Nor does it address the core issue of why the Japanese are building better automobiles than Americans, even in American plants with American workers. Nor does it solve the problem of the profits from these plants building Japan's industrial might, not America's.

Those who study the automotive industry say there's no cause for optimism, and that things could become much worse. In mid-1991 a Brookings Institution study conducted in conjunction with the University of Washington estimated that, based on current buying trends, the Big Three will lose ten more percentage points in U.S. market share by the end of the 1990s, and Honda, Toyota, and Nissan will pick up most of that lost share. The study also revealed that American buyers who switched to the Japanese imports have developed intense brand loyalty—and that's not easy to overcome.

Since the automobile industry, with its dealers, vendors, and associated products, represents America's largest single industry by far, this issue has more than passing significance for the national well-being—even leaving aside the ramifications for other industries. Given that the basic differences flow from the contrasts in management approaches, those ramifications for other products are plentiful, even ominous, as the Japanese penetration of many other industries continues. Also, there's lots more of that to come as globalization unfolds, with the competition coming not only from the Japanese.

One course of action is to opt out of the competition in some industries, as America largely has done in the consumer electronics business. Go to the annual *Electronic Industries Association* convention in the United States sometime, as I have. Japanese, Koreans, and others from Oriental countries so overwhelmingly dominate the sales personnel and the rows on rows of display booths it's as if some exotic malady wiped out the American suppliers. In a sense, that's the case. And its final stages are reflective of poor immune system resistance to globalization. Obviously an approach of dropping out of competition as we've largely done in consumer electronics holds dramatic consequences for America's future health. We must, and we can, compete.

Though I'm worried about these trends, I sympathize with union workers on these issues—they're between a rock and a hard place in devising how to hold on to the gains of the past. And it seems increasingly true that both the management of their company—and of their union—are letting them down. Regardless, we simply cannot continue with the old confrontational methods of reaching agreements or with partnerships marked by alienation rather than cooperation. The current dynamics just aren't working, and GM's financial bleeding and the closing of plant after plant make that abundantly clear. Pine for the old days if you will. But the stark fact is these are new days calling for new ways—and a new partnership between management and labor, everywhere.

Both sides must change their policies and practices. Management must take the lead—which in its case means giving up the long-standing arrogance about the superiority and professed vitality of the traditional American management style. As a way of underscoring what is perpetuating the old ways, let me recast—in business terms —a memorable American poem about the bitter fruit of arrogance.

CASEY AT THE BAT—GENERAL MOTORS STYLE

THE OUTLOOK wasn't brilliant for America's team that day;
Japan's team led by one big run, with one inning left to play
And when Harvester died at first, and Philco did the same,
A sickly silence fell upon the patrons of the game.

Some felt fear, and muttered their despair—the rest
clung stoutly to the hope that springs in every human breast;
They thought once General Motors would get its whack at bat—
They'd lay lots of money that would be the end of that.

Then from the throats of millions there rose a lusty yell;
It rumbled through the valley, it rattled in the dell;
It knocked upon the mountain and recoiled upon the flat,
For good ole Number One, GM, was coming to the bat.

There was ease in GM's manner as it advanced upon the plate;
There was pride in GM's bearing and a spring in GM's gait.
And when, responding to the cheers, it lightly doffed its hat,
No stranger in the crowd could doubt 'twas a mighty one at bat.

All eyes were on GM as it rubbed its hands with dirt;
And all were heard applauding as it billowed out its shirt.
Then as the pitcher waited—with hands upon his hips,
Defiance gleamed in GM's eyes, a sneer curled GM's lips.

And now the leather spheroid came hurtling through the air,
And GM stood a-watching it—in haughty grandeur there.
Close by the sturdy batsman the ball unheeded sped—
GM said, "That ain't my style." "Strike One," the umpire said.

From the benches full of people there arose a muffled roar,
Like the beating of the stormwaves on a stern and distant shore.

"Kill him! Kill the umpire!" shouted many on the stand,
And it's likely they'd have killed him had not GM raised a hand.

With the arrogance of ages, great GM's visage shone,
It stilled the rising tumult, it bade the game go on;
After signaling to the pitcher once more the spheroid flew;
But GM still ignored it, and the umpire said "Strike Two."

"Fraud!" cried the maddened millions, and echo answered fraud;
But one scornful look from ole GM and the audience was awed.
They saw its face grow very stern, they saw its muscles strain,
And they knew that mighty ole GM wouldn't let it by again.

The sneer is gone from GM's lips, the teeth are clenched in hate,
As it pounds with mighty gusto its bat upon the plate.
And now the pitcher holds the ball, and now he lets it go,
And now the air is shattered by the force of GM's blow.

Oh, somewhere in this favored land the sun is shining bright;
The band is playing somewhere, and somewhere hearts are light,
And somewhere people laugh, and somewhere children shout;
But there are no jobs in Mudville—mighty GM has struck out.

The moral of this parody, as all should plainly see—You have to change your haughty ways or the umpire says "Strike Three." I end with thanks to Ernest Thayer for the use of his poem to say: We must learn this global ball game or we won't get to play.

GM is but an example. There are lots of companies, previously successful, that are "striking out" these days because of arrogant adherence to the old ways of managing—resulting in job losses across the nation.

"LABOR" OF ALL KINDS—PARTICULARLY UNION LABOR—SHARES THE OBLIGATION TO FORM A NEW, MORE PRODUCTIVE PARTNERSHIP

Even in the face of all these new competitive realities, and the growing specter of jobs being lost and plants closing, it's not surprising that nationwide unions like the UAW are reluctant to give up the tools that have worked for them over many decades. As an example of the success of those traditional bargaining methods, UAW leaders have bragged over the years about achieving wages and benefits that are some 20 percent higher than those for comparably skilled workers in other manufacturing industries, and that claim has a basis in fact. *Pattern bargaining*, for example, has worked extremely well for the UAW over the years. That's the practice of first negotiating wages and benefits with one company under threat of a strike that would put it at a competitive disadvantage, and, once achieved, using those gains as a benchmark for wresting the same wage and benefit levels from others in that industry. (Is that *whipsawing* the involved companies? Not according to the UAW. More in chapter 11.)

The reaction of the unions to the idea of pay-performance linkage has been mixed at best, and in some places every bit as hostile as the strong resistance to the team concept. For example, both GM and the UAW have been making a concentrated effort to forge a new partnership at the "different" Saturn plant in Spring Hill, Tennessee. And, the organizational approach and management-labor relationships there, based extensively on the NUMMI model, have made the plant a paragon of cooperation compared to other GM plants. Among the other novel features at Saturn (at least novel for GM and the UAW) is an agreement that gives the workers and the UAW a voice in all management decisions. Also, the entire plant is organized in accordance with the team concept. Thus far, it appears to be working very well. It's reported, for example that in the first five years of the Saturn operation the UAW filed only three grievances, all involving employee dismissals. As this was being written the Saturn dealers simply couldn't get enough cars to meet the eager demand. (And the J.D. Power mid-1992 quality satisfaction ratings ranked *Saturn* right behind *Lexus* and *Infiniti*—an extraordinary achievement for the GM/UAW Saturn team.)

The Saturn labor agreement prospectively calls for linking 20 percent of pay to quality, productivity, and profitability, the targets to be set jointly by the company and the union. If the workers exceed those targets, they are to be eligible for bonuses. However, that aspect of the agreement hasn't come to pass. In fact, in 1991 the UAW persuaded the Saturn management to wait and phase in those provisions over the next four years rather than adhere to the original schedule. And certain UAW leaders, according to *Business Week* in its August 17, 1992, issue, have made it known that they won't accept a contract with similar team concept and compensation provisions elsewhere in General Motors. In fact, a UAW spokesman was quoted as saying, "We've seen lots of fads come and go at GM. Now we have the Saturn fad." (The union official is right about the fads coming and going. However, I recommend the UAW take another close look at this Saturn "fad" and its success in many other settings—in the best interests of all its members.)

Most other major unions stoutly reject any conversion of traditional compensation methods (even though when you look at the numbers and trends, it's very difficult to argue that they've been in the workers' best interests). There are many reasons for the opposition, mainly steeped in past practices. Some union chieftains—not all— see a vastly diminished role for themselves in a system of performance-reward links. They also understand that benefits traditionally are tied to wage scales, including the retirement benefits, not to wages plus bonuses. That also provides a strong vested interest in perpetuating the status quo. These union leaders are elected officials, after all, and they have learned to prefer a system in which higher wages, improved benefits, and better working conditions come from intransigence at the bargaining table, pattern bargaining, and threats to kill the company's competitiveness with slowdowns or walkouts. It's worth repeating that during most of American business history these have been the tactics, and the only tactics, that have produced "fairness" from the standpoint of the union members.

Therefore, I'm sure we will see much more of that. But no one should harbor any illusions in that respect. In an expanding global marketplace, and an era of ever-expanding alternative sources, the workers pay as high a price as the managers and "owners"—or a higher price—for actions that cripple competitiveness, however briefly. Simply stated, we need new definitions of winning and losing in management and labor relations. These biases and habits are deeply

ingrained, and changing isn't easy. However, there is a road map out
of the dilemma, and ample evidence that this array of two-class policies and the problems they yield can be fixed. Those fixes admittedly
are countercultural, even counterintuitive to many, but the best companies show it takes no less to succeed. We also must realize, and in
"we" I include the unions, that there is a limit to how long companies
can be coerced into following the old practices when they're losing
money. Ask the workers from Eastern, Pan Am, International Harvester, LTV, and others who have joined the growing parade to the
bankruptcy courts.

Union employees, shrinking in numbers over the years, now comprise 11.5 percent of the American nongovernment work force. However, nearly all American companies that deal substantially in
international competition are unionized. So as those relationships go,
so goes our international competitiveness. In my view there's still a
strong role for the unions to play. But it's high time both management
and the unions assessed where they've been and where they're going,
or we're in for even rockier days ahead. I don't know about the rest
of this fractious and contentious world, but that's where America most
needs a peace treaty.

It's been said by a number of observers that when you ask Toyota
employees to talk about "*we and they*," they think in terms of Toyota
versus Honda, or Toyota versus Nissan—but that in America the
same question evokes images and responses in terms of labor versus
management. The Japanese have turned their attitudes around. So can
we. I choose to leave the last word on this matter to New York
governor Mario Cuomo. He may seem a curious choice to most managers because his pro-labor sympathies are well known, and he is
highly unlikely to be elected Man of the Year by the *Business Round-
table*. But along with many others sympathetic to union agendas, he
recognizes that new practices are needed to fit the new realities. In
an interview in the April 11, 1988, *Business Week*, Cuomo said:

> There is no denying that were it not for the union movement,
> chances are we would not have had the level of decency and prog-
> ress in this country that we've had. The only case you could really

make against unions now is that they are anachronistic. We must move toward some sort of intelligent engagement of working people in the economic process. More participation. They should be more tied to the benefits of production than to wages. They are reluctant to give up their wage increases because it's a habit they've developed. They have to gradually be taught that by participating in enhanced productivity, bonus arrangements, and some kind of ownership where possible, this in the long run is better for them. I think this is the future.

It is the future—or at least it had better be. With effort, America's managers can make it so. In that spirit, let's return to solutions.

MANY COMPANIES ARE BUILDING STRONGER COMMITMENT BY BROADENING INCENTIVE COMPENSATION POLICIES TO INCLUDE ALL EMPLOYEES

Let's first revisit the matter of compensation policies to see how the few exceptions, the best companies, do it. Earlier I explained that Motorola, under Bob Galvin's influence, long ago changed its compensation approach to provide pay-performance links and to be far more inclusionary of frontline employees. I also referred to Jack Welch's moves in the same direction at General Electric, and I covered the linkage and inclusionary compensation policies at Honda. Toyota uses similar policies, as do many of the Japanese companies. For example, at the Toyota Motor Manufacturing, U.S.A., assembly plant in Georgetown, Kentucky, which produces a new Toyota every minute, the base wages are 10 percent below those paid by American automakers. However, the Toyota employees also receive performance awards as high as 12 percent of their wages, and bonuses with no set limits. In a variation of Honda's approach, Georgetown employees with 100 percent attendance each year attend a gala at which ten new Toyotas are given away. It costs Toyota $250,000 or more each year to do that. But it's worth it. On average, more than 60 percent of Georgetown employees qualify to attend the party.

In the previously cited study *Made in America* by the MIT Commission on Industrial Productivity, the commission found the more successful companies "sharing success" through variations of worker bonuses and other forms of incentive compensation. The commission's members also spoke to the benefits they observed from the awarding of team as well as individual bonuses, as a means of fostering cooperation and teamwork. As they put it, "This has already been tried by some best-practice companies with good results." Indeed it has. A bonus system won't create miracles on its own. (That's why there are Five Pillars, not one.) But it helps, especially where it's one element in a family of inclusionary techniques.

One can find new and innovative pay practices popping up in many forms—and working—in various companies. The successful retail chain *Nordstrom* brags about paying its employees 20 percent more than its competitors. Nordstrom pays more—and it also expects and gets more. *Mayflower* trucking pays its drivers more when customers advise they "used care" with the shipment. (The costs are more than offset by avoiding claims that result from indifferent handling.) At *Domino's Pizza*, supervisors are authorized to pay monthly bonuses to employees based on measures of customer satisfaction. Some argue such practices are tantamount to paying workers what they're already "well paid" to do, and thus "should be unnecessary." But the same critics don't frown on incentives for managers. Such incentives work with everybody. That's not an indictment of human nature, it's a recognition of how it operates.

Bank of America, floundering badly in the eighties, has recently made a recovery. Richard Rosenberg is the chairman and CEO who came in and radically changed its fortunes. Among the many new practices he implemented was *pay for performance* for lower-level officers. That, analysts say, gave major impetus to the other changes. The changes worked. The bank went from three years of record losses directly to three years of record earnings. Sam Walton, whose Wal-Mart success needs no elaboration, years ago initiated profit-sharing and stock-purchase plans for all employees. (They nicely complement other inclusion measures, giving substance to Wal-Mart's use of the term "*associates*.")

Besides monetary incentives, it's important to recognize the psychic reward that comes to frontline workers from the various aspects of being *included*. So, let's turn to a discussion of the *motivators* as well as the *demotivators* as seen from the worker's perspective. The two are of equal importance, and astute leaders understand and address both sides of that important commitment equation.

THERE'S NOT MUCH MYSTERY ABOUT WHAT WORKERS LIKE AND DON'T LIKE— BUT OUR MANAGEMENT PRACTICES DON'T PIVOT OFF THEM

First of all, it's easy to fall into the trap of dwelling on the negatives in the American culture. However, when one looks with an open mind there also is a great deal that is positive, much of it rooted deep in the American psyche. And it is of great *potential* benefit to us in the Globalization Age. As one example of our positive cultural perspectives, Robert J. Samuelson, in his *Newsweek* column in October 1988, said, "When Americans are asked whether it's government's responsibility to reduce differences between the rich and the poor, only about 36 percent say yes. In Europe, the proportions are much higher: 63 percent in West Germany, 70 percent in Britain, and 81 percent in Italy. The United States is different. People believe in opportunity, not equality. Faith in individual effort and reward remains strong."

Having lived nine years in Europe, and having traveled extensively there for many years, I can readily believe those statistics. I've seen those attitudes in action in those cited countries. So a key question in the new global ball game is "*Compared to what?*" We're not as bad off as we think we are, at least not in potential terms. However, our underlying American beliefs in individual effort, and their implications for the work ethic when unleashed, are helpful only to the extent that our management policies take advantage of them. Many say there has been a discernible, even radical shift in the balance between asserting *rights* and accepting *responsibilities*. I agree there has been such a shift but I don't believe it's permanently damaging to our future if positively addressed.

At this point I'm tempted to comment in detail on the sage observations of Douglas McGregor and Abraham Maslow, and others who have contributed much over the years to our understanding of employee attitudes and what creates them. I won't do so because their work boils down to the fact that if you treat people fairly and justly they will respond in positive ways. A brief word on Maslow and his needs hierarchy theory is in order, though. Maslow, whose work from the early fifties is still cited, ordered human needs into a hierarchy of five distinct groups: physiological, security, belongingness or love, status or esteem, and self-actualization, with each emerging as the other leaves off. Whether needs are arranged in a layer cake or in a complex, shifting mosaic I will leave to the psychologists. However, we all know, at a gut level, that everyone wants to *matter*. And policies that in effect tell people they don't matter are a big turnoff. (Taylor, wherever you are, are you listening?) Conversely, those that make people believe they do matter inspire loyalty and commitment in return.

Surveys show inclusion is an aspiration of frontline workers that ranks alongside involvement and empowerment. In fact, it's the stepping-stone to the other two. I don't find companies adopting policies of "ownership" and "empowerment" without first changing their traditional attitudes regarding "inclusion." There is even strong evidence that psychic pay greatly outweighs monetary pay. In that context it is useful to briefly address the work of Frederick Herzberg.

A decade and a half after Maslow presented his needs hierarchy theories, Herzberg, as Chairman of the Psychology Department of Case Western Reserve University, did research into motivational and demotivational factors as they are viewed by U.S. workers. Based on his extensive interviews and surveys, Herzberg ranked the job factors that lead to "extreme dissatisfaction" and, on the other hand, "extreme satisfaction" as seen by those frontline workers. He found the top 5 *dissatisfiers* to be: Company Policy, Supervision, Supervisor, Work Conditions, and Salary. The top 5 *satisfiers* turned out to be: Achievement, Recognition, Work Itself, Responsibility, and Advancement. "Company Policy" was the runaway leader as a dissatisfier, and none of the other four top producers of dissatisfaction will defy your intuition. Note that the grand prize as a satisfier went to "Achievement," and a close runner-up was "Recognition." Note also that Responsibility outpaced Advancement on the scale of satisfiers—other samplings show the employees want responsibility whether it comes with a promotion or not.

Herzberg's enlightening research dates to the seventies; however, human nature hasn't changed since then—and neither have our management practices (except by a few). Moreover, we are not wholly dependent on Herzberg's work because we can put together similar calibrations from more recent polls and surveys. From his lengthy study of worker perspectives, Herzberg developed his own theories regarding the ways to create "job enrichment." In explaining his use of that term he drew a sharp distinction between "horizontal job loading" (more work without motivators) and "vertical job loading" (providing many motivators in the new job makeup). The best companies understand that distinction well.

At the bottom line, the message that McGregor, Maslow, Herzberg, and other behavioral psychologists have provided us over the years is direct: Company leaders need to pay lots of attention to the satisfaction index. And we simply don't do that well in America. If the reader will stop to reflect, it was through *job enrichment* that we were able in TAC to dramatically increase the satisfaction index at all levels, especially at the frontline. Under the centralized system the employees had voted on "company policy" with their feet. When our reenlistment rate increased by 136 percent they were saying we had moved company policy to the satisfaction side of the ledger. They expressed their greater satisfaction in many other ways as well, verbal and nonverbal, and our productivity and quality soared along with that satisfaction. Also, take a moment to reflect on how our *Five Pillar TQM* highlighted and championed Herzberg's "satisfiers" of *achievement, recognition*, and *responsibility*. There also was more *advance-*

ment than before. All took a vast turn for the better in the TAC work force. That's because they were given far more say-so over their work conditions, rules, and scheduling. Also contributing were the new forms of ownership and the much broader means of bestowing recognition and reward for achievement. In short, they were included, empowered, and enriched as never before.

I believe it instructive in this regard that my transformation successes in the government were not based on changes in compensation policy. (I couldn't affect that; it was controlled by the Congress.) So I'm among the last to argue that it boils down to a matter of monetary compensation only, or even that money is the primary motivational tool. You ignore monetary incentives at your peril, but they fit into a broader mosaic of inclusion policies. Those broad-based inclusionary policies, including compensation changes as appropriate, can be found in the exemplary companies I have discussed. There's really no mystery about it. It's getting the guts and gumption to do it that's the missing ingredient.

We pay a big price when common purpose and commitment become the missing ingredients because of shortsighted management policies and practices. Some surveys show that employees admit to spending up to 20 percent of their time, perhaps more, doing *absolutely nothing*. We're not talking work breaks here, we're talking dawdling and daydreaming. Kate Ludeman, an organizational psychologist and author of *The Worth Ethic* (1990), a book that addresses issues of worker motivation, sagely observes that the *work* ethic is suffering in America because managers pay too little attention to the *worth* ethic. She says, "Right now, the deliberate and persistent waste of paid time costs American business $170 billion annually—12 percent of the payroll of businesses." She states that's because managers "keep employees in the dark" and "say one thing and do something else." As she puts it, "No wonder employees reciprocate by using work time for conducting personal business." And Ludeman says this about inattention to the matter of worth:

> The work ethic—producing goods and services through hard work
> —is no longer serving America well. The reason is that the work

environment found in most American companies discourages people from working from the heart—from caring about the job they do and the people with whom they work. As a result, the work environment—the way we manage and define our jobs—discourages what we used to call "labors of love." . . . Wherever I find employees who work from the heart, I also find managers who dedicate themselves to building up the self-worth of their employees. . . . Unfortunately, few managers see the connection between productivity and building self-worth.

Well said. I find the same. Leaders also must work to instill a sense of group worth, and of the importance of each person's contribution to the success and well-being of colleagues. In fact, that's one of the key ways you put their business in their hearts so they in turn will put their hearts in the business.

Many others have discovered and used that formula for success. Vince Lombardi, legendary coach of the *Green Bay Packers*, was fond of saying there are three key elements to winning in any human endeavor—be it sports, business, or life. The first is talent. The second is discipline. And the third, Lombardi said, is "You have to care for each other." And that spirit must come from the top. In fact, all the coaches who have built legendary dynasties, such as Bear Bryant at Alabama, John Wooden at UCLA, and Red Auerbach of the Boston Celtics, have paid great attention to the humanistic aspects—and to the ways of building team-oriented motivation in every team player.

Auerbach's inclusionary policies were legend, as was his ability to build the famous "*Celtic pride*." Insight into Auerbach's techniques comes from Tommy Heinsohn, the well-known TV sports analyst who played nine years for the Celtics. During those nine years the Celtics won eight NBA championships, so he writes as a discerning insider on what created that Celtics dynasty. In sports circles Red Auerbach has long had the reputation of being a stickler for details, discipline, and determination—all keys to his success. However, Tommy Heinsohn focused on still another aspect of Auerbach's genius, and that was "getting everyone involved." Heinsohn put it this way in his entertaining 1988 book, *Give 'em the Hook*:

One of the first things I noticed about playing for Red, it was obvious he was interested in what I thought, in what we all thought. There'd be a timeout and Red would say, "Okay, Cooz [Bob Cousy], what do you think?" Or, "Let's try Tommy's play now." We were all allowed to have creative input. We weren't just robots, just hired hands waiting to be told what to do. We were urged to get involved in the thought process, to look for things that might work and then bring them to the team's attention. Some suggestions were readily embraced, while others were rejected, but you never had to fear that something you recommended would be rejected out of hand. . . . The point is, we all got to make our statements, and this quickly became a very significant factor in the personality of our team. . . . As much as he wanted us to be physically well conditioned, he was even more of a stickler for making sure we were all well-grounded in the fundamentals of the game. He wanted us to become engrossed in the technical aspects of basketball . . . and the best way to accomplish that, he felt, was to get us actively involved in the decision-making process.

Heinsohn's point (and Red Auerbach's) is crystal clear. It is by such inclusionary policies that the best leaders build self-worth, interest, creativity, and commitment in every player on the team, whatever the team pursuit might be. The success—and the dynasties—grow from that.

Another who succeeded hugely by paying close attention to these same humanistic principles is Frederick C. Crawford, who brought the "T" to the TRW Corporation. (His Thompson Products and Ramo-Wooldridge merged to form TRW.) In March 1991 Crawford celebrated his 100th birthday. The following passage comes from his reminiscences about working his way up from common laborer through sales engineer, plant manager, general manager, president, and finally chairman of the board of TRW. (He retired in 1958.) Crawford's account of the way he built motivation and commitment after taking over a failing plant makes a rich and instructive addition to this narrative. (This account comes from an interview by Davis Dyer in the November–December 1991 *Harvard Business Review*.) As Crawford tells the story:

When I took over our Detroit plant, it was having a terrible time. . . . The year before, it had lost more money than it brought in in revenue. . . . When I got there I spent a lot of time talking to the employees, and I was surprised to find that they had no idea that anything was wrong. The place was operating without discipline, so everything was careless. People came late and loitered in the rest rooms. We produced as much scrap as we did finished product. . . . Well, my interests being human, I felt so sorry for these people that I decided to tell them what my orders were. . . . I'll never forget the look of shock and disappointment on their faces when I said the company wanted to close the plant. Then, on impulse I said, "If I disobey orders and try to save this plant, how many of you will go all out to help me?" Every hand went up. Then I said, "Wait a minute. Do you know what you're voting for? If you vote yes, that means you'll be here on time and work a full day. No making scrap. No smoking breaks in the toilet room." They all voted yes again.

Then I said, "Wait a minute. I want you to vote again. Will you come in here—everyone—and work as if you own the business and you are fighting for yourself?" Everyone voted yes again. It was like a religious revival. In the days that followed, those people looked different. They walked different. They talked different. They were in early, and they were working when the bell rang. The response was amazing. Fantastic things—the kinds of things that the Japanese are doing now—began to happen. . . . I could tell a dozen stories about that experience in Detroit. We used exactly the same work force, equipment, and resources that had been used before and resulted in failure. The only change was in using the worker's brains.

I know how Fred Crawford felt, and why he never forgot that experience. He had tapped into, and vitalized, the human spirit that determines whether the human system of the organization works well or poorly. With the resulting change in employee focus and commitment, the plant's quality and productivity soared. It was then unnecessary, even silly, to close the plant.

I've seen the same results over and over. Unfortunately, what Crawford's predecessor was doing in that plant to create the condition Crawford inherited was what America's managers continue to do: Ignore the human aspects. Keep the employees out of the information loop. Leave motivation and involvement out of the loop. In contrast, Crawford had put the business in their hearts. Said another way, he had radically improved their commitment level, and the turnaround in the performance was a natural consequence. In this case it just required including workers in the information loop and carefully explaining their stake in the outcome. Usually it takes a bit more than that to put the business in their hearts, but it's never complicated or difficult to do.

Motivation and commitment involve issues of the human spirit, and that operates independently of the business you're in, the job you're in, and the level you toil on. None of this insight is new. People like Fred Crawford have been discovering the truth about employee commitment—and the key role it plays in determining business outcomes—ever since there was such a thing as a business organization. Winston Churchill left us the timeless observation, "Man often stumbles across the truth, but then gets up and hurries on as if nothing had happened." That certainly applies to the poor managerial attention that's been paid over the years to the way organizational structures and systems affect commitment.

Some companies, but all too few, have paid full attention to it, and in every aspect of their management style. Let's look at a few of them, because they're still out there, going strong, and their continued success holds lessons for all companies—particularly those that haven't quite gotten the drift of this employee motivation business.

THERE'S BEEN NO SHORTAGE OF GOOD EXAMPLES AND GOOD ADVICE—JUST A SHORTAGE OF WILLINGNESS TO LISTEN, LOOK, AND LEARN

Many books since *In Search of Excellence* have illuminated the problems stemming from the traditional centralized style. They also have provided insight into exemplary companies that are prospering from abandonment of that style (or continue to prosper by having avoided it in the first place). Unfortunately, the American business culture has largely shrugged off the lessons those books and those companies provide, just as it did with the message from Peters and Waterman in 1982. The same basic message was skillfully conveyed in a 1985 book, *Vanguard Management*, by James O'Toole, a professor at the University of Southern California's business school. (Before that O'Toole was a correspondent for *Time* and *Life* and a management consultant for McKinsey & Company, and chaired an HEW task force on "Work in America.") He emphasized that the "Vanguard are people oriented," the "Vanguard provide a sense of ownership," the "Vanguard are future oriented," and the "leaders of the Vanguard are visible." Other decentralization-oriented, team-structure–oriented, ownership-oriented, quality-oriented, leadership-oriented, people-oriented themes permeate his book. He sets these forth as the principal themes distinguishing the "Vanguard" from their corporate brethren. O'Toole said about his examples:

> Life in the Vanguard corporations is neither simply good nor simply bad. It is like real life: simply complicated. It is sometimes rough and tumble and always marked by the tension of moral choice—an inescapable tension in a world fraught with differences of values, perceptions, and objectives and inhabited by people with human frailties. Because they are not perfect the Vanguard companies are, in many ways, like the organizations in which most of us work. Because they are not unapproachable ideals, they can serve as *achievable* models of what the organizations in which most of us work can realistically become.

I echo his sentiments, and I offer my exemplary models in the same context. Among the companies O'Toole singled out as the practitioners of "Vanguard Management," holding lessons for other companies all over America, were *Motorola, Hewlett-Packard, Weyerhaeuser,* and *Johnson & Johnson.* Let's look at the last one and examine why it has been such a consistently strong performer over the years.

THE ORGANIZE SMALL, EMPOWER BIG APPROACH TO BUILDING STRONG COMMITMENT IS NOT A NEW ONE, AND THERE'S AMPLE HISTORY TO SHOW IT WORKS—JOHNSON & JOHNSON IS ANOTHER CASE IN POINT

Johnson & Johnson is one of those rare companies that since its founding more than a hundred years ago never succumbed to the seductive precepts of organizational Centralism. Quite the contrary. Johnson & Johnson was a key exemplary model used by Peters and Waterman in *In Search of Excellence* to illuminate the great effectiveness of a decentralized management style. Why was Johnson & Johnson not a practitioner of Centralism like most of the *Fortune* 500? In part that's because its leaders from the very outset, including General Robert Wood Johnson, established the company's character, culture, and climate as the antithesis of the centralized style. In part it is because a succession of leaders were groomed to head the rapidly growing Johnson & Johnson in full concert with those principles— no matter how big the company got.

In Search of Excellence contained a quote from then chairman and CEO James E. Burke on that very matter:

> We have periodically studied the economics of consolidation. Let's just take our consumer business and consolidate the distribution network. There would be some dollar efficiencies on paper. But we say to ourselves that these efficiencies would have to be enormous before we go with them, because we believe if the manager can control all aspects of his business it will be run a lot better. And we believe that a lot of the efficiencies you are supposed to get from economies of scale are not real at all. They are elusive. Once you get your big monster going, you're going to create inefficiencies that you don't know are there. And if the management does see them, it won't be aggressive in rooting them out because it doesn't have control of them.

Jim Burke, a superb leader, deftly summarizes what's wrong with the beguiling but befuddled precepts of Centralism. As that Burke quote appeared in print in 1982, Johnson & Johnson was a $5-billion company. As this was being written annual revenues stood at well over $12 billion, and net earnings had tripled. And the steady growth continued unabated. Even in the face of the worldwide recession, Johnson & Johnson averaged a 11.43 percent growth rate from 1989 through 1991. Not only that, but like the other exemplary companies that have taken the decentralized approach to heart, its growth curves in sales, earnings, capital structure, and stockholders' equity have been an impressive model of consistency. The reason according to Burke is, "We believe the consistency of our overall performance as a Corporation is due to our unique and dynamic form of decentralized management, our adherence to the ethical principles embodied in our Credo, and our emphasis on managing the business for the long term."

The pharmaceutical and health care giant that is Johnson & Johnson (headquartered in New Brunswick, New Jersey) is a far-flung global collection of 166 companies in more than fifty countries. Each of those companies, exercising authority over its own business strategy and P&L balance sheet, is given "considerable autonomy." In fact, Burke and all the other CEOs over the years have made this point quite clear: "The responsibility for our success as a corporation rests in the hands of the Presidents and Managing Directors of our companies. Each must assume Leadership in every facet of the business." And the decentralization philosophy the corporation has long followed extends downward within each of those companies. Besides the decentralized autonomy Johnson & Johnson believes in so deeply, its management principles emphasize that all of the decentralized companies share the "same set of values and a common mission." And they match their words with their actions—scrupulously. For example, they repeatedly emphasize putting ethical conduct foremost in all of their business and management decisions—and they do. A classic example is the way they handled the Tylenol cyanide tampering episode a few years ago. There was no equivocating and no hand-wringing. Tylenol came off the shelves, period. And the corporation made clear that ethical considerations would guide its actions, even if that meant Tylenol would never be sold again.

I vividly remember discussing that episode with Jim Burke on a visit to Johnson & Johnson in New Brunswick not long after it occurred. (I went there at Burke's invitation to address the top corporate officials on some ins and outs of TQM, Five Pillar–style. I was preaching to the choir.) Burke deflected any praise for the forthright way he had stepped forward to handle the incident. He said simply, "I just acted in keeping with our credo and our beliefs, so I didn't even have to think about it." That's what instilling the right character and culture in an organization is about: when it's adequately embedded, the employees at any level, at the very top or the very bottom, *don't even have to think about it.*

That famed Johnson & Johnson "credo" by which every company, every division, and every frontline element operates could productively serve as the model for every business in America. And the company prides itself on walking the talk. For example, when the credo says "everything we do must be of high quality," and "everyone must be considered as an individual—we must respect their dignity and recognize their merit," and "we must experiment with new ideas"—they mean it and they practice it. I won't dwell on the ample proof of that, but if you're skeptical, visit Johnson & Johnson and see for yourself.

I cannot overemphasize what it does for an organization when the employees look on it as not belonging solely to a set of "managers" and "owners" far removed from the fray and the everyday realities there. When all employees are included and involved they respond by acting like an *owner* themselves. And you simply cannot achieve that with slogans, or new and imaginative ways to force compliance and conformance. Human nature just doesn't work that way.

Jim Burke, after twelve years as CEO, became chairman emeritus in 1989. His replacement as chairman and CEO is Ralph S. Larsen. As were all Johnson & Johnson CEOs, Larsen was carefully groomed in the company's decentralized, leadership-oriented, quality-oriented management style. So Johnson & Johnson continues resolutely down the management path it has followed for more than a hundred years. The company's people understand all about quality management, how to perpetuate a management system that carries it out, and that a company builds commitment from its customers by creating commitment in its employees to quality, productivity, and the principles for which the company stands.

I wrote earlier that I would return to the subject of *cost control* —an imperative for every organization, public or private, large or small. And I pointed out the ways the old-time religion just doesn't hack it. We did it differently in TAC, and in the other organizations I was privileged to head, and in each case we achieved well-documented cost savings that were dramatic when compared to similar organizations being managed in the centralized way. It wasn't all that difficult to do. That's because it was a natural by-product of our decentralized, leadership approach. Our decentralized *Five Pillar TQM* system lent itself perfectly to spreading cost-consciousness throughout the organization—and transformed the cost-value trade-off decisions from a top-down to a bottom-up matter. You must involve those at the frontline if the decisions are to be properly focused and cuts made in the right places. Cost-consciousness and control must be everyone's job. To make that work you must have a system that *makes* it everyone's job. But you won't find such a system in the nation's centocracies, because that's all centralized, too.

COST-CONSCIOUSNESS AND CONTROL—EVERYONE'S JOB, BOTTOM TO TOP

Let's start with some observations. As quality is to performance and product decisions, value is to cost and funding decisions. Every business, private or public, needs to control costs. Cost control quite obviously starts with cost-consciousness—and that's a necessarily complex process that works best when everyone is involved interactively, bottom to top. That means involving everyone in the cost-value trade-off decisions—which, of course, is not the style in centocracies, nor anything resembling it. Centocracies leave the business of cost control almost exclusively to those far removed from the front. I've said enough about *beancounters* in that respect, but that's where they hang out—at the rear. We might even invent a few more Murphy's Laws to illustrate what happens as a result of the centralist approach:

- *When only senior management is involved, cost savings come in the wrong places in the wrong way for the wrong reasons.*
- *The fewer the people who care about the costs, the more they go up, not down.*
- *The less the involvement of the organization's frontline, the more the unseen and hidden costs are overlooked.*
- *The more people who directly benefit by reducing costs while enhancing value, the more it takes place.*

As a consequence, in the traditional management approach the cost-value decision process operates incompletely and inadequately. That, in turn, creates all sorts of inefficiencies. Most businesses take too narrow a view of the matter: They place strong emphasis on the controlling of costs, not the production of value. Sometimes they're the same; sometimes they're not. Let me give examples.

After forming the teams in TAC, we educated them on the costs of their activities. For example, we provided cost data to each black-box repair team on its own set of black boxes and their component parts. We also made them aware of the various "wraparound" costs, such as those involved in sending a component back to an Air Force depot for repair. That new cost-awareness, alongside their newfound authority over their part of the total system, triggered a stream of value-oriented recommendations on practices to change or abandon —and other revisions to make "their business" more productive of value. In several cases that involved suggesting that they could repair a black box, if given the authority, rather than send it back to the depot as "not repairable this station"—a category comprising a long list of black-box maladies. In most cases we got authority to do so, and saved the government a good bit of money. (Mind you, this meant more work for them. But that's the kind of commitment that providing such empowerment and authority can engender.) In other cases they came up with ways to reduce inventory, and means of speeding up the repair cycle—all of which yielded savings as well. The team-based approach lends itself well to this value consciousness because it provides the context and commitment that makes it work. My earlier story about the cost-sensitivity of the Boeing Irving production team when it redesigned the 767 handset fits the same mold.

As another example, on a visit to a TAC engine shop (after cost data was provided to the workers) one of the young engine technicians said, "General Creech, these parts at the end of the engine tailpipe cost an awful lot of money, and I'm not convinced we need them." They did cost a lot. They were made of *titanium*, which is very expensive to create and to form into parts. Only titanium sufficed because of the extremely high temperatures involved. The troops called the parts "turkey feathers"; they surrounded the tailpipe and moved in and out with changes in engine thrust. He gave his reasons. I promised I would check it out. The turkey feathers were there for a reason. They matched the tailpipe to the airframe, and provided an aerodynamic face to the surrounding airflow. Without them, the aircraft "boat tail drag" rises, requiring more fuel for a given range and speed. (It also reduces both, affecting combat capability.)

After jousting with some beancounters and turf-protectors elsewhere in the bureaucracy, I took the turkey feathers off twelve of one squadron's 24 F-15s and asked them to tell me what difference it made. They couldn't tell enough difference to make them worth the cost. So we took them off all TAC F-15s. Everyone else soon followed suit. (There are 950 F-15s in the Air Force, and there were thirty "turkey feathers" on each one, so we're talking lots of costly parts here.) They're still off. At the last count, that step had saved the government more than $70 million. Before someone jumps to the conclusion that this was another dumb government exercise, let me point out that the turkey feathers are also on the single engine in the F-16—it's the same engine. They remain on the F-16 because in its case they do make a big difference; the costs, including fuel costs, would outweigh the savings in taking them off. They weren't imperative on the F-15, so we saved lots of money. That all started because a frontline worker was given cost visibility—and the idea that controlling costs was his job, too.

We didn't require frontline workers to fill out all sorts of paperwork accounting for every piece they used. We were making those workers a part of the management, not a part of the clerical force. This was a program to make them more cost-conscious, and to get them involved in cost-value trade-off decisions. That got everyone working for continuous improvement in value efficiency as well as quality effectiveness. When the cost-value decision system is run solely from on high, and those at the frontline are mere inventory-takers, it creates great frustration—and continued inefficiencies. None of the centralist cost-chasing techniques are new, of course. Perhaps no one has captured the frustration stemming from those techniques better than the Duke of Wellington in a letter to London during the Napoleonic wars:

Gentlemen:
   Whilst marching to Portugal to a position which commands the approach to Madrid and the French forces, my officers have been diligently complying with your request which has been sent by H.M. ship from London to Lisbon and then by dispatch rider to our headquarters.
   We have enumerated our saddles, bridles, tents and tent poles, and all manner of sundry items for which His Majesty's Government holds me accountable. I have dispatched reports on the character, wit and spleen of every officer. Each item and every farthing has been accounted for, with two regrettable exceptions for which I beg your indulgence. Unfortunately, the sum of one shilling and nine-pence remains unaccounted for in one infantry batallion's petty cash and there has been hideous confusion as to the number of jars of raspberry jam issued to one cavalry regiment during a sandstorm in western Spain. This reprehensive carelessness may be related to the pressure of circumstances since we are at war with France, a fact which may come as a bit of a surprise to you gentlemen in White-hall.
   This brings me to my present purpose, which is to request elu-cidation of my instructions from His Majesty's Government, so that I may better understand why I am dragging an army over these barren plains. I construe that perforce it must be one of two alter-native duties. I shall pursue either one with the best of my ability but I cannot do both; 1. To train an army of uniformed British clerks

in Spain for the benefit of the accountants and copy-boys in London or perchance, 2. To see to it that the forces of Napoleon are driven out of Spain.

> Your most obedient servant,
> Wellington.

There are good ways to create cost-consciousness and control throughout the organization. But they're not the traditional ways.

The management system, structure, and style in any organization—however large, however small—determine whether there is respect and harmony of purpose between the front and the rear. And that's precisely why commitment plays such a pivotal role as an indicator of the effectiveness of the management approach, and why it also serves as the principal determinant of each organization's relative success or failure.

THE NAME OF THE BUSINESS SUCCESS GAME IS EMPLOYEE COMMITMENT—CENTOCRACIES DON'T UNDERSTAND OR PURSUE THAT, SO THEY LEAVE ENORMOUS POTENTIAL UNDISTURBED AND UNREALIZED

Rosabeth Moss Kanter of Harvard brilliantly defines a key source of the lackluster commitment to be found in organizations featuring traditional centralized management: "Powerlessness corrupts. Absolute powerlessness corrupts absolutely." Other good wisdom on the subject has been provided by the *Pasadena Weekly Journal of Business*. It came up with a graphic way to underscore the vital importance of every single employee and why each should be treated as important. The *Journal* hit the heart of the matter in a short essay titled "You Arx A Kxy Pxrson."

Xvxn though my typxwriter is an old modxl, it works vxry wxll— xxcxpt for onx kxy. You would think that with all thx othxr kxys functioning propxrly, onx kxy not working would hardly bx noticxd; but just onx kxy out of whack sxxms to ruin thx wholx xffort. You may say to yoursxlf—Wxll, I'm only onx pxrson. No onx will noticx if I don't do my bxst. But it doxs makx a diffxrxncx bxcausx to bx xffxctivx an organization nxxds activx participation by xvxry onx to thx bxst of his or hxr ability.

That gets to the heart of it; so the changes must be shaped to elicit the most from *all* the organization's human resources. Alas, nearly all books these days leave the frontline work force out of the change equation—they speak instead of remedies to how you "manage the managers." (Or how you manage "processes.") And that narrow focus is why those remedies fail.

Johann von Goethe left us this wisdom to explain why Commitment must infuse every level of the organization:

> Until one is committed, there is hesitancy, the chance to draw back, always ineffectiveness. Concerning all acts of initiative (and creation), there is one elementary truth, the ignorance of which kills countless ideas and splendid plans; That the moment that one definitely commits oneself, then Providence moves too.

It can't be phrased better. That's why organizational greatness requires a Commitment Pillar. Your *succxss dxpxnds* on it. Indeed, a company's success in building commitment shapes its total success. Accordingly, commitment should get star billing. To explain further how that is best done, chapter 11 returns to management system matters. As promised, it provides a summary of the stark human-system differences between the centralized and decentralized management approaches. It also recaps how to build a successful organization—in the Five Pillar way.

A TQM Path to Tomorrow: New Ways for New Days

Product is the focal point for organization purpose and achievement. Quality in the product is impossible without quality in the process. Quality in the process is impossible without the right organization. The right organization is meaningless without the proper leadership. Strong, bottom-up commitment is the support pillar for all the rest. Each pillar depends upon the other four, and if one is weak all are.

THE FIVE PILLARS PROVIDE THE NEEDED FOUNDATION

I repeat the above formulation to emphasize that these Five Pillars provide the foundation on which the TQM system rests, and also to emphasize that the principles which each embodies must suffuse every element of the management system. Everything I've experienced, and everything I've seen in the best companies, convinces me that success depends on the effectiveness of the management system by which a business operates—including the structure and style that shape its operations. Some management systems work well and some don't; some are well defined and some aren't; some adequately address human system issues and some ignore them; some flounder on structural issues; some flounder on style issues; and all flounder, sooner or later, when the system is based on the precepts of Centralism. There's a far better way. And to adequately delineate it for you I speak in these pages not only about each foundation *pillar*, but also about an organizational *model* and about a management *system*—all working in conceptual harmony to produce impressive day-to-day system effectiveness. This chapter reviews how you can pull all of that together to produce a new way of managing that's been well proven in many challenging settings—a management system approach that is fully suited to our trying and troubling times.

THE HARDEST CHOICE OF ALL IS DECIDING WHAT TO DO; THE HARDEST OBSTACLE TO OVERCOME IS TO HAVE THE GUTS TO DO IT

Piecemeal application of a few quality principles yields little real change, and paltry results. The returns are already in on that. And they portend a largely dismal outcome for the quality movement if that piecemeal trend continues. So how do businesses make real improvements in quality and productivity? It requires system changes, and that requires people who are determined to make a change. Obviously it's best if the leader at the very top of the organization sees the need for a holistic change approach and leads the charge. But it can also happen from within, starting in one part of the organization. From small acorns grow mighty oaks. Therefore, *you* can make a difference. *You* can be a principal catalyst for change—whatever your particular level might be.

And there's a way to do that without breaking faith with your boss by ''opening up your own store'' (which is hard to do in a centralized organization because it's constantly on the alert for that). I did it in the nation's largest, and in many ways most staid, bureaucracy. And in every case, I kept my boss informed, at least generally, on what I was doing. That's only fair, and it's the principled thing to do. But I also operated on the principle that I had full latitude and empowerment to do *anything* that made sense to me—so long as it was not *specifically* ruled out by a regulation. When I ran into any regulation (or policy) that created a partial roadblock, I worked hard to be relieved of it. And in every case I succeeded. If other ways didn't work, I got permission to conduct a special "test."

I've found top leaders much more likely to approve a "test" than they are to grant a priori approval for one part of the organization to be a completely different duckling. And I've found that equally true in the public and private sectors. Convince your bosses to let you try, and then go for it. Where there's a will there's a way.

A lot of the barrier to change is in the mindset. I vividly recall going to an Air Forces, Europe "Commander's Conference" while I was running the wing at Madrid. At an impromptu get-together of wing commanders the night before, several in the group I was sitting with were complaining about their lack of leadership latitude. I said I didn't feel that way at all—that I had all the maneuvering room needed—and I asked them to give me some examples. So they told me about things they perceived they couldn't do. I was doing all those things. That doesn't mean that the centralized approach being devoutly practiced above all of us, all the way to the top of the Air Force, wasn't a problem, because it was. (And I wouldn't see that alter until we started the charge for change from TAC seven years later.) My point is, a lot of the barriers to change are to be found in the minds of those who could carry it out, if only they would. *No guts, no change. No guts, no glory.*

EVERY BUSINESS MUST DESIGN ITS OWN SYSTEM, AND ITS OWN PACE OF CHANGE, BUT IT MUST CREATE THE VISION AND THEN CARRY IT OUT

If nothing else comes through clearly in this book I hope it's that I'm a steadfast foe of *"one size fits all"* when it comes to the management system, structure, and style. (This is one of Centralism's most grievous faults.) So suit yourself. Go wholeheartedly into the

Teams, Outputs, Product, Leadership system model as I describe it, or adopt and adapt major parts of it. (I recommend the former.) Also, I recommend it be done on a measured but steadfast basis if you're now in a centralized system. (And most who read this are, even if they don't recognize it as such.) It will produce shock waves, not good results, if you walk in one morning and announce that you're going to a totally different style management the next day. As I've said, we used an *evolutionary* method to bring about *revolutionary* change at TAC, creating models, conditioning people to change, winning converts as we went. The GE and Boeing stories reflect a similar "make haste in deliberate fashion" approach in implementing their transformations.

However, no matter how measured the approach, it's important to have a clear vision of where you're going—and to share it with everyone in the organization. It need not be a written, step-by-step plan, but the direction and ultimate reorganization goal should be well understood by all. Then you need to get all the employees involved in crafting as well as implementing the new organizational vision. Variations by location and activity should be allowed, even welcomed, so long as they are consistent with their special circumstances and the new vision. You don't want the employees banging off the walls, or hunkering down in resentment. That will result in everything from creative incompetence in carrying out the change to outright guerrilla warfare against it.

The heavy-handed approach used by *McDonnell-Douglas* when it introduced a new "TQMS" system to its Douglas Aircraft subsidiary is a case in point. McDonnell put a new boss in charge (out of its St. Louis headquarters) who, according to news reports and accounts from insiders, had schemed out his "Total Quality Management System" approach for Douglas in advance. He began its implementation by gathering over 5,000 of the most senior Douglas managers into a hangar and telling them they were all fired—but that they could submit their résumés for new jobs in the new Douglas. The managers were then interviewed by outside "personnel specialists," and they had to convince those outsiders they should stay on where they had worked for years. That, and other overbearing techniques, soon precipitated widespread dissatisfaction and even some guerrilla warfare. As an example, "TQMS" banners had been put up all over the plant. Covertly, people went around and wrote in "Time to Quit and Move to Seattle" (the home of Boeing). Douglas has slowly overcome that lousy start, but as this was written it was still struggling financially, and its "TQMS" approach was still less than a rousing success.

I emphasize that the McDonnell-Douglas executives have the right to call that Total Quality Management if they want to, but it certainly doesn't fit my definition of what TQM is all about. In fact, the way they implemented it violated the most treasured precept of all in *Five Pillar TQM*: The top leader should include all the employees in crafting the architecture—and build up the dignity and self-worth of each, not tear them down. Admittedly, resistance to change is built into the human condition. So no matter how skillfully and humanistically you go about it you can expect some opposition—even a few hard-core pockets of it—as a few protect their turf and the status quo ante with which they are comfortable. You should use logic, example, and persuasion first, and to every possible extent. (You'll find that peer pressure from the majority who like the new approach will help in that regard.) Challenge individuals who are impervious to all that to get all the way in or all the way out. If you go about it right, that will be a trivial percentage, in TAC a fraction of a percent. It's both the worth of the vision and the way it's carried out that count.

The growing competition accompanying globalization doesn't allow most companies to let any grass grow under their feet. So the need is now. But that still means that organizational transformations must be led, not driven. And companies must go about implementing decentralization in a decentralized way. That's a piece of advice based on experience—not a cliché. In that regard, even a studied and measured approach—if it's built on a solid foundation of TQM principles—begins producing positive results immediately. I've seen numerous cases of rapid transformations in business outcomes as those principles take hold. Going from worst to first doesn't mean you've become perfect. It means you're far better than you were, and better than your competition. The "*Relentless pursuit of perfection*" (Toyota's Lexus motto) can begin right away—but can be fine-tuned as you settle into the new system. GE didn't get better all at once. GE did start getting better right away. The same at Boeing. The same at TAC and in many other organizations I have observed. Once system change is started properly it takes on a momentum of its own.

I'm not sanguine that thousands of America's managers are going to rush out and reorganize into teams just because of this book. (Some 95 percent of them are not using teams in that way now, much to the delight of the Japanese.) I am intimately familiar with organizational inertia, and with the widespread reluctance to decentralize for fear of losing control. Perhaps some readers, however, will find the logic presented here persuasive—and tip the scales toward considering a decentralized, TQM-style system. So let's review briefly the *decentralized, leadership* model introduced in chapter 1, and depicted once again below. It's not mysterious or complicated. It does involve the use of teams—the day-to-day, hands-on, get-the-job-done type of teams as the basic structure for the decentralized model. I've discussed at length the depersonalization that results from organizing by *Functions*. Organizing by *Teams* fixes that. It humanizes the system in terms the employees can understand and appreciate. It also is the ideal way to extend leadership to the very bottom of the organization.

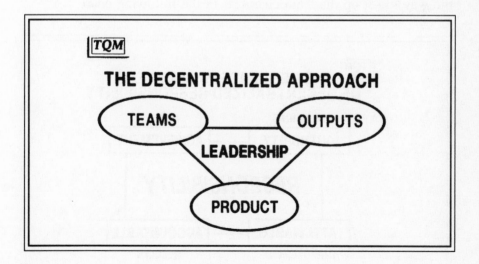

ORGANIZING BY TEAMS HELPS TO MAKE ALL THE OTHER DECENTRALIZED AND TQM SYSTEM ELEMENTS WORK—AND WORK TOGETHER

There are not a lot of hard-and-fast rules on how to form the teams. But there are four general rules to keep in mind. First, we're talking about permanent organizational structure, not ad hoc team overlays. Second, the teams should be designed to exercise ownership over a specific product, and each team given adequate authority to carry out that charter. Third, each team should have a leader as the focal point of responsibility. (And the leadership style should create leadership involvement by every single team member.) Fourth, the teams should be small. That's to give content and meaning to the team product and to the relationships, interpersonal and organizational. How big should the teams be? Depends on the industry, the company, and the product. In general, they should be kept as small as possible—as few as three or four and as many as fifteen, but no more. Boeing says an overly large team doesn't have the same flavor, focus, and spirit. So do the Japanese. Suit yourself, but mind the relationship between team size, team product, and team customer.

The charter must be defined and the outputs measurable. I describe the way to set up the team character in the following chart:

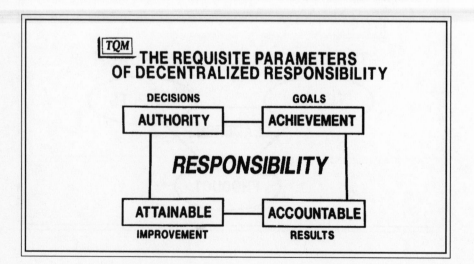

TQM THE REQUISITE PARAMETERS
OF DECENTRALIZED RESPONSIBILITY

DECISIONS	GOALS
AUTHORITY	ACHIEVEMENT

RESPONSIBILITY

ATTAINABLE	ACCOUNTABLE
IMPROVEMENT	RESULTS

It largely speaks for itself. I was not surprised later to hear Boeing talk of "sizing the box," because that's an important part of defining as well as delegating responsibility. And managers in traditionally managed organizations will find, just as they did at Boeing, that they've never really done that before. And *achievement goals*—in a context of attainable improvement—are not established in ways that are meaningful to frontline employees in traditionally managed businesses either. At least they're not in terms of the level, specificity, clarity, and individual responsibility that the team approach provides. This approach also gives life and meaning to *accountability*—at every level. Centralized organizations try to hold everyone (vaguely) responsible and accountable, but that doesn't work. The employees know who is accountable for the problems, but the managers don't —so they tend to blame everything and harangue everyone when things go wrong. Indeed, that's a major source of employee alienation. The team approach helps avoid that.

Forming the teams is just the start. This chart highlights the actions that bring the team concept to life:

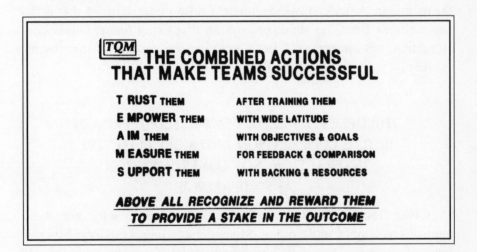

TQM	THE COMBINED ACTIONS THAT MAKE TEAMS SUCCESSFUL

T RUST THEM   AFTER TRAINING THEM

E MPOWER THEM   WITH WIDE LATITUDE

A IM THEM   WITH OBJECTIVES & GOALS

M EASURE THEM   FOR FEEDBACK & COMPARISON

S UPPORT THEM   WITH BACKING & RESOURCES

*ABOVE ALL RECOGNIZE AND REWARD THEM
TO PROVIDE A STAKE IN THE OUTCOME*

Yes, it spells "TEAMS." It starts with "Trust" and ends with leadership "Support" enabling the teams to carry out their ownership free of micromanagement. This approach helps eliminate the *trust gap*, the well-recognized contributor to employee apathy and alienation. In fact, a good share of the precepts of Centralism are based on *distrust*, and that permeates the policies and practices of the organization. Employees recognize when they are distrusted—and they resent it, as well they should. Moreover, they simply won't accept responsibility (or accountability) without adequate authority to carry it out—nor should they.

Therefore, a principal advantage of the team-based approach is that it allows managers to build trust and respect into the system, while also providing for accountability at every level. That's a far cry from the distrust and stifling rules that mark the centralized system —all designed to have the employees support the leadership, not vice versa. But many managers shy away from the team approach for the very reason that they have become comfortable with collective condemnation, and have developed neither the skills nor the stomach for dealing with specific accountability. Admittedly, it requires more interpersonal leadership skill. But that's easily learned.

The proven worth of the team approach is verified by success in many different organizations. I have merely cited some in these chapters. Despite such examples of its effectiveness, it is not spreading far or fast in American management. And a good share of that resistance comes from the shopworn notion that using teams builds confrontation, not cooperation. Let's examine the validity of that notion.

THE DECENTRALIZED, TEAM-BASED APPROACH BUILDS COOPERATION AND MORE EFFECTIVE INTERACTION, NOT CONFRONTATION AS SOME ALLEGE

Given the accumulating persuasive evidence, why not more teams? Tradition. Conditioning. Misunderstanding. Lethargy. Myopia. Fear of change. Denial that problems exist. Comfort with the old ways. Belief that maximum organizational potential already is being obtained. (Many of these, particularly the last, are self-serving beliefs on the part of managers I find to be quite common.) The answers vary, of course, from manager to manager and company to company. However, part of the reluctance to use permanent structural teams is created by those who speak out forcefully against them. It's no big secret that a good many management seers are dead set against team-style permanent organization. They're even more outspoken in opposing the use of measurement and comparison in the team context. Most never ran anything themselves. Nevertheless, their views have resonance and attract disciples within the various management circles, so they must be addressed.

Those critics say the team approach, and the comparisons it naturally yields, invariably create *"workplace competition."* They further assert that this competition effectively rules out cooperation. Many choose to believe what they say. As a result, one more obstacle to change is created. Those who make such assertions are wrong. Cooperation improves. I acknowledge that you must be sensitive to the issue. Everyone should be for cooperation, not confrontation. I certainly am. But that rules the decentralized, team-based approach in, not out.

As but one example, when we went to the empowered team approach in TAC, organizational harmony greatly improved. We also found that the new team-oriented comparison systems helped rather than hurt overall cooperation and integration. In fact, we found that the centralized TAC had far more impulses toward workplace competition than did the decentralized TAC. Success at the intersections of the building blocks depends on common purpose, common focus, harmony, and mutual respect. All that flowered under decentralization. In contrast, the larger, functional building blocks stifled rather than fostered those very qualities. Indeed, a peculiar form of elitism and a we–they mindset ran rampant between the previous functional arrays. "We supply specialists," "we electricians," "we munitions specialists"—and divisions within those divisions—were all too common. TAC's "radar specialists" frequently told "aircraft mechanics" they wouldn't take the aircraft panels off to get to the radar—because that was not *their* job.

Unusual, you think? No, it happens all the time with the centralized, functionalized approach. Consider GM's problems with functional fiefdoms. Also, ask *any* of the U.S. automakers about their problems with the functional alignments and narrow specialties built up over the years in the UAW. All say, even union members, that those arrangements worked as a serious inhibition to the employees' *pitching in* as needed to get the job done. (The UAW had reached a level of more than 125 separate specialties, with no UAW member allowed to cross specialty boundaries.) With NUMMI's team approach those myriad job classifications were reduced to only four. Centralization had created that problem; the team-based approach solved it. And the local union likes it. So much for the notion that decentralization and organizing by teams creates workplace competition. It's actually the other way around.

In the TAC case, that functional elitism dropped away quickly as we adopted the team-based structure, and a bonding took place in pursuit of the team goals. In my years running the *Electronic Systems Division* I encountered the same factors at work in American industry. As previously explained, at ESD we annually bought some $6 billion of high-tech electronic products. Accordingly, our interaction with U.S. businesses large and small, in goods and services, was extensive. Time after time when we examined ESD's supplier companies that were having serious troubles, we found a centralized organizational structure. We also found the inevitable walls between the functional departments. The pattern became so persistent that before dispatching a government *"Tiger Team"* to investigate one mess or another I would predict it would find the troubled company was a practicing centocracy.

Invariably, that prediction was right. And how did we get them to fix it? By insisting that they give the overall project manager real authority, and tear down those functional walls. It always worked, when they would do it. One such company, whose name is a household word, was in deep trouble on a major government program. Their performance was so inept that we were considering cancellation and a new procurement. At our considerable urging, they decentralized and turned matters completely around. They are now lions on the business talk circuit on the merits of team-based management.

COMPANIES CAN'T SHUT OUT COMPETITION; IT'S A FACT OF LIFE—AND THE COMPETITIVE SPIRIT CAN BE A KEY TO SUCCESS

It's well understood that a propensity to reflect a tribe mentality with an accompanying we–they orientation is built into the human condition. So be it. If that's properly channeled it can be very helpful, not hurtful. If workers want to outdo their competitive counterparts, or even outdo the sister division in the same company, what's wrong with that? It's wrong if it creates confrontational behavior and lack of cooperation—but that won't happen if each team benefits when all improve. It's a competitive world. Those who think they can build a moat around their business and shut out competition's influences are living in a dream world. *Everyone* must worry about the organization's comparative capabilities and competitive position, know where it stands, and pull together if it is to succeed. That can't be left, as before, to a few folks in senior management.

Not only that, Centralism breeds far more distrust and disharmony than any other system. People in the former USSR came to understand that very well. One of their many stories about the negative effects of Communism and Centralism goes like this: The God who is not supposed to exist nevertheless one day appeared to a Russian peasant—and said he would grant him one wish to make his life better. The peasant, long accustomed to the workings of a centralized system, thought for just a moment and came up with his fondest wish for comparative improvement: "Kill my neighbor's cow!"

The team approach makes it far easier to channel those tendencies in positive not negative directions. Far from suppressing team pride and team competitive spirit within TAC, we encouraged both. However, we also worked hard to channel that spirit and orientation beyond each frontline team's own product and on to the product of the broader team of teams. Measurement, comparison, feedback, and scoreboarding helped tremendously in creating that broader perspective. Thus, companies ought to enhance and exploit the competitive spirit, not shrink from it. Indeed, a key *strength* of our American society is its love of competition and achievement. In all my travels around the world, and in living twelve years of my life in foreign countries, I have never seen a society as competition-oriented, as team-oriented, and as results-oriented. And that is a considerable strength, when put to proper use. Trouble is, most companies don't even see the potential, much less put those American traits to good use for the benefit of everyone.

The centralized structure operates on such a broad scale it's most unlikely that individual workers will be moved by "teamwork" exhortations served up in a slogan not a system context. To use a sports analogy: It's good for the Atlanta Braves to have competitive zeal and a desire for dominance over the Los Angeles Dodgers. However, it's decidedly bad if the Braves' infielders seek dominance over the outfielders, or the pitchers over the catchers. The key to harmony and efficiency is the smooth integration of the various specialties, at a meaningful team level, and with clear-cut goals. The omnipresent scoreboards and statistics reminding them of their team results helps put the focus on that integration. It's no different in any organization.

Cooperation stems from giving people reasons and incentives to look at their endeavors in a team context. The functional approach just does not produce the same spirit or perspective. Teams do. They do, that is, if they are installed throughout—as the organizational building blocks. Pseudo-teams don't. Quasi-teams don't. Ad hoc committees (called teams) don't. And cross-functional teams make marginal not primary contributions. In fact, the American management culture largely has responded to the Japanese challenge by a lot of team talk and bestowing the team name in new ways—but has done almost nothing to utilize teams as an organizing principle. Don't be confused by such "teams" rhetoric that leaves Centralism principles intact—or let the naysayers talk you out of the team-based approach.

There's also much talk these days about "metrics." That too is more rhetoric than reality. A few indeed are measuring more, but most are using it in old ways—not in ways to decentralize and create front-line empowerment and ownership. Old fears about that, and comparison, die hard. Let's look at the flawed logic.

A MEASUREMENT AND FEEDBACK SYSTEM BENEFITS ALL EMPLOYEES, INCLUDING ON THE FRONTLINE, BY INCREASING JOB SECURITY

Why so little measurement and feedback to be found in American businesses? The short answer is the old-time management religion and its superstitions and shibboleths regarding performance measurement. It's certainly not because the tools aren't available. And that bias against measurement doesn't benefit the frontline employees, it penalizes them. Among the many powerful reasons for overcoming that long-standing prejudice is greater employee *job security*. That's a matter of increasing concern to employees at every level as globalization unfolds, and rightly so because they can see it eroding all around them. The only real job security as competition intensifies comes from being better at what you do than your competitors down the street, in the next state, or across the water. That's a new and growing reality, and it's not going to go away. Lee Iacocca, writing in *Talking Straight*, went to the heart of the matter: "The only job security anybody in this company has comes from quality, productivity and satisfied customers. Without them you don't put meat on the table." So job security must be looked at in a new light. Many already are doing so. Among the many is Jan Carlzon, the highly respected president and CEO of Scandinavian Airlines System (SAS).

Carlzon has been called "Sweden's Iacocca" because when he took over SAS in 1981 it was losing lots of money, employees were being laid off, and services were being curtailed. He brought it new spirit and new vigor in what he calls the *"50,000 moments of truth every day"* when SAS employees interact with the customers. SAS now is rated one of the top airlines in the world in every category. So there's reasonable basis to attach credibility to what Carlzon has to say on this matter of measurement, assessment, and employee security. In an extensive interview in the May 1989 *INC.* magazine, he said:

A positive example is the best way to create the right atmosphere.
. . . Really there are many things you can do to give people the

security to take responsibility. Over time, you do it by measuring and rewarding performance.

INC.: Not by show biz?

Carlzon: For a year or two you can motivate people through emotion and show biz. They are hyped up for awhile. But, for the long run, people must know they will be measured in an accurate way in relation to the responsibility they have been given. That's a good way of spreading security among people, and it's one area I didn't always understand as well as I do today.

Subjectively, most people think they're doing great, and that can provide a false sense of security. Then they feel betrayed when the roof caves in. Here's another case in point. Earlier I discussed GM's December 1991 bombshell announcement that it would slash 74,000 more jobs and close twenty-one more plants by 1995. The plants to be closed were not announced, touching off all sorts of speculation in the media and among GM employees as to whether it would be this one or that one for big cars, and this one or that one for other GM product lines. Late in February 1992, GM ended some of the suspense by announcing the locations of twelve of the twenty-one plants to be closed. The plant at Willow Run in Ypsilanti, Michigan, was on the closure list; a plant in Arlington, Texas, (building like products) was to remain open. A *Washington Post* article said that confounded the analysts because the Texas plant is more distant from suppliers, which increases costs. The same article quoted a longtime GM worker at Willow Run: "Right now we are shocked. We feel we were cheated. Nobody was expecting it. We thought Texas didn't stand a chance." Ponder the import of those last two sentences. They help make the point.

Sure, some management gurus, particularly those of the centralist persuasion, allege that measurement and comparison are unfeeling and unproductive. OK, so they don't want comparative scoreboards. But how about if you're a worker at any of those plants facing closure, and your first report card says you've flunked the course? I believe they should have been told where they had specific competitive short-comings and given the opportunity and incentive to improve. I don't think that's being unfeeling at all; I think it's being realistic and help-ing all of the employees, the frontline specifically included.

Some argue that the UAW would strenuously object if you tried to make such comparisons, and simply would not go along. (In UAW parlance that's *"whipsawing,"* long considered the greatest *manage-ment sin* of them all by the UAW leadership. Accordingly, it has been forsworn by all the GM CEOs—to keep the peace.) Perhaps the UAW would block it. But if so, it's time for the unions to also awaken to the growing conflict between the old practices and the unrelenting new realities. Again, you can't build a wall against competition at company boundaries or factory gates. The old rules no longer apply. The inefficient will fall by the wayside. Better they know their prob-lems, and do something about them, than labor in the dark under the mistaken assumption they're bulletproof. No one is. Not anymore.

The frontline employees do benefit from measurement, compari-son, and feedback, perhaps more than anyone else. And both union and nonunion employees will readily accept it when they see it's in their best interests. Its acceptance at Boeing's unionized (IAM) Texas plants, and at the unionized (UAW) Toyota-GM venture at Fremont are but cases in point. There's room for quality and productivity im-provement in *every* organization—embedded in all sorts of untapped potential. And tapping it not only requires a new partnership between management and labor, it also requires an entirely new level of *ob-jectivity* regarding the organization's strengths and weaknesses in the competitive context. Objectivity has not been one of America's strong suits either.

OBJECTIVITY: YOU CAN'T BUILD A WINNING ORGANIZATION WITHOUT IT, AND AS MUCH OF IT AS YOU CAN GET AT EVERY LEVEL

As one of the indicators of America's glaring weaknesses in na-tional objectivity, let's go back to the 1992 round of mathematics tests that were administered internationally. Before the test the students in the fourteen participating countries were asked, "Who are the best mathematicians in the world?" The American students ranked themselves first. However, they came in last. The Koreans ranked themselves near the bottom. They came in first. That tells us a lot about the wide gap between our view of ourselves and the way we actually stack up against the capabilities of those in other nations. And those American students' attitudes—as those of the Koreans— came from their elders. We simply don't do enough to provide real-world objectivity—and therefore the motivation to do better—in either our school systems or our management systems.

Objectivity springs from facts—in a context of comparison. It's not the American way to provide that. That's not because we can't provide factual comparison or don't know how. It's because we don't even try. Those superstitions and shibboleths aren't easy to overcome. Maybe some homespun philosophy can help. So let's look at what an *Outputs* oriented system brings to an organization—through the prisms provided by some of America's favorite management bromides.

If it ain't broke, don't fix it. That's right, but you should add to it: *If you don't know it's broke, it don't get fixed.* Another is: *Find the anomaly and fix it.* That's good advice. But I augment that also: *Find the anomaly. If it's wrong, fix it. If it's better than expected, praise it. Even copy it.* To achieve that, you obviously need some breathing room for anomalies. I have found that once you decentralize effectively you end up identifying far more things that are right and to be praised, than the few things that have gone wrong. (That certainly happened in TAC, and we developed methods to praise and cross-pollinate those good ideas, including *Best in TAC* awards for a host of activities and processes.) Moreover, when you do find bad anomalies you find them earlier, while they are still localized. You can then get them fixed without a big fuss, and before they can do widespread collateral damage. Nothing about the previous centralized system in TAC provided any of those benefits.

One of the oldest bromides of them all is: *If you're going to kill the alligators, you first have to drain the swamp.* Good advice. At least the sense of it is right; if you're going to kill the alligators, you first have to find them. However, it's rarely practical or possible to *drain the swamp*. That's where modern technology comes in. There are uncomplicated, inexpensive ways to collect data that will show you where the bad anomalies are (the "alligators" if you will) so you can cope with them. If you do it right, when you look out over the surface of a business it need not be opaque. I know how frustrating that lack of visibility can be. I've taken over my share of organizations where the surface was opaque because those organizations had no means of providing the required insight. There simply were no good tools for enlightened leadership—at any level. I had to live with that—and manage by intuition—until I could fix it. Intuition is fine, but it's no substitute for keen perception based on ample facts.

That absence of adequate insight is more usual than unusual in American businesses. Lee Iacocca said in his book *Iacocca* that the greatest shock of his professional life was when he took over Chrysler and learned how little its managers knew about what was going on in the organization. As he put it: "Never mind the answers, these guys didn't even know the questions." Adequate factual information is the lifeblood of intelligent decision-making. You especially need visibility into the outputs, so that you can localize the alligators as they appear on the scene. When objective facts are not available, decisions are formed through subjective opinion, bias, and habit. Consequently, they inevitably are ill suited to the actual circumstances. It's also a lousy way to go alligator hunting.

It is for all these reasons that the *Outputs* element of the decentralized, leadership organizational model is so important. *Outputs, Orientation, Objectivity, Ownership*, and *Obligation*—those, among others, I described in chapter 8 as the important synergies the outputs orientation provides. I now expand on ownership and obligation—because the decentralized model brings meaning and substance to those organizational concepts as well. Let's start with employee ownership and the psychic and material rewards that flow from it—for everyone in the organization.

CHANGING THE SUPERVISORY FOCUS TO OUTPUTS PROVIDES DIRECT LINKAGE TO OWNERSHIP—AND MAKES IT REAL, NOT A SLOGAN

There's lots of talk these days about "ownership." But when you look more deeply into most of the management literature it turns out to be a very slippery concept indeed. (Or as the Texans would say, *All hat and no cattle*.) We all know how to define it and understand it in a private sense. But what is its meaning in the workplace? I know how I have used it in transformations at TAC and elsewhere, but that's not how most of the sloganeers in centralized organizations use it. When we assigned a *"Dedicated Crew Chief"* to each TAC fighter we were giving them "ownership" of that aircraft, along with the authority, accountability, and pride that went with it. We did the same when we formed teams from functions, and gave each team ownership over its product—along with the obligations of that ownership.

I could never figure out a way to do that when TAC was centralized and organized by functions—though I flirted for a while with the idea of somehow repairing rather than changing that organizational approach. I finally decided it couldn't be repaired. It just didn't lend itself to imparting ownership and instilling commitment. And I have yet to see it successfully done in a centralized structure, no matter how much the avowed commitment to employee ownership.

Some, when pressed, change the subject by citing another kind of "ownership" everyone should support. That's stock ownership through 401K plans, or ownership of stock through a tax-leveraged ESOP, or the like. I strongly support those various approaches to "ownership," and have made it a point to educate myself on those important aspects of modern business management. In fact, one year I keynoted the annual convention of the *Employee Stock Ownership Association*. As you would expect, I addressed in some depth the various approaches to ESOPs and how they do and do not contribute to employee commitment depending on how they are approached.

(Frequently they're viewed as part of the "benefit package" that goes with the job, but not as practical ownership that increases employees' voice in the company's day-to-day activities. Why? That's the way it is, and it's not a matter of rocket science to figure that out.)

Those kinds of ownership are valuable, and I recommend them. They do provide a stake in the outcome (of sorts) and anything of that nature helps—particularly since frontline employees usually are frozen out of other forms of sharing greater success. However, I'm speaking of a different dimension of ownership here. Companies of all sizes, whether or not they have an ESOP or other stock ownership plan, also need an everyday brand of workplace ownership—through inclusion, involvement, and empowerment—to get the motivational juices flowing and to get the employee sense of obligation operating that produces greater commitment and professionalism. Both those ownership themes were well received by the ESOP Association. In many such settings I have found frontline employees every bit as interested as managers are in that broader form of ownership. And they realize it entails a new level of *obligation* on their part.

ORGANIZATIONS CAN'T BECOME WINNERS WITHOUT A STRONG SENSE OF OBLIGATION THROUGHOUT

Obligation is the fifth "O" that works synergistically with the outputs-oriented approach. It's a particularly apt word to use because it conveys the dual ideas of commitment and accountability. It's also apt because it involves an obligation from supervisors up the organizational chain to provide more trust and greater latitude to the "owners" down below. A great many companies that believe they are decentralizing stop the delegation of ownership at the "first-level reports" below the CEO. It simply goes no further, unless the top executive insists on it—and follows through. I've seen (and advised) a large number of companies that preach and practice decentralization, but are having difficulty in certain parts of the organization to get those managers to carry it on down below them. And those centralized portions struggle, even wither on the vine, for a simple reason: *If you don't have real ownership, you won't get real obligation.*

Outputs, Orientation, Objectivity, Ownership, and *Obligation*— that's the synergy to be achieved, using small group outputs as the pivot point for all the rest. Try doing the same with the *inputs* approach so prevalent in the American management style. It just doesn't work in the same way.

DECENTRALIZATION AND MEASUREMENT SYSTEMS GO TOGETHER

Decentralization, empowerment through distributed authority, and measurement systems all go together. And measurement provides all the "important results" I have listed on the following chart:

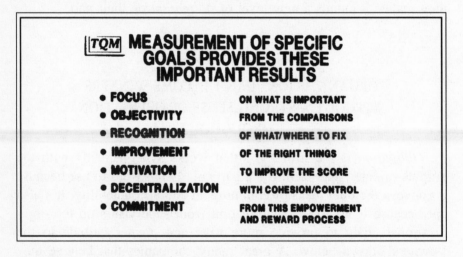

TQM **MEASUREMENT OF SPECIFIC GOALS PROVIDES THESE IMPORTANT RESULTS**	
• FOCUS	ON WHAT IS IMPORTANT
• OBJECTIVITY	FROM THE COMPARISONS
• RECOGNITION	OF WHAT/WHERE TO FIX
• IMPROVEMENT	OF THE RIGHT THINGS
• MOTIVATION	TO IMPROVE THE SCORE
• DECENTRALIZATION	WITH COHESION/CONTROL
• COMMITMENT	FROM THIS EMPOWERMENT AND REWARD PROCESS

Each result is highly important, and you simply won't get them without means to measure, compare, analyze, and feedback to those doing the work. Also, managers must be given means to track performance—for visibility, coherence, and "control"—or they won't even consider empowerment. That is a practical fact of life the unions should keep in mind. Once you decide to do it, it isn't a difficult or expensive transition to make. The abundance of information-processing technology now available makes it much easier, and cheaper, than in the old days of manual data handling and display.

There's lots of room for improvement—because the measurement tools that fit decentralization simply are not found in traditionally managed companies. I know. I've looked and looked for them in vain. So have others. The leaders of decentralized organizations realize that when you decentralize you also need means of keeping track. Why? Because they know you can bet your boots it will all get better—but that it won't get better, and stay better, in all places all the time. Thus, you need means to provide detailed, comparative insight so that you can spot problems and trends in their formative stages. I would add these convictions: When performance is measured, it improves. When performance is measured and compared, it improves further. When performance is measured, compared, and appropriately recognized and rewarded, it improves even more—dramatically more.

MEASUREMENT SYSTEMS FOR THE PURPOSES DESCRIBED ARE NOT FOUND IN THE NATION'S CENTOCRACIES—CENTRALISM CATECHISM SAYS IT ISN'T NECESSARY AND CAN BE DESTRUCTIVE TO COOPERATION

The Centralism catechism says there is no need for a system of measurement, feedback, and reward of the type I've described. (This is partly because Centralism disdains many of the benefits I've also described. And I've already addressed the cooperation argument—it's spurious.) In fact, you might logically surmise that when a centocracy holds a company picnic the boss announces, "We're going to divide into two teams for slow-pitch softball. We'll play for two hours. We won't keep score for each side. We don't believe in keeping score in this company. So choose up sides, and everybody have a good time." So much for goals, achievement, and recognition. And so much for attitude and the human-system dynamics. Measurement systems—and the ideas of empowerment that go with them—are not to be found in those businesses because that's the way they want it. And they want it that way because they've been conditioned to that point of view. Centralism's book of organizational *potions and poisons* speaks out against using measurement in the ways I have described. That's why you'll find it in Japanese companies but not in America's centocracies.

Indeed, the centralist litany says if you get all the inputs right through prescribed behavior, the outputs will take care of themselves. But that's just not the case. One of the most popular and devoutly believed centralist articles of faith is that employees won't accept measurement systems. True, if it's done in isolation, you can expect resistance. But I have found that employees will welcome measurement, even champion it, when it works to their benefit and not to their detriment. They even quickly grow to prize it if it's designed and structured as their system, and is used primarily for self-improvement, recognition, and reward. Moreover, if being measured is the price exacted for giving them a level of involvement and ownership they never had before, they can understand that. I've seen that again and again also.

So one of the many ironies to be found in the traditional American management style is that most managers think nothing of their reams of conformance rules and lack of empowerment, but become resistant, some even indignant, when you discuss tracking performance in small group and individual ways. (Which also would measure their comparative performance.) They usually provide a humanistic rationale to place a noble face on their indignation. And that produces a double irony—because their own management approach (and the approach that governs their own work) is anything but humanistic. You simply cannot improve productivity and quality with such outworn management ideas.

MOST WHO SPEAK SAGELY ON QUALITY MANAGEMENT PRAISE MEASUREMENT AND COMPARISON AS A KEY TO BUILDING QUALITY AND PRODUCTIVITY, BUT A FEW SPEAK AGAINST IT AND STIFFEN RESISTANCE TO CHANGE

Most of the quality management experts with famous names believe in the benefits of measurement and comparison, but Deming and his many disciples do not. Let's discuss that briefly, because that's another subject that causes confusion over what to do. Peter Drucker, in his book *Managing for Turbulent Times*, said:

> It is not easily possible to assess, let alone to test scientifically, the spirit of an organization and the development of the people in it. But it is quite easy to test the results of that spirit and development. . . . All it needs is a "scorecard" that judges results against expectations. . . . The performance of management can and should be measured against its business strategies. Did the things that the strategy expected to happen in fact take place? And were the goals set the right goals, in light of actual development? And have they been attained? To judge strategies against performance requires that expectations be defined and spelled out, and that there be organized feedback from actual events on the expectations.

I heartily agree, as my representations in these pages attest.

I've already mentioned Tom Peters's views on the necessity of measurement, of the "soft stuff" as well as the hard stuff. Additionally, I've covered in detail how measurement, comparison, and feedback are being pervasively and effectively used in successful companies like Motorola and Boeing—as well as by all the Japanese companies I've studied. In fact, it's a big part of the Japanese style. So if you, too, believe it's a bad idea, please tell the Japanese—maybe they will lose sight of one of the prime reasons they're beating us so badly in the quality derby.

If asked the most recognizable names among the "quality gurus" in our country, most observers in quality-related disciplines would come up with the four I've already mentioned: W. Edwards Deming, Joseph M. Juran, Armand V. Feigenbaum, and Philip B. Crosby. All are eminently worthy of that distinction. Deming and Juran, as previously explained, are associated with planting the early seeds for the emphasis on quality in the current Japanese style. Feigenbaum also influenced the Japanese with his *"Total Quality Control"* concepts and methods. Feigenbaum says he realized, early on, that quality was "not a group of individual techniques or tools" but rather "a total field" and that all the employees had to be adequately trained and involved if quality control was to work.

At about the same time, in Japan, Kaoru Ishikawa was developing a Japanese version of Total Quality Control which he portrayed as not unlike that of Feigenbaum but also different in substantial respects. As Ishikawa put it, some of the same basic "QC" ideas were involved, but his TQC had a special *"Japanese seasoning."* He was especially adamant that the feedback from the widespread measurement and comparison that was a principal part of his TQC approach had to go to *everyone*, not to a few of the managers. Indeed, his inclusion of the frontline employees in the definition of who was to manage the TQC system went well beyond the managers orientation to the quality control techniques then being espoused and practiced in the United States. (Alas, that orientation still holds true in the United States.) Ishikawa died in 1989. His influence on the current holistic, humanistic Japanese management style was extensive.

(Incidentally, my use of the term "Total Quality Management" owes nothing in its lineage whatsoever to the Total Quality Control of either Feigenbaum or Ishikawa. I had heard of neither one, nor of their concepts, when I was practicing the Five Pillar variety of TQM successfully—or when I chose the terms Total Quality Management—and TQM—to describe what my quality-focused and decentralization-oriented management style was all about. That doesn't mean, however, that TQC is not an appropriate part of a successful TQM approach. As I look on it, the various family members of quality control techniques, including TQC, are a valuable part—but only one part—of a holistic approach to the management system, structure, and style that TQM entails. So it's important not to confuse TQC with TQM, or vice versa.)

Joseph M. Juran spreads his message on quality and productivity through the *Juran Institute* in Wilton, Connecticut. He no longer owns it, having sold it to others, but he stays in touch with what is being taught there. Classes are conducted at the Connecticut location and on site in the businesses that avail themselves of the Juran Institute's consultancy services. As Juran puts it in discussing statistical methodology and the associated quality control tools and techniques, "I got started in that soon after 1924, and I know the merits of it, and the limitations, and it has both. But achieving quality involves a great deal more than the tools you use. It involves finding out what the customers need, how to design goods and services to respond to those needs, and how to produce them using the proper technology. There's a great deal in it."

In his books, Juran discourses knowledgeably on such themes as the *"Cost of poor quality,"* the *"Anatomy of processes"* (along with all sorts of measurement and diagnostic tools), and the key role played by *feedback*, involving, he says, "communication of data on quality performance to sources which can take appropriate action." In the "Juran Trilogy" approach he has developed he explains there are three managerial processes used in managing for quality: "quality planning, quality control, and quality improvement." He says it's the interaction of the techniques of all three—not just quality control—that yields success.

Juran candidly admits that what he now teaches is a large step beyond what he taught the Japanese in the fifties, his concepts having undergone "continuous revisions"—and expansions—in the years since. Those revisions, he says, took on special vigor (and broadened in scope) when the subject of quality control, and associated techniques, came out of the deep doldrums in the American business world circa the early eighties. (For more details see his 1989 book *Juran on Leadership for Quality.*) There are numerous clues that the same can be said for W. Edwards Deming. This is not to say that what Deming and Juran taught the Japanese did not have broad dimensions—rather that a gradual progression from *"quality con-*

trol" to a broader context of *"quality management"* occurred in their thinking and in their teachings—just as it did (independently) with the Japanese.

Armand V. (Val) Feigenbaum, who got his start in the quality business as a reliability engineer at GE, spreads his quality management advice through his Pittsfield, Massachusetts, based *General Systems Company*, a consultancy firm of about thirty well-trained professionals. Go to one of the permanent clients of GSC, like the Union Pacific Railroad, and you find pervasive measurement vis-à-vis standards, goals, and targets. To ensure proper leadership focus, usually not more than ten categories are involved in the micromeasurement and macroscorekeeping that GSC-style TQC involves. One of Feigenbaum's treasured tools is the detailed measurement of the *"Cost of Quality"* as a way of setting priorities and determining progress.

Philip B. Crosby, who left ITT in 1979, now spreads his management teachings with a staff of more than 300 through *Philip Crosby Associates, Inc.* Headquartered in Winter Park, Florida, his consultancy group provides "Quality College" courses on quality management issues and approaches there at Winter Park, and also at schools teaching the Crosby theories in eight foreign countries. Phil Crosby developed "fourteen points" that set forth his quality improvement philosophy. Point number three is "Measurement. To provide a display of current and potential non-conformance problems in a manner that permits objective evaluation and corrective action." Point number four addresses "Cost of Quality. To define the ingredients of the Cost of Quality (COQ) and explain its use as a management tool."

W. Edwards Deming was different from the other three in at least two major respects. First, he operated as a one-man consultancy, out of his home in Washington, D.C., with a single longtime secretary. Famous for his four-day seminars on various means of achieving quality control, Deming discoursed on the need to establish "profound knowledge" about quality tools and a proper "management culture" in which quality will thrive. A second distinction is that Deming was a steadfast foe of broad-based measurement and comparison. Among *his* "Fourteen Points," point ten says, "Eliminate slogans, exhortations, and numerical targets.'' Point eleven says, ''Eliminate work standards (quotas) and management by objective.''

Deming held such strong beliefs on the subject that he spoke out forcefully, every chance he got, against testing and grading in the nation's public schools. He saw no benefit to measurement, testing, grading, and feedback (except, of course, as measurement relates narrowly to variations from stipulated process parameters). In fact, Deming said measurement destroys cooperation in the workplace (and in the schoolroom). Many of his disciples are holier than the Pope on the same subject. And those views, widely quoted and disseminated, stiffen the natural centocratic resistance to performance measurement. As I've pointed out, you find Peter Drucker, Tom Peters, and the other three of the ''Big Four'' in specific disagreement with Deming on this subject. So, too, are the Japanese. In fact, if Deming issued all those admonitions about not using broad-based goals and measurement to them, they certainly have not listened to him. Their practices reveal they believe exactly the opposite.

Admittedly, they are the first to agree it's not just a numbers game, as do I, but that's a frail reason to rule out goals and measurement against those goals entirely. Further, the Japanese do not worship solely at the shrine of ''process improvement'' through advanced quality control techniques, as so many of the Deming disciples do. In fact, the Japanese view is immensely broader than that—and they are unambiguous in saying so. Because it's so important to placing TQM and quality control techniques in the proper perspective (as they relate to one another), let's further examine the issues involved.

THE JAPANESE HAVE TAKEN "QUALITY CONTROL" TO A DIFFERENT PLATEAU, AND APPLIED THE CONCEPTS IN A DIFFERENT WAY THAN THAT WIDELY PRACTICED IN THE U.S.—TO THIS VERY DAY

The previously mentioned Dr. Kaoru Ishikawa wrote a most informative account of the different brand of ''QC'' being practiced by the Japanese in his book *What Is Total Quality Control? The Japanese*

Way. (It was first published in Japan in 1981, and translated into English in 1985 by David J. Lu and published by Prentice-Hall.) On the matter of measuring across the entire spectrum of management activities, Ishikawa said this:

> In management the most important concern is the exception principle. If things are progressing according to the goals set and unusual events occur, then the manager must step in. The purpose of checking is to discover these exceptions. In order to perform that task efficiently, the basic policies, goals, and standardization and education procedures must all be clearly understood. Unless these are clearly stated, and unless there are reliable standards, one cannot tell which are exceptions and which are not.

That's my view too. And that's what one finds as the guiding principle at work in the majority of Japanese companies—and in all the successful ones.

Ishikawa also draws a clear distinction in his book between what the Japanese learned from their Western mentors and where they took the entire subject of *"Quality Control."* He wrote in that regard:

> Japan's QC originally came from the West. If it had been adopted without modification, it would not have succeeded. . . . There are many differences between the QC activities in Japan and those in the United States and Western Europe. . . . [In those countries] great emphasis is placed on professionalism and specialization. Matters relating to QC therefore become the exclusive preserve of QC specialists.

(By "professionalism" he means the kind associated with pursuit of a particular narrow discipline, not the caliber of conduct of that pursuit.) Ishikawa then further dwells on the differences between the *"Characteristics of Quality Control"* in Japan versus the United States, as he had studied them in *both* countries. His list is too long to repeat here, but it starts with what Ishikawa terms the number one difference: In Japan they emphasize "company-wide quality control; participation by all members of the organization in quality control."

In that same spirit of contrasting Japanese- and American-style QC Ishikawa writes:

> In manufacturing high quality products with full quality assurance, the roles played by workers must not be overlooked. Workers are the ones who actually produce, and unless workers and their foremen are good at what they do, QC also cannot progress. . . . Quality control begins with education and ends with education. To promote QC with participation by all, QC education must be given to all employees, from the President to assembly line workers. QC is a thought revolution in management, therefore the thought processes of all employees must be changed.

Indeed, they must be.

To make sure the readers won't miss his point about the differences, Ishikawa says,

> There are many reasons for the failure of America's Zero Defects Movement, one being that the movement was made into a mere mental exercise that used people as machines and disregarded the fact that people are people.

Phil Crosby was a principal instigator of the "Zero Defects" movement in the United States, and it's clear from Crosby's writings that he didn't intend that result at all—quite the contrary. However, as a matter of practical application of the *Zero Defects* approach in businesses across America, Ishikawa is right on target. It largely has sputtered out and faded from the scene just like other past quality crusades. That's because America's managers wouldn't give up their centralist ways, insisting on trying to graft its concepts onto their centocracies as they have done with *Quality Circles, Management by Objectives, Participatory Management*, and every other quality and productivity improvement idea to come down the pike. The bottom line is as Ishikawa describes it: too little emphasis on treating people as people.

In this same context Kaoru Ishikawa attributes a great deal of the problems in achieving quality in a total organizational context in

America (and Western Europe) to continued adherence to centralized management ideas, just as set down by Frederick W. Taylor (a view I fully share, and reached independently). The translator of Ishikawa's book, American David Lu, summed up Ishikawa's treatment of that subject in this way:

> We must take Dr. Ishikawa's criticism of our continued reliance on Taylorism seriously. Managers and engineers establish work standards under Taylorism, and line workers simply obey the commands. Have we not treated our workers for too long as exchangeable and expendable commodities? It is dehumanizing both for the workers and for those who oversee them, and it creates cause for labor unrest and dissension. In its place, Dr. Ishikawa speaks of respect for humanity and of treating each worker as a whole person.

Based on the important message in these excerpts, if any reader still doesn't understand the differences that I have drawn and that Ishikawa draws between the Japanese and American approaches—and their implications for America's future success—then I recommend perusal of Ishikawa's book. For that matter, everyone with a strong interest in this subject would profit from reading it. The fact is that *Policy Deployment* as now practiced by the Japanese is a substantial departure from American-style QC—either that of yesteryear or of today.

I dwell on this for several reasons. First, even with my considerable respect for and deference to W. Edwards Deming, based on his novel contributions to quality improvement techniques for more than five decades, I can't remain silent on that subject in these pages and let pass unchallenged the sheer nonsense about not testing and grading in our schools, or not measuring the ins and outs of what's working and what's not in the nation's businesses. That view contradicts everything I have learned—and proved again and again in practice—about creating greater employee commitment, focus, and teamwork at all levels, especially at the frontline (and thereby creating far greater quality and productivity in that same work force). In this respect I can assure you what the Air Force fighters accomplished in the skies over Iraq wasn't based on lots of luck with a little bit of

"SPC" mixed in here and there. We're talking about a management system at work, not a control system.

If Deming had been off alone on this particular kick (don't test, don't measure, don't compare, don't have goals and targets) I wouldn't even raise the subject. But those same ideas are spread by his numerous disciples, and then picked up and further disseminated by the nation's various associations devoted to the matter of quality and the quality disciplines. Also, because of the way "quality management" came to America's attention (via the Japanese cleaning our clocks in product quality) most of the uninitiated readily believe the rampant representations that the "Deming way" is the only way. But giving someone a broad destination and some process improvement tools is a far cry from a detailed roadmap and specific insight into how to get there. In Ford's case, its executives say they had to work that out on their own. Deming got their attention about changing their culture, and they give him full credit for that. But he didn't design their new management system. As a related and relevant piece of history, in 1982 Ford also started what Ford's president termed in the foreword of the cited Ishikawa book "a long and fruitful relationship with Dr. Ishikawa." Ford borrowed ideas from everywhere for its quality revolution. Everyone should.

By sheer weight of numbers what I call the *process school* of quality management advocates have seized the high ground in the United States on what, when, and how to change. That primacy also comes because the process-oriented theories and tools resonate strongly with the many who toil in the nation's companies in *Quality Control, Reliability Engineering, Quality Assurance*, and like disciplines. So I can readily understand that the nation's managers become confused over what productive change is all about. There's general agreement on the need for change, but then the consensus breaks down.

Indeed, the Big Four American quality experts have not been averse to sniping at one another, and Deming had a feud going in one way or the other with each of the others. Phil Crosby, for example, says that the Deming view is a "theory" about management that is "primarily based on statistics." Crosby goes on to say that the Deming tools are not management tools—they are technical tools for process control. In Crosby's words, "They're wonderful, but they have nothing to do with running a company." Deming and his many disciples, of course, fired back. In fact, Deming became noted for caustically trashing everything from the Baldrige Award to just about anyone or anything that ventured into his gunsights by offering differing views on quality management, and his most devout disciples are of a similar bent. Obviously this book will qualify me for that target list. So be it. The issue is too important to be ignored, or to be treated with kid gloves.

The quality movement has now become so popular that consulting firms of all types are adopting new buzzphrases to describe what they've been teaching all along. (You want it; I've got it.) That's clear from the blizzard of promotional literature that crosses my desk. Despite these new brand-names, I find little or no change in course content. That still focuses, in virtually all cases, on "process" as the star of the show, just as I have described. To break the code on that, look for what those firms do to address all Five Pillars I prescribe for effective change. Missing usually are: *Organization* (the makeup of the basic structure as opposed to ad hoc arrangements), *Leadership* (its importance and how to get it working from the bottom up), and *Commitment* (how to enhance it to create quality not just control quality, and to spur productivity as well).

As but one example of old ideas posturing in a new name, one can find increasing references these days that tie Deming to "TQM" and vice versa, some even asserting that TQM and Demingism are synonymous. (I've explained why I resist any such notion.) Given that growing trend, Japanese observers are now saying "American-style TQM doesn't go far enough." It sure doesn't, not at the moment. And it will not if it continues to wander off down "process avenue," leaving unaddressed the beliefs that have created, and perpetuated, this nation's centocracies. Read the books of the gurus, study the offerings of the consulting firms, and then make up your own mind —don't just take my word for it. I've warned you about the consequences of a narrow focus, and others are issuing the same warnings, and that should be sufficient to at least pique your interest in studying the matter further.

QUALITY CONTROL AND QUALITY CREATION ARE TWO DIFFERENT SUBJECTS. THE "CONTROL TOOLS AND TECHNIQUES" CREATE INSIGHT ABOUT WHAT TO FIX, THEY DON'T CREATE QUALITY

This distinction between quality control and quality creation is rarely made. I make it because I see, in my management advisory activities, all sorts of confusion resulting from a blurring of the two subjects. Granted, they're related. But they're still quite different, and you must think in sweeping management terms, not just about tools and techniques, if you're to be effective in *creating* quality. Indeed, if you think back to the very beginnings of what writers now call the "quality movement," its language has been riddled with one central reference word—"control." (Statistical Quality *Control*, Statistical Process *Control*, Total Quality *Control*, and so on.) And as you study the tools and techniques involved in that control, you find that those tools, no matter how sophisticated, create insight about what to fix—but they don't create quality.

Therefore, can those process-oriented means of control find a happy home in a centocracy? Of course they can, and they do. But they don't change the outcomes very much. I gave an example earlier: TAC, when it was a centocracy, believed it was rigorously applying the most modern tools of quality control—and saw no inconsistency between those control means and its other centralist means of control. Am I splitting hairs? Not at all. Look at what's happening to the quality crusade. (Phil Crosby addresses this same distinction. He says it's the "difference between prevention and playing catch-up.")

Thus, a principal problem is that those hooked on the control measures Centralism promises take readily, even enthusiastically, to the control means that the process-oriented quality movement promises. They see those vaunted quality-control tools as natural allies to the way they manage. That decidedly is counter to what I believe in, and how the companies that are most savvy about TQM view the matter. So let me be crystal clear about one thing in my message.

The kind of Total Quality *Management* I'm talking about is not simply another, more fulsome variant of Total Quality *Control*—or any other control philosophy. QC, SQC, SPC, and their ilk have been around a long time. Neither alone nor in combination do they provide a roadmap to a successful new system—as many companies are now finding to their chagrin. The conceptual makeup of *Five Pillar TQM* most certainly includes quality in all things at all times and the use of process analysis tools to make that happen (an idea for which there is no sole inventor). However, it owes the most in its lineage to the issues of frontline worker competence, creativity, and commitment—and to the issues of how to organize and lead to realize their full potential. Since we've already taken liberties with Murphy's Laws in the interests of clarity, let's invent a few more on this subject:

- *Quality requires creation methods as well as control tools.*
- *The way you empower matters more than the way you control.*
- *The best process control tools won't make managership work.*
- *The best process control tools won't make functionalism work.*
- *Those who control processes lose to those who create quality.*
- *Those controlling behavior lose to those creating commitment.*
- *The more employees who care deeply about quality creation, the more you will find it in the organization.*

Quality control is both a science and an art. There's lots of literature available on how to go about it, and many consultants standing at the ready. Quality creation also is both a science and an art. The art predominates because quality starts in the minds of the customers who want it and the employees who produce it. That places it in the realm of the management art, not the statistical control art. It all boils down to this: Quality creation is more than quality control. Productivity creation is more than productivity control. Behavior creation is more than behavior control. Commitment creation is more than apathy control. Ingenuity creation is more than innovation control. Creation language is different from control language. Creation methods are different from control techniques. So all the QCs piled together won't get you there—or even get you started right.

There are four reasons why I have dwelled on the *Outputs* element of the decentralized model. First, well under 15 percent of American companies measure the right activities to provide the required insight tools for effective decentralized leadership. Second, most American companies—with their centralist cultures of long standing—are dead set against even trying small-group performance tracking, analysis, feedback, and scoreboarding. Third, I repeatedly have found that those very insight tools are the key to getting managers long conditioned to Centralism to allow decentralization to happen, to embrace it, and to make it work. Fourth, a decentralized, leadership approach is the most productive way to manage any organization. If the American management culture (and there is one) doesn't address the first three issues, we'll never get to four, and then we'll stay mired in the centralized, managership style, long America's favorite. If we do, we can look forward to a day when the only two growth industries in America will be *health care* and *Japanese language instruction.* An exaggeration to be sure, but one with a ring of truth that serves as a bell of warning.

Do I overstate the case? Not at all. Only one American business in twenty, at best, manages as the Japanese do, as GE does, and as Boeing does—even though many believe they do because they've adopted a few pieces of those same principles in some places in some ways. Clearly, that's not enough. In chapter 6 I quoted John Betti, who was a key Ford executive during its quality turnaround and who later saw lots of TQM in action as a DOD official. I remind you what he said:

[Many] latch onto [only] one or two of TQM's characteristics. . . . The unfortunate result is that, like the blind men with the elephant, [they] are convinced their view of TQM is correct and complete, and cease to pursue any deeper understanding. . . . TQM truly is a cultural change. It involves a change in both the stated and unstated rules which govern the behavior and beliefs of an organization. Adopting new techniques, tools, or programs can be important—but in themselves do not represent cultural change. Slogans and simplistic solutions will not help; they will make matters worse. TQM can make a significant difference, but all of us need to exert the effort to understand it.

To better understand what must be involved, let's return to the matter of the organizational models. The centerpiece of *Five Pillar TQM* is a team-based structure. There's a good reason for that.

TEAMS ARE THE BEST CHOICE FROM A SYSTEM ENGINEERING STANDPOINT

I've expounded at length on the usefulness of teams when one looks at organizational structure from the bottom-up point of view. Teams also turn out to be the best choice, by far, when looked at from a top-down, system architecture point of view. That's because there is no better way to ensure the effective interface, integration, and harmonious interaction of the organization building blocks. I can best illuminate the point by turning to an analogy from the world of system engineering.

The bulk of my Air Force career was not only spent running large, complex organizations of ever-increasing size, it also was spent being heavily involved in the conceptualization, building, and fielding of the various hardware-software systems that were the tools by which we carried out our overall mission. Therefore, not only at the *Electronic Systems Division* in Boston, but also in the *Pentagon* and at *TAC*, I was heavily involved with the contractors and subvendors across America that build those various systems for the Department of Defense. I saw where they did it well—and why. I saw where they did it poorly—and why. (They got the credit when they did it well. We took the blame in the press when they didn't. I'm not complaining about that; it comes with the territory. I'm pointing out that in all cases it was a joint effort, and if either side of that government-contractor team was weak or inefficient, the outcome fell well short of expectations and needs. That's true today, as it always has been.) Those experiences—most good, some bad—have strongly reinforced my views on the value of using structural teams, not vertical functions, as the organizational building blocks. Let me explain.

Any organization is a combination of structural modules. The key to harmony and efficiency is to get those modules interfaced and integrated in ways that create smooth, trouble-free interaction between those modules. That might well be called the imperative of the *Three I*'s in overall system design. That's for any system, including an organization. I've seen the results in our major "weapons systems" (as the Pentagon calls them) when one or more of the system's modules functions poorly. I've also seen how that affects not only the other modules on which it depends or which it supports (or both), but also how it drags down overall system effectiveness. Often the faulty module can be fixed, sometimes with minor redesign, and the system thereafter performs well. However, I've also seen cases (fortunately the exception) in which the overall system is poorly conceived, designed, and built. Some of its individual parts might perform extremely well, but as a system its modules do not work well together at all. Then you have to start over.

There are many examples around of that, and most people understand it intuitively, so I won't discuss specific cases. However, I emphasize that I'm not talking only about a major piece of equipment such as a fighter, a bomber, or a helicopter. I'm also talking about the more complex kinds of military systems, such as a *command and control system*. Those far more complex systems, with many more modules and connections, present the conceivers, designers, builders, and users with all sorts of daunting and complicated integration challenges. Those challenges specifically include what designers call *the human interface*—which usually presents the most vexing challenges of all. That human interface is, of course, an integral part of the system—indeed, it's the most important part. The point is this: If any one of the major modules is poorly designed and built, the entire system is affected, but can be fixed. If a large number of the modules do not harmoniously interact you have a whale of a problem on your hands—because it involves major redesign and reengineering.

In like manner, when the human interface aspects have been poorly conceived and addressed in the overall system design, it might "work well" in all but the most critical test of all: It doesn't get the job done that the human operators want it to do and need it to do. I've seen many examples of those system engineering realities in action. And I've found organizations—regardless of the setting and endeavor—no different. In fact, I've found the centralized, functionalized organization to be a nightmare from the *Three I*'s standpoint —and from the human interface standpoint as well.

Those system engineering experiences didn't shape my beliefs on how to organize and lead, but they strongly reinforced them. Specifically, they confirmed that I was using the right approach to management system design—and provided still more rationale for why the decentralized, team-based approach unfailingly produced such positive results. Additionally, they further convinced me of the merit of approaching overall management system design as consisting of two primary challenges.

The first challenge lies in effective integration engineering, the second in human psychology. The team approach makes it far easier to meet the dictates of both disciplines. Indeed, it's the ideal way to blend those disciplines to create harmonious interactions among all the organizational modules. In this regard, a portion of the Peter Drucker quote from chapter 6 again comes to mind: "The modern business enterprise is a human and social organization." That's why the psychological and human interface aspects must come into strong play in the system design. Thus the value of teams.

Note that I don't use the term *"autonomous work teams,"* as some who favor the team concept do. I'm certainly not quarreling with them, because we're on the same side of this important issue, and they are trying to make a point by the use of the word "autonomous." (They use it, among other reasons, to emphasize they are addressing specific permanence and empowerment, and therefore something quite different from the cross-functional, ad hoc "teams" that most of the quality management literature goes on and on about.) I avoid use of the term "autonomous" because it has not one but two primary meanings. First, it can pertain to *self-government.* That meaning I have no problem with. Second, according to Webster's, it can mean *"functioning independently from others."* And it's that very issue of

independence that the critics of teams seize on as a means of articulating their derision and fear of the concept.

That criticism is misplaced because there's ample evidence that
teams integrate far better—in a customer-supplier sense and in every
other aspect of organizational synergy—than do functional building
blocks. If you want to give them a name, an appropriate one is *Integrated Work Team*, or *Integrated Product Team*. That's appropriate
because each is integrated as a single team and integrated and bonded
within a team of teams. Actually, if you use the decentralized model
you don't need a special name. But don't call such teams *"cross-
functional"* as that name has already been taken by those grafting
patchwork ad hoc teams onto the centralized, managership model.
And we already know that such *adhocracy* does little to correct the
flaws of a *centocracy*—or to come to substantive grips with the issues
of Centralism.

In this respect, I repeat what I said earlier: *The workers aren't
letting the managers down; the managers are letting the workers
down*. But that's not meant as an indictment of all of America's managers. Indeed, based on my own experiences, and the examples I've
provided in these pages, I'm convinced that the great majority of
America's managers are ready, willing, and able to switch from their
centralist approach if they are given the opportunity and the supportive leadership from the top that makes it happen. So it's appropriate
to expand on my earlier formulation in this way: *The senior managers
of businesses using the traditional American management style are
letting everyone down, from midlevel managers on through the last
frontline worker*. They're doing so by passing on the same bad managerial habits they were taught. Experience shows if the top leader
will break that mold, the entire organization will swing into step, and
will do so with increasing vigor and enthusiasm. If the transformations I have told about in these pages teach nothing else, they teach
that.

Since this chapter, as explained at its outset, is meant as a review,
a recap, and a summary, its themes may seem redundant. That's deliberate, because these are lonely ideas adrift in a sea of traditional
management catechism (and "process improvement" rhetoric that

does little to change that traditional style). And I've found in my management advisory activities that the more clarity and emphasis I give these themes, the more likely they are to penetrate the fog of the conventional wisdom. Thus, some additional emphasis seems well justified.

Throughout this book I have tied certain principles and practices to the centralized approach—and tied quite different ones to the decentralized approach. Their results are quite different as well. The stories of transformations and of exemplary companies I have provided speak to those very differences. As promised in chapter 1, I now turn to a summary of the two models, and the principles, policies, and practices associated with each. Those features are sufficiently consistent that I have come to call them *"The Hallmarks of Centralized and Decentralized Management."* On the two pages at the end of this chapter I show those hallmarks. This side-by-side comparison helps to highlight the profound differences between the two. The features of each fit snugly together and reinforce one another. So trying to mix and match a centralist approach with a few decentralization principles ends up being a largely futile exercise—they simply don't fit together.

This wrap-up comparison admittedly involves simplifications and generalizations, and neither of the two descriptions can be made to fit every organization. You can find a blend of structural and behavioral patterns in most businesses. However, one or the other of these philosophical approaches predominates. And that in turn determines the organization's health and vitality.

Oliver Wendell Holmes left us this: "Man's mind stretched to a new idea, never goes back to its original dimensions." Stretching to the new idea is, therefore, the key part. But as the examples in the earlier chapters illustrate, it can be done; and it's not difficult to do. These examples also show that once managers' minds are stretched to their full change dimensions, they will never go back to indifference to the subject—or to a narrow interpretation of the principles and policies that must be applied for success.

I earlier used Albert Einstein's rueful observation, "Everything in the world has changed except for our thinking." I reprise it here to emphasize that very problem as it relates to the challenges of the late twentieth century—and the challenges that will face America in the twenty-first. However, I'm the eternal optimist—even when the portents provide little reason for optimism. Einstein left us some valuable wisdom in that respect, too:

> Times such as ours have always bred defeatism and despair. But there remain, nonetheless, some few among us who believe man has within him the capacity to meet and overcome even the greatest challenges of this time. If we want to avoid defeat, we must wish to know the truth and be courageous enough to act upon it. If we get to know the truth and have the courage, we need not despair.

No, we need not despair—indeed there's no room for that. And managers, at all levels, needn't despair about their own case either— they must keep pounding away at the old ways, and doing all they can within their own sphere of influence. Sooner or later, let's all hope, these new notions will spread. And then vastly more of the nation's managers (and academicians) will *"get to know the truth"* about what the Globalization Age has brought us. However, in order to succeed on the scale of the best companies I've cited, we cannot continue to *overlay* those old ways while clinging steadfastly to them—in the illusion that we've changed things. And we cannot continue finding refuge in a stream of fads that simply don't address the management fundamentals that globalization has now brought to a reckoning. Yes, change you must. But it's clear: *You cannot replace a system without passion with passion without a system.* And that's what chapter 11, indeed the book, has been all about.

Chapter 12 summarizes the intensifying imperatives for a change in our traditional ways. It also underscores the value that comes from getting to know the truth, and from having the willingness and the courage to change. Success takes all three.

THE HALLMARKS OF CENTRALIZED AND DECENTRALIZED MANAGEMENT

THE CENTRALIZED, MANAGERSHIP APPROACH

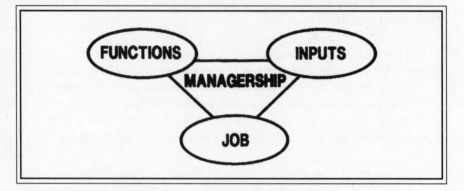

The Overall Structure Is Based on Functions
The Supervisory Focus Is Centered on the Inputs
The Work Accomplishment Mindset Is on Each Person's Job
A CLEAR DIVISION EXISTS BETWEEN "MANAGEMENT" AND
"LABOR"

THE HALLMARKS:

Centralism Principles Are Everywhere
Every Activity Possible Is Consolidated
A Few Top Executives Set All of the Policies
The Authority Is Closely Held—by the Managers
The Accountability Is Diffused, and It's Untraceable
There's Little Quality Focus, and Only on a Few Things
A Cost Fixation Controls Quality—"Quality Is Expensive"
There's Very Little Measurement, Comparison, and Feedback
Productivity and Quality Are the Expectation; "Do Your Job"
Performance Is Tied to Compliance—So "Do Things Right"
Management Has Its Set of Goals, but Labor Has Another
The Culture Is One of Distrust and Tight Supervision
The Climate Reflects Austerity and Cost Obsession
Only a Few Profit from Productivity Improvement
The Customer Linkage Is Frail—and Unfocused
The Motivation Tools Emphasize the Negative
Involvement Is Only a Suggestion Program
Commitment Is Expected, Not Fostered
The Human System Matters Little

THE HALLMARKS OF CENTRALIZED AND DECENTRALIZED MANAGEMENT

THE DECENTRALIZED, LEADERSHIP APPROACH

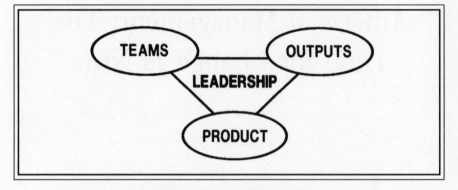

The Overall Structure Is Based on Teams
The Supervisory Focus Is Centered on the Outputs
The Work Accomplishment Mindset Is on the Team Product
A TOTAL TEAM PROCESS OPERATES IN A SEAMLESS
LEADERSHIP NETWORK

THE HALLMARKS:

Decentralization Principles Abound
Diseconomies of Scale Are Understood
All Employees Are Involved in Leadership
Authority Is Widely Distributed Throughout
Accountability Is Inseparably Tied to Authority
Quality Is a Way of Life at All Times, in All Things
Quality Reduces the Costs—"Unquality Is Unaffordable"
Measurement and Comparison Are Widely Used, at All Levels
Productivity and Quality Flow from Commitment; "Be Involved"
The Performance Is Tied to Empowerment; "Do Right Things"
Common Purpose Elicits Strong Commitment and Achievement
The Culture Emphasizes Dignity, Respect, and Cooperation
The Climate Features Strong Commitment to Excellence
Success Is Shared: There's a Stake in the Outcome
The Paramount Focus Is Every Customer's Needs
Involvement and Reward Breed the Motivation
Empowerment and Ownership Reach Everyone
Commitment Is the Aim of All the Policies
The Human System Is the Cornerstone

12

American Management: The Time for Change Is Now

I tell you naught for your comfort
Yea, naught for your desire
Save, that the sky grows darker yet
and the sea rises ever higher.
—G. K. Chesterton

OUR NATION'S PROBLEMS GROW BY THE DAY

Tom Peters spoke out ten years ago about a "rising sea of despair." He was not exaggerating. Now the sky grows darker yet, and the sea rises ever higher. Can we cope with, even benefit from the intensely competitive dynamics of globalization, and stave off the many new forms of economic imperialism? Yes, we can—if we will. There's a proven path. But America's pundits, managers, and soothsayers must awaken to the problem. The effects of globalization are all around us, yet the nation at large remains insensitive to its full ramifications. There's no shortage of signs of our increasingly troubled times. By 1991 it was estimated that twenty cents on every dollar spent by Americans on products ends up in the treasury of a foreign-owned company. The Japanese penetration alone is substantial, and growing.

As one of many examples of the Japanese economic incursion, Sony is now establishing manufacturing facilities in the United States to build a variety of consumer electronics products. To orchestrate its overall effort, Sony has taken over the "AT&T Building" in New York City for its U.S. headquarters. AT&T had put it on the market because "it's too big for us, and too ostentatious." If that isn't a sign of the times, I don't know what is. Sony also is spending $300 million to renovate a mothballed Volkswagen assembly plant on a 600-acre parcel of land in western Pennsylvania where American employees will build Sony products. (Another sign of the times. Volkswagen never made "transplanting" work. The Japanese do.)

And Sony is not alone. Mighty Mitsubishi, the biggest of them all, is investing heavily in American operations also. That includes everything from buying a parcel of Eastman Kodak, to investing in a $400-million power plant in Virginia, to being the deep pockets behind the purchase of the famous Pebble Beach golf course in California. Another giant of Japanese industry, Matsushita (producer of Panasonic and other brand names) is building a huge "manufacturing campus" in north-central Texas. Indeed, the Japanese are jostling one another in their haste to get through the door. And they play product hardball, no doubt about it. For example, Fujitsu, another major player in microelectronics, computers, and communications, boasts in its advertisements in American media that it spends more each year on R&D "than most of the *Fortune* 500 will make in sales." In short, the Japanese are exporting good management practices all over the world, including to the United States, and in doing so are cleaning up on the local competition.

Akio Morita, chairman of Sony, addressed that very issue in an interview in the October 9, 1989, *Newsweek*:

> Forty percent of Sony's employees are not Japanese. Nearly 70 percent of our business is overseas. If we talk about consumer goods, 40 percent are produced overseas. We are still expanding our facilities. I don't like the word "multinational." I don't know what it means. I created a new term: "global localization." That's our new slogan.

We should listen intently. Morita was not only describing the present, he was portraying the future. Indeed, he was saying in effect: *We're coming on your own turf and beating you at your own game.* They sure are. That means tremendous leverage of some kind. And their primary leverage is that they have developed ways of managing employees, of whatever nationality, that enable them to overpower competition still managing in the traditional ways.

In this same overall vein, shortly after Sony announced that it had bought CBS Records, Akio Morita said this about the Columbia pictures part of the package: "We don't know whether present management will stay or not. We are seeking good management—the best management." He then issued a wakeup call to America on its ways:

> Maybe I sound arrogant to the American people. Some people say I'm an America-basher. But since I came to this country, I learned from American friends to speak frankly. Unless American industry changes its attitude, that will be a problem for all of us. The United States is the center of our free economic system, which I believe in. So for our whole free world, we need strong American leadership, and a strong American industry.

And the Japanese are not alone. The list of "NICS"—newly industrialized countries joining in international competition—grows and grows. And that poses vast new challenges for the U.S. and the other "PICS" (Previously Industrialized Countries). Times have changed. The old ways worked then; they don't now. And the evidence of that is everywhere. And it's going to get worse. Jack Welch of GE, who's amply proved his vision, said in a recent *Fortune* interview: "There's going to be global price competition like you've never seen. It's going to be brutal."

The moral in all this? We're paying a big and growing price for our outdated management practices still found all over the place. And they've proven to be deeply embedded and resistant to change, despite all the talk about change. We need not, we must not, go on as we are. The sea rises ever higher.

TRENDS IN AMERICAN SOCIETY SHOW THAT IMPROVING QUALITY AND PRODUCTIVITY IS IN *EVERYONE'S* BEST INTEREST

Everyone in America is familiar by now with the gap between our national income and our national spending to support what we perceive as our entitled lifestyle. And there are only two ways to close that gap, or even to narrow it substantially. We either increase the income or reduce the spending to subsidize the lifestyle. So far, the latter has proved to be a practical political impossibility, and there's no change on the horizon. Indeed, most of the nation's "organization language" (the political variant, that is) has to do with what we still don't have, and with those who don't have what the others already have.

As this was written, the United States of America was entering its twenty-fifth year—a full quarter century—of spending far more than it takes in. In fact, since we embarked on the course of not matching entitlements to enablements in the sixties, our government has provided, on average, $1.22 worth of services for every $1 collected in taxes and other revenue-raising measures. Our soft, squishy euphemism for that difference is the "annual deficit." A far more accurate descriptor would be the "annual subsidy" of the American lifestyle, through borrowing and a constantly growing load of debt. This state of national affairs is analogous to a profligate couple who spend wildly beyond their means and sink deeper and deeper into debt, all the while increasingly seeking the things *they don't have*. But as with this metaphorical couple, all such aspiration games must come to an end, and in a way that's not pleasant to contemplate.

A subgame in all this, of course, is the *blame game* in our national political dialogue. One of our two political parties says it's all in the hands of the White House—which, its leaders point out, the other political party continuously occupied during the twelve years the national debt skyrocketed from $1 trillion to $4 trillion. They contend, in essence, that the White House sets those forces in play and then refuses to control them. That being the case, they allege that what the American people have been witnessing in this entire deficit and debt game is *Repubonomics*. The politicos of the other party say, "Not so fast." They point out that not a single dollar can be spent by the government, and not a single penny in taxes raised or lowered, without empowering legislation by Congress. (A unique power invested in Congress by the Constitution.) They then point out that Congress has been controlled by "that other party" during the quarter century when all the nation's massive spending and borrowing has been going on. So, they say, what we are actually seeing in action in all of our growing debt and deficit troubles is *Demonomics*. Actually, both are right. *Or, more correctly, both are wrong.*

Given an increasingly strident electorate that demands more government services and fewer taxes to pay for them, what we're actually witnessing is *Electonomics*. Does anyone reading this expect that to change—at least by much? Don't hold your breath. It's been repeatedly observed that the entitlements for the elderly—Medicare and Social Security—constitute the *third rail* of American politics; touch it and you're dead. A better metaphor for the total problem is that *every* politician in America rides on the back of a subsidy tiger—a tiger that grows larger, hungrier, and more ferocious by the day. Get off its back as a politician and *you* get eaten—not a politician's favored outcome.

As entitlements steadily grew over the past quarter century, and enablements didn't, the scoreboard started showing us the folly of our ways. From the world's largest creditor nation we had become, by 1990, the world's largest debtor nation. From the biggest investor in other countries we have fallen to number four. (Japan is number one.) Once we had most of the world's top banks; now we have only one in the top 30, at number 29. (Citibank.)

Worse yet, the debt rhythm we have established speeds up with each passing year. On October 1, 1981, the national debt passed $1 trillion. It reached $2 trillion on April 3, 1986. Four years later, on April 2, 1990, it hit $3 trillion. In midyear 1992 it passed $4 trillion. As 1995 drew to an end it was nearing $5 trillion—still climbing steeply. If one were to count $5 trillion dollars out a dollar a second, it would take them 160,750 years to reach that exalted number. And, as Al Jolson used to say, *"You ain't seen nuthin' yet!"* At least you haven't unless we change our ways. It isn't easy to turn the entitlements off, or the enablements on. And, if there is one thing we know about subsidies it's that they are very easy to start but virtually impossible to stop. Indeed, those who start them become our heroes and those who try to stop or trim them are villains. And most so-called "entitlements" (including Social Security and Medicare) are a mixture of true entitlements (pay-outs derived from pay-ins by/for the individual) and "subsidies" (augmenting the pay-outs from the general tax revenues). Our politicians have totally blurred these two lines over the years for self-serving reasons. So, it's not hard to understand why Americans feel "entitled." ("I've paid for everything I'm getting"—which simply isn't so.) Unscrambling them, and means-testing the subsidy component, seems vital if a viable solution is to be found. But don't hold your breath that will happen.

After long being ignored, the continuous annual borrowing finally got some attention. And the new administration in 1993 passed budget projections designed to cut borrowing by one-third ($1 billion a day to $660 million a day). Even that was highly controversial. Then in 1995 a big fight erupted over proposals to zero the deficit by 2002. And the issues of what, where, and when to cut were as polarized, and as heated, as ever. This underscores the issue's intractability. So the subsidy game, the debt game, and the blame game are to go on and on. Meanwhile, most everyone, no matter their circumstances, feels they're richly entitled to the subsidies; indeed, many are arraying themselves in powerful lobbies to get even more.

Given all this, the debate rages about whether the entitlements we cooked up in the sixties, and have added to progressively ever since, are warranted or unwarranted. Some allege they have gone for naught—that our huge debt has bought us little. Also, there's no shortage of people willing to point to their favorite culprits for the growing national debt—but never to themselves.

Even the politicians willing to confront the issues do so by treading ever so gently when it comes to the "middle class"—or by exempting that group from the solutions entirely. No surprise in that. Polls show that some 92 percent of Americans, when asked, place themselves in the middle class. I say this to underscore my point that improving quality and productivity is in *everyone's* best interest. Otherwise, everyone is going to be affected, and substantially so, by the wreckage inevitable in our present course. Are the entitlements justified? Who's going to pay for them? Those are the central questions. With regard to the worth of the current entitlements, this may not yet be a "Great Society" in the view of those clamoring for more (and who loudly criticize the society's various blemishes), but that government largesse certainly has provided a far better life, for all Americans, as contrasted with the first half of this century.

Let's look at those contrasts briefly. In the first half of this century, almost no one retired; now essentially everyone does. Then, most Americans in most places did not have access to electricity, now everyone does. Then, most roads were dirt or gravel, now we have paved streets, and an interstate highway system maintained by the federal government. Then, almost everyone depended on outdoor "privies"; now virtually all enjoy the comforts of indoor plumbing. Then, heat came from a potbelly stove, kept going by great individual effort to stoke it with wood or coal, now virtually everyone has central heating, and air-conditioning, too.

Then, only a few Americans had access to skilled, up-to-date medical care; now, with but a few exceptions, the entire society does. Then to be on a medication (other than aspirin or Carter's Little Liver Pills) was rare at any age; now everyone over fifty is on at least one medicine to make life more livable, and the number of medications increases dramatically with age. Then, complex procedures to keep people with terminal diseases alive longer and longer were available to none; now they're available to almost everyone. Then, aged parents were supported by their children, more often than not by taking them into their homes; now the need to do that is the exception not the rule.

Anything wrong with any of that? My own answer is there's only one thing wrong with it for certain: It's an American lifestyle that our quality, productivity, and ingenuity as a society have been unable to support without massive borrowing. If the U.S.A. is going to hell in a handcart, as many say, it's not because there's anything wrong with living better than those who went before us; it's that we haven't figured out a way to pay for it—a national problem reaching epic proportions.

Virtually all the solutions held out by the nation's economists hinge on the good old *rosy scenario*—the solution of substantially increased growth in both productivity and income. The idea is that if we can stimulate growth we'll increase the national income base, thereby increase the tax base, and thereby close the gap and eliminate the deficit—even if we have to leave debt reduction to another day. However, those rosy scenarios never come to pass. Why not? Largely because we haven't come to grips with what is causing our productivity problems. There are potential solutions, but they don't lie in a nostrum associated with macroeconomic theory, even if we could find it in the welter of differing opinions. In that respect, a wag once said that if we were to lay all of America's economists end to end they would still all point in different directions.

It's indeed confusing to follow the widely divergent opinions emerging from that community on what's wrong with the American economy and what we can and should do about it. On the one hand, few economists disagree about *what* we need to make happen as a nation by way of restoring robust economic health through greater productivity. However, when it comes to the matter of *how*—the actions to be taken and by whom—the consensus breaks down completely. There's an abundance of opinion, but little of it lies in the realm of the practical. I've avidly read those notions on how to ''rev up'' American productivity, and I don't put hope in any of them.

In that respect, I'm a strong supporter of the government taking actions to rev up investments in R&D, in plant and equipment, and in the other trappings that make greater productivity possible. Experience shows that tax policies do exert a beneficial—or detrimental —role in those respects. However, we know that even the newest plants sometimes have the lowest productivity, so there's much more to it than that. Remember the story about the Ford plant in Mahwah, New Jersey, I told earlier?

As I see it, there's one huge, overpowering piece of our national productivity dilemma that can be solved only by the nation's managers. (With, of course, government support and encouragement, not obstructionism.) That matter is quite straightforward, based on the rationale and evidence I have provided in these pages. What we need, and need now, is to forge a far more harmonious and productive partnership between management and labor in the workplaces of this nation. That must be a partnership based not on the tired old ways that don't work but on new ways that do. But times a-wastin'! That's because the problem feeds on itself. Indeed, the problem far exceeds the rapidly growing debt load and interest load because there are worrisome signs all over the business landscape of their many side effects. As but one example, surveys now show that annual wages (and fringe benefits) of new workers are dropping, not rising, compared to their predecessors. So our borrowing is adding to the problems that created the need to borrow in the first place, thereby setting up a self-perpetuating and ominous cycle.

There is an end, even if it's an abrupt and altogether unpleasant end, to how far a nation can carry its dependence on OPM (Other People's Money) and OCM (Other Countries' Money) to cover huge annual gaps between its income and its outgo. But the beat goes on. Two-thirds of the national budget is now on autopilot, to cover the entitlements everyone has learned to love and the growing debt service payments that continue to make them possible. Moreover, as the baby boomers dramatically swell the ranks of the elderly early in the next century—and as we live longer at greater and greater cost to the society at large—entitlements spending goes ballistic.

When the Social Security program began in the Franklin Roosevelt administration in 1935, the eligibility age was sixty-five. Life expectancy then was just under sixty. It now averages seventy-six years, and is climbing. If we still had the same relationship between life expectancy and eligibility age we had when Social Security began, Americans wouldn't be eligible until age eighty-one. I'm certainly not suggesting that, but it is relevant to note that eligibility age has not climbed since the program's inception—instead, it has dropped to sixty-two. (And, if you make it to sixty-two you can expect, on average, to make it to eighty-five.) Most retirees take advantage of the age sixty-two eligibility. In fact, the average retirement age, nationwide, was just over sixty-one as this was written. The first Social Security retiree, Vermont native Ida Made Fuller, paid in $22 and—at her death at age ninety-nine—had taken out $20,000. Ever since, retirees in the aggregate have taken out more than was paid in on their behalf (roughly twice more). Who pays the balance? Current workers.

That brings in other important arithmetic. In 1935 the peak retiree-to-worker ratio at program maturity was forecast to be 1 retiree for every 15 workers. With the changing life-expectancy versus retirement age dynamics the ratio now is 1 to 3—and will head quickly toward 1 to 1.5 as the baby boomers retire, starting early in the next century. Given these trends, the *mother of all oxymorons* soon may be the phrase "trust fund." There goes trust when there's no fund behind it! In fact, the government levies special taxes for any number of "trust funds" related to highways, airports, and various other national infrastructure needs. But there isn't any money in any of them. It's all a bookkeeping exercise.

To be sure, the government bureaucrats have worked out more intricate bookkeeping methods for the "Social Security trust fund." It's a highly ritualized *Kabuki* dance in credits and debits. But you still can't go visit your money in that trust fund because the government has no way to save money—not with total outgo exceeding income. Some of the politicians take to the airwaves to assert: "The Social Security trust fund is solvent into the foreseeable future; we fixed that back in 1983." Small solace in that. The fact is, the money raised through Social Security taxes is going for other purposes, and the government borrows to boot. I won't repeat all the stark arithmetic here, but it adds up to one bottom line for the American lifestyle: *Either start earning it or lose it.*

Indeed, we may well find ourselves talking five to ten years hence of the *General Motors Syndrome* the nation has fallen into. As I write this book, GM is on the credit watch list for downgrading which would make raising capital far more costly. Also, GM's retiree-to-worker ratio, and the growing unsupportability of all its overhead costs, are but a microcosm of what faces the nation as more companies fall into the same downward spiral. In fact, the more the *Fortune* 500 companies downsize, because of the loss of their competitive edge, the more costly the effects of the retirements used as the only device available to hold on to declining profitability. That's not the formula that makes America financially strong; it never was, and we all know it.

All this should inspire sobering thought by every American, especially by the nation's managers, in whose hands the solution lies. The politicians, you say? Not so. They run the government, not the nation's businesses. And the electorate has made the government a big part of the problem, not a principal part of the solution. But there is a constructive role for government to play.

THE GOVERNMENT CAN'T DO IT ALL, BUT ITS ROLE HAS NEVER BEEN MORE IMPORTANT: ITS ROLE MUST BE RESHAPED TO OUR TIMES AND INCLUDE CONSTRUCTIVE INVOLVEMENT IN THE BUSINESS OF AMERICA

There are two key things the federal government needs to do if America is to become more productive and competitive. First, it must get its own house more in order. TQM offers workable solutions to many of government's classic problems. I've given tips on how to go about it. For all those interested in what governments can do to become more productive, I recommend the acclaimed 1992 book *Reinventing Government* by David Osborne and Ted Gaebler. The key theme is the power of decentralization and the entrepreneurial spirit in government agencies large and small—local, state, and federal. In studying governments across that spectrum, the authors say governments are best when they are: *Mission-Driven, Customer-Driven, Anticipatory, Market-Oriented, Results-Oriented, Competitive, Catalytic, Enterprising, Empowering*, and *Decentralized*. Entire chapters are devoted to each of those characteristics, and the authors provide many examples to reinforce the importance of developing them.

The authors' conclusions and recommendations are in harmony with those I have presented. As examples, their findings on the value of competition, and of measurement, reinforce the points I make. They devote a special section to "The Art of Performance Measurement." And as I do they point out "There is a vast difference between measuring process and measuring results." Regarding the design of the management system they say "Decentralized institutions have a number of advantages over centralized institutions," including being "more flexible, innovative, and effective"—and thereby "generate higher morale, more commitment, and greater productivity." With regard to useful role models they say: "Perhaps the starkest example of decentralization we came across occurred in the nation's largest and most centralized bureaucracy: the Department of Defense." They tell how TAC led the charge to decentralization within the DOD, and why TAC's new organizational model is the right pattern for success. Anyone who toils within government would greatly benefit by reading the book. So would all who are interested in seeing government become more effective.

The second thing the United States government must do is to reorient its thinking about its relationship with the businesses of America. Specifically, it must adjust its long-standing attitudes about the role government must play vis-à-vis the business community to better suit the realities of our times. If the *business of America* is not the business of its government, how are we to compete with those economic powerhouses, and economic blocs, that look on the government-business relationship in precisely that way?

Some historical government biases, and government posturing to exert those biases, will have to change if that partnership is to help solidify America's future. And if the nation's managers will make each of their businesses the business of *all their employees*, it will be much easier for the government to make that transition. It has long served as the grand adjudicator between the warring factions of business and labor; so it comes by its many biases and its standoffish stance toward business quite naturally. Said another way, a more productive partnership between management and labor can help facilitate a more productive relationship between business and government.

And anyone who thinks we don't need better partnerships and less confrontation in both those respects just hasn't been paying attention to the realities of our times.

WHO KEEPS THE TRADE FAIR? HOW IS IT KEPT FAIR?

The economic competition that accompanies globalization is not only between companies, it's between *socioeconomic systems*—each with its own history, laws, capabilities, and motives. Thus, the governments are competing along with the companies. Who wins, who loses? That will depend on each government's management savvy in spurring national productivity—and in ensuring that its trade policies help, not hurt. Experience tells us that government policies do either help or hinder, and our companies need fewer, not more, handicaps in globalized economic jousting. This is another lesson the Japanese are providing. But we haven't been astute in grasping that lesson— its import—or in adapting our own ways. How our nation faces up to this intensifying struggle must be at the very top of our national agenda as we go forward.

Every nation "manages" its multinational trade; it always has, and it will continue to do so into the foreseeable future. So let's not be taken in by our own rhetoric and confuse the ideal with the practical as we evolve, slowly, toward a different global economic system. For example, the *North American Free Trade Agreement* (*NAFTA*) among the United States, Canada, and Mexico simply takes the trading concept of *most favored nation* to a broader application, and sets out ground rules on how, in that trading bloc, we will each manage our trade policies to provide fuller access to one another's markets in ways that are to our mutual and collective advantage. However, that's to be on a "fair" and evolutionary basis, not a "free" basis—at least not for many years to come.

In that respect, the difficulties in managing the transition to "Free Trade" within any regional bloc, much less the world, should not be underestimated. Witness the problems the Europeans are having in cobbling together the European Common Market and its companion stalking-horse, the European Economic Community. Serious problems already exist in that projected paradise, problems that aren't easily overcome as each nation attends to its own interests and attends to the varied domestic political realities shaping those interests.

This is an important piece of the puzzle the Globalization Age brings to our national policies. There, too, we need to recognize that it's a new age calling for new ways. I don't pretend to be an expert on economic and trade matters; however, I do know a great deal about the machinations of our government at the interdepartmental level, and about the ways of maintaining awareness and moving aggressively in forestalling or coping with military forms of conflict between nations. As George Washington reminded us at the time of our nation's founding, "To be prepared for war is one of the most effective means of preserving peace."

That was very good advice. However, we haven't always heeded it. For example, we did our level best to sit out World War II, making a national pastime of *unpreparedness* and drilling our troops with broomsticks instead of rifles even while most of the world was on fire—until one shattering Sunday morning in Hawaii shook us out of our lethargy and isolation from the realities of those times. When we bestirred ourselves we were a powerful force to be reckoned with, as the later surrender ceremonies on the deck of the battleship *Missouri* clearly demonstrated. Indeed, it turned out—somewhat to our surprise—that we were a world superpower when we put our mind to it. But we certainly had not been preparing ourselves like one, or conducting ourselves like one. I make these points because they provide a parallel for a period of intense global economic competition. That competition—some prefer the word "conflict"—has already started. And thus far we're not exactly showing as an economic powerhouse. Indeed, the spectacle of the U.S. government going to Japan, hat in hand, to plead for voluntary restraint is not a comforting one. And in this new global economic conflict if that's not defense rather than offense, I don't know what is.

To bring home the ramifications of globalization, on occasion during a speech I'll conduct a "hands in the air" poll. I start by asking each of the audience members to put a hand in the air and leave it there if I name a Japanese product used within his or her immediate family—including children, grown or otherwise. I start with Japanese cars. More than one-third of the hands go up, often as many as half. I then add TVs and VCRs. Lots more hands shoot up. Then I add computers, printers, faxes, and home copiers. By then nearly all hands are in the air, and I don't even have to go on to cameras and kitchen appliances. My poll results are remarkably consistent in audiences large and small, no matter what the industry or business involved. I then point out that a similar poll taken of a Japanese business audience could exhaust America's entire array of durable products and not get 15 percent of the hands in the air, if it got that. The moral of the story? There are several.

First, the effects of globalization are pervasive, as we can vividly see in nearly every American home. Second, part of our trade imbalance with the Japanese is culturally influenced in that American society readily accepts foreign-made products, even seeks them out and bestows special status on them. The insular Japanese society, on the other hand, is slow to accept foreign things (except for good foreign management ideas). But the issue doesn't stop there. The third moral is that the enormous trade disparity between America and Japan flows from the policies of the two.

Much has been written about the devices used by the Japanese to keep foreign products out. They range from outright barriers and tariffs to far subtler forms such as making it difficult to enter their distribution networks, and on to regulations on product performance and safety that are disadvantageous to products built on foreign shores. I won't repeat all that here, but there's not much doubt that Japanese government trade policies are major players in ensuring that market penetration is largely a one-way street.

Let's look at a related example. Earlier I spoke of Europe's Airbus Industries and how it has consistently lost money, how aggressive it is in bidding low prices in the global marketplace, and how the founding governments prop up all that seemingly contradictory behavior. Let's suppose that the American government with all its financial clout (while it still has it) went to Boeing and said, ''Go after Airbus.

They're taking jobs from Americans by using unfair tactics and government subsidies. We'll cover all your losses. Just drive them out of the marketplace.'' Any doubt that Boeing could do that? Not at all. Boeing would make chopped liver out of Airbus in no time (at least in global markets; the nationally owned airlines of those same countries would still find reasons to buy from Airbus, of course). I use this admittedly fanciful scenario simply to point out that economic conflict, and the thrust for national economic advantage, take many forms.

Given those realities and their growing implications, our government needs to be far more proactive than it has been in the past. To provide perspective on a major part of those needed actions, Washington's famous admonition regarding war deserves a parallel that fits our international trade policy: *The surest way to avoid a trade policy disadvantage is to be prepared for it, to be well organized to cope with it, and to simply not stand for it.* In that context, many believe we're drilling with broomsticks and making our usual mistakes of underestimating the problem and the solutions. For all those who believe that reciting the free trade mantra is enough, and who advocate that Uncle Sam set a benevolent example for the world to follow, I reprise a saying regarding preparedness whose truth we learned the hard way: *It does no good for the sheep to pass resolutions in favor of vegetarianism so long as the wolves are of a different persuasion.* I provide the examples of techniques employed by Japan, and of wheeling and dealing by Airbus Industries, to point out a cold, hard reality in global economic life: *Bet on the wolves.*

We will need to manage our way through the shallows and shoals of *fair trade* before we can ever hope to get to *free trade*, notwithstanding all the high-flown rhetoric to the contrary. And, to be honest about it, our nation is nearly as often the transgressor as the one transgressed against, simply proving that trade barriers, tariffs, and subsidies created for domestic political reasons yield only to outside, not inside, pressures—and that's true everywhere. So, as the world slowly discards the practices of the past, there's little doubt we must stay prepared for the economically aggressive and the advantage-takers among the world's nations. Indeed, the government's role is a pivotal one if this nation is to be a force to be reckoned with as we sort who wins and who loses in the Globalization Age. Maybe we should never try to become a *U.S.A., Inc.*, on the *Japan, Inc.*, model. However, at the least we must drop our disposition to the view that the government is policeman and kibitzer of the nation's business activity rather than supporter and facilitator.

A step in the right direction is the formation of the National Economic Council, the equivalent of the National Security Council. Since its formation and embodiment in law, the NSC has been highly useful in helping the President and other Cabinet officials to stay informed on defense matters—and to help orchestrate the defense-related activities of the many Cabinet-level departments. The NEC can be—and needs to be—no less of a force on economic and trade matters. I would hope also that a strong international and bilateral trade focus in its fact-gathering and deliberations is maintained. History suggests there will be a tendency for it to turn inward and primarily focus on domestic economics, budget policy, and fiscal policy.

The formation of an NEC is just a start. We must also address the way the entire government is organized in the light of our changing times. Specifically, we need to sort out a new and far more important role for the Department of Commerce, analogous to that of Defense for military matters. Commerce needs to maintain global situation awareness (far more than now), to have much stronger Cabinet clout, and to have the array of talented people (and other required resources) to make all that happen. We must also ensure that our heads are up and alert, not buried in the sand. It was Germany's Bismarck who once observed, "Every time I look for the United States of America I see the rear end of an ostrich." Let's be sure our naive past is not prologue. The stakes are too high.

This, the twentieth century, is variously called the *"Industrial Age,"* the *"Technology Age,"* the *"Information Age,"* the *"Globalization Age,"* and a few others of that ilk. All those names, of course, are used to signal various aspects of the technological and informational developments that make this the most remarkable period in human history. As one comparison benchmark, the differences between the nineteenth century and all those which preceded it pale by comparison to the differences between the nineteenth and twentieth centuries. (Automobiles, airplanes, telephones, telefaxes, televisions, computers, exploration of space—the list goes on and on.) And clearly the rate of that change is accelerating—an acceleration away from the strictures of the past. Technology breeds new technology. New means of studying physical phenomena spawn new knowledge. New knowledge in turn spawns more new knowledge. And the increasing worldwide distribution of that knowledge brings more and more countries into a smaller and smaller orbit measured in terms of time and easily spannable distances.

Some things, though, haven't changed much. Certainly humans are more knowledgeable and more aware than ever before (in the aggregate). However, human nature hasn't changed much at all. And because of the stubborn persistence of human nature and our propensity for clinging to the old ways, there has been little change in the preferred American management style. As a consequence, there is ample justification for the view that we continue to live in the *Centralism Era* of American management—with all the varied trappings and troubles that go with it. Everything else is changing around us, but that isn't, at least not by much.

In chapter 7 I spoke of some new developments in management theory in the sixties (namely, matrix management) that are still with us. But those were changes on the margin—and they perpetuated the centralized style. Before that the most discernible theoretical watershed came with Frederick W. Taylor's conceptual framework of "Scientific Management" at the turn of this century. In essence it was a theory of the ways to make management centralization work as we entered the Industrial Age—with all its implications for organizational dynamics. The theory was successful in that respect, since it did provide the means and methods to perpetuate a centralized style; in fact, it defended it, dignified it, and embellished it. For that reason, if no other, it was widely admired and copied.

In this regard, I freely admit that we cannot lay all of modern centralist thinking and practices at Taylor's door. Most of those among our millions of modern managers practicing the traditional centralized, managership management style have never heard of Frederick W. Taylor. Most wouldn't know his *Scientific Management* concepts from a bale of hay—and couldn't care less. Still, Taylor's ideas remain in our management theory warp and woof, and they continue to define the way most businesses are managed. Therefore, let's briefly review the central ideas in Taylor's theories as a way of providing insight into why things haven't changed all that much. The atmospherics and slogans are quite different, to be sure, but the core ideas remain.

IT'S TIME TO PUT THE LEGACIES OF CENTRALISM AND MANAGERSHIP ASIDE—SUCCESS IN A GLOBAL ECONOMY DEPENDS ON IT

Frederick Winslow Taylor more than anyone got the idea started for *"multiple functional foremen"* as a way of specializing and supervising work. Indeed, he took the time to set down any number of various *functions* by which work should be divided—and closely supervised. Taylor also fathered the notion of taking any and all *"brain work"* away from the workers. In fact, he was adamant that *planning and working* had to be completely separate activities.

Following the same general line of reasoning, Taylor had a theory that what he called the *"first-class man"* was he who was best at doing exactly what he was told to do, without giving any thought to it one way or the other. Taylor even bragged about singling out for his experiments a poorly educated and slow-witted "first-class man" who would do just as he was told—and that specifically included when and how hard to work and when to rest. If that's not getting the centralization and dehumanization ball rolling, and laying the groundwork for the Centralism of today, I don't know what is.

It's only proper to acknowledge that a few of Taylor's theories made positive contributions, especially his application of scientific study methods to work activity. Also, it's not altogether fair to hold Taylor, writing from his nineteenth-century perspectives, responsible for the negative motivational aspects of his techniques in the hands of others. Given that, I'm willing to excuse Taylor for his oversight of those *human psyche* aspects as our country entered the 1900s, at the start of the Industrial Age. However, I'm far less understanding, as all should be, of those who leave aside those human psyche aspects today. You'd think we would be sufficiently enlightened by now that the same kind of myopia and insensitivity wouldn't happen. Unfortunately, it not only still happens, it's rampant.

In this regard, Peter Drucker, in his usual insightful way, has written about Frederick W. Taylor's management ideas and said, "The need today is neither to bury Taylor nor to praise him. It is to learn from him." Along with bestowing praise where appropriate on Taylor's useful contributions, Drucker points out two blind spots in Taylor's "Scientific Management" methodology and approach. The first is "the belief that because we must analyze work into its simplest constituent motions we must also organize it as a series of individual motions, each if possible carried out by an individual worker. This is false logic." Drucker goes on, "Scientific Management purports to organize human work. But it assumes—without any attempt to test or to verify the assumption—that the human being is a machine tool, although a poorly designed one. . . . The human being does individual motions poorly; viewed as a machine tool, he is badly designed." He sure is. So you can't treat him or her like a machine tool, or isolate work activity down to each individual as distinct from the group.

The second blind spot, according to Drucker, came from Taylor's having "laid aside the personality, emotions, appetites, and soul issues that make up the human psyche" in developing his theories of management and worker supervision. As usual, Peter Drucker hits exactly the right keys to understanding Taylor's work, and placing it in modern perspective. Indeed, a great lack of attention to the ramifications and consequences of management systems, structures, and styles on the human psyche—and thereby on the entire *human system* of an organization—still is more characteristic than uncharacteristic of today's management literature. More importantly, it's characteristic of the management policies and practices in most of America's businesses. It seems high time to put Taylor's ideas to rest along with those of Lenin, while continuing to learn from both of them—about what *not* to do. Their ideas have caused far too much damage to have any remaining worth or staying power.

As you read about Taylor's theories, did any of them sound familiar? They should. Indeed, if Taylor could have come back before our transformation he would have been very proud of the centralized, functionalized Tactical Air Command—and the other DOD elements similarly organized. Such organizations, in either the public or the private sector, are expert at separating the planning and the working —and at organizing by Taylor's beloved "functions," "functional foremen," and precise rules about how to carry out the work.

Taylor also would have seen his fondest dreams in action in the centralized, functionalized General Motors. Indeed, it seems safe to speculate that he would have bestowed on GM's Fred Donner and his many successors as GM CEOs the "Taylor Prize" for distinguished accomplishment in centralization! Beyond that, it would be a delight for Taylor to see the staying power of his ideas throughout America. That's true in many other countries, too, but that's not our concern. In fact, it helps us if we're smart enough to change our ways before they do. But change won't be easy. As I've pointed out, defenders of the traditional management culture abound in our society. That's a primary reason it has hung on even in the face of compelling evidence it is no longer appropriate to our times. Those attitudes won't change quickly, so a bit more on that issue is appropriate.

THE CENTRALISM DEFENDERS SEIZE ON EVERY EXCUSE TO CHANGE THE SUBJECT OR DEFLECT THE IDEA THAT CHANGE IS REQUIRED

Most will recall that the national business press—giving equal voice to the defenders of the status quo—helped gleefully play the "Oops" game with Peters and Waterman in criticism of their landmark book *In Search of Excellence* when any of the exemplary companies they cited faltered, however slightly. (Most examples they used, like Johnson & Johnson, did not falter, but a few did.) Based on past experience, I'm sure the keepers of the Centralism faith will challenge and critically dissect the remedies offered in these pages.

Obviously, I cannot guarantee companies adopting these remedies will be runaway financial successes if they are in struggling industries. For example, I have praised *American Airlines* and *The Boeing Company*. As this book was going to press all the airlines continued to struggle financially—including American Airlines. And, because of a worldwide recession (and too many passenger seats chasing too few passengers at too low a seat/mile price) orders for new aircraft were being postponed, delayed, or canceled right and left. As a consequence, Boeing found it necessary to lay off 20 percent (27,000) of its workers—at least until there's a resurgence in orders. Such industry woes should not be confused with poor management practices by Boeing, or used as rationale to shoot down the merits of decentralization and team-based management.

In that regard, U.S. companies competing head-to-head with the Japanese (autos, electronics, etc.) have staged a comeback. Improved U.S. quality played a part, but the major reason has been the plunging dollar/soaring yen (*endaka*). That tripling of the yen's value (since 1985) dramatically drove up their production costs—thus making the U.S. more competitive. However, Japan is adapting itself to this dramatic development. And they remain more efficient. (Chapter 2.) So what's next? We can't ride this *endaka* horse for very long. Also, those who profited the most (Ford and Chrysler) have done the most to change their old ways. Thus, the evidence remains clear: The traditional U.S. management style is unsuited to our times.

Further, I cannot guarantee that each of the exemplary companies cited in these pages will prosper eternally. Faces change at the top, and even the best companies sometimes wander away from the management system principles that made them what they are. (Witness my earlier story of wings within TAC turning sour or sweet, often very rapidly, as the person at the top changed.) What I can guarantee is that businesses that diligently apply (and stick with) the *Five Pillar* principles will get better—and stay better—than their competitors. And this book is about the competitive edge, not perfection.

At this book's beginning I pointed out the bewildering variety of advice available now on "quality management" under various names, TQM included. I said about that advice: Some of it is quite good. Much of it is off the point. And some of it is the worst advice you could take. By now you have more insight into why I say all three kinds of advice are to be found in the current management literature. I also said that in dispensing (and accepting) management advice credentials matter—or at least they should.

The sad fact is the American management culture is awash in defenders of the traditional style. They deflect the idea of change, or drown it in a sea of rhetoric, or suggest minimal changes that address only part of the problem. So, when the Centralism defenders mount their pulpits to decry, deflect, and deter grander remedies such as these, and they do and will, I suggest you examine their credentials, their credibility, and their motivation before making up your own mind. You should also ask yourself what remedies they are offering for our vexing problems in global competitiveness and economic vitality. Most who snipe from the sidelines are very strong on what not to do but soft or silent on what to do. So don't be hornswoggled by those who offer contempt for change—not change itself. That's why we're so deeply mired in the traditional style.

There's a better alternative to Taylorism cum Centralism. It's called TQM. However, to succeed it must be based on all Five Pillars of TQM not some pieces in some ways in some places. *The TQM approach must be holistic and it must be humanistic.* Without both aspects strongly at work in the application of TQM principles within any organization it becomes "quality management" in name only— all slogans, no substance. That's why I've linked the words "holistic" and "humanistic" repeatedly with the term TQM throughout these pages. Some may think it's overdone. I admit I beat that drum strongly and incessantly. I do so because change is imperative—and the response by America's managers is tepid.

THE PROFIT BUSINESS IS THE PEOPLE BUSINESS; THE SUCCESS BUSINESS IS THE HUMAN SPIRIT BUSINESS— AND THE SUCCESSFUL LEADERS CONDUCT THEIR ORGANIZATIONS ACCORDINGLY

I've wondered a lot during my lifetime about what makes organizations tick. And I've concluded there's no great mystery to it. That's because it comes down to what makes people tick. It isn't how big the organization is, it's how small its leaders choose to run it— small in the sense that when all's said and done it's all up to each Bob and Betty, each Harriet and Homer, each Julietta and José, each Simon and Samantha. They are the organization—not its name, not its heritage, not its products. And they determine its success, its image, and its future. How big the organization is has nothing to do with how big their feeling for it or how big their willing contribution to it. That has to do with how big are the trust, empowerment, dignity, and fulfillment that the organization bestows on each of them. Trust little and you get little in return. Empower little and you get little in return. Dignify little and you get little in return. Fulfill little and you get little in return.

The centocracies have never quite figured that out. They manage, not lead. They distrust, not trust. They demand, not delegate. And then they wonder, and wonder why they aren't doing better than they are. The lessons aren't complicated and they can be reduced to two. First, any organization that wants to get in and stay in the profit business must get in and stay in the people business. Second, put the business in their hearts if you expect them to put their hearts in the business.

There's really no other formula for leadership success that amounts to anything or has any staying power. If you agree with any of this, you should have no lingering doubt about why centocracies fail. Granted, many look back and say they had no problems with their traditional style in the past—that it must be other factors at work. And they come up with a wide array: an eroding employee work ethic, our education system, our trade policy, our governmental regulations—the list goes on and on. Far too few stop to consider that, while these factors increase the leadership challenge, the real problem is that they succeeded because it was centocracy against centocracy, flawed policies against flawed policies, insensitivities against insensitivities. What's needed now is to bring the organizational *dinosaur* approach to an end. Why do I call the centocracies dinosaurs? Because they feature large lumbering bodies, pea brains, and a poor instinct for survival in changing times.

TAC did poorly along with the other Air Force centocracies before a lot of enthusiastic TAC people got behind the idea of changing it for the better by ending its dinosaur days. We didn't change the faces, we changed the culture—and the dramatic results came from our tapping the slumbering potential that was there all along. All the transformations in which I've been involved fit that same pattern. In fact, nearly all the turnarounds I've observed fit that same pattern. Why *"nearly"*? Because there are exceptions worth emphasizing. Those are the cases in which the centocracy was simply world-class stupid compared to its fellow centocracies, but then got smart enough and just agile enough to move to the head of the dinosaur class. That worked then; it doesn't work now. Turnarounds and big success in the fast moving Globalization Age don't happen by chance. Enthusiastic people operating in a seamless network of proactive, sensitive leadership make it happen. And new, more enlightened management principles and policies make the leadership happen.

Earlier I quoted Tadashi Kume of Honda: "It is usually true the larger an organization becomes, the more conservative it becomes, the more bureaucratic it becomes, and the more rigid it becomes." Centocracies specialize in all those problems. In this respect, however, I once again emphasize that my use of the terms "Centralism" and "centocracy" are meant to portray a frame of mind and a way of doing business—not a way to describe the size of the business. While the bigger the organization the more prone it is to the lingering disease of Centralism, you can find its manifestations everywhere, in small organizations as well as in large ones. In today's world no company, whatever its size and market niche, can long survive the detrimental effects of Centralism. Every manager should examine his or her own organization in that light. The battering ram of globalization is busy working on the *Fortune* 500 now. However, it's headed toward *every* business—whatever its presumed immunity from globalization's perils and pitfalls.

THE TQM PRINCIPLES MUST EMANATE FROM THE TOP DOWN AND OPERATE BOTTOM UP IF THEY ARE TO BE FULLY EFFECTIVE. THAT CALLS FOR CONTINUOUS ASSESSMENT OF HOW THEY ARE WORKING AT EVERY LEVEL

As I've explained in some detail, you need good ways to assess how those principles are operating from bottom to top. There's lots of talk these days about various assessment tools and models for analyzing process and product quality. For example, most of America's managers have now heard about the uses and benefits of the *"Plan-Do-Check-Act"* (*P-D-C-A*) cycle approach that was first set forth by Walter Shewhart decades ago, and dubbed the "Shewhart cycle." These days this same analysis methodology is more often called the "Deming Cycle." That's because Deming popularized its use and expanded its applications. By any name it's a useful tool in creating continuing process-product improvement.

However, beyond those process-oriented analysis tools companies also need ways to assess their entire management system—to assess it, that is, in terms of how that system is affecting every process and every employee and, by extension, how it is affecting each product and sub-product. In other words, every organization needs a way to assess how the "human system" is responding to the "management system" from the bottom to the top—in every part (every structural module) of the organization. Turn the page to see depicted the conceptual model a savvy business should use to assess its organizational vitality and where it needs to be improved. Based on all I've said up to now, I believe this model—founded as it is on the principles of *Five Pillar TQM*—requires no further explanation.

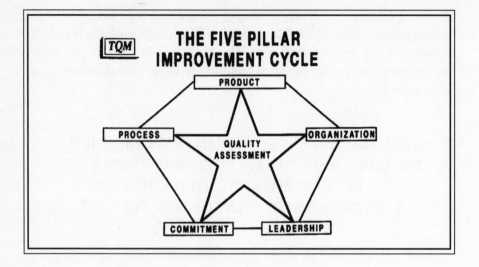

The bottom line is this: If the overall organizational foundation for TQM is weak, you can tinker with individual processes to your heart's content without creating any lasting improvements in quality and productivity. So every structural module of your business, large or small, must be examined—and made better—in each of the elements at the five points of the quality assessment star. Note that process improvement is a precursor to product improvement, but that it depends on the health and vitality of three other critical elements. If any is weak, all are. And that's why process improvements grafted onto a centocracy produce such paltry results.

There is much in American society, and in our management culture and its achievements, to be proud of. This, after all, is the nation that sent successive teams of astronauts to walk on the moon and brought them all home safely. That was an extraordinary technological and management achievement no other nation could have duplicated. And the United States produces the most innovative products, and the widest variety of consumer choices, of any nation on earth. In traveling the world over I have found no nation that can hold a candle to us in the diversity of our marketplace, or in the renewal dynamics of our business culture. Merely by walking into a neighborhood supermarket you can see an example of those dynamics, constantly yielding a stream of new ideas, new products, new marketing concepts, and yes, even new businesses to replace the old, imaginative ones to replace the unimaginative. Wal-Mart quickly rode from an empire of only five Ben Franklin stores to the nation's largest retailer by striking out on a new course, one that used imaginative new ideas to give much more vigor and vitality to the retailing ideas of old. So we don't have to start with a clean sheet of paper in making our management approach far better than it is.

Various surveys carried out by a U.N. agency and other study samplings set forth evidence the surveyors say proves the American worker in 1992 was the ''most productive'' on earth. So we have nothing to worry about, right? Wrong. Our view must be based not on how good we are now but on what American workers can produce when their creativity and commitment are unleashed. Our declining economic vitality also provides food for somber thought.

Finally, we must decide how we are to support the new lifestyle we've built. Americans of all ages and callings devoutly believe they're entitled to that lifestyle, even to have it enhanced. But if we don't change our ways, we most assuredly will prove that feeling entitled can't make it so. We earn it or we lose it. It's no more complicated than that.

Kaoru Ishikawa, after a great deal of thought and study, told us that the United States' problems in quality and competitiveness are caused by ''reliance on Taylorism'' by America's managers. I've featured the same point. I've also shown the ways we can unleash America's enormous potential if we will but overcome our steadfast affection for the centralized, managership approach that Taylorism cum Centralism has brought us. The blueprint for successful change is not mysterious or difficult. We just need to follow it.

As we adopt those new ways for our new days, we should not blame the managers who think in the old ways. After all, they've been trained to think that way, and are doing what has been expected of them all along. So no one adopting *Five Pillar TQM* should declare war on the managers; declare war instead on the old ways. The only finger-pointing to be done is to point forward.

I chose the word "Total" in devising the phrase "Total Quality Management" to emphasize the all-embracing issues that quality management must address if it's to succeed. In like manner, I chose the metaphorical representation of Five Pillars as a way of setting forth the broad reach of holistic, humanistic elements that must make up the TQM foundation if it is to have a total effect, positive effect, and a lasting effect. If you remember nothing more about the word Total in TQM and the Five Pillar foundation I hope you remember that—because it gets to the crux of why this current quality management crusade is sputtering and in danger of dying out.

With regard to this and my earlier references to theories, configurations, and models, Henry Mintzberg in his perceptive 1979 book *The Structuring of Organizations* said this about his own use of those same means to get his points across:

> In one sense the structural configurations do not exist at all. After all, they are just words and pictures on pieces of paper, not reality itself. Real structures in all but the most trivial organizations are enormously complex. What they constitute is a theory, and every theory necessarily simplifies and therefore distorts the reality. . . . But that should not lead to a rejection of the configurations. For the reader's choice is not between theory and reality, so much as between alternative theories. No one carries reality around in his head; no head is that big. Rather, we carry around thoughts, impressions, and beliefs about reality, and measures of it we call facts. But all of this is useless unless it is ordered in some way. So, we carry around in our heads comprehensible simplifications—concepts or models or theories—that enable us to catalog our data and experience. The reader's choice then becomes one of alternative systems of cataloging—that is—of alternative theories.

It is on this Mintzberg insight that I rest any apology I owe for the simplifications I've used in presenting the configurations, models, and theories involved in *Five Pillar TQM*. In fact, I have tried throughout to make those TQM concepts (as I and many others have put them into successful practice) as uncomplicated and unadorned as the intricacy of the subject matter permits.

You're not obliged to accept all of those concepts, or any of them, for that matter. However, I feel obliged to be sure you aren't mystified at the end of this book about what they entail. Any criticisms I leveled here and there I found justified for that reason. If I failed in my effort to provide a clear, ungarbled account of what a system for our times should and should not be, it wasn't because I didn't try. If my representations provide you, as I hope, with a clear view of a proven alternative to America's traditional management style, those simplifications have been justified. And if you find them useful, the effort I have spent to research and write this book has been worthwhile.

From time to time in these pages I've turned to the world of baseball for some down-to-earth philosophy. Perhaps the right note on which to close this book is to draw upon another famous baseball sage, Charlie Brown, who said about his *Peanuts* baseball team: *"It's tough to bear the awesome burden of permanent potential."* That is an awesome burden, and now is the time to unlock that dormant potential in America's businesses. The potential is not there some say. They are wrong. Case after case proves it's always there, slumbering and awaiting the right wake-up call.

It all boils down to this: The old ways no longer work. And change efforts don't succeed when they get sidetracked into one of the new fads with captivating names. J. M. Juran scorns those fads as mere "buzzwords" set forth by "opportunitists"—empty of meaningful content. He also says: "TQM is different, but few understand it." I agree. But must you call it TQM? No. It's your choice. But it's people behind the processes. So, if you wish to succeed, you must change the very *basics* of how you manage, a point Peter Drucker makes clear in the Introduction.

The Epilogue reviews the main themes and principles of this book, as *"The Guidelines for Organizational Greatness."* They also will yield personal success, whomever and wherever you are. The principles set forth in these guidelines have produced huge success in a variety of settings in all kinds of industries. Experience shows they will work for all. All, that is, who are wise enough to use them. Let's hope you're among the wise ones.

Epilogue

GUIDELINES
for
ORGANIZATIONAL
GREATNESS

For a Management System Suited to New Times
Use These Guiding Principles

1. **BUILD YOUR APPROACH, AND ITS PRINCIPLES, ON FIVE SYSTEM PILLARS:**
   PRODUCT—PROCESS—ORGANIZATION—LEADERSHIP—COMMITMENT.

   PRODUCT IS THE FOCAL POINT FOR ORGANIZATION PURPOSE AND ACHIEVEMENT.
   QUALITY IN THE PRODUCT IS IMPOSSIBLE WITHOUT QUALITY IN THE PROCESS.
   QUALITY IN THE PROCESS IS IMPOSSIBLE WITHOUT THE RIGHT ORGANIZATION.
   THE RIGHT ORGANIZATION IS MEANINGLESS WITHOUT THE PROPER LEADERSHIP.
   STRONG, BOTTOM-UP COMMITMENT IS THE SUPPORT PILLAR FOR ALL THE REST.
   EACH PILLAR DEPENDS UPON THE OTHER FOUR, AND IF ONE IS WEAK ALL ARE.

2. **FIRMLY ESTABLISH THE CHARACTER AND CULTURE OF YOUR ORGANIZATION.**

   DEVELOP THE OVERARCHING PRINCIPLES. KEY THEM TO THE HUMAN SPIRIT.
   ENSURE THEY ARE WHOLLY UNDERSTOOD AND WIDELY PRACTICED—BY ALL.
   GIVE THEM VIGOR THROUGH INSISTENCE, PERSISTENCE, AND CONSISTENCY.
   STRESS ETHICAL CONDUCT, INTEGRITY, AND COURTESY IN ALL ENDEAVORS.
   THE PRINCIPLES FLOW TOP DOWN BUT THEIR POWER MUST FLOW BOTTOM UP.

3. **USE A DECENTRALIZED, INTERACTIVE SYSTEM THAT INTEGRATES ALL LEVELS.**

ORGANIZE FOR THE NEW REALITIES. *CENTRALISM* IS A BANKRUPT APPROACH.
BUILD A DECENTRALIZED STRUCTURE ON THE *TEAMS-OUTPUTS-PRODUCT* MODEL.
REPLACE THE *I AND MY* MINDSET USUALLY FOUND WITH THAT OF *WE AND OUR*.
FOSTER BELIEF IN THE RICH REWARDS OF TEAMWORK, AND PROFESSIONALISM.
BUILD STRONG COMMITMENT BY ALL TO HIGHEST QUALITY AND PRODUCTIVITY.

4. **ORGANIZATION IS THE CENTRAL PILLAR—IT INFLUENCES EVERYTHING ELSE.**

CREATE WIDESPREAD OWNERSHIP. DECENTRALIZE THE AUTHORITY THROUGHOUT.
COMBINE AUTHORITY AND ACCOUNTABILITY. MAKE THAT UNAMBIGUOUS TO ALL.
ELIMINATE UNNECESSARY LAYERS. TEAR DOWN ALL OF THE FUNCTIONAL WALLS.
RECAST THE RULES. STREAMLINE THE PAPERWORK. SHORTEN THE CYCLE TIMES.
MAINTAIN COHERENCE AND CONTROL WITH INCENTIVE, NOT AUTHORITARIANISM.

5. **BASE THE STRUCTURAL BUILDING BLOCKS ON SMALL TEAMS NOT BIG FUNCTIONS.**

ORGANIZE BY TEAMS FOR INVOLVEMENT, AGILITY, AND AN OWNERSHIP FOCUS.
KEEP EACH TEAM AT A MANAGEABLE SIZE. PROVIDE EACH ITS OWN IDENTITY.
EVERY TEAM HAS A PRODUCT. IDENTIFY IT. DIGNIFY IT. CELEBRATE IT.
FORM TEAMS OF TEAMS. CLEARLY IDENTIFY THE INTERFACES BETWEEN TEAMS.
PROVIDE EACH TEAM AMPLE AUTHORITY OVER ITS OWN PART OF THE PRODUCT.

6. **ORIENT EMPLOYEE FOCUS AND ACTIVITY TO THEIR PRODUCT, NOT THEIR JOB.**

ONE'S *JOB* IS SELF-CENTERED. BUILD A GROUP-CENTERED *PRODUCT* MINDSET.
DEFINE EACH PRODUCT IN TERMS OF ITS CUSTOMER, INTERNAL OR EXTERNAL.
IDENTIFY EACH PRODUCT SUB-ELEMENT. IDENTIFY ALL INVOLVED PROCESSES.
CREATE PROCESS IMPROVEMENT BY MEASUREMENT, ANALYSIS, AND INCENTIVE.
USE THE PRODUCT AS THE FOCAL POINT, AND RALLYING POINT FOR QUALITY.

7. **PLACE THE PRIME LEADERSHIP FOCUS ON THE OUTPUTS, NOT THE INPUTS.**

INHIBIT MICROMANAGEMENT OF THE INPUTS. CHAMPION OUTPUT OWNERSHIP.
DEVELOP OUTPUT GOALS ITERATIVELY WITH THE TEAMS DIRECTLY INVOLVED.
MAKE THE GOALS UNDERSTANDABLE, RELEVANT, ATTAINABLE—AND WANTED.
PROVIDE AMPLE INCENTIVE FOR INITIATIVE, INGENUITY, AND INNOVATION.
CREATE STRONG DESIRE FOR CONTINUOUS IMPROVEMENT IN EVERY ACTIVITY.

8. **KEEP SCORE, ASSESS, AND PROVIDE TIMELY FEEDBACK TO ONE AND ALL.**

MEASURE QUALITY AND PRODUCTIVITY AT VARIED PRODUCT/PROCESS POINTS.
USE QUANTIFICATION BENCHMARKS TO JUDGE YOUR PROGRESS—AND NEEDS.
AMPLIFY OBJECTIVITY THROUGH BROAD USE OF DATA, FACTS, AND SURVEYS.
USE COMPARISON TO BRING LIFE TO THE DATA AND TO PROVIDE RELEVANCE.
USE GOALS AND SCOREBOARDING TO DECENTRALIZE, AND CREATE OWNERSHIP.

9. **KNOW YOUR MARKETPLACE INSIDE OUT AND CREATE STRONG CUSTOMER LINKAGE.**

CONTINUALLY ASSESS YOUR STRENGTH AND COMPETITIVENESS IN YOUR NICHE.
BE SURE YOUR EXPERTISE IS SUITABLY MATCHED TO EACH OF THE PRODUCTS.
PAY CLOSE ATTENTION TO THE BUSINESS OF YOUR BUSINESS. STICK TO IT.
CREATE A PRODUCT-CUSTOMER LINKAGE. ASSURE EVERYONE UNDERSTANDS IT.
ENSURE THAT EVERY DECISION, EVERY ACTION, IS KEYED TO THE CUSTOMER.

10. **PROVIDE A CLIMATE OF QUALITY WHICH PROMOTES PRIDE AND PROFESSIONALISM.**

MOBILIZE DEDICATION TO HIGHEST QUALITY IN ALL THINGS, AT ALL TIMES.
PRIDE IS THE FUEL OF HUMAN ACCOMPLISHMENT. CREATE IT. SUSTAIN IT.
MAKE CONTINUOUS RENEWAL AND REJUVENATION EVERYONE'S RESPONSIBILITY.
CALIBRATE YOUR REVISIONS ON THE LEVEL OF MOTIVATION AND ENTHUSIASM.
QUALITY BEGETS QUALITY. PROVIDE THE MEANS, TOOLS, AND MOTIVATION.

11. **BASE ANY AND ALL DECISIONS ON THE INSEPARABILITY OF COST AND VALUE.**

GET EVERY ORGANIZATIONAL LEVEL INVOLVED—FROM THE VERY BOTTOM UP.
PROVIDE COST DATA TO TEAMS. INSTILL VALUE CONSCIOUSNESS THROUGHOUT.
BE WARY OF CUTS THAT AFFECT THE QUALITY MINDSET. DON'T DISABLE IT.
THE LINE CUTS THE COSTS NOT THE STAFF, TO ENSURE VALUE SENSITIVITY.
USE QUALITY TO DRIVE COSTS DOWN, NOT SAVINGS TO DRIVE QUALITY DOWN.

12. **PROVIDE DETAILED, FOCUSED TRAINING TO EMPLOYEES AT EVERY LEVEL.**

ON-THE-JOB AND AD HOC TRAINING ARE KEY PARTS, BUT ARE ONLY PARTS.
FORMAL TRAINING IS VITAL FOR PROPER QUALITY MINDSET AND KNOW-HOW.
MAKE ALL TRAINING SPECIFIC ON KEY PRINCIPLES, METHODS, AND GOALS.
TRAIN ALL EMPLOYEES AT EVERY LEVEL—INCLUDING AT SENIOR LEVELS.
LEADERS AT ALL LEVELS MUST BE TEACHERS. LEADERS CREATE LEADERS.

13. **GIVE HIGH PRIORITY AND PAY GREAT ATTENTION TO THE COMMUNICATION FLOW.**

ON KEY ISSUES AUGMENT THE HIERARCHICAL FLOW. GO SEVERAL LAYERS DEEP.
TALK NUMBERS AS WELL AS WORDS. ENSURE FULL COMPREHENSION THROUGHOUT.
REPLACE ALL INHIBITIONS TO UPWARD COMMUNICATIONS WITH FULL OPENNESS.
PROVIDE THE REQUISITE MEANS AND ADEQUATE INCENTIVES TO MAKE IT WORK.
LISTENING, HEARING, AND CARING ARE THE CATALYSTS WHICH MAKE IT THRIVE.

14. **WORK UNCEASINGLY TO INSTILL COMMON PURPOSE FROM THE BOTTOM TO THE TOP.**

CLOSE THE CLASSIC MANAGEMENT AND LABOR GAP. MAKE LEADERSHIP SEAMLESS.
ASSURE THE COMMON PURPOSE IS KEYED TO THE PRODUCT, AND THE CUSTOMER.
GET ALL OF THE EMPLOYEES ENTHUSED, AND FULLY INVOLVED TO SUPPORT IT.
STAY IN TOUCH AND IN TUNE WITH ALL OF THE EMPLOYEES ALL OF THE TIME.
INSTILL IN ALL THAT COMMITMENT FROM ALL DETERMINES SUCCESS FOR EACH.

15. **BUILD THE COMMITMENT THROUGH GENUINE OWNERSHIP, AND SHARED SUCCESS.**

EMPHASIZE THE DIGNITY AND THE WORTH OF EACH JOB AND EVERY EMPLOYEE. MAKE WIDE USE OF RECOGNITION AND REWARD, FOR INDIVIDUALS AND TEAMS. MAKE INVOLVEMENT REAL. PROVIDE THE OPPORTUNITY AND THE INCENTIVES. MAKE OWNERSHIP REAL. THE TEST IS IF THEY FEEL IT—AND APPLY IT. *PROVIDE A CLEAR STAKE IN THE OUTCOME FOR EVERYONE. SHARE SUCCESS.*

16. **ABOVE ALL, BUILD YOUR NEW MANAGEMENT APPROACH ON ALL FIVE PILLARS.**

IT'S NOT COMPLICATED OR MYSTERIOUS. IT NEED NOT ALL BE DONE AT ONCE. BUT IT REQUIRES ACTIONS—NOT JUST WORDS. A SLOGAN IS NOT A SYSTEM. THE SYSTEM ISN'T DIFFICULT TO IMPLEMENT. START WITH THESE PRINCIPLES. THE VERY BEST COMPANIES, WORLDWIDE, USE THEM TO BEAT THE COMPETITION. *ALL WHO USE THEM REAP FAR GREATER QUALITY, PRODUCTIVITY, AND SUCCESS.*

**A HOLISTIC SYSTEM IS A PROVEN ANSWER TO THE NEW REALITIES
OF THE '90S AND BEYOND**

IT WILL HUGELY BENEFIT ANY ORGANIZATION WHATEVER ITS SIZE OR ITS BUSINESS

Index